# The Interface of Domestic and International Factors in India's Foreign Policy

This book investigates the interplay of internal and external constraints, challenges and possibilities regarding foreign policy in India.

It is the first attempt to systematically analyse and focus on the different actors and institutions in the domestic and international contexts who impose and push for various directions in India's foreign policy. Rather than focusing on any one particular theme, the book explores the myriad aspects of foreign policymaking and the close interface between the domestic and external aspects in Indian policymaking. In turn, this relates to the structural issues shaping and reshaping the Asian regional dynamics and India's connectivity within a globalized world.

This book will be of great interest to postgraduate students; scholars of Asian Studies, development, and political science and international relations; and all those involved in policy – especially foreign policy – within India and South Asia. It will also be useful for people working in professional branches of consultancy and the private sector dealing with India and with South Asia in general.

**Johannes Dragsbæk Schmidt** is an Adjunct Associate Professor in Development and International Relations at Aalborg University, Denmark. He is also a Senior Expert at the Nordic Institute for Asian Studies (NIAS) at Copenhagen University, Denmark, and Senior Research Associate at the Global Policy Institute (GPI) in London, UK.

**Shantanu Chakrabarti** is Professor in the Department of History and Convenor of the Academic Committee at the Institute of Foreign Policy Studies at the University of Calcutta, India.

**Rethinking Globalizations**

*Edited by Barry K. Gills, University of Helsinki, Finland and Kevin Gray, University of Sussex, UK*

This series is designed to break new ground in the literature on globalization and its academic and popular understanding. Rather than perpetuating or simply reacting to the economic understanding of globalization, this series seeks to capture the term and broaden its meaning to encompass a wide range of issues and disciplines and convey a sense of alternative possibilities for the future.

**Challenging Inequality in South Africa**
Transitional Compasses
*Edited by Michelle Williams and Vishwas Satgar*

**Between Class and Discourse: Left Intellectuals in Defence of Capitalism**
*Boris Kagarlitsky*

**Questioning the Utopian Springs of Market Economy**
*Damien Cahill, Martijn Konings and Adam David Morton*

**The Interface of Domestic and International Factors in India's Foreign Policy**
*Edited by Johannes Dragsbæk Schmidt and Shantanu Chakrabarti*

**Unity on the Global Left**
Critical Reflections on Samir Amin's Call for a New International
*Edited by Barry K. Gills and Christopher Chase-Dunn*

**Reglobalization**
*Edited by Matthew Louis Bishop and Anthony Payne*

**Rising Powers, People Rising**
Neoliberalization and its Discontents in the BRICS Countries
*Edited by Alf Gunvald Nilsen and Karl von Holdt*

For more information about this series, please visit:
www.routledge.com/Rethinking-Globalizations/book-series/RG

# The Interface of Domestic and International Factors in India's Foreign Policy

Edited by
Johannes Dragsbæk Schmidt
and Shantanu Chakrabarti

Routledge
Taylor & Francis Group
LONDON AND NEW YORK

First published 2021
by Routledge
2 Park Square, Milton Park, Abingdon, Oxon OX14 4RN

and by Routledge
52 Vanderbilt Avenue, New York, NY 10017

*Routledge is an imprint of the Taylor & Francis Group, an informa business*



*British Library Cataloguing-in-Publication Data*
A catalogue record for this book is available from the British Library

*Library of Congress Cataloging-in-Publication Data*
Names: Schmidt, Johannes Dragsbaek, 1960– editor. |
Chakrabarti, Shantanu, editor.
Title: The interface of domestic and international factors in India's foreign policy / edited by Johannes Dragsbaek Schmidt and Shantanu Chakrabarti.
Description: London ; New York, NY : Routledge/Taylor & Francis Group, 2021. |
Series: Rethinking globalizations | Includes bibliographical references and index.
Identifiers: LCCN 2020046549 (print) | LCCN 2020046550 (ebook) |
ISBN 9780367641320 (hardback) | ISBN 9781003122302 (ebook)
Subjects: LCSH: India–Foreign relations–20th century. |
India–Politics and government–20th century.
Classification: LCC DS448 .I688 2021 (print) |
LCC DS448 (ebook) | DDC 327.54–dc23
LC record available at https://lccn.loc.gov/2020046549
LC ebook record available at https://lccn.loc.gov/2020046550

ISBN: 978-0-367-64132-0 (hbk)
ISBN: 978-0-367-64135-1 (pbk)
ISBN: 978-1-003-12230-2 (ebk)

Typeset in Times New Roman
by Newgen Publishing UK

# Contents

# Contributors

**Riddhi Bhattacharya** is Head of the Department of History at Scottish Church College, India. Email: bhattacharyarid@gmail.com

**Shantanu Chakrabarti** is Professor in the Department of History and Convenor of the Academic Committee at the Institute of Foreign Policy Studies at the University of Calcutta, India. Email: chakrabartishantanu@hotmail.com

**Tridib Chakraborti** is Professor and Dean at the School of Social Sciences, ADAMAS University, Barasat, India. He is an expert in South Asian, Southeast Asian and Asia Pacific affairs, Indian political thought and foreign policy, and strategic studies. Email: tridibchakraborti2001@yahoo.com; tridib.chakraborti@gmail.com

**Shibashis Chatterjee** is Professor in the Department of International Relations at Jadavpur University, India. His areas of interest are international relations theory, Indian foreign policy and South Asian politics. Email: shibashis.chatterjee@gmail.com

**Aleksandra Jaskólska** is a PhD Scholar and Research Assistant at the Faculty of Political Science and International Studies at the University of Warsaw, Poland. Her areas of interest include the foreign policy of India; the political and party system in India; international relations in South Asia; and the influence of culture, religion and identity on the internal and foreign policy of states. Email: a.jaskolska@uw.edu.pl

**Catarina Kinnvall** is Professor in the Department of Political Science at Lund University, Sweden. Her research interests involve political psychology, international relations and critical security studies, with a particular focus on nationalism, religion, gender and populism in Europe and South Asia. Email: Catarina.kinnvall@svet.lu.se

**A. Vinod Kumar** is Associate Fellow at the Manohar Parrikar Institute for Defence Studies and Analyses (MP-IDSA), India. Email: vinujnu@gmail.com

**Sreya Maitra** is Assistant Professor at Maulana Azad College, India. Her areas of interest include contemporary issues of domestic politics in India and Indian foreign policy, conflict and internal security in India and Sri Lanka, and securitization theory. Email: shreya.maitra@gmail.com

**Jørgen Dige Pedersen** is Emeritus Associate Professor in the Department of Political Science at Aarhus University, Denmark. His areas of interest are global development issues and India's economic, social and political change and its international relations. Email: dige@ps.au.dk

**Sashinungla** is Professor in the Department of Philosophy at Jadavpur University, India. Her areas of interest include ethics, feminist philosophy, environmental philosophy, insurgency, ethnic conflict, and tribal philosophy and culture with a particular focus on the Indian context. Email: sashi.phil@gmail.com

**Johannes Dragsbæk Schmidt** is an Adjunct Associate Professor in Development and International Relations at Aalborg University, Denmark. He is also a Senior Expert at the Nordic Institute for Asian Studies (NIAS) at Copenhagen University, Denmark, and Senior Research Associate at the Global Policy Institute (GPI) in London, UK. Email: jds@dps.aau.dk

**Langpoklakpam Suraj Singh** is Associate Professor in the Department of Political Science at the D.M. College of Arts at Dhanamanjuri University, India. His areas of interest include the socio-political and economic dynamics of Myanmar, and its relevance to India's Northeast. Email: slangpok@yahoo.co.in

**Ted Svensson** is Associate Professor in the Department of Political Science at Lund University, Sweden. His research interests include state formation, identity politics, cultural heritage and rituals, contemporary South Asia, and issues broadly related to constitutive moments. Email: ted.svensson@svet.lu.se

# 1 The interface of domestic and international factors in India's foreign policy

## Introducing the issues*

*Johannes Dragsbæk Schmidt and Shantanu Chakrabarti*

### Introduction

Foreign policy-making is inherently dynamic and determined by external geo-political and geo-economic challenges but in most cases it is the result of internal societal contradictions and power politics. The multi-polar setting of the globalized world with rising incidences of intra-state conflicts and growing convergence between security and development issues has generated fresh as well as severely mutated old challenges confronting unipolar hegemony in the post-Cold War period. While there is a growing scholarly consensus on the long-term decline of the United States, China and India, on the other hand, have been marked by observers as re-emerging key entities setting the course of the new 'Asian century'. In this context, as a rising power, foreign policy-makers in India have also had to make significant changes in their old style as well as substance of policy-making in order to cope with the evolving challenges.

With the contours of a new multi-polar world polity and a fading US hegemony, India's diplomacy and foreign policy has been taking a number of sharp U-turns in recent years. As 2020 fades out, the world faces a multitude of unprecedented challenges mainly in the form of non-traditional security issues (climate change, economic recession and global economic meltdowns along with the spreading of the coronavirus pandemic) which have generated new points of conflict as well as opportunities for co-operation. Overall, a new discernible trend is reduction in global interactions and a visible trend towards autarchy and nationalism. This has affected democracies as well, as the popular trend indicates emergence of popularly elected conservative/authoritarian leadership capable of making 'tough' decisions and initiating hard action. While there has been a lot of criticism (Eichengreen 2018; Germani 1978; Chacko 2018a) on the emergence of authoritarianism and disappearance of 'consensus-building' approaches in democracies, there is yet no indication of waning of popular support for authoritarianism yet perceived to be 'effective' leadership. Historians may record these times as the era of muscular political leaders who symbolize a renewed focus on nationalism and antidemocratic populism. 'Make in India', 'China-first' and not least 'America-first' have become slogans signalling a spiralling away from multilateralism and interdependence towards brute power in geo-economic as well as geo-political relations. The questions boggling academia and commentators are whether we are entering a period with beggar-thy-neighbour policies, bilateralism and protectionism and erosion of the so-called US-led liberal world order (Parmar 2018).

## Whither India?

India's international positioning has for a long time been characterized by 'strategic autonomy'[1] and shifting domestic configurations and complexities. Some analysts have argued that, acting under cross-pressure, India's foreign policy appears to vacillate between appeasement and aggression, rather than converging onto the assertion of national self-interest (Mitra and Schöttli 2007, 21). According to yet another opinion, while India has been a mildly revisionist state at the level of the international system, its regional agenda for the past several decades has been to buttress the regional status quo for the simple reason that the current configuration of regional capabilities suits it (Sahni 2005, 219). The post-Cold War period and the onset of globalization during the 1990s have witnessed the phenomenon of India 'crossing the Rubicon' and the two major aspects of 'rising India' have been India's economic growth since the onset of the liberalization process since 1991 and its expanding military links, particularly with new partners like the US and Israel. While policy-making has continued to suffer from a certain degree of inertia, a level of confidence about its historical position as a great power and the projection of its re-emergence are also discernible. Understanding the complexities involved in Indian policy-making requires one to remember the colonial legacy inherited by the new nation state, restricting her attempts to initiate foreign policy-making on a clean slate since 1947. The Indian nationalists, on the one hand, rejected the colonial state's foreign and military policy-making as an 'imperialist scheme' which must be rejected after independence. On the other hand, the assertion that India would continue to play a leading role in global politics after decolonization, not as a military power, but as a benevolent leader of the developing countries, continued to be expressed in nationalist thinking on foreign policy which influenced Nehruvian thinking after independence.

Jawaharlal Nehru, in fact, firmly believed that India's destiny is to gain its rightful position among the world's major powers. His ambition was for India to promote 'real internationalism' that enhanced global peace and shared prosperity. Much water has flown down the river Ganga since then and there has been a steady dilution of the Nehruvian focus on internationalism and Non-Alignment-led Third World solidarity. Though the Indian state continues to officially endorse the principle of Global South solidarity, keeping in with the evolving global dynamics and new intellectually dominant priorities today, the focus is almost entirely on domestic reforms of the economy and the pursuing of a pragmatic and realist approach to international affairs.

No Indian government has, historically speaking, produced a blueprint or a vision for its foreign policy though one of the most important constants in India's foreign relations, as mentioned before, has been the promotion and preservation of 'strategic autonomy'. Some analysts see foreign policy-makers tending to 'split the difference' by mouthing traditional nationalist rhetoric serving a perceived domestic constituency while at the same time pursuing a largely pragmatic course, which is also illustrated in policy shifts at both regional as well as international level. Domestic factors determining foreign policy is a well-established fact and Delhi's options and choices in this regard have become increasingly impacted by a variety of actors, institutions and issues related to internal but also external affairs.

India's foreign policy-making has in many cases clashed with other strands of public discourse. The media, influential business groups, think tanks, social movements and sub-national actors at local state level and external actors, institutions, norms and regulations to varying degrees affect the most important aspects of decision-making and goals of foreign policy. The internet, social media and television have become mobilizers for civil society movements' influence on foreign policy, but also a tool and medium for the political class in Delhi and governments who reach out, leveraging their influence (Mohan 2009, 155). Since the launch of neo-liberal reforms at the beginning of the 1990s, the private sector has played a decisive role in shaping India's relations with other countries as well as influencing domestic public opinion and media on a range of political issues including foreign policy.

As Jaishankar notes, media and especially television often view developments in isolation and are prone to preconceived notions and prejudices being reflected in their news presentation and analyses. Pakistan and more recently, after the Doklam issue and the Ladakh border clash between the Indian and the Chinese armed forces leading to casualties on both sides, China bashing, has become a full-time preoccupation with some media channels. There are more fractious and self-serving discourses on many areas despite the remarkable continuity and consensus. In this connection, Jaishankar stresses that "evaluating India's advancement of its international interests will require a clearer assessment of its objectives, the progress made, and India's continuing limitations. That challenge will be all the more difficult in a fast-evolving and unpredictable world" (Jaishankar 2016).

The number of think tanks in Delhi, Mumbai and elsewhere in India has exploded and many receive funds from abroad. They feed into the articulation of policies related to external affairs especially when the debate is about Pakistan and China. As commentator Bhadrakumar notes, some of these media 'hawks' advocating a more aggressive policy *vis à vis* the neighbours like China or Pakistan are also getting encouragement from foreign countries – if one were to examine the credentials of publications such as *The National Interest* or *Nikki Asian Review* or *The Diplomat* – which are known to be stakeholders in fuelling India–China tensions. It is unfortunate – even tragic – that some Indians could be so utterly delusional about India's capacity at its present stage of development to sustain a confrontational policy towards China, which has an economy five times the size of India's and is a formidable military power. Fortunately, Bhadrakumar notes, "the government can ignore these maverick opinions as there is a broad consensus of national opinion behind the government's recent overtures to China" (Bhadrakumar 2018), although this may have changed lately due to recent border tensions and the clash at Doklam.

This essay starts out with a discussion about what defines the interface of domestic and external factors in theoretical terms followed by a specific case study of India's policy-making process. It then concentrates on the debate about what defines 'national interest' and attempts to deconstruct the concept, which seems to be quite unclear in the evolving theoretical literature. The next section gives a brief assessment of the three phases of India's foreign policy with focus on interlocking conflicts in historical perspective. Further, the next section discusses how domestic and international factors intermesh in foreign policy and how the articulation of national interest in itself becomes the core issue in defining and understanding how competing views clash. The last section introduces the chapters with a focus on the interface as the main denominator of foreign policy-making in India.

## The interface of India's foreign policy – a conceptual framework

In substance, foreign policy, like the state itself, may be perceived as Janus-faced – full of contradictions and multi-layered complexities in its democratic basis and with a steady open space for contestation, and in the end based on a fluid discourse of 'national interest' and a pragmatic approach to global affairs. As mentioned before, domestic factors, to a very high degree, shape the modus operandi of external relations among international entities. As one analyst mentions,

> In the literature of International Relations, it is fast becoming commonplace to assert the importance of domestic politics ...Some even contend that realism's dictum about the 'primacy of foreign policy' is wrong, and that the domestic politics of states are the key to understanding world events. Innenpolitik is in.
>
> (Zakaria 1992, 177)

The entire decision-making structure of any given country is primarily, though not exclusively, shaped by the domestic political environment, and economic and ideological or political and cultural sentiments. External socialization and international dynamics may also affect the articulation of foreign policy by upholding it to international norms and rules and the way international institutions function.

Traditionally, the incorporation of foreign policy analysis into mainstream international relations theory has not taken place despite its focus on domestic decision-making factors. Carlsnaes convincingly notes, "The divide between domestic and international politics…is highly questionable as a feasible foundational baseline for a sub-discipline that needs to problematize this boundary" (Carlsnaes 2002, 342). This is why it is a daunting task to investigate the blurred lines between the domestic and the international levels as "FPA [foreign policy analysis] research has consistently shown the significance of domestic politics and decision making to issues central to international politics, including international interventions, state cooperation in financial crises, regional dynamics, and nuclear proliferation" (Kaarbo 2015, 195).

International and domestic variables such as culture, ethnicity and political and economic interests are complementary to each other and influence the process of policy formulation, planning and implementation together with geography, history and tradition, social structures and organizations. States take on different roles and actions relying on expectations and this affects the government's responses. The interplay between these variables is in many cases additive in nature and directly and indirectly influences foreign policy-making, and is furthermore related to challenges to the legitimacy of the state and the unfinished state-building process in India. In sum, the relationship between internal and external ideational factors is complex, sometimes operating independently, pushing the state in opposite directions and sometimes in particular directions. At other instances, external factors provide the right conditions to manifest themselves in the foreign policy process and even feed into alterations in the domestic context, and thereby indirectly affect the planning and execution of foreign policy (Beasley et al. 2013, 333–336).

Examples of the blurring between domestic and international ideational factors are legion. What starts as a domestic issue quickly escalates into a foreign relations issue. The conflict in Kashmir has been an example of this since 5 August 2019, when the autonomous status of the state was lost when the central government of Modi brought in a parliamentary resolution revoking Article 370 and 35A of the Indian constitution and suspended the Jammu and Kashmir constitution. Interestingly, in spite of criticism coming from the opposition parties, the government managed to carry through the resolution with sufficient majority in both houses of the parliament indicating that many members of the parliament, belonging to opposition parties, had voted independently, defying party lines on the issue. This happened despite the possible international ramifications as critics mainly highlighted the Indian promise of a plebiscite in Jammu and Kashmir to allow the local population to determine their own future as per the UN Security Council Resolution 47 in 1948. Also, article 370 of the Indian Constitution had provided special status for Jammu and Kashmir, with a degree of autonomy which came to an end through the new legislation. To many analysts, however, the promise of plebiscite was also associated with the question of the exercise being undertaken in the entire state. The division of the state, with one portion under Pakistan's control and supervision and a section being leased to China by Pakistan, had ended the prospects of holding any plebiscite for all practical purposes. This is particularly true as there is increasing anti-Chinese and anti-Pakistani ferment among the residents of Gilgit and Baltistan. An article in *The New York Times* reporting on a demonstration of over five thousand people in Azad Kashmir (Pakistan-Occupied Kashmir) quoted a demonstrator mentioning that "We want freedom on this side and we want freedom on the other side", and "Foreign oppressors, leave us alone" (Habib et al. 2019). On 5 August 2019 a bill was passed in the Indian parliament stripping the state of Jammu and Kashmir of its autonomy and special status enshrined in the Indian constitution. It was stripped of statehood, and converted into two union territories, Ladakh, and Jammu and Kashmir. Ladakh has no legislature and is now governed directly by New Delhi while Jammu and Kashmir has a legislature. The Indian government has maintained that it aims at restoration of statehood at 'early opportunity', and assured no demographic change and the release of all political prisoners in 'due course', as revealed in an interaction between the Indian home minister Amit Shah, regarded as one of the chief architects of the legislation, and a political delegation of the Jammu and Kashmir Apni Party (*The Economic Times* 2020). The arrangement has, however, been rejected by the two major political parties in the state and the region continues to be engulfed in a blanket of security including massive presence of military and paramilitary forces with large-scale restrictions on civilian rights.

The other major domestic development has been enactment of the new domicile law by the Modi government in the form of the Citizenship Amendment Act (CAA) passed in December 2019 amending the older Indian Citizenship law, which prohibited illegal migrants from becoming Indian citizens. The new Act adds an exception for members of six religious minority communities – Hindu, Sikh, Buddhist, Jain, Parsi and Christian – if they can prove that they are from Pakistan, Afghanistan or Bangladesh. They will only have to live or work in India for six years to be eligible for citizenship by naturalization, the process by which a non-citizen acquires the citizenship or nationality of that country. Opponents of the bill say it is exclusionary and violates the secular principles enshrined in the constitution by excluding Muslims coming from the neighbouring countries (*BBC News* 2019). A further piece of legislation was the National Register of Citizens (NRC), which is, according to critics, supposed to detect and flush out 'Bangladeshi infiltrators', particularly located in East and Northeast India, and targeting of Muslims (Roy 2020).

These issues have huge spillover effects on the immediate regional balance of power since these contested areas are located between three nuclear armed powers, Pakistan, India and China. The actions of the Bharatiya Janata Party (BJP) government in Delhi may easily be seen as provocations for the immediate neighbours and have international repercussions as well, though the protests against the CAA have faded away because of the impact of the corona epidemic. For instance, Bangladesh's pivot towards China and recent overtures to Pakistan along with a growing powerful anti-India lobby in the country are, to an extent, also a reflection on the CAA along with other geopolitical dynamics which may lead to an exodus of Muslims from Assam and other states in the eastern parts of India into that country. However, recently Delhi has approached Dhaka and some alignment appears to have taken place. The Sheikh Hasina government still continues to be a key regional ally for India in spite of such domestic spillovers.

There was a fear as to how the legislation would influence India's relations with the countries with Muslim majority in the South Asian neighbourhood (Pakistan, Afghanistan, Bangladesh and Maldives) as well as hamper her relations with Muslim majority countries in Southeast Asia like Indonesia and Malaysia and also upset her key allies in West Asia. While there has been some criticism in the local press and curt reactions at some official levels, by and large the CAA has not resulted in any major disruptions in India's relations with such countries. While India's relations with Iran have been affected by growing US–Indian bonhomie, and in Southeast Asia, there has been some disruption in Indo–Malaysia relations, India's relations with partners like the UAE and, more significantly, Saudi Arabia have witnessed an upswing. This is a clear indication that in the context of rapidly changing regional and global dynamics, India's foreign relations continue to dominate over spillover of domestic developments in the global arena.

These developments also illuminate the complicated relationship with Bhutan and especially Nepal. The recently raised Nepalese claims of Lipidhura, Lipulekh and Kalapani belonging to Nepal and not India, along with demands for restoration of these territories and accusations in certain circles of India targeting the Nepalese government, first by supporting the Madhesi claims for better representation in the political set-up, and also clandestinely supporting internal hardline demands for restoration of Nepal's status as a Hindu state, have in all probability worsened the otherwise fragile relationship between Nepal and India. These issues are further exacerbated by India's bandwagoning and alignment with the US and the Quad (Australia, the US, Japan and India) to form an alliance against China. To complicate these matters even Iran has teamed up with China, leaving India's regional strategy in West Asia with renewed challenges.

These examples illustrate the 'interface' well since they illustrate the feedback mechanisms involved when government- (in this case the BJP) controlled domestic and foreign policies affect the international context of that state and those changes in context subsequently impact on the state's future foreign policy decisions.

Related to such developments, contested territorial borders may be difficult to judge if the issues involved become a foreign relations problem and involve other states or civil society actors such as ethnic, linguistic or religious communal groups. Armed ethnic, tribal and political conflicts and calls for local autonomy and independence across India's borders, with its intimate and fragile neighbourhood, illustrate the problem. Systematic discrimination and injustice related not only to material grievances but also to cultural, religious, caste and ethnic practices at the domestic level may impact the conduct of foreign policy and in this way illuminate the interface of internal and external relations.

One more issue with important effects on the interface between domestic actors and institutions and foreign policy is related to party coalition politics and federalism versus local state politics.[2] The basic and relevant question scholars ask is whether regional parties form coalitions in order to influence foreign policy. Three chapters in this volume give important new insights into these issues and claim that there are important instances of local state-level parties creating bargaining coalitions across the political centre; that they do in fact try to impact foreign policies at the federal level; and, at the same time, in many cases, with support from the BJP government, they perform independent foreign policies especially, but not exclusively, in the political economy sectors.[3]

For all its public image of strongman politics, the BJP government has been an ardent supporter of neo-liberal reforms and privatization of state assets. The Modi government has implemented radical deregulation or corporate rule and reinvented statism (Chatterjee 2020). One key example was the shock-and-awe decision on 8 November 2016 to junk India's two largest-denomination rupee bills overnight, launching shock therapy for the country's cash-driven shadow economy. The demonetization policy came as a shock but in an interview three years later PM Modi claimed it was done in the name of 'national interest' and that it had an impact on the financing of terrorism from abroad, including the hawala,[4] mentioning also Jammu and Kashmir. The alibi of demonetizing the economy was done in accordance with the national interest and to stop funding of illicit activities, and had huge ramifications at the international level (Shekar 2019). The idea was, furthermore, to emulate China's anti-corruption drive and catapult India's informalized economic structures into global competition and create a new growth miracle. Interestingly, a proposed data protection bill has been introduced as well, which has been cast as a new surveillance system very much copying China's Big Brother' approach towards privacy and civil liberties (Parkin and Findlay 2020).

The question is whether the blurring of the external and internal ideational and material factors in reality is reinforcing a state-centric version of foreign policy, strategy and security. Does it reinforce the communal and ethnic lines in terms of India's national, regional and global security concerns? At a broader level, if theorizing in international relations and policy implications in international security studies seek to move towards a normative goal, then should the role of ideology and ethnicity in the form of religious nationalism and communalism be deconstructed? Finally, it is important to go beyond the observable geo-strategic factors (which are so over-emphasized by mainstream international relations theorists) and delve into more intrinsic factors such as the role of ideology, culture, material factors and interests that may shape state-building practices, foreign policy and security discourses in international relations.

## The interface and three phases in Indian foreign policy

Varieties of state-building may result in foreign policy contestation or what Ogden refers to as the symbiosis of national identity and security or 'security identity' as transmitting domestic and foreign policy precedents (Ogden 2009). The first phase, which may be called the period of non-alignment, was characterized by the norms of internationalism, non-intervention, self-reliance and Third Worldism but the reality also showed a willingness to intervene in civil conflicts partly referring to humanitarian and democratic values (Chacko 2018b, 347). It is also interesting to stress the 'independence' of India's foreign policy and the importance of norms related to sovereignty, democracy, secularism and the reference to India as a great civilization with the attainment of great power status.

After the break-up of the Soviet Union in 1991, when the compulsions of having to avoid competing alliances at all costs evaporated, India entered into the second phase of its foreign policy evolution. Pursuing a variety of strategic partnerships with more than thirty different countries, India sought to expand specific forms of collaboration that would increase its power and accelerate its rise. As a senior US statesman stated, "The domestic economic reforms unleashed in the very year of the Soviet Union's collapse paved the way for consolidating India's path toward higher growth" (Tellis 2016). A more prominent pro-US tilt was complemented by a new state-building strategy revealing a move away from non-alignment to a more resilient foreign policy. India's foreign policy has been lying low and has only focused on "short-term value maximizing", as mentioned by former Indian prime minister Dr. Manmohan Singh, and the country is still without a national foreign policy vision (Karnad 2015, 86).

The third phase is also characterized by a hard-core realist approach to foreign policy. With the landslide victory in the 2014 election subsequently repeated in 2019 for another term and the BJP governing a huge majority of constituent states in India, Indian politics has witnessed the dominance of a single party long after the 1980s. The new state-building 'make in India' project signals a move away from a reactive state-building project towards a more opulent, muscular and optimistic drive towards modernization and the achievement of international respect and legitimacy. However, according to some observers the BJP exercises a more authoritarian and illiberal approach towards domestic affairs and this has had important spillover effects on foreign policy though the rhetoric during the election campaign was pretty straightforward. This has ominous implications for the federal set-up in India which, according to some observers, has been steadily weakening since the assumption of power by Modi in 2014. The BJP's undiluted power at the centre, it has been argued, has created the political context for greater centralization of power which has weakened the role of regional parties in national politics, both in electoral terms and in bargaining power, as regional parties rarely have well-defined, credible national policy platforms in India.[5]

The regional parties, however, continue to remain strong in several parts of India and thus have to be consulted by the central government while taking important decisions particularly related to border issues and regional dynamics. Moreover, the BJP's attempts to spread its influence in new areas like Jammu and Kashmir and Northeast India have led the party to negotiate with regional and local political groups and regional satraps.[6] One important example was the short-lived alliance of the BJP with the People's Democratic Party (PDP) following the assembly elections in Jammu and Kashmir held in 2014. As no party gained absolute majority, the two most unlikely political partners came together to form a coalition government based on a common minimum programme in 2015. While the running was not very smooth due to various political developments like the death of senior leader Mufti Mohammed Sayeed and the succession of her daughter Mehbooba Mufti as the party leader and next chief minister, the issue of army operations against the terrorist groups, etc., the coalition did linger on till June 2018, when it collapsed due to the BJP's withdrawal of support and reimposition of the president's rule in the state.

Similarly, the BJP's attempts to politically penetrate into virgin territories of Northeast India has seen it regularly try to co-opt powerful local leaders or wean away sections of the local regional parties. While this could, on one hand, be described as a process of imposition of political centralization and uniformity, it must, on the other hand, be kept in mind that the BJP has often had to dilute or mute its key agenda and issues like Hindutva in order to maintain political connectivity and accessibility in these new areas, particularly in the Northeast with its substantial Christian and animist tribal populations.

As previously mentioned, the other aspect of post-2014 Indian domestic politics which has caught global attention is the implementation process of key issues within the BJP's political agenda like the uniform civil code (through the implementation of the NRC and the CAA); abolition of the special status of the state of Jammu and Kashmir and division of the state into federal units; and the inauguration of the Ram temple project at Ayodhya at the disputed site where the Babri mosque was destroyed through mob action during the Ram Mandir agitation of 1992, after the Supreme Court judgment on the long dispute was delivered. As one analyst critically comments:

> The rabid focus on identity is a piece of a global pattern, of course, but it is especially dangerous in a country that is as tenuous a construct as India. This is still, as it was in 1947, a land teeming with so many identities – plotted multi-dimensionally along the axes of caste, gender, class, religion, language and ethnicity – that the only way to make it work is to accept that everyone belongs equally to India.
>
> (Subramanian 2020)

Influential sections of the global media in fact have taken a critical stand on such developments in India. While *The Economist* titled one of its issues published in January 2020 as 'Intolerant India: How Modi is endangering the world's biggest democracy', there were several more critical reviews and opinions which came out in other influential publications.

But has there really been an irreversible turn in India's political set-up, turning India into a more 'authoritarian' state? In our view, while some of these critical comments are indeed valid, the recent developments cannot completely overturn the local dynamics acting as shock observers to any political adjustment process deemed as centralization. Moreover, the key question, to what extent these developments have impacted upon India's foreign relations, would produce a more complex answer. India's relations within its own South Asian neighbourhood and India's global engagement continue to reflect the earlier patterns which have been followed since the 1990s, with a key focus on economic diplomacy and expansion of military (particularly naval) power in order to complement the economic growth and expansion. The other aspect of India's foreign policy is growing proximity to the US, reflected in numerous economic and defence partnerships and engagements. This, however, has prevented India from exercising her option to retain autonomy in her foreign policy decision-making process. For instance, though the US has started projecting India as a key partner in the Indo-Pacific region, India is yet to give her consent to formalize the QUAD maritime group consisting of the US, Australia, India and Japan. India's increasing engagement with the Southeast Asian and East Asian partners also has its own dynamics which are only marginally affected by the Indo-Malaysian bilateral dispute over the status of the Indian (particularly Hindu Tamil) minority in Malaysia, from time to time.

What has affected the foreign policy dynamics more significantly has been external developments like the rise of China within the post-Cold War setting rather than India's domestic developments. The confrontation and disputes between India and her neighbours, for instance, have their own regional and local dynamics but China's emergence as a powerful neighbour with deep pockets and its initiation of the Belt and Road Initiative (BRI) have led to increasing competition and challenges for India's diplomatic ability in retaining her importance. Such tension is evident in India's Indian Ocean projection in terms of naval exercises with countries like the US, Australia, Japan and several Southeast Asian countries. The China factor is also noticeable in India's bilateral relations with her South Asian neighbours like Nepal, Bhutan, Bangladesh and, of course, Pakistan, regarded as a vital player in the BRI initiative. China also plays a major role in shaping up Indian policy-making in Southeast Asia and also East Asia. The domestic developments in India do generate political ripples in the external world but, by and large, not to the extent of changing India's positioning within the global order, and external factors still dominate the foreign policy agenda.

## Domestic and international factors intermesh: the national interest

Culture, identity and ultimately ethnicity have always played a unique role in the evolution of India's foreign relations. The two dominant political parties, Congress and BJP (or People's Party), rely on a specific reading of state identity, national interest and post-independence history, and a blend of civilizational exceptionalism, post-colonialism and democracy. Some scholars note that Congress has been influenced by non-violence and non-alignment while BJP relies on a more organic and nationalist version of identity and culture based on a specific reading of 'Hindu values' founded on '*Hindutva*'. National prestige and pride are intermeshed with a double-bound construction of identity and culture as the main denominators of 'secular nationalist' and 'ethno-nationalist' interpretations of Hinduism, respectively. The understandings and internalization of these values are embedded in both parties' political discourse and are promoted in the domestic context and the near-environment, regional and global context; and reflect the different layers of history and foreign domination that have shaped India's rise in the world system (Schmidt 2017, 1894).

Congress constructed a secular and 'civic nationalism' distinguished by its reference to territorial identity defined by residence, geography and culture. This interpretation has been articulated by the use of voluntarism and is concerned with the present. BJP, on the other hand, has referred to 'ethnic nationalism' as an organic political–cultural construct based on ethnic descent and tradition centred on cultural communities and their histories. Geography and religion are the main denominators of ethno-nationalism (Adeney and Lall 2005, 260–261, 263) and this has several repercussions for the framing of the 'national interest' and for foreign policy analysis in India.

The discourses, strategies and objectives of India's current and past foreign policies rely on the legacy of post-independence struggles to re-create a new nation inherited from one of the world's oldest civilizations and British colonialism. Strategic debates and policy-making about security and external relations have been nourished upon the basis of readings of historiography, population size and location, geography, the democratic and secular nature of constitutionalism, political culture, ethno-religious identity, nationalism and Third World solidarity. The strategic and ideological context in which India's foreign policy-making has been framed shows paradigmatic shifts from non-alignment to more assertive positions regarding the country's place in the international polity, but always embedded in a framework of domestic diversity and grievances. Indeed, foreign policy in India has tended to pale 'relative to domestic political and security concerns' (Malone 2011, 6). These concerns are neatly illuminated by a speech Jawaharlal Nehru made to the Constituent Assembly of India on 8 March 1948: "External affairs will follow internal affairs. Indeed, there is no basis for external affairs if internal affairs go wrong" (Mukherjee and Malone 2010, 147).

This notwithstanding, external relations discourse has, historically speaking, been an elite project. The claims according to the dominant explanatory variables within and outside India have been that a tiny and insulated vanguard network within the elite and bureaucracy or the leadership itself has been solely responsible for the evolution of the narratives, discourses and identity preferences underlying the articulation of policies towards the external environment. In this way, decisions have been highly individualistic and rarely based on strategic thinking or planning about long-term goals (Miller 2013, 14–19) and thus neatly fit mainstream concepts of foreign policy as "the strategy or approach chosen by the national government to achieve its goals in its relations with external entities" (Hudson 2008). India's foreign policy is often characterized as reactive and formulated incrementally, case by case, and this type of explanation complies with early conceptions of how internal factors may or may not affect foreign policy patterns. In line with this description, the inside-out literature asks whether domestic political openness or closeness affects foreign relations, what effect national self-images have, and whether national role conceptions originating from domestic politics shape foreign policy.[7]

Among several aspects of public policy-making, the globalization process has also affected foreign policy-making, making it more inclusive in character. The theoretical exclusivity of sovereignty enjoyed by the state over foreign policy-making has been questioned, both academically and in reality, leading to several fallouts. This has particular implications for federally organized state structures, particularly in developing/under-developed parts of the world where state-building continues to be an ongoing process, leading to blurred or often under-defined categorizations of sovereign authority and exclusivity, leaving room for contestations. In the post-Cold War period, one important trend which is becoming particularly discernible, in this context, is the process and manner in which the component units within the Indian federation are articulating or even challenging/opposing 'official' foreign policy options of the Indian state. While input from local constituent units of a state in determining the direction of foreign policy-making has not been altogether absent before, its rising incidence in global affairs has been marked since the ending of Cold War during the 1990s.

The focus of Indian diplomacy has been on communicating India's *raison d'être* for its foreign policy decision, while domestic politics require an internal focus. Modi's government has energized engagement with the international community to achieve these domestic objectives. In short, India still focuses inwardly: in actions, however, India is beginning to feel its way outside its borders. Reacting to India's recent proactive foreign policy behaviour, one observer notes, "after more than a half century of false starts and unrealized potential, India is now emerging as the swing state in the global balance of power" (Mohan 2006, 17).

Shifting government statements clearly indicate a wish for global power status and see India as one pole in a multi-polar world. The continuing quest of Indian decision-makers for hegemonic ascendancy has been supported by the country's expansion of its military, economic and technological capabilities and the continuing hostility with neighbouring Pakistan and partly China. India's gradual rise is most evident in the field of security where strategies of co-optation and co-operation have been employed. As an advanced nuclear power with a military comprising more than one million men, and being Asia's number one purchaser of weapons and weapon systems, India is at the forefront of the Asian arms race, though its spending on defence continues to be much lower than that of China. Modi is utilizing foreign policy as a means to promote inward investment, business and technology for domestic growth and development. One aim is to enhance regional co-operation and stability in South Asia. As the Prime Minister Modi himself noted on one occasion, "India positions itself in a leading role, rather than just a balancing force, globally" (Press Information Bureau 2015). Related to this observation, the foreign secretary, Subrahmanyam Jaishankar (currently foreign minister in the Modi government), later noted that Modi's dramatic international initiatives reflected India's growing self-confidence, declaring that the country now "aspire[s] to be a leading power, rather than just a balancing power" (Jaishankar 2015).

## Opening the field and introducing the book

The present volume focuses on the interface of Indian foreign policy-making within the context of how some key variables are shaped through domestic dynamics and the obliteration of the gaps between the external and the internal (if it ever existed). Clubbed into four parts, each part containing three chapters, the twelve chapters and the introduction itself bring out the diverse dimensions and aspects of policy-making and the contextualization of such policy-making *vis à vis* local, regional and global settings.

Following the Chapter 1 introduction, Part I is titled 'The evolution of reactive and proactive foreign policy'. A. Vinod Kumar's essay in Chapter 2 elaborates on how India's nuclear policy and nuclear outreach essentially gave life to the national global identity and its conception of the power system in grand strategic terms – be it for balancing, challenging or bandwagoning. The author concludes that the process of Indian nuclear policy-making was always regulated and leveraged by the push-and-pull factors that determined the nation's grand strategy. At the same time, the eventual shape that nuclear policies have taken over the years has given a distinct flavour and identity to the country's grand strategy. The chapter explains the struggles of policy-making and the challenges the Indian leaderships faced in framing the country's nuclear policy, constantly shaped by a handful of exogenous and endogenous factors. The third chapter, by Sashinungla, focuses on the nature of India's foreign policy and domestic compulsions with emphasis on the theorization of the marginal, pointing out the dangers of getting deluged under the meta narrative of the nation. The chapter authors argue that India should embrace its cultural, religious, racial and ethnic diversity capital and use it as a strategic advantage for foreign policy purposes. Chapter 4, by Jørgen Dige Pedersen, focuses on the complex nature of the evolution of India's foreign aid policy with India evolving its unique double role as a recipient of global development aid and also as a donor of development aid to the global South. The chapter analyses some of the complexities – even contradictions – involved in this unique double role for India. Both the provision of aid and the donation of aid are by their very nature intrusive activities that establish relations between internal actors and external agencies, thus crossing the borders between external and internal affairs.

Part II is titled 'Global ambitions, internal and regional constraints'. Chapter 5 by Tridib Chakraborti focuses on India's evolving bilateralism in its historical context using a case study of the status of Malaysian-Indians in the Malaysian social matrix and how that relates to domestic politics and also impacts upon foreign policy-making. In Chapter 6, through her detailed analysis of the Eastern South Asian Community, Riddhi Bhattacharya looks at the phenomenon of sub-regionalism as an emerging layer of economic governance between the nation-state and the global economy – a mechanism through which the domestic meets the international and the global. In Chapter 7 Johannes Dragsbæk Schmidt analyses the relationship between India and China by looking inside-out and outside-in. He argues that similar interests are shared in opposing the US and EU in climate change policy, world trade and to a certain extent in security and energy matters. However, disagreement persists on unresolved problems in terms of attracting foreign direct investment, border issues, the near-environment and contradictions with regard to energy security policies. Coming to the regional Asian setting, the global alignment and foreign policy convergence appears to be partly replaced by a more competitive relation in strategic terms and the two entities act more as rivals for regional dominance than as potential allies, especially in relation to accessing energy resources.

Part III is titled 'Identity, migration and structural dimensions'. In Chapter 8 Aleksandra Jaskólska analyses a key aspect of domestic policy-making through the evolving multi-party structure within the Indian domestic political milieu. She argues that regional parties still play a very important role in the Indian party system and also conduct some influence on foreign policy. In Chapter 9, the authors Catarina Kinnvall and Ted Svensson look at the important dimension of how emotions and foreign policy are closely intertwined and are most visible through national gendered identity constructions that aim to reconstruct a civilizational Hindu narrative at the expense of other competing narratives, and how such representations are likely to reproduce a governing process that makes religious groups appear natural, authentic and essential – thus ignoring religious diversity as well as those other groups who exist outside this narrative. The last chapter in this section, Chapter 10 by Shantanu Chakrabarti and Johannes Dragsbæk Schmidt, looks at the evolving nature of the federalization of Indian foreign policy-making and how the 'state nation' and Indian federalism give more importance to 'diversity claims' rather than 'equality claims'. The argument of the authors is that, in spite of the *de jure* control of the central government over the process of foreign policy-making, historical trajectory and the onset of globalization have led to sub-national governments having a huge and determining impact on India's policies particularly towards its South Asian neighbours over the past years.

The last section of the book, Part IV, is titled 'Looking in – outside out: Northeast of India related to India's foreign policymaking'. Chapter 11 by Langpoklakpam Suraj Singh focuses on the inter-Asian dimensions of cross-cultural and social linkages based on pre-colonial heritage through a detailed analysis of the Manipur dynamics within the context of India's policy towards the neighbouring country of Myanmar. The author is of the opinion that a mechanism linking top-down and bottom-up initiatives is a must even when it comes to foreign policy. Besides, the socio-political atmosphere should also be such that the general masses as well as the civil societies of the state should be receptive to the developmental dynamics encompassing the region with the ever-changing geo-political realities. Chapter 12, by the authors Sashinungla, explores the idea of a cultural interconnection through ethnic, linguistic and anthropological categories of migration of concepts and ideas across East and Southeast Asia to Northeast India that happens to be at the centre of India's Look East/Act East policy.

The last chapter in this volume, Chapter 13 by Sreya Maitra and Shibashis Chatterjee, argues that internally India's tight federal model has tried to be accommodative and inclusionary and the turn towards coalition politics has only strengthened this trend. It has remained sensitive to its neighbourhood and got involved when groups have been excluded in the political process in states like Sri Lanka, Bangladesh and Nepal. This is not necessarily because there is a strong commitment to liberal multiculturalism in India's democracy. Federalism was necessary to accommodate the country's many diversities so that people enjoyed constitutional guarantees and might claim a share in the operating dynamics of the state. The chapter also highlights as to how the so-called seamless national interest parleyed by the Indian state has often been strongly critiqued if not resisted by the bordering provinces, which are sensitive to resource sharing and economic forces across territorial lines. Federal calculations have, therefore, often been at variance with those of the provinces on the border. Immediate consequences and short time horizons have motivated the political decisions of such states far more than the abstract and sanitized approach of the centre. This has exposed the implications of the operational dynamics of federalism, rendering clear that it is not just the constitutional division of powers as etched in black and white. It involves the actual dynamic of co-ordination between the two levels of authorities and its illustrations in everyday politics. In essence, this study describes the evolution of India's federalism and traces how this process has impacted on a range of foreign policy issues both in South Asia and beyond by looking at both the domestic changes and their broader effect.

The present volume, outcome of an international research project and collaborative efforts, was planned as a published record and outcome of intense and interesting debates and discussions ranging across the institutional and praxis-level analyses of policy-making with principal focus on the nature of Indian foreign policy-making. The editors deliberately adopted a policy of not trying to introduce a thematic boundary as they felt that focusing on any one particular theme would miss out the myriad aspects of foreign policy-making and the close interface between the domestic and external aspects in Indian policy-making which, in turn, is also related to the non-solidified structural issues shaping and reshaping the Asian regional dynamics and their nature of connectivity within a globalized world.

## Notes

* The authors acknowledge comments to earlier versions of this chapter by participants and commentators at international workshops at Nordic Institute for Asian Studies, Copenhagen; Jadavpur University, Kolkata; and the South Asia Centre, Oxford University. We also thank three anonymous reviewers for useful comments and critique.

1 Here understood as both a transactional and transformative government seeking a guaranteed permanent freedom in its foreign policy, combined with the fear of becoming a junior partner of a greater power.

2 For debates about the theories involved, see Kuznetsov (2014) and Schiavon (2019).

3 See also Blarel (2019).

4 Money transfer system popular in the Middle East and across the Indian subcontinent which uses a network of money brokers to transfer funds.

5 For details, see Aiyar and Sircar (2020).

6 The Western Satraps were contemporaneous with the Kushans who ruled the northern part of the Indian subcontinent and were possibly their overlords, and the Satavahana (Andhra) who ruled in Central India. The meaning of 'Satrap' is regional governor.

7 See in particular Rosenau (1966) and Holsti (1987).

## References

Adeney, Katharine and Lall, Marie. 2005. Institutional Attempts to Build a 'National' Identity in India: Internal and External Dimensions. *India Review* 4, no.3–4: 258–286

Aiyar, Yamini and Sircar, Neelanjan. 2020. Understanding the Decline of Regional Party Power in the 2019 National Election and Beyond. *Contemporary South Asia* 28, no.2: 209–222

*BBC News*. 2019, December 11. Citizenship Amendment Bill: India's New 'Anti-Muslim' Law Explained. www.bbc.com/news/world-asia-india-50670393 (accessed: 21 August 2020)

Beasley, Ryan K., Kaarbo, Juliet, Lantis, Jeffrey S. and Snarr, Michael T. eds, 2013. *Foreign Policy in Comparative Perspective. Domestic and International Influences on State Behavior*: New Delhi: CQ Press and Sage

Bhadrakumar, M. K. 2018, March 21. Modi, Xi Jinping to Enhance Strategic Communication. *Indian Punchline, Reflections on Foreign Affairs*.

Blarel, Nicolas. 2019. Coalition Politics and the Making of Indian Foreign Policy: A New Research Program. *India Review* 18, no.5: 582–595

Carlsnaes, Walter. 2002. Foreign Policy. In *Handbook of International Relations*, ed., Walter Carlsnaes, Thomas Risse and Beth A. Simmons, 331–349. London: Sage

Chacko, Priya. 2018a. The Right Turn in India: Authoritarianism, Populism and Neoliberalisation. *Journal of Contemporary Asia* 48, no.4: 541–565

Chacko, Priya. 2018b. Foreign Policy, Ideas and State-building: India and the Politics of International Intervention. *Journal of International Relations and Development* 21, no.1: 346–371

Chatterjee, Elizabeth. 2020. New Developmentalism and its Discontents: State Activism in Modi's Gujarat and India. *Development and Change*. https://onlinelibrary.wiley.com/doi/abs/10.1111/dech.12579 (accessed: 14 May 2020)

Eichengreen, Barry. 2018. *The Populist Temptation: Economic Grievance and Political Reaction in the Modern Era*. Oxford: Oxford University Press

Germani, Gino. 1978. *Authoritarianism, Fascism, and Populist Nationalism*. London: Routledge

Habib, Maria Abi, Mughal, Jalaluddin and Masood, Salman. 2019. In Pakistan-Held Kashmir, Growing Calls for Independence. *The New York Times*. www.nytimes.com/2019/09/19/world/asia/pakistan-kashmir-independence.html (accessed: 20 August 2020)

Holsti, K. J. 1987. National Role Conception in the Study of Foreign Policy. In *Role Theory and Foreign Policy Analysis*, ed., Stephen G. Walker, 5–44. Durham: Duke University Press

Hudson, Valerie M. 2008. The History and Evolution of Foreign Policy Analysis. In *Foreign Policy: Theories, Actors, Cases*, ed., Steve Smith, Amelia Hadfield and Tim Dunne, 13–34. New York: Oxford University Press

Jaishankar, Subrahmanyam. 2015. IISS Fullerton Lecture by Dr. S. Jaishankar, Foreign Secretary in Singapore, speech presented at the International Institute for Strategic Studies, Singapore, 20th July, 2015

Jaishankar, Subrahmanyam. 2016, May 26. India's Five Foreign Policy Goals: Great Strides, Steep Challenges. The Wire

Kaarbo, Juliet. 2015. A Foreign Policy Analysis Perspective on the Domestic Politics Turn in IR Theory. *International Studies Review* 17, no.2: 189–216

Karnad, Bharat. 2015. India's Strategic Diffidence. In *What Does India Think?*, ed., François Godement, 85–89. Brussels: ECFR. www.ecfr.eu/page/-/ECFR145_WDIT.pdf (accessed: 15 November 2019)

Kuznetsov, A. S. 2014. *Theory and Practice of Paradiplomacy: Subnational governments in International Affairs*. New York: Routledge

Malone, David M. 2011. *Does the Elephant Dance? Contemporary Indian Foreign Policy*. New Delhi: Oxford University Press.

Miller, Manjari Chatterjee. 2013. India's Feeble Foreign Policy: A Would-be Great Power Resists Its Own Rise. *Foreign Affairs* 93, no.3: 14–19

Mitra, Subrata K. and Schöttli, Jivanta. 2007. The New Dynamics of Indian Foreign Policy and Its Ambiguities. *Irish Studies in International Affairs 18:* 19–34

Mohan, Raja C. 2006. India and the Balance of Power. *Foreign Affairs* 85, no.4: 17–32

Mohan, Raja C. 2009. The Re-Making of Indian Foreign Policy: Ending the Marginalization of the International Relations Community. *International Studies* 46, no.1–2: 147–163

Mukherjee, Rohan and Malone, David M. 2010. Polity, Security, and Foreign Policy in Contemporary India. In *South Asia's Weak States: Understanding the Regional Insecurity Predicament*, ed. T. V. Paul, 147–169. Stanford: Stanford University Press

Ogden, Chris. 2009. Post-Colonial, Pre-BJP: The Normative Parameters of India's Security Identity, 1947–1998. *Asian Journal of Political Science* 17, no.2: 215–237

Parkin, Benjamin and Findlay, Stephanie. 2020. India: Is Modi's BJP Introducing Big Brother? *Financial Times*. www.ft.com/content/c626fd96-4db3-11ea-95a0-43d18ec715f5 (accessed: 20 March 2020)

Parmar, Inderjeet. 2018. The US-Led Liberal Order: Imperialism by Another Name? International Affairs 94, no.1: 151–172

Press Information Bureau, Government of India, Prime Minister's Office. 2015. 07-February-2015 15:7 IST PM to Heads of Indian Missions

Rosenau, James N. 1966. Pre-Theories and Theories of Foreign Policy. In *Approaches to Comparative and International Politics*, ed., R. B. Farrell, 27–92. Evanston: Northwestern University Press

Roy, Arundhati. 2020. Modi's Brutal Treatment of Kashmir Exposes His Tactics – and Their Flaws. *The Guardian*. www.theguardian.com/commentisfree/2020/aug/05/modi-brutal-treatment-of-kashmir-exposes-his-tactics-and-their-flaws (accessed: 19 November 2020)

Sahni, Varun. 2005. The Protean Polis and Strategic Surprises: Do Changes within India Affect South Asian Strategic Stability? *Contemporary South Asia* 14, no.2: 219–231

Schiavon, J. A. 2019. *Comparative Paradiplomacy*. New York: Routledge

Schmidt, Johannes Dragsbæk. 2017. The Internal and External Constraints on Foreign Policy in India: Exploring Culture and Ethnic Sensitivities. *Third World Quarterly* 38, no.8: 1894–1908

Shekar, Shashi. 2019, April 6. Demonetisation Was Done in National Interest: PM Narendra Modi. *LiveMint*. www.livemint.com/elections/lok-sabha-elections/demonetisation-was-done-in-national-interest-pm-narendra-modi-1554504639418.html (accessed: 16 August 2020)

Subramanian, Samanth. 2020, February 20. How Hindu Supremacists Are Tearing India Apart. *The Guardian*. www.theguardian.com/world/2020/feb/20/hindu-supremacists-nationalism-tearing-india-apart-modi-bjp-rss-jnu-attacks (accessed: 4 August 2020)

Tellis, Ashley J. 2016. India as a Leading Power. *Carnegie Endowment for International Peace*. https://carnegieendowment.org/2016/04/04/india-as-leading-power-pub-63185 (accessed: 16 August 2019)

*The Economic Times*. 2020, March 15. J&K Statehood to Be Restored Soon, No Demographic Changes: Amit Shah. https://economictimes.indiatimes.com/news/politics-and-nation/jk-statehood-to-be-restored-soon-no-demographic-changes-amit-shah/articleshow/74638939.cms (accessed 20 August 2020)

Zakaria, Fareed. 1992. Realism and Domestic Politics: A Review Essay. *International Security* 17, no.1: 177–198

# Part I

# The evolution of reactive and proactive foreign policy

# 2 The struggle between political idealism and policy realism

## The making of India's nuclear policy

*A. Vinod Kumar**

India's grand strategy has evolved since its independence through various dimensions that defined its status among the comity of nations. Its approach to the international system was shaped by the inherent metamorphoses in its own national identity – initially as a third-world state struggling to tide over the colonial hangover, its subsequent growth into prominence as a developing nation with enhanced leverage in its neighbourhood, and its eventual elevation as a major power with the concomitant rise in its economic strength and military capabilities. This evolution was also represented by the multitude of roles that India assumed for itself: as a poster-boy of former colonies that sought a distinct identity from their erstwhile imperial masters, as a crusader against the division of the world into superpower blocs through a mentoring role in the non-aligned movement (NAM), and as a country that exercised realist statecraft by breaking away from its idealist foundations when its national interests were at stake.

The transformation in India's power profile has reflected through the variations in its grand strategic standing as illustrated by its numerous contributions and interventions towards shaping global discourses on multipolarity and collective security structures in the post-War years, as also its post-Cold War efforts to explore a place for itself at the high tables – be it on economic interdependence, non-proliferation, climate change, or reforming the UN Security Council to reflect the new power equations. A notable aspect of India's transformation from a third-world actor to a major power is the contest and transformation of dominant ideologies, namely the political conceptions of leaderships about the world order and how such variances had influenced the process of framing India's approach to the world.

The history of India's nuclear policymaking fits into this backdrop and remains an integral part of the grand strategic tradition of over seventy years, though also replete with its high symbolism of political idealism being often contrasted by realist pursuits of national interest and realpolitik. For a country that religiously espoused the cause of nuclear disarmament and total elimination of nuclear weapons and then went on to undertake two rounds of nuclear tests – first in 1974 and later in 1998 – India's nuclear decisions and actions have had a significant impact in the shaping of the global non-proliferation regime and its associated normative structures. This history is made unique by the fact that few actors in post-War global affairs could replicate the Indian record of being at the forefront of formulating normative structures (as a norm entrepreneur) and subsequently undertaking deviant actions (and ending up as an outlier) that were intended to challenge the character of those same structures with the hope of changing the status quo or their normative basis.

Positing that nuclear politics occupied a prominent space in the global security landscape, this chapter seeks to address a key puzzle: how has the role India played in global nuclear affairs determined or influenced its standing in the international system? Put differently, how could India's nuclear history be explained – as a template reflection of India's foreign policy the way it evolved in the seven decades or as one of the prominent policy fields that were moulded by the grand strategic paradigms the leaderships developed over the decades? Furthermore, should India's nuclear history be viewed through the prism of its sustained attempts to influence the politics of the global nuclear order or should it be analysed through the conflicts and struggles the Indian leaderships underwent in charting a nuclear policy that mirrored its grand strategic outlook? This chapter approaches these questions by examining the 'nuclear' leg of Indian foreign policy traversing three political epochs, and arguing that national interest remained a constant through these phases irrespective of their ideational nature or slant.

## The 'nuclear' in India's foreign policy

The evolution of India's foreign policy has been ideational as well as epochal; the same applies to its nuclear policy record as well. The ideational course has traversed through three paradigmatic models, namely (a) the initial quest to promote a post-colonial order bereft of imperialism and attain third-world leadership in the post-War global order, (b) non-alignment as a means to position India amid global politics of bloc rivalry, power balancing, military containment and alliances, and (c) a realist shift towards elevating itself towards the central balance of great powers backed by advances in its economic and military profile. Three perceptible epochs, influenced by the above-listed paradigms, could be identified in India's nuclear journey: (a) when India opted for nuclear disarmament and total elimination realising how global power balancing in the post-War years was being determined by nuclear powers, (b) when the desire to shape an egalitarian and non-discriminatory nuclear order propelled its actions to challenge the emergent normative structures, and (c) when the emergence of a tumultuous post-Cold War world along with fading hopes of disarmament and rising security challenges formalised its pursuit of a credible nuclear deterrent, conditioned its renewed engagement with the non-proliferation regime and drove aspirations for an elevated position at the nuclear high tables. All three paths had their inevitable foreign policy or grand strategic calling, analysed below.

### *The post-colonial and anti-imperialism paradigm*

The quest for a post-colonial world order in the immediate post-War years formed the contours of India's foreign policy from the outset, which is largely attributed to collective vision of the Gandhian worldview and Jawaharlal Nehru's internationalism. The resolution of the All India Congress Committee of 8 August 1942, jointly drafted by Mahatma Gandhi and Jawaharlal Nehru, had called upon the British to quit so that India could defend itself as a free nation and look ahead to the formation of a world federation. The resolution said:

> [T]he future peace, security and ordered progress of the world demand a world federation of free nations, and on no other basis can the problems of the modern world be solved. An independent India would gladly join such a world federation and cooperate on an equal basis with other countries in the solution of international problems.
>
> (Parthasarthi, 1994)

It was, however, Nehru's concept of internationalism depicted by his idea of One World centred on the United Nations that defined India's grand strategy in the initial years. Nehru's internationalism comprised five elements: (a) shaping a post-colonial world by countering colonialism, imperialism and racialism, (b) non-alignment by staying away from the superpower bloc rivalry, (c) peaceful co-existence for a cooperative international order, (d) preventing internationalisation of conflicts, and (e) disarmament (Kalyanaraman, 2014; Kumar, 2011; Dar and Dar, 2016). While there is no denying the Nehruvian commitment to campaigns against imperialism and promotion of third-world causes, there are differing views on the actual intentions behind the conceptualisation of the 'peaceful co-existence' slogan and how he saw the implications of nuclear politics gaining centrality in global affairs. The dominant, and largely substantiated, narrative glorifies the impact Nehru's internationalism had in shaping the post-War global order and particularly in carving space for the third world in a global power spectrum with India as the spearhead. Nothing exemplifies this better than the fact that the 'peaceful co-existence' principle was institutionalised – first through the 'Panchsheel Agreement', as part of the India–China agreement in 1954 by adding specific ideals like mutual respect for territorial integrity and sovereignty, mutual non-aggression, non-interference in internal affairs of the other, equality and respect etc. That these principles were reiterated in Indo-Soviet relations during the visit of Nikita Khrushchev to India in 1955 and subsequently adopted by the UN in a resolution in 1957 embodied the global acceptance of the Nehruvian model.

While espousing his brand of internationalism, Nehru was lucid about where India has to place itself in the evolving global political system. Through various elucidations during the 1950s at home and abroad, Nehru asserted that India has a prominent space in world politics by virtue of its geographical (as a bridge between East and West) and political positioning (as a former colony that had a tradition of nationalist struggle against imperialism and promise to rise on the global scene), and also then had some influence and potential for a prominent role in global affairs. He conceived of India's future trajectory by asserting that India needs to strengthen economically and militarily to defend from external attack, but not to become an imperialist power and that security was obtained not just by military power but also by policies of friendship. In a speech to the Parliament in February 1953, Nehru remarked thus:

> [T]he strength which limits or conditions the foreign policy of a country may be military, financial or, if I may use the word, moral. It is obvious that India has neither military nor financial strength. Furthermore, we have no desire to and cannot impose our will on others.[1]

T.N. Kaul, who served in both the Nehru and Indira Gandhi governments, described this policy as driven by the deep traditions of tolerance of an ancient country and its belief in peaceful co-existence and the peaceful solution of problems. Kaul contended that India's anti-colonialism and opposition to military alliances are based on the assumption that supporting all movements that uphold sovereign equality of nations will be in its own national interest.[2] This approach was seemingly also driven by Nehru's aversion towards a military- or power-centric framework of world politics and his belief that states have to avoid war and engage in a lasting search for peace. Ashok Kapur, however, feels that more than an exercise in idealism, peaceful co-existence is a strategy based on national interest and opportunism to address the transitional phase in Indian foreign relations until it gains military and economic strength to defend its interests (Kapur, 1976). Kapur quotes a statement by Nehru to point out that he had rejected the Gandhian approach in foreign and defence matters: "We are moved by these arguments, but for us, the non-violent method was not and could not be a religion or an unchallengeable creed or dogma. It could only be a policy promising certain results … to be finally judged" (Das, 1961).

Will that be to say that the disarmament advocacy too came across as a clear political strategy? That disarmament figured in Nehru's principles of One World and that he brought it to the centre-stage of global debate right from the end of World War II onwards signified the importance he gave from the beginning to challenges caused by nuclear weapons. Yet there are varying views on the ideational spirit or strategic calling behind Nehru's disarmament activism even if existing documentary evidence by and large underlines his aversion towards nuclear weapons. In fact, India under Nehru had started putting forward her views on disarmament as early as the third session of the United Nations General Assembly (UNGA) in September 1948, where Vijaylakshmi Pandit described the problem of atomic energy control and disarmament as "one of the most important items and momentous questions" for discussion (Jain, 1974). That she talked about ending the nuclear race as well as outlawing biological and chemical warfare in itself was viewed as illustrating the farsightedness and knowledge of the leadership at that point of time.

Yet, for a man known to be influenced by Gandhian thought about nuclear weapons – as a diabolic use of science – as much as his awe for the atom's many manifestations, Nehru's disarmament advocacy seemed to be a mix of idealism and pragmatism, along with a bit of surrealism (Mirchandani, 1978). In one of his early letters to chief ministers, Nehru wrote thus:

> Disarmament should be the first and vital issue before everyone, not only disarmament in the physical sense of putting an end to the vast armed forces, but even more so in its effects on the mind. We have to disarm our minds of hatred and the spirit of violence. When that will be, I don't know. But unless this comes about a disaster on an inconceivable scale is inevitable.
>
> (Singh and Sharma, 2000)[3]

Parthasarthi pointed out that the nuclear problem had bothered Nehru at entirely two different levels at the same time. At one level, it was the issue of a global nuclear war leading to planetary devastation, which, he felt, had to be prevented at all cost and machinery devised within the parameters of an existing global organisation to prevent the outbreak of such a conflict between the great powers. At another level, the continuing environmental hazards posed by atmospheric tests bothered him (Parthasarthi, 1994).

The actual Nehruvian imprint on global disarmament discourse began with his 1954 proposal for a standstill agreement to halt nuclear testing.[4] Nehru's approach towards disarmament seemed to have been shaped by two key factors: (a) propensity of the superpowers to determine the character of the international system by relying on military power, especially nuclear weapons, and (b) the actions of nuclear powers to dominate and monopolise all affairs of the atom. Accordingly, the standard theme that reverberated in Nehru's campaign was his urge to challenge this nuclear monopoly and devise a more egalitarian international system to manage the affairs of the atom, a principle that has remained constant in India's nuclear outreach ever since. Despite his vigorous campaign against nuclear testing, Nehru's approach reflected a realistic appreciation of global power politics and the realisation that his crusade would make only marginal influence on the race for nuclear supremacy.[5] While sounding pragmatic in his declarations that disarmament could only be achieved in a phased manner, Nehru also evoked amusement (and alarm) by suggesting ambitious timelines like four to five years for nuclear abolition to be accomplished, though not specifying how this could happen.[6] His vision for general and complete disarmament by prohibiting all conventional as well as biological and chemical weapons, and his seemingly exaggerated claims on the impact of ongoing nuclear testing, carried a tenor of idealistic rhetoric.[7]

On the other hand, this activism also proved effective in parroting the third-world voice and propelling their interests as a post-colonial collective, especially when the Atoms for Peace plan was floated by US president Dwight Eisenhower, and when the structure of the International Atomic Energy Agency (IAEA) was being negotiated.[8] The Indian campaign against the safeguards systems was based on the argument that it was discriminatory against the aspirations of the third world and also that the Agency's representation was lopsided. In fact, the most significant Indian contribution was the formula it proposed for the constitution of the IAEA Board of Governors, which ensured representation for every region and has since remained the organising principle of the Board (Fischer, 1997). By the time Nehru was leaving the scene, the scenario was sharply transforming with the aggravating superpower rivalry leading to flashpoints like the Cuban Missile Crisis and the inevitability of a Chinese nuclear bomb looming large in the background. As new proposals came up at the UNGA and its disarmament bodies, the Indian delegation followed up its campaign for a grand disarmament instrument, as conceived by Nehru, which would prohibit the production of nuclear stockpiles, mitigate their spread and lead to disarmament and total elimination.[9]

While the public statements Nehru made throughout his life were profound expressions of his disarmament vision, echoing the superpower arms race and their propensity to monopolise the affairs of the atom, there is a parallel line of argument that suggests Nehru being receptive towards keeping the nuclear weapons option open (Karnad, 2002). Bharat Karnad has been the foremost votary of this argument which is based on various less-publicised statements of Nehru, his policy decisions, and the manner in which the nuclear establishment has been structured, as well as many personal accounts. Karnad points to Nehru's 'awe' of the atom's gigantic manifestations based on a speech delivered to the 34th session of the Indian Science Congress on 3 January 1947 in which he talked of "Hiroshima heralding all kinds of enormous changes … (and) producing a conflict in people's mind about ends and means". Karnad cites a reference in this speech to science having "two faces like Janus, both destruction and constructive", as embodying Nehru's thinking in favour of both civilian and military applications of the atom. Also listed is another speech in which Nehru had likened the atomic bomb to the invention of gunpowder, as the heralding of a new age, and hoping that India would harness the opportunity provided by the atom.

Karnad attributes Nehru's purported fascination with a nuclear deterrent as influenced by four personalities: Field Marshal Sir Claude Auchinleck, India's first Commander-in-Chief, who espoused the possibility of a formidable Indian force structure; Lt. Gen. Sir Francis Tuker, then General Officer Commanding-in-Chief of Indian Army's Eastern Command, who had identified India among the countries with large landmass and one that could play a singular military role in maintaining peace in Australasia; PMS Blackett, the British physicist, who had vouched for a small nuclear deterrent for Britain (that India could emulate); and Homi Bhabha, the architect of the Indian nuclear programme, who had talked about India's ability to produce a nuclear weapon in the shortest possible time. Beyond these influences, Karnad feels Nehru's decision to keep the nuclear programme secretive and under his direct control, and the conscious choice of a pressurised heavy water reactor (PHWR) to harness the promise of plutonium for a potential military application, exemplified his desire to keep this option open.

Thus, in Karnad's words, Nehru's approach was about the weaving of three policy streams: the utility of nuclear weapons, disarmament and nuclear energy as a source of electricity. He attributes Nehru's desire to acquire competence in nuclear technology as driven by his belief that it could provide India with bargaining power in the international system. Though Karnad quotes many statements to draw inferences about Nehru's bomb interest, the closest Nehru seems to have come to indicating his future consideration of nuclear weapons was his statement of 24 May 1957 (for a resolution on nuclear explosions) that "if one has these fissionable materials and resources, then one can make a bomb, unless the world will be wise enough to stop (its) production" (Singh and Sharma, 2000). Karnad also cites a statement by Krishna Menon in July 1956 when he said countries like India could produce nuclear weapons cheaply, which could complicate the problem if great powers did not expedite a satisfactory agreement on disarmament.

It is not just Karnad who interprets such statements to premise Nehru's purported interest in nuclear weapons. Ashok Kapur, for instance, quotes Nehru's speech of 22 November 1960 to insist on an active link between India's disarmament activism and its nuclear policy (implying its security angle). Nehru had remarked in that speech: "If nothing effective is done in regard to disarmament in the course of the next three or four years, it may perhaps become too late to deal with it" (Kapur, 1976). Despite such assertions, the context Nehru (and Menon) provided for such lines of opinion was seemingly to warn the international community about the impending armament race if nuclear powers did not adopt a path of disarmament. Many such warnings have been sounded in the course of India's disarmament outreach, which cannot be convincingly connected to a security intention or plans to keep the nuclear option open. Yet Kapur thinks some of Nehru's statements were with a reference to the Chinese nuclear programme. He argues that Nehru's disarmament policy was not simply guided by an altruistic concern to save humanity, but instead was intended to secure a purposive disarmament agreement that could contain China's programme and, failing that, to retain India's nuclear option. Kapur, like many others, feels Nehru kept his thoughts on nuclear policy options ambiguous, especially the boundaries he set between peaceful and military uses of nuclear energy.

Another addition to this line of thought is by Sampooran Singh, who claims Nehru said in 1946 that India would develop nuclear power for peaceful purposes only, "so long as the world was constituted as it was, every country would have to develop the latest scientific devices for its protection" (Singh, 1971). Singh cites various examples to contend that Nehru had put India's interests first and hence could have modified his views on nuclear weapons after knowing of Chinese nuclear plans. The apparent impression projected here is that Nehru was not the 'peacenik' he was made out to be and that his dependence on military power is evidence that he had not excluded the role of force from his statecraft. Notwithstanding the fact that even an idealist leader could rely on military force to defend his nation, such contentions, in fact, provide for an alternate paradigm in explaining the evolution of India's nuclear policy, especially to illustrate the extent of policy options the leadership contemplated in their quest to maintain an idealist outlook without detaching from the means to secure its strategic interests. In fact, this flexible policymaking matrix is abundantly evident during the decades when non-alignment became the pivot of India's grand strategy.

### *Non-alignment as the guiding principle*

Though non-alignment was a Nehruvian conception, its actual relevance was in determining the space for India and the third world in the Cold War spectrum from the early 1960s, when the superpower competition began to acquire many dynamic and sometimes contrasting dimensions – of conflict, cooperation and détente. After its initial mobilisation as an anti-colonial and anti-imperial voice, the movement has been about the struggles of members to confront and reconcile with the normative structuring of the global order as shaped by superpower politics. India's own non-aligned postures remained contested and subjected to varied interpretations as it evolved in the next four decades of pivoting India's foreign policy, including its interaction with the emergent nuclear order that came into being with the Treaty on the Non-Proliferation of Nuclear Weapons (NPT).

Nehru evidently had two streams of thought on the virtues of being non-aligned: as a model of third-world self-sufficiency, if not supremacy, bereft of influences of imperialism or colonial elements, and as a platform to safeguard the interests of those who wished not to align with the superpowers in the Cold War rivalry. Nehru said in a 1953 speech:

> To become part of a power bloc means giving up the right to have a policy of our own and following that of somebody else. We should co-operate with others or consult them but at the same time must follow an independent policy.[10]

Kaul fashions this further by stating that non-alignment was seen more as a bridge between two hostile ideological blocs and a policy of independence to judge issues on its merits, irrespective of external pressure.[11]

Though it needed courage of conviction to adopt an independent policy against power blocs, as Kaul puts it, there was considerable confusion on where NAM members placed themselves in the global pecking order – as a third alternative or a neutral group. Nehru attempted an early explanation on this:

> My approach to foreign policy … you may call it neutral or whatever else. But I fail to see how this approach is neutral. Neutrality as a policy has little meaning except in times of war. If you think there is a Cold War today, we are certainly neutral. We are not going to participate in a Cold War which is worse than a shooting war.[12]

In a speech to the US Congress in 1949, which Kaul highlights, Nehru stated that "India is not neutral. India cannot and shall not be neutral where peace is threatened and freedom is denied, for to be neutral in such circumstances would be the denial of all that India stands for".[13] M.C. Chagla, who was Indira Gandhi's foreign minister, expounded this further in 1967:

> India's policy of non-alignment did not mean neutrality. By not aligning herself with any power bloc, she was not subservient to any country and reserved the right to pass judgment on international issues. At the same time, she was aligned to certain principles and certain causes: to disarmament, to doing away with nuclear weapons, to anti-communalism, apartheid, and so on.[14]

Such elucidations notwithstanding, the West essentially saw India's non-alignment as a negative policy, with the then US Secretary of State John Foster Dulles terming it as immoral, as a policy of expediency, of sitting on the fence, alongside his argument that those who are with us are with us and those who are not are against us. In fact, most Western analyses of non-alignment treated it in relation to the bipolar world, as an effort to mediate superpower rivalries or to prevent global war, along with other conceptions like it being a repudiation of traditional machinery of power politics, reactive diplomacy, representing itself as a posture of moral superiority, substituting balance of power model, and so on. Kapur, though, differs with these dominant prognoses and argues that, rather than staying away from bloc conflicts, non-alignment was about getting involved in global politics, as a 'low-risk' strategy to gain influence despite the condition of material weakness and to gain influence through diplomatic means. Neutralism and equidistance, Kapur thinks, only meant a rejection of military alliance, not any other politico-economic or cultural-intellectual relations, as India did with both major powers of both blocs.

Despite non-alignment being fashioned as India's foreign policy ideology for over four decades, India found itself indulging in realist statecraft involving both blocs with significant policy swings that could be counted as everything from neutrality to alignment. The decision to seek US assistance when the Chinese attack happened in 1962, the efforts to obtain military equipment from both the superpowers, the food aid from the US and the Friendship Treaty with the Soviet Union are notable examples of the policy initiatives that transcended the non-alignment ethos.[15] In fact, the Indian outreach during the 1960s was largely shadowed by two key aid issues –food aid and arms supplies. While being dependent on the US for food aid, India also had to grapple with its balancing games when it came to US arms supplies to Pakistan, which illustrated Washington's preferential policies towards Pakistan as a Cold War ally even while humouring India so as to ensure that it did not veer towards the Soviets.[16]

An outcome of this manoeuvring was Indira Gandhi's decision to sign a Treaty of Peace, Friendship and Cooperation with the Soviet Union.[17] Though the US endorsed it as a peace treaty, Gandhi used the aggravating crisis with Pakistan over Bangladesh as a rationale for the treaty, terming it as 'additional deterrent'.[18] Yet the impact of the peace treaty was not just the credibility of India's non-alignment advocacy being eroded, but also India's hyphenation with the Soviets. This shaped India's subsequent international interactions till the end of the Cold War, with the US and allies taking an inimical approach on many issues, be it on India's peaceful nuclear explosion (PNE) of 1974, the sanctions imposed on the missile development programmes, the dispute over Jammu and Kashmir, cross-border terrorism, trade policies, and so on. India's non-alignment was thus seen as an idealist façade to exercise statecraft and pursue national interests, with neutrality and alignment with the superpowers conditioned by the strategic environment.

If, in practice, non-alignment meant preserving the autonomy to take decisions pertaining to one's own national interest, free of superpower influence, pressure or enticement, what has it meant for India's nuclear policy? From the Nehruvian times, Indian political leaderships have looked at nuclear weapons as the most potent symbol of great power dominance as well as a means to gain leverage in global affairs. Nehru's initial disarmament activism, for that matter, was not just about limiting the role of nuclear weapons in the imperial imprints of the superpowers, but also about inhibiting the possibility of aspirant states using them as means to great power status. Yet, even while spearheading the resistance against nuclear monopoly, early Indian leaderships were seemingly concerned about the possibility of non-alignment becoming a hurdle in the pursuit of national interests, especially if it demanded at some stage a shift towards military applications of nuclear technology.

Nonetheless, non-alignment remained a key factor in framing India's nuclear policy, which was driven by overlapping objectives – being detached from the nuclear politics of superpowers, pursuing nuclear policies that were in India's national interests, and promoting third-world interests in the emerging nuclear order or, rather, an egalitarian nuclear rules system. Accordingly, principles that defined non-alignment – be it neutrality, equidistance or autonomy – had significant meanings for India's nuclear policies, outreach and activism from the 1960s onwards. In fact, two parallel streams influenced nuclear decision-making during the 'non-aligned' decades from the 1960s to the 1990s: one involving India's disarmament diplomacy and the other about a nuclear policy that could secure India's strategic interests.

*NPT and India's disarmament dogma*

A defining feature of disarmament diplomacy in the non-aligned period was the struggles faced by the leadership: one, about balancing Nehruvian ideals with realist policymaking when it came to institutionalising the non-proliferation norm, and second, delaying the certitude of a weapons programme in the hope of a disarmament breakthrough. India's nuclear outreach from the early 1960s was preoccupied with fears of the Chinese bomb, dealing with domestic pressure for a strategic response and the effort to safeguard the idealist disarmament outlook. India's campaign at the Eighteen Nation Disarmament Committee (ENDC), which was formed to negotiate and draft a comprehensive disarmament instrument (but ended up formulating the NPT), was centred on the hope that the disarmament treaty would formulate a time-bound process towards total elimination, which would affect existing and prospective nuclear powers. Accordingly, by the time of China's first nuclear test in October 1964, India had adopted the strategy of demanding a "prohibition of the manufacture, acquisition, receipt or transference of these weapons" for a comprehensive treaty that could address both vertical and horizontal proliferation.[19] In fact, it was the Indian representative, V.C. Trivedi, who introduced the phrase and concept of 'proliferation' in the lexicon, which became the nomenclature for the treaty – the NPT.[20]

The NPT, howsoever flawed its creation, did not just emerge as the cornerstone of the global non-proliferation regime and its associated normative structures, but also became a decisive factor in determining India's nuclear status in the years to come. The three years of NPT negotiations (1965–1968) were marked by the contest between the superpowers on one side exploring a treaty that secured their arsenals while promoting non-proliferation, and the non-weapon states, on the other, pushing for a treaty that balanced non-proliferation with disarmament timelines and enabled uninhibited access to peaceful uses of nuclear energy. While attempting to shape the treaty text through initiatives like Resolution 2028,[21] the final months of the NPT negotiations witnessed India's attempt to secure security guarantees from the superpowers, retain the right to conduct peaceful nuclear explosions and invoke a timeline for reductions and elimination in the final text (Kumar, 2016). In fact, India's unique activism – a mix of resistance to superpower dominance, advocacy for nuclear rights of the third world, and forming a neutral bloc – patently carried the symbols of India's non-aligned positioning.

An example of its determined resistance was the belligerence India showed against curbing rights to conduct peaceful nuclear explosions, calling the US proposal for commercialising this technology an "atomic commercial super-monopoly" and affirming that "the civil nuclear powers cannot tolerate atomic apartheid in their economic and peaceful development".[22] At the same time, India was ready for adjustments while seeking security guarantees from the nuclear powers, largely driven by the Chinese threat in mind, which some Indian parliamentarians described as a sort of alignment. It is another matter that the superpowers were not willing to enshrine security guarantees in the NPT nor was India inclined to accept 'nuclear umbrellas' that could undermine its non-alignment stand, besides its lack of faith that the superpowers would come to its rescue in the event of a nuclear attack by China.[23] An equally significant non-aligned posture was India's leadership of the NAM bloc at ENDC to raise the third-world voice, whether it was on Resolution 2028, opposition to the US–Soviet joint draft (which became the NPT text) or the decision to abstain on the UNGA resolution on the treaty text.

Though India was among 21 countries that abstained, the decision to undertake a PNE in 1974 was seen as a demonstration of a nuclear weapon capability, which invited censure[24] from the West, with Canada withdrawing support to the nuclear programme and the US going slow on supplies for Tarapur nuclear power plant.[25] The period from 1974 to the mid-1990s was marked by the struggles of the Indian leaderships to convince the world that it had no plans to produce nuclear weapons while remaining committed to the disarmament cause. Starting with the Morarji Desai government's declaration that India would desist from any further PNEs,[26] India remained at the forefront of the disarmament movement, especially at the Special Sessions on Disarmament (SSoDs), where it sought a 'nuclear freeze', end to the production of weapons and fissile materials, and the prohibition of nuclear weapons.[27] Throughout the 1980s, India spearheaded or was part of various initiatives including the Six-Nation Initiative on peace and disarmament that culminated in the Stockholm Declaration of January 1988, the Palme Commission and eventually the Rajiv Gandhi Action Plan. The Action Plan, in fact, was a landmark initiative through which Prime Minister Rajiv Gandhi proposed measures towards total elimination by 2010.[28] The final turn in this course of India's disarmament diplomacy was its co-sponsorship of the resolution 48/70 for a comprehensive nuclear test ban treaty in November 1993, though it eventually opposed the final text for the same reasons as the NPT – that it was a discriminatory text that favoured the interests of the nuclear weapon states.

### *Nuclearisation – the strategic option*

Even while India's disarmament diplomacy was in action, the leadership was constantly challenged by the imperative of having to secure its security interests in the light of the Chinese threat. That the NPT turned out to be a discriminatory treaty that mitigated India's right (as a non-nuclear weapons state (NNWS)) to develop nuclear weapons, while allowing the nuclear powers (including China) to retain and expand their arsenals, also propelled the leadership's resolve to stay out of the treaty and explore other options to secure its interests. Certainly, the two decades (from 1974–1995) were also witnessing a distinct form of statecraft displayed by the Indian leadership through policy formulations that could be interpreted in different ways –either as a circumvention of non-alignment or a distinctive pursuit of national interests without appearing to jettison the idealist values. This condition, as either a preferred choice of action or an existential predicament, amply embodied nuclear policymaking from the 1960s till around 1998. Chagla described this condition aptly:

> There had been considerable apprehension as to what India should do in response to China having exploded the bomb. There was a section which insisted that this should not be allowed to go unanswered and that since India had the technological knowledge, equipment and men, she should manufacture the bomb. India stood for certain values … created by Gandhiji through non-violence and although the national interest must come first, those values could not be lightly thrown aside.[29]

For the diplomatic overdrive, which intensified after the Chinese test, coincided with the emergence of the pro-bomb lobby within the country – initially propelled by the right-wing parties and later joined by voices from other parties, media and the nascent strategic community. At the forefront was the Bharatiya Jana Sangh, which had demanded the production of nuclear weapons soon after the 1962 war with China.[30] Besides building pressure for a nuclear deterrent, the lobby also sought withdrawal from the Limited/Partial Test Ban Treaty (LTBT/PTBT) in light of China's non-adherence. Adding to the clamour was the statement by Homi Bhabha that a nuclear weapon device could be readied in 18 months.[31] The government's measured response to these demands was that though India had the technological capability to develop such weapons, it would use nuclear energy only for peaceful purposes; this policy, however, might not remain static and would be reviewed based on the security environment.[32] This approach, though initially driven by the hope of a disarmament instrument, was subsequently maintained in order to quell the pro-bomb voices even as the government explored the means to deal with the security environment.

Between 1966 and 1968, when NPT negotiations were at their peak and China was testing on a regular basis, there were numerous statements and developments that pointed to the Indian leadership seeking more proactive options to deal with the enveloping security environment. While Indira Gandhi declared that "we are increasing our know-how and that China cannot attack any country with impunity", Swaran Singh assured the Parliament that the policy (of making a bomb) was kept under constant review and that not just China but other factors including progress made at the disarmament negotiations would be taken into consideration.[33] Indira Gandhi, in an interview to *Le Monde*, stated that "we may find ourselves having to take a nuclear decision any moment and it is therefore not possible for us to tie our hands". Sarabhai had remarked to Robert McNamara in April 1967 that "if disarmament is not going to be the next step, then India is reluctant to give up the option of building the bomb" (Noorani, 2001). Indira Gandhi also made statements in November 1967, when the NPT text was being finalised, that "our policy is constantly under review and first consideration is to safeguard national security".[34] Later, she declared in the Lok Sabha that "we will now be driven by our self-enlightenment".[35] Most of these statements, however, seemed a balancing act as Indira Gandhi continued to reject the possibility of a weapons pursuit.

At the other end of the spectrum are a handful of reminiscences that indicate that the government wanted to keep its options open on the weapons programme. M.G.K. Menon, who headed the Tata Institute of Fundamental Research (TIFR), talked about Bhabha hinting at the possibility of his joining the Indira Gandhi cabinet (implying dramatic changes in the nuclear programme).[36] B.G. Varghese points to an Atomic Energy Commission (AEC) meeting in 1966 where tentative approval was given for the study of a nuclear weapons programme and delivery system (Varghese, 2010). The nuclear weapons debate had intensified by 1965 with various studies conducted on the cost and feasibility of a weapons programme, with Bhabha's estimate of Rs 18 lakh being debated (and contested by some scientists) along with those done by Subramanian Swamy and others.[37] A 1964 US Intelligence Estimate stated that India had capabilities for plutonium separation and could produce its first device in 1–3 years after a decision, determined by factors like the pace of the Chinese programme and assurances from the superpowers.[38] K. Subrahmanyam describes the three schools that shaped this debate thus: the first opposed a weapons programme, the second demanded a full-fledged deterrent and the third favoured a "crash programme" of weapons and delivery means for a limited mission (Subrahmanyam, 1970).

The defining aspects of nuclear policymaking at that point of time were: (a) the decision to reject the NPT (conveying a desire for strategic autonomy and moderating the pro-bomb pressure),[39] (b) the refusal to discard the PNE option (as announced in Parliament on various occasions),[40] and (c) the Sarabhai Plan, which initiated the nuclearisation phase. The NPT decision underlined the dominant thinking among all sections that the treaty would be inimical to India's interests, especially with China's fledging arsenal lurking in the neighbourhood and the treaty failing to enshrine obligations on the nuclear powers to reduce and eliminate their arsenals. Further, the refusal of the superpowers to include security guarantees in the treaty text and the prohibition on the right to undertake PNEs convinced the leadership of the need to devise a strategy – of a middle path – that provided a strategic balancing without compromising on its ideational standing. The middle path was the Sarabhai Plan, which entailed the establishment of a self-reliant and advanced nuclear infrastructure that could provide for a sustainable nuclear energy programme, and enable a shift to a military version when the need arose. Though it looked like a blueprint for nuclear energy and space research, a closer look reveals the game plan to build an advanced infrastructure of nuclear, space and electronics, all with dual-use implications.[41]

Subrahmanyam described this as part of a multi-faceted strategy that was to define India's nuclear policy from the 1970s. It include: (a) reliance on the general deterrence exercised by superpowers, (b) a weapons programme or a 'peaceful' or plutonium explosion, (c) research and development with regard to atomic energy, space and electronics to reach 'a balanced weapons capability' as early as possible, and (d) to seek security in a treaty with one of the superpowers – a strategy that was to be entwined with the disarmament campaign. While many of these strategies were pursued in due course, it remains an enduring mystery as to why Indira Gandhi decided to sanction the PNE six years after rejecting the NPT. Raja Ramanna mentions how Indira Gandhi, while approving the PNE, had "decreed that the experiment should be carried out for the simple reason that India required such a demonstration" (Ramanna, 1991). Although the meaning of these words is yet to be discerned, the official reasoning for the test – of using nuclear explosives for development purposes – was hardly convincing as India showed no concrete plans for using this technology, either for gas and mineral exploration, deep-sea mining or blasting mountains to build tunnels.[42] With the scientific reasoning finding few takers, the Western world saw it as a demonstration of a weapons capability, with Canada refusing to differentiate between PNE and nuclear weapons technology, while the US saw it as India's prospective course towards weaponisation.[43]

The pressure from the Western world and dramatic change in India's domestic politics, though, constrained the scope for any political or developmental exploitation of the 1974 test, with the Morarji Desai government committing not to undertake any further tests, as quid-pro-quo for receiving uranium supplies for the Tarapur plant.[44] It was not until the mid-1980s, when the Pakistani nuclear programme was seen to be considerably progressing with Chinese help and India's disarmament forays were not attaining the desired results that the leadership decided to revisit the possibility of a strategic weapons option. Though there are different narratives of Rajiv Gandhi sanctioning the weapons programme following a cold reception to his Action Plan presented to the UNGA, it was not until the supposedly aborted attempt by the Narasimha Rao government to undertake a test in 1995 that indications of a nuclear weaponisation process came to the limelight, which was subsequently confirmed by the 1998 tests conducted by the National Democratic Alliance (NDA) government. That these tests came after the NPT's indefinite extension and India's rejection of the Comprehensive Test Ban Treaty (CTBT) was a testament to how India sought to balance its non-aligned values with imperatives of national interest.

### *Nuclear power seeking legitimacy*

The 1998 tests came at a crucial juncture – the global order was in turmoil with the Cold War ending; non-alignment was beginning to lose its raison d'être and lustre; India too was in flux trying to figure where it stood in the emerging international system, who its allies could be and what policy it needed to frame for the emergent order. This was also a period when India was undergoing massive transformations marked by the advent of economic liberalisation that meant discarding not just its socialist models but also transcending the third-world matrix to fashion its power pursuits. The nuclear tests, though marking a continuity of policy going by the supposedly aborted attempt in 1995, was thus seen as a realist turn in the way the leadership began to see its national interests from a power-centric paradigm. While some could perceive the idealism followed until then as also being shaped by evolving conceptions of national interest (and indicative of some form of policy realism), the nuclear test marked a decisive shift that signified not just India's rising power profile, commensurate with economic growth and rise in military capabilities, but also the beginning of a calculated grand strategy to harness these 'symbols of strength' to carve out a role and space in great power politics.

The transition from a third-world leader to a great power though was not an easy journey. Despite liberalisation triggering sweeping changes in India's economic policies, the process of global economic integration came with inherent challenges on issues such as World Trade Organization instruments like General Agreement on Trade and Tariffs (GATT) and Quantitative Restrictions, and opening up of various sectors to free-trade agreements and foreign direct investment. Many of these trade-relatedissues added to the existing political divergences, especially with the US, over matters like the Jammu and Kashmir dispute (with enduring American bias towards Pakistan) and continuing sanctions on India's high-technology and missile programmes, among others. The nuclear tests, undertaken in this backdrop, invited international censure, and sanctions from the US and the liberal security community. Yet, despite such initial criticism, it was this demonstration of nuclear weapon capability that marked India's advancement to the ranks of great powers. India's rise on the global scene, and acceptance among great powers, was, however, marked by a process of assimilation – not merely as an economic powerhouse, but also of mainstreaming a nuclear outlier into a nuclear-armed political heavyweight.

Numerous policy formulations and initiatives could be listed to validate what is supposed to be a realist shift in Indian grand strategy: opening a bilateral relationship with Israel, the rapprochement with the US, forging new politico-regional coalitions (like BRICS[45] and BASIC[46]) beyond the NAM framework, the Look East policy (intended to create strategic inroads into the East Asian periphery), attaining power projection capabilities (Cold Start and expeditionary orientation attained by the Indian Navy), anti-piracy operations and acting as a security provider in the Indian Ocean region, cooperating with rivals for common objectives (Paris Agreement, Shanghai Cooperation Organisation, BRICS Bank), and lately, the inclination and determination to undertake cross-border military operations when national security is involved. Despite this broad matrix that supposedly represents the realist shift in India's grand strategy, it is the nuclear arena – embodied by the nuclear tests, the India–US nuclear deal, membership in export control regimes, and so on – that potently represented the power pursuits and realignments that India sought. While nuclear policymaking covers a larger ambit including nonproliferation and disarmament, nuclear doctrine and postures, and nuclear energy, this section encapsulates the post-Cold War realist orientation by analysing two streams: a) returning to the non-proliferation mainstream and reframing its disarmament advocacy, and b) establishing the nuclear deterrent and legitimacy of India's nuclear arsenal and doctrine.

*Mainstreaming non-proliferation and disarmament policy*

Once the initial animus over the 1998 tests subsided and major global actors began to recognise the rationale driving the nuclear tests, a process of dialogue and reconciliation was initiated, most notably the Jaswant Singh–Strobe Talbott talks. Officially described as the India–US dialogue on security, non-proliferation, disarmament and related issues, the interaction was aimed at reducing divergences and harmonising mutual perceptions, especially on nuclear issues.[47] Though different views prevailed on the utility of this dialogue process, three notable outcomes need mention: (a) the talks enabled an endorsement of India's security concerns (especially on the Chinese threat) in the US administration, which was until then sympathetic to the Pakistani narrative on the South Asian security situation; (b) the US side opened up to appreciate India's grouse against the discriminatory nature of the non-proliferation regime, though at the same time laying the initial seeds for its assimilation into the non-proliferation system;[48] (c) the dialogue facilitated the visit to India by President Bill Clinton, the first visit by an American president in 25 years, which was considered as a creeping recognition of the nuclear status as well as setting the ball rolling for the revival of ties, leading all the way to a strategic partnership in 2004. That such a dramatic turnaround happened in the India–US relationship within five years of the nuclear tests indicates the impact it had on the power realignment.

On the other hand, a perceptible change marked India's projection of its nuclear status, with the country seeking global recognition as a state with nuclear weapons. When the 2000 Review Conference (RevCon) of NPT was in session, then External Affairs Minister made a *Suo Motu* statement in Parliament:

> India is a nuclear weapon state. Though not a party, India's policies have been consistent with key provisions of NPT that apply to nuclear weapon states. The NPT community needs to understand that India cannot join the NPT as a non-nuclear-weapon state. Statements about India rolling back its nuclear programme are mere diversions to prevent focussed attention on the basic goals of the NPT. India has been a responsible member of the non-proliferation regime and will continue to take initiatives and work with like-minded countries to bring about a stable, genuine and lasting non-proliferation.[49]

The statement clearly affirms India's post-1998 posture: that it needs to be recognised as a nuclear weapons state and that its policies have been consistent with the NPT (despite rejecting and opposing it for thirty years), though India cannot join it as an NNWS anymore. The highlight of the statement is not just about India espousing the cause of its nuclear weapons, but also its formal declaration of adhering to NPT principles, implying endorsement of the non-proliferation norm (though it opposed its implementation) and rejecting calls to join the treaty as an NNWS (implying clearly its nuclear status). Also discarded in this process was India's historic disarmament positioning – of concurrent efforts, facilitated by or transcending the NPT, to pursue disarmament and total elimination. Instead, post-1998, India took a leaf out of its proposals at the SSoDs to demand a Nuclear Weapons Convention (NWC) that could formulate a non-discriminatory and verifiable elimination treaty by "prohibiting the development, production, stockpiling and use of nuclear weapons".[50]

This quest for legitimacy, on the other hand, coincided with dramatic developments in the global system, notably the 11 September 2001 attacks in the US and the advent of the George W. Bush administration, which came with the promise of unravelling traditional US non-proliferation policies by rejecting the CTBT and putting the NPT in a freeze. Following the 9/11 attacks, the Bush administration proposed a series of new initiatives under his 'forward policy against proliferation' to address the emergent threat matrix under the rubric of a counter-proliferation strategy. These included ventures to cover a broad spectrum of areas: a proactive strategy for military tools (Proliferation Security Initiative and Container Security Initiative) and nuclear terrorism (Global Initiative to Combat Nuclear Terrorism), and securing a fuel cycle under the Global Nuclear Energy Partnership (Kumar, 2014). While many of these initiatives endured controversies over their unilateral character and criticism that they undermined the NPT-centric order, the actual relevance for Indian nuclear policy from the Bush doctrine was its organising principle that countries which violated access to nuclear resources for peaceful uses need to be penalised (reference to Iran, North Korea) while those with a clean non-proliferation record (like India) need to be rewarded. Further, the spectre of nuclear terrorism, along with exposing nuclear-trading black markets (traced to Pakistani scientist A.Q. Khan as mastermind), made a decisive shift in the US approach towards terrorism.

All these factors enabled an India–US convergence on strategic issues leading to a formal partnership, with the 'Next Steps in Strategic Partnership', announced in January 2004, identifying three specific areas to expand cooperation: civilian nuclear activities, civilian space programmes, and high-technology trade, besides dialogue on missile defence.[51] This was a major indicator of India's mainstreaming process as many entities in India's space, missile and nuclear domains which had been facing sanctions for decades were now being invited to partner with US counterparts. Yet the most significant epoch in the evolution of India's nuclear policy was the decision for civil nuclear cooperation, as announced in the 18 July 2005 Joint Statement, which observers termed as India's return to the non-proliferation mainstream or ending three-and-a-half decades of isolation from nuclear commerce.[52] According to the agreement, popularly known as the Indo–US nuclear deal, the US was to facilitate India's access to global nuclear commerce, in return for India's commitment to play a major role in global non-proliferation efforts, besides harmonising its civilian nuclear programme with the norms of the nuclear non-proliferation regime, which included the separation of civilian and military nuclear facilities, commitment to join the FMCT talks and synchronising its systems with international export control norms.

Accordingly, India became the only non-NPT state permitted to participate in nuclear trade despite not subscribing to the IAEA's full-scope or comprehensive safeguard agreement as required by the 1992 (Warsaw) guidelines of the Nuclear Suppliers Group (NSG). A new safeguards agreement was signed with the IAEA in August 2008, following which the NSG gave an India-specific waiver from its guidelines in September 2008. The fledging Indian nuclear energy market was also allurement for many countries like France, Russia and Kazakhstan to take the first plunge in signing nuclear cooperation agreements with India while many erstwhile critics of the Indian programme, including Canada, Japan and Australia, also followed suit. The process towards a 123 Agreement with the US, signed in 2008, came after intense debates in the US Congress and represented the sharp divisions over the special treatment given to India.[53] While the flow of uranium into Indian reactors was an instant spin-off of the deal, an important aspect was the allotment of sites for new nuclear power plants to be constructed with foreign assistance. This was supposed to leapfrog the Indian nuclear energy capability from the around 5000 MW at that point towards the 10,000 MW target and beyond, as originally conceived by the three-stage programme.[54] However, the efforts to gallop towards these projects were stymied by the opposition to stringent provisions in the *Civil Liability for Nuclear Damage Act* (CLNDA) of 2010, which, though, was resolved during President Barack Obama's visit to India in 2015 (Kumar and Patil, 2014; Mohan and Abraham, 2013).

The almost two decades from the time of the 1998 nuclear tests was witness to a unique transformation process of an outlier returning to the centre-stage of global nuclear politics, and a resurgent effort to be at the high tables of global nuclear leadership. From recognising the security imperative behind India's nuclear test to arranging an India-specific waiver enabling its participation in nuclear commerce, and from initiating a strategic partnership to promoting India's membership in export control forums, this Indian journey from being a proliferation problem to being part of the solution has been termed as a distinct case of nuclear exceptionalism (Mohan, 2007; Malik, 2010). This is true on many accounts – India becomes the only non-NPT state that could keep its nuclear arsenal intact (and expand uninhibitedly) and yet participate in nuclear trade without formally attaining the status of a nuclear weapon state; the only non-NPT state to get the NSG waiver; the only country to have a stand-alone safeguards agreement, and so on.

While many NPT state-parties and critics warned that such waivers will weaken the non-proliferation system (besides citing discrimination against NNWS who discarded nuclear weapon ambitions), the US rationale was that this was meant to integrate a "responsible state with advanced nuclear technology"[55] into the nuclear mainstream, in order to strengthen the system, though the allure of the fledgling Indian market was inherent in the reasoning. Yet, despite such tremendous transformations in India's nuclear status and the burgeoning of its nuclear industry, the integration process has remained inconclusive over the question of whether India could be deemed to be integrated sans an NPT membership, and as an NNWS. Though much of the above benefits granted to India circumvented the NPT, its status vis-à-vis the treaty has come to the fore with China opposing India's entry into the NSG and demanding a criteria-based approach for membership. The integration question thus will remain alive in the long haul even as India pursues alternative ways to enhance its global nuclear standing.

### *Seeking nuclear deterrence and legitimacy*

The nuclear deal and NSG waiver were symbols of India gaining recognition as a state with nuclear weapons. Yet, as a nuclear-armed state, India had struggled to instil legitimacy of its nuclear arsenal and postures owing to various factors: first, India operates in a unique environment with two nuclear dyads involving China on the one and Pakistan on the other, with the latter being designated as highly unstable and a nuclear flashpoint with the maturity of the actors in this region to handle nuclear weapons being challenged; second, India's nuclear doctrine, despite being defensive in character and supporting the pursuit of a minimum deterrent, has not been seen as credible owing to the No-First-Use posture (NFU) and inconsistent projection of retaliatory capabilities and intentions; third, India's strategic weapons policy has had a bearing on India's approach to disarmament as it opposed recent efforts for a nuclear weapons ban treaty even while remaining inactive on this front.

That India and Pakistan came face-to-face on a conventional conflict in Kargil within months of their nuclear tests spurred arguments that the region has been pushed to instability that could trigger a nuclear war. While proliferation pessimists termed nuclear weapons as causal for the historic rivals to slip towards conflict, proliferation optimists argued that nuclear weapons will ensure such conflict will not escalate to full-fledged conventional or nuclear war (Sagan and Waltz, 1995; Ganguly, 1995; Hagerty, 1998; Raghavan, 2001; Sridharan, 2007). Both arguments gained traction as the nuclearisation of the region was inherently linked to the four major crises that symbolised its vulnerability towards a major conflict. While the first crisis over the insurgency in Jammu and Kashmir in 1990 was in the covert nuclearisation phase (when both countries had nuclear latency but denied the existence of nuclear weapons), the next three – Kargil (1999), Parliament attack (2001–2002) and Mumbai terror (2008) happened in the overt nuclearisation phase and placed considerable stress on India's deterrent (Ganguly and Kapur, 2010).

It was assumed that Pakistan had successfully exploited India's NFU (which inhibited an Indian first use of nuclear weapons) to run a low-intensity conflict under a nuclear overhang and mitigated an Indian response with its ambiguous nuclear thresholds (threatening nuclear response for a conventional or sub-conventional attack). India soon responded to this asymmetry by signalling a willingness to cross the border in response to a terror attack originating from Pakistan and challenge the nuclear threshold. The Army doctrine of 2004, termed Cold Start in popular discourse, projected the intent for maximum thrust under a nuclear environment and achieving asymmetry using integrated battle-groups.[56] While the Indian government refused to endorse its existence, its signalling spin-off was that Pakistan began to doubt the credibility of its brinkmanship behaviour and instead resorted to an assortment of campaigns (by hyping Cold Start as escalatory) and technological responses (Nasr tactical nuclear missile, Babar and Ra'ad cruise missiles).

Though India signalled that it made no difference between tactical and strategic nuclear weapons (Saran, 2013), implying 'massive retaliation' for any nuclear use,[57] the India–Pakistan theatre seems to have since evolved to a level of nuclear maturity which enables space for sub-conventional conflicts, as evident in the continuing terror attacks as well as India's 'surgical strike' of September 2016. The decision of proactive Indian leadership to undertake cross-border 'surgical strikes' against terrorist camps in Pakistan-occupied Kashmir was, in fact, a defining moment that marked the inclination to test Pakistan's purported redlines for nuclear use and open the space for 'sub-conventional' military operations under a nuclear overhang. That another military-level confrontation of similar nature, this time involving the use of air-power, happened in February 2019 was a testament to the fact that the space between sub-conventional and conventional conflict was to witness greater action with the Indian determination to respond to Pakistan-aided low-intensity conflict targeting Indian territory and assets (Kumar, 2019).

The second aspect flows from the above condition – about the credibility of India's nuclear doctrine. To convey to the world that it is a responsible nuclear weapon state, India announced its nuclear doctrine in 2003, which elucidated the objectives of its nuclear weapons as the pursuit of a credible minimum deterrent (CMD) to meet its security challenges pending nuclear disarmament, and sticking to an NFU in order to convey India's defensive posture of using nuclear weapons only in retaliation.[58] The doctrine aims at creating a Triad – of nuclear delivery systems from land, naval and aerial platforms with the objective of creating a survivable second-strike capability. Nearly two decades after the 1998 tests, India has moved from existential to retaliatory deterrence with capabilities to target key counter-value (population) and counter-force (military) targets in both China (Agni-V) and Pakistan (most Prithvi and Agni platforms), with the naval leg (K5 and K-15 Submarine Launch Ballistic Missiles) expected to fulfil the survivability part when deployed.

Notwithstanding the progress in operational maturity, the doctrine is supposed to be beset by postural deficiencies. According to the document, credibility is achieved when the adversary knows that India can and will retaliate with nuclear weapons to inflict (unacceptable) destruction. Despite great advances in delivery capability, including the supposed integration of thermonuclear warheads, the dynamic security environment constantly pushes the concept of 'minimum' to tumult along with the operational disparity created by two dyads in which India's CMD has to operate. Notable is the impact created by Nasr with India refusing to trigger any doctrinal shift as a riposte or project its technological response (Prahaar), fearing dilution of the deterrent and its original objectives.

Another aspect of the doctrine whose credibility is constantly doubted is the NFU posture, especially the flexibility to pre-empt a potential first-strike.[59] While Pakistan rejects India's NFU as merely declaratory, many feel that India cannot absorb the cost of a nuclear attack on a population centre and hence could go for a pre-emptive strike in the event of credible intelligence of a potential nuclear attack. On the other hand, Pakistan's exploitation of the NFU had prompted calls for discarding of this posture or a theatre-specific revision though the defence establishment believes its missile defence capability could effectively negate the first-strike advantage that Pakistan had held hitherto. Another topic that raises constant debate is massive retaliation. That India has maintained this as a consistent posture, even for a tactical nuclear scenario, is seen as inherently escalatory and showing incertitude on tactical options. While the Indian logic is to reject Pakistan's attempt to drag it into a theatre nuclear conflict, doubts also exist as to whether India could realistically attain the capability of undertaking massive retaliation against China (Nagal, 2014).

In fact, a clear exemplar of national interest always guiding India's nuclear policy, particularly the strategic programme, is the unwavering continuity that has been followed by all Indian leaderships irrespective of their ideological moorings. As a consequence, the nuclear deterrent has progressed according to the original plan, notwithstanding logistical and developmental delays, with the political leaderships staying away from influencing the process to establish a CMD and its concomitant infrastructure. Like the discourses in the 1960s when domestic pressure had intensified on the government to initiate a nuclear weapons programme, the governments since 1998 have also consistently resisted the pressure and temptation to review and upgrade the nuclear doctrine in order to stand up to the dynamics transformation of the strategic environment embodied by two nuclear dyads, or two nuclear-armed adversarial neighbours. Accordingly, the security establishments under each political dispensation had been endowed with the wherewithal to realign and improvise on the postural structures to address these challenges without having to alter the basic doctrinal framework. As a result, even the current dispensation under Narendra Modi, who is known to favour a muscular strategic posturing, has desisted from the pressure for doctrinal reviews, in spite of numerous statements from his own ministers towards this end (Kumar, 2019). Much of the developments in the strategic programme under his watch have largely adhered to the ongoing schedules, which included the operationalisation of the naval leg of the Triad and planned advancements in development and deployment of various delivery platforms (with only the demonstration of the ASAT capability in 2019 – in the midst of the general election campaign – denoting a personal imprint of the Prime Minister).

The third issue is about perceptions and dichotomies that define the fine balance India seeks between its nuclear weapons status and its disarmament advocacy. After rejecting the NPT, India took the line that disarmament should be pursued in a concurrent manner through various UN platforms like the Conference on Disarmament and SSoDs. Soon after the 1998 tests, India adopted the Nuclear Weapons Convention but hardly made any decisive campaign, unlike in the pre-1998 years, to promote this cause, even while preferring to be identified among weapon powers. In fact, India's disarmament standing remains sticky after its refusal to join the efforts to formulate a nuclear weapons ban treaty[60] that materialised through the initiative to project the humanitarian consequences of nuclear weapons (Kumar, 2015). Having aligned itself with the position of nuclear weapon powers against the ban treaty (despite being a model similar to the NWC) and continuing to remain outside the NPT, India's disarmament activism should now be deemed to be on the backburner.

## Conclusion

This chapter attempted to narrate and explain the evolution of India's nuclear policy and the dynamics of decision-making that influenced this policy. Part of this exercise was also the effort to place the 'nuclear policy' in the larger foreign policymaking that has formed the grand strategy of the country since formation to date. The chapter explained the struggles of policymaking and the challenges the Indian leaderships faced in framing the country's nuclear policy, constantly shaped by a handful of exogenous and endogenous factors. The narrative spread over three eras – the Nehruvian phase, the non-alignment period and the post-Cold War years – thus attempting to explain India's contribution to global nuclear politics and the global discourse on norms and structures which eventually shaped the global nuclear order from the earliest to contemporary times.

Three broad conclusions could be culled out from this attempt to place India in the global nuclear collective: the multitude of roles India played in shaping or influencing the system, determining interests in the struggle between political idealism and policy realism, and discerning the significance of 'nuclear' in determining India's grand strategy.

**India's nuclear record** is unique for the fact that it had donned a variegated range of roles that few actors had in global nuclear politics. A dominant set of narratives identify India's initial role as a norm entrepreneur (standstill agreement, NPT, CTBT) but it later slipped into a pariah status after the 1974 test and struggled as an outlier until the 2005 India–US nuclear deal facilitated its gradual return to the mainstream. The insight from this chapter is about other undefined rules, like that of a challenger (1974 and 1998 tests, rejecting the NPT and CTBT) who constantly contested the non-proliferation and disarmament status quos, or that of a catalyst (Resolution 2028, Rajiv Gandhi Action Plan, nuclear deal) who pushed for normative transformations that could address systemic flaws and protect its vital interests.

**The pursuit of national interest** is indisputably reflected in, or defined, the struggle between political idealism and policy realism that echoed throughout this chapter as the fundamental characteristic of nuclear policymaking through the three eras. The struggle that reverberated in the exterior could thus be explained as the inquisitions of the leadership in determining where the interest lay – a demonstration (or façade) of political idealism and high moralism or a subtle execution of policy realism through intelligent statecraft. It might be ironic that the form of (Nehruvian) idealism practised in the initial years was criticised in later years, though many commentators have pointed out how that suited Indian interests best for those times. The practice of models like non-alignment were perfect examples of how national interest was pursued within an idealist framework without compromising the nation's vital interests, as illustrated in the withdrawal from NPT and the nuclear tests.

**Placing nuclear in the grand strategy** will never be a difficult endeavour, though the challenge is to explain whether nuclear policymaking was the most accurate depiction of Indian grand strategy over these epochs or was it shaped and aligned to fulfil the requirements of strategic thinking over the eras. The difficulties the leadership faced at various points of time – be it on the NPT decision, the actual factor determining the PNE decision, the delay in determining whether to go nuclear and the manner in which traditional disarmament advocacy was discarded in favour of securing interests as a nuclear weapon state – are a testament to the fact that the nuclear policymaking was always regulated and leveraged by the push and pull factors that determined the nation's grand strategy. At the same time, the eventual shape that nuclear policies have taken over the eras has given a distinct flavour and identity to the country's grand strategy. In other words, nuclear policy and nuclear outreach essentially gave life to the national global identity and its conception of the power system in grand strategic terms – be it for balancing, challenging or bandwagoning.

## Notes

* The author wishes to thank Jaya Ravindran and her team at the National Archives of India and the staff members of the Manuscript Division at the Nehru Memorial Museum and Library.

1 *Defining Foreign Policy*, Speech during debate on the President's Address in Parliament, New Delhi, 17 February 1953, in *Jawaharlal Nehru's Speeches 1949–1953* (New Delhi: Publications Division, Ministry of Information and Broadcasting, Government of India, 1954).

2 Speech to Georgetown University delivered on 21 January 1975, T.N. Kaul Papers (II and III Instalments), Subject File No. 3 (Part – I), Nehru Memorial Museum and Library (NMML), New Delhi.
3 Also see collection of Nehru's speeches at: *Jawaharlal Nehru's Speeches 1949–1953* (New Delhi: Publications Division, Government of India, 1954).
4 Jawaharlal Nehru made this proposal in the Lok Sabha on 10 May 1954, which was forwarded to the UN Secretary General in a letter (DC/44 and Corr.1).
5 Nehru's understanding of the ground realities is marked in his speech to the Closed Session of the Asian-African Conference at Bandung on 22 April 1955, where he challenges the notion of 'peace through strength' and rejects the proposal for bloc formation of smaller and less-industrialised states. In his speech to the Lok Sabha on 22 May 1957, he expresses inability to influence the super powers to end testing and force them to disarmament (Singh and Sharma, 2000).
6 Nehru had remarked that "it is a question of trying to achieve it not all in one fine morning or in one piece, but as one piece with so many stages within it for the accomplishment of the whole thing in a short period of four or five years". See speech to the UNGA on 30 October 1960 (Singh and Sharma, 2000).
7 India demanded the addition of chemical and biological weapons and small arms in order to make the disarmament process comprehensive. See debates of ENDC/P.V.37, 15 May 1962 and ENDC/P.V.47, 1 June 1962. Quoting a Western scientist, Nehru told the Parliament on 2 May 1962 that the ongoing atmospheric tests would cause over three million deaths, in terms of genetic damage.
8 The proposals in Eisenhower's speech of December 1953 included establishing the IAEA under the UN, requesting the nuclear powers to make contributions of stockpiles of uranium and other fissionable materials that could be allocated for peaceful pursuits, and urging all countries to end the race for armament. See text of speech at: www.iaea.org/about/history/atoms-for-peace-speech (last accessed in May 2017).
9 The prominent proposals were Ireland's draft resolution and the US and Soviet drafts for a disarmament treaty. Ireland submitted drafts on 'non-dissemination' and for measures against 'relinquishing control or transferring information on nuclear weapons manufacturing' in 1959 and 1960, which led to UNGA resolutions 1664 (Question of Disarmament) and 1665 (Prevention of Wider Dissemination of Nuclear Weapons). Failing to agree on a common draft, the superpowers instead released the US–Soviet Joint Statement on Agreed Principles for Disarmament Negotiations of September 1961. See text at: www.nucleardarkness.org/solutions/mccloyzorinaccordstext/ (last accessed in November 2020).
10 See *Jawaharlal Nehru's Speeches 1949–1953*, n.3.
11 Kaul Papers, n.4. The latter elucidation comes from Kaul's speech at the Asia Society on 25 September1974, T.N. Kaul Papers (II and III Instalments), Subject File No. 2, 1974, NMML.
12 *The Larger Scheme of Things*, Speech in reply to debate on Foreign Affairs in Lok Sabha, 12 June 1952, n.3.
13 Kaul Papers, Subject File No. 2, n.4.
14 Insights from The Proceedings of the Conference of Governors Held at Rashtrapati Bhavan on 30 November–1 December 1966, M.C. Chagla Papers, File No. 92, NMML.
15 Much of the discussion between Indian and US governments (involving Indian Defence Minister Y.B. Chavan and US Defence Secretary Robert McNamara) on

military sales happened after the Sino-Indian conflict with the US showing inclination to support modernisation of Indian armed forces. The B.K. Nehru papers give a glimpse of these discussions, which included India's request for the F-104G aircraft, which the US declined, later focussing on the F-5s and F-6s. While showing willingness to supply the AMX tanks lying redundant after the Korean War, the US side was perturbed that India was already buying and producing the Soviet MIGs and hence had apprehensions over 'intermingling' of US military equipment with those of the Soviets. For a detailed consultation, see Subject File No. 18, B.K. Nehru Papers, NMML, New Delhi.

16 For more on the food aid and arms supplies files, see Subject Files in P.N. Haksar Papers (Installments I, II & III), NMML, New Delhi. For more insights on military supplies to South Asia, see AMS Files in the MEA Transfer List at National Archives of India, New Delhi.

17 For a draft of the treaty text that was negotiated between the two parties and the conversations Indira Gandhi's representative, D.P. Dhar, had with Soviet leaders, see Subject Files No. 49 and 51, P.N. Haksar Papers (Installment III), NMML.

18 Gandhi told this to US President Nixon in a meeting at the Oval Office on 4 November 1971. See Memorandum of Conversation, P.N. Haksar Papers, Subject File no. 277, (Installment III), NMML, New Delhi.

19 ENDC/P.V.174, 12 March 1964.

20 Trivedi defined the concept of proliferation to point out that the main issue is about "the proliferation that has already taken place", and that "a prohibition applies first to those who are in a position to proliferate, and only secondarily to those who may subsequently be doing it" (ENDC/P.V.223, 12 August 1965). Also, in a letter to the Secretary General dated 10 October 1964, Ambassador B.N. Chakravarty requested an item entitled 'Non-proliferation of nuclear weapons' be inscribed in the agenda for the 19thsession of the UNGA.

21 The five principles of Resolution 2028 (XX) were that (a) the treaty should be void of any loopholes which might permit states to proliferate; (b) it should embody acceptable balance of mutual responsibilities and obligations; (c) it should be a step towards general and complete disarmament, particularly nuclear disarmament; (d) there should be acceptable and workable provisions to ensure its effectiveness; and (e) it should not adversely affect the right to conclude regional treaties to ensure total absence of nuclear weapons in respective territories. The joint memorandum on non-proliferation (ENDC/158) was submitted to the 233rd meeting of UNGA by Brazil, Burma, Ethiopia, India, Mexico, Nigeria, Sweden and the United Arab Republic. See Disarmament Commission, (Official Records) Supplement for January to December 1965, New York 1966.

22 Indian submissions at ENDC/P.V.298, 23 May 1967, and ENDC/P.V.370, 27 February 1968.

23 The government sent L.K. Jha to Moscow and Washington to seek a guarantee from the superpowers while Prime Minister Shastri broached the topic with British PM Harold Wilson during his visit to the UK in December 1964. The Soviets conveyed to Jha that India would be protected against a nuclear attack if it renounced the right to make nuclear weapons. A draft of the Soviet declaration was carried by Jha to Washington for discussion with President Johnson, who was advised by his aides of the constitutional problem of giving a guarantee to India only as a treaty with Senate's approval. They instead suggested supporting the Soviet proposal of "acting through the UNSC if a non-nuclear NPT state

is subject to a nuclear threat or attack". See Memorandum of Conversation, President Johnson with L.K. Jha, B.K. Nehru, V. Sarabhai and W.W. Rostow, Washington, 19 April 1967, Foreign Relations of the United States (XXV), South Asia, Document 440, and Telegram from Special Assistant (Rostow) to President Johnson, Document 438 (Noorani, 1967).

24 The whole range of global reactions to the PNE has been captured in the MEA (AMS) file WII/103 (18) 74, National Archives of India (NAI).

25 Different reactions emerged in the US, with one section terming the PNE as a nuclear weapon test and those in the government including Kissinger recording that India had not violated any agreement through the PNE. Yet the second shipment to Tarapur was delayed owing to petitions at the US Nuclear Regulatory Commission, and eventually cleared with pressure from the State Department. For a glimpse of these events see Telegram No. 171 from the Indian Ambassador in Washington to the Foreign Secretary dated 22 June 1974 and T.N. Kaul's letter to Henry Kissinger (6 July 1974) in WII/103 (18) 74, NAI. Also see Kaul–Kissinger conversations in Subject Files No. 2, Kaul Papers, n.4.

26 Reference to Desai's assurance in debate on Lok Sabha No. 17 Answered on 13 July 1977, in File No.WII/504/3/77 (I-V) – Nuclear Matters, Tarapur Plant, Indo–US Agreement for supply of Uranium, etc. (MEA/AMS), National Archives of India, New Delhi.

27 India's statements at the SSoDs included: Morarji Desai, "Quest for Peace", Speech at the Special Session of the United Nations General Assembly, New York, 9 June 1978; P.V. Narasimha Rao, "Disarmament: An Urgent Concern", Statement made at the Second Special Session on Disarmament on 11 June 1982.

28 Also known as the Comprehensive Plan for Phased Elimination of all Nuclear Weapons, the text of RGAP titled "A World Free of Nuclear Weapons: An Action Plan," 9 June 1988, available at: http://meaindia.nic.in/cdgeneva/?pdf0611?000 (last accessed in November 2020).

29 Chagla, n.14.

30 The Jan Sangh had passed this resolution at its Bhopal session of December 1962.

31 Bhabha's declaration was made in an All India address on 24 October 1964 (Jain, 1974). Also see "Bhabha: India Can Make Atom Bomb in 18 Months", *National Herald*, 5 October 1964.

32 Expressed by both Shastri and Indira Gandhi as Prime Ministers in the parliament debates (Poulose, 1978).

33 Rajya Sabha debates on the Chinese program at: www.idsa.in/npihp/document.html

34 See statement at: http://idsa.in/npihp/documents/RS_21-November-1967.pdf (last accessed in July 2017).

35 Lok Sabha Debate on Foreign Affairs, 5 April 1968.

36 Bhabha died in a plane crash the day the Indira government took over. Menon made the revelation in a lecture at the Dr. Homi Bhabha Birth Centenary Symposium organised by the TIFR in 2008 (Ghosh and Grover, 2009).

37 Swamy talked of producing around 200 bombs by 1970–1971 using plutonium from all facilities (despite being under safeguards). Speech to the Jana Sangh Parliamentary Study Group, 19 August 1968.

38 National Intelligence Estimate Number 4-2-64, "Prospects for a Proliferation of Nuclear Weapons over the Next Decade", 21 October 1964, available at: http://digitalarchive.wilsoncenter.org/document/115994 (last accessed in May 2015).

39 The pro-bomb pressure continued even after rejecting the NPT. Following the Chinese satellite test of April 1970, two major conferences were organised in Delhi (7–10 May), first by a Parliamentary Committee and another by two think tanks, where an overwhelming consensus emerged in favour of a weapons programme.

40 The government remained non-committal on PNEs until November 1972, when Indira Gandhi told the Parliament that the "AEC is constantly reviewing progress in the technology of underground nuclear explosion both from theoretical and experimental angles, and assessing its economic value". Nine months before the 1974 test, the minister in charge of atomic energy, K.C. Pant, confirmed that studies were being done, stating that "we have to identify the broad applications which are viable". Debates in Rajya Sabha on 7 December 1972 and 2 August 1973: http://idsa.in/npihp/documents/RS_2-August-1973iii.pdf and http://idsa.in/npihp/documents/RS_7-December-1972.pdf (last accessed in May 2017).

41 The Plan announced on 25th May 1970 include projects like advanced thermal reactors to lower cost for plutonium production, fast breeder reactors, heavy water facilities, gas centrifuge technology, development of uranium mines, construction of facilities for solid propellant, rocket fabrication and in-flight guidance, and communication and remote sensing satellites. Press handout reproduced in *IDSA Journal* (Subrahmanyam, 1970).

42 Official statements insisted that the test was for scientific purposes and that India did not intend to make nuclear weapons. Kaul, as ambassador to the US, was at the forefront giving explanations on the test. Besides constantly elucidating its developmental applications, Kaul insisted that the IAEA had encouraged the use of PNE technology. He also demanded an international agreement which would regulate the use of nuclear explosives for peaceful purposes. Kissinger rejected this proposal, stating the technology used by the US and USSR for PNE was different from the Indian device, which was closer to a nuclear weapon device. See files on Kaul's outreach at Subject File No. 2: 1974, T.N. Kaul Papers (Installments I, II and III), NMML. For official Indian statements on and international response to the PNE, see WII/103 (18) 74, (MEA/AMS Division), NAI.

43 In a subsequent conversation, Kissinger told Kaul that he believed India would be making nuclear bombs and that it had to the right to do so considering that other great powers already possessed them.

44 Though the Indian government had denied giving any formal assurances to the Carter Administration, Prime Minister Desai declared at the Special Session on Disarmament of June 1978 that India would abjure nuclear explosions entirely even for peaceful purposes. Meeting withPrime Minister Morarji Desai, The Oval Office and Cabinet Room, 12 June 1978, Office of Staff Secretary; Series: Presidential Files; Folder: 6/13/78; Container 80, www.jimmycarterlibrary.gov/library/findingaids/Staff_Secretary.pdf (accessed in July 2020).

45 BRICS is the acronym used to refer to the group of five large emerging economies comprising Brazil, Russia, India, China and South Africa. Jim O'Neill, an economist at Goldman Sachs, is said to have coined this term, initially as BRIC (without South Africa) in 2001, by contending that these four economies would dominate the global economy by 2050. South Africa was added to the list in 2010, giving the group its current name. See James Chen, "Brazil, Russia, India, China and South Africa (BRICS)," *Investopedia*, 25 August 2020, available at: www.investopedia.com/terms/b/brics.asp (last accessed in November 2020).

46 BASIC is a grouping of four emerging economies – Brazil, South Africa, India and China – that was formed as a bloc for collective bargaining during the climate change negotiations, and has since expanded its mandate to cooperate and consult on various other matters of trade and politics. For a description, see "Explained: Who Are BASIC, the Climate Change Alliance Whose Meeting India Just Attended?", *Indian Express*, 18 August 2019, available at: https://indianexpress.com/article/explained/explained-who-are-basic-the-climate-change-alliance-whose-meeting-india-just-attended-5914424/ (last accessed in November 2020).

47 There were fourteen rounds of talks between the Indian Foreign Minister and the US Deputy Secretary of State. The dialogue itself was peculiar as by protocol the US Secretary of State was supposed to be the corresponding official who should have had the dialogue with the Indian minister.

48 While Strobe Talbott claims in his book that Singh had agreed to India's accession to the CTBT in return for support to full-scope lending by multilateral banks, the other proposals that were discussed – like commitment on the Fissile Material Cut-off Treaty (FMCT) (supposed to have shortened the list of Indian entities covered by US sanctions), and the implementation of stricter export controls (which was to facilitate government-to-government dealings and military cooperation) – actually formed the contents of subsequent agreements of India–US strategic partnership (Talbott, 2004).

49 Statement of 9 May 2000 available at: www.mea.gov.in/in-focus-article.htm?19220/Suo+Motu+Statement+in+Parliament+by+the+EAM+on+the+NPT+Review+Conference (last accessed in February 2013).

50 A draft NWC was crafted in 1997 in response to the Advisory Opinion of the International Court of Justice (ICJ) and was updated in 2007 by an international consortium of lawyers, scientists and physicians. For an assessment on the NWC process, see Jürgen Scheffran, "The Nuclear Weapons Convention as a Process Umbrella Negotiations as a Framework for a Nuclear-Weapon-Free World", *The Atlanta Consultation III* (Middle Powers Initiative), 20–22 January 2010, available at: www.baselpeaceoffice.org/sites/default/files/imce/oewg/scheffran_the_nwc_as_a_process.pdf (last accessed in November 2020). A Model NWC submitted by Costa Rica and Malaysia to the UN in 2007 can be accessed at: http://inesap.org/sites/default/files/inesap_old/mNWC_2007_Unversion_English_N0821377.pdf (last accessed in November 2020).

51 See joint press statement of 17 September 2004 at: www.mea.gov.in/bilateral-documents.htm?dtl/7461/ (last accessed in June 2017).

52 Joint Statement available at: www.mea.gov.in/bilateral-documents.htm?dtl/6772/Joint_Statement_IndiaUS (last accessed in November 2020).

53 For an FAQ on the 123 Agreement, see https://mea.gov.in/Uploads/PublicationDocs/19149_Frequently_ Asked_Questions_01-11–2008.pdf (last accessed in July 2017).

54 The sites (suppliers) include: Jaitapur (Areva), MithiVirdi (Westinghouse), Kovvada (GE) and Haripur (Rosatam). Kovvada was subsequently allotted to Westinghouse after GE's withdrawal. Following the Kudankulam agitation, many of these designated sites have also witnessed public protests over safety concerns of nuclear projects (Kumar, 2013).

55 This was how India was described in the 18 July 2005 Joint Statement. See n.52.

56 Drawn from mobilisation lessons during Operation Parakram, Cold Start entailed the ability to launch quick strikes across the border without prior warning by

moving rapidly to battle positions by penetrating the border areas over a wide front. See "Section 14: Low intensity conflict and counter-insurgency operations", Chapter-4, Part II, *Indian Army Doctrine*, Headquarters Army Training Command, Shimla, October 2004.

57 The Indian signalling came through two expositions of the then Chairman of the National Security Advisory Board, Shyam Saran. See his lecture of April 24, 2013 delivered in New Delhi titled: "Is India's Nuclear Deterrent Credible?", available at: http://ris.org.in/images/RIS_images/pdf/Final%20Is%20India's%20Nuclear%20Deterrent%20Credible-%20rev1%202%202.pdf (last accessed in November 2020).

58 See *Draft Report of the National Security Advisory Board (NSAB) on Indian Nuclear Doctrine*, 17 August 1999, www.indianembassy.org/policy/CTBT/nuclear_doctrine_aug_17_1999.html, and the confirmation note, *Cabinet Committee on Security reviews progress in operationalizing India's nuclear doctrine*, 4 January 2003, http://pib.nic.in/archieve/lreleng/lyr2003/rjan2003/04012003/r040120033.html (both last accessed in July 2017).

59 The shift from the Draft Nuclear Doctrine's position that nuclear weapons will not be used against non-nuclear states, to the inclusion of the biological and chemical conditionality in the 2003 press release, as well as a reported interpretation by a National Security Advisor, Shiv Shankar Menon (at a closed-door session at the National Defence College), that the NFU will only be valid for NNWSs is cited as an example of inconsistency or timely doctrinal shifts.

60 The UNGA resolution for a nuclear weapons ban treaty was backed by 122 countries on 7 July 2017. See www.reachingcriticalwill.org/images/documents/Disarmament-fora/nuclear-weapon-ban/documents/voting-record.pdf (last accessed in July 2017).

## References


Dar, Mohd Yousuf and Dar, Jahangir Ahmad. (2016): "Nehru as an Internationalist," *Mainstream*, Vol. IV(24), 4 June.

Das, M.N. (1961): The Political Philosophy of Jawaharlal Nehru, George Allen and Unwin, London.

Fischer, David. (1997): History of the International Atomic Energy Agency: The first forty years, IAEA, Vienna, www-pub.iaea.org/mtcd/publications/pdf/pub1032_web.pdf (last accessed April 2017).

Ganguly, Sumit and Kapur, Paul. (2010): India, Pakistan and the Bomb – Debating Nuclear Stability in South Asia, Penguin, New Delhi.

Ganguly, Sumit. (1995): "Indo-Pakistani Nuclear Issues and the Stability/Instability Paradox," *Studies in Conflict and Terrorism*, Vol. 18.

Ghosh, Dipan K. and Grover, Arun K. (eds.). (2009): Tribute to a Titan, Indian Physics Association, Mumbai.

Hagerty, Devin T. (1998): The Consequences of Nuclear Proliferation: Lessons from South Asia, The MIT Press, Cambridge.

Jain, J.P. (1974): India and Disarmament: Vol.1 – Nehru Era: An Analytical Study, Radiant Publishers, New Delhi.

Kalyanaraman, Shankaran. (2014): "Nehru's Advocacy of Internationalism and India's Foreign Policy," in Kanti, Bajpai, Saira, Basit and Krishnappa, V. (eds.), India's Grand Strategy: History, Theory, Cases, Routledge, New Delhi.

Kapur, Ashok. (1976): India's Nuclear Option: Atomic Diplomacy and Decision Making, Praeger Publishers, New York, Washington, London.

Karnad, Bharat. (2002): Nuclear Weapons & Indian Security: The Realist Foundations of Strategy, Macmillan India, New Delhi.

Kumar, Suneel. (2011): "Nehruvian Internationalism: Principles, Features and Relevance," *Pakistan Horizon*, Vol. 64(2), April.

Kumar, Vinod A. (2013): "India's Nuclear Energy Renaissance: Stuck in the Middle?" *Journal of Risk Research*, Vol. I.

Kumar, Vinod A. (2014): India and the Nuclear Non-Proliferation Regime – The Perennial Outlier, Cambridge University Press, New Delhi.

Kumar, Vinod A. (2015): "Reframing the Disarmament Discourse: Can the Humanitarian Paradigm Make a Difference?" *IDSA Strategic Comment*, 26 May, www.idsa.in/idsacomments/ReframingtheDisarmamentDiscourse_avkumar_260515 (last accessed in July 2017).

Kumar, Vinod A. (2016): "Between Idealism, Activism, and the Bomb: Why did India reject the NPT?" in Popp, Roland et al. (eds.), Negotiating the Nuclear Non-Proliferation Treaty: Origins of the Nuclear Order, Routledge, London.

Kumar, Vinod A. (2019): "No-First-Use Is Not Sacrosanct: Need a Theatre-specific Posture for Flexible Options," *IDSA Issue Brief*, 27 August, https://bit.ly/2W0HqLG (last accessed in July 2020).

Kumar, Vinod A. and Patil, Kapil. (2014): "Resolving India's Nuclear Liability Impasse," *IDSA Issue Brief*, 6 December 2014.

Malik, Priyanjali. (2010): India's Nuclear Debate: Exceptionalism and the Bomb, Routledge, New Delhi.

Mirchandani, G.G. (1978): "India and Nuclear Weapons," in Poulose, T.T. (ed.), Perspectives of India's Nuclear Policy, Young Asia Publications, New Delhi.

Mohan, Raja, C. (2007): "India's Nuclear Exceptionalism," in Sverre, Lodgard (ed.), Nuclear Proliferation and International Security, Routledge, Oxon.

Mohan, Ram and Abraham, Mohit. (2013): "Don't Waver Now on the Nuclear Liability," *The Hindu*, 20 September.

Nagal, B.S. (2014): "Checks and Balances," *Force*, June.

Noorani, A.G. (1967): "India's Quest for a Nuclear Guarantee," *Asian Survey*, Vol. 7(7), July.

Noorani, A.G. (2001): "India's Nuclear Guarantee Episode," *Frontline*, Vol. 18(2), 9–22 June.

Parthasarthi, G. (1994): "Foreword," in Reddy, S. and Damodaran, A.K. (eds.), Krishna Menon on Disarmament, Sanchar Publishing House, New Delhi.

Poulose, T.T (ed.). (1978): Perspectives of India's Nuclear Policy, Young Asia Publications, New Delhi.

Raghavan, V.R. (2001): "Limited War and Nuclear Escalation in South Asia", *The Nonproliferation Review*, Vol. 6(3), Fall–Winter.

Ramanna, Raja. (1991): Years of Pilgrimage, Viking, New Delhi.

Sagan, Scott D. and Waltz, Kenneth N. (1995): The Spread of Nuclear Weapons, A Debate, W.W. Norton, New York.

Saran, Shyam. (2013): "Weapon That Has More Than Symbolic Value," *The Hindu*, 4 May.

Singh, Gopal and Sharma, S.K. (eds.). (2000): Documents on India's Nuclear Disarmament Policy, Volume-I, Anamika Publishers & Distributors, New Delhi.

Singh, Sampooran. (1971): India and the Nuclear Bomb, S. Chand & Co. (PVT) Ltd., New Delhi.

Sridharan, E. (ed.). (2007): The India-Pakistan Nuclear Relationship, Routledge, New Delhi.

Subrahmanyam, K. (1970): "The Path to Nuclear Capability," *IDSA Journal* (*Special Issue*), Vol. 3(1), July.

Talbott, Strobe. (2004): Engaging India, Penguin Books, New Delhi.

Varghese, B.G. (2010): First Draft, Tranquebar, New Delhi.

# 3 India's foreign policy and domestic compulsions

## Theorizing the margins of exclusion

*Sashinungla*

## Introduction

India's foreign policy today emerges as a global umbrella of the Hindu nationalist rhetoric juxtaposed on racial subtexts, both at home and abroad, that develops into a rivalry structure in the state-to-state relations. Such a structured and hegemonic discourse of foreign policy institutes a process of linking discourses of national development and national security with a discourse of political superiority at the international level. A genealogy of such a 'supremacist intentionality' is purely instrumental as it appeases the home-grown sectarian forces and projects a notion of 'national interest' in security and economic terms, which is serviced from below by India's domestic cultural pluralism, civilizational linkages and electoral multi-party politics. The instrumentality of foreign policy lies in subsuming overtly racist, anti-minority and anti-marginalized nationalist rhetoric of exclusion by projecting common national ideals and staking claims on universal covenants of human rights, justice and fairness. This shows a disjunction between ideological nationalism and proclaimed compliance of Indian nation-states to international normative order. This chapter aims to analyse this disjunction in terms of how the minority discourses are excluded by nationalist rhetoric and how such a nationalist rhetoric is utilized to eliminate concerns of minority groups in India's foreign policy. How India's discourse of economic and security supremacy in foreign policy eschews the vulnerable and marginalized groups both within domestic and foreign policy discourses and apparatuses is discussed from a normative-evaluative standpoint.

An overemphasis on economic growth, balance of trade and balance of payments and strategic military superiority in India's foreign policy discourse polarizes the vibrant cultural pluralism from below by neglecting human rights and concerns of marginalized peoples and regions in areas of border management, neighbourhood, fair use of natural and cultural resources, climate change, healthcare and higher education, to name a few. A large part of the people's concerns are subsumed and submerged within the discourse of economic and military superiority by leaving them to market forces and at the same time by wielding a diabolic view of control and authority to decide the national and international interest. This paper argues that India must incorporate human rights standards more robustly into foreign policymaking disciplinary methods/practices and its professional code of ethics as India needs to respond to the legal, ethical, human and political implications of its policies and actions.

## Nation, national identity as ideal-critical concepts

The nationalism, national identity and unity-in-diversity of India is often assumed and taken as a given. However, it is important to subject these notions to a critical examination in a diachronic framework. As ideal-critical concepts, these have to be differentiated and defended from cultural solipsism, narrow chauvinism or hyper-nationalism. The ideal of national identity is reflected in the secular-democratic framework which is enshrined in the republican Constitution of India. Consequently, this ideal is reinforced by the cultural pluralism and broad 'civilizational ethos'[1] of the country. Hence, critical interpretation and reinterpretation of traditions in the light of the secular-democratic ethos of modern India is necessary. It is in this context that the concept of national identity should be seen as essentially an ideal-critical concept which is embedded in a broad humanistic framework. Such a concrete universal of national identity assumes a form of abstract particularity of a specific identity that remains subsumed within the larger framework of Indian nationalist discourse. India's foreign policy discourse represents this act of subsumption within its articulation of a supremacist rationality.

At the pan-Indian level, two major perspectives on what is being understood as the idea of India, national identity or Indian nationalism may be delineated. From the first perspective, the idea of India is one in which every Indian of different faith, culture, caste, region, language and race is an equal and important component with equal opportunity under the law, according to the Constitution. Here, the Indian nation-state is based upon a pluralistic view of culture and a federal system of government, where both the wishes of the majority, as expressed by free democratic elections, and the rights of the minorities can be accommodated. The second perspective conceives the idea of India as a Hindu *rashtra*, or a combination between existing state structure and the Hindu nation – in which every Indian of different faith, caste, region, language, culture and race can be absorbed and integrated within the dominant Hindu religion and culture. Here, the Indian nation-state is based not only on 'common' culture but also upon the religion of Hinduism, leading to a discourse of *Hindutva* that otherizes difference and specificity into the abstract particularity of being Hindu. Under this idea of Indian identity, the 'unity' of India among the various communities and sections is articulated through the common heritage of living within a 'Hinduized' land. With its accent on homogenization and regimentation and its "identification between Hinduism and nationalism" (Momin, 1996), this version tends to be xenophobic and exclusivistic, which is at variance with the secular-democratic ethos of the Indian Constitution. This brand of ideology and its consequent domestic politics is in "constant tension with India's multi-cultural character, and often attempts to resolve this dissonance through bouts of severe violence against religious minorities" (Malone and Mukherjee, 2010: 149), particularly Muslims and Christians.

Having a common national identity and vision should not make us oblivious of our diversity and tolerance. In the prevailing climate of globalization, a participatory and collaborative approach would be prudent, rather than imposing oversimplified straitjackets on the inherent complexity of life. Accepting and respecting diverse cultures coexisting together strengthens and broadens our views on every aspect of life, rather than jeopardizing Indian solidarity. If one culture insisted on dominating all others, the result would be continuing disunity and strife. A policy of integration that attempts to impose uniformity and homogeneity not only disregards the contributions of different groups but also ignores the fundamental Indian constitutional principles of justice and equal citizenship.

## Cultural politics of India's 'power'

The issues of national identity and 'national interest' are closely intertwined with foreign policy. An aggressive nationalist approach tends to be exclusionary in its framework. Underlining the Bharatiya Janata Party's (BJP's) vision of exclusionary Hindu nationalism, political theorist Rahul Sagar observes that, in their vision, national power relies upon the nurturing of an "assertive and exclusionary nationalism" (Sagar, 2014: 237). In September 2015, the then BJP chief Amit Shah promised to fulfil its *Hindutva* pioneer Vinayak Damodar Sarvarkar's "one nation, one culture, one nationality" dream of India (Ramasehan, 2015). He then went on to say he believed in a democratic India where followers of all religions and faiths would be treated equally and where nobody would be allowed to dominate others. One can only wonder how these two diametrically opposing ideas of "one cultural value" and "democratic India" can be reconciled. This exclusionary brand of Hindu nationalism can be traced back to when, from within the Congress party, the powerful conservative voice of a Marathi Brahman, Bal Gangadhar Tilak, emerged, who perceived in the increasing Westernization of India's elite the seeds of the destruction of Hindu culture (Schwartzberg and Stoddard, 1995). As Sumit Ganguly has written:

> In the BJP's vision, the presence of various religious and cultural minorities in India can contribute to social fissures. More to the point, such minorities may not be suitably loyal to the Indian state.
>
> (Ganguly, 2015: 6)

In 2015, the BJP's minister for culture, Mahesh Sharma, aptly articulated such an anti-minorities mindset when he spoke of late President APJ Abdul

Kalam being a patriot and a humanitarian "despite being a Muslim" (Keeler, 2015). He was simply articulating his party's political philosophy – the belief that being a non-Hindu (a Christian, Muslim and so on) gets in the way of being Indian. An incident such as the murder of Akhlaq[2] needs to be seen as an assertion of a rightist political mindset. He was killed for being the 'other', for being different. The beating of Dalits at Una in Gujarat too is an expression of a rabid ideological sense of othering that creates anger amongst those who are otherized.

Closely linked to the exclusionary nationalism project is the clever exploitation of 'majoritarian' Hindu emotional sentiments on controversial issues. The BJP has been able to project to a large section of people the sense that it stands for the 'true' India. Such tactics elicit their appeal from a shared sense of patriotism and nascent nationalism, which is then articulated and presented to the masses in the nationalist semantic as 'national interest'. Apart from its rejection of Western influences and anti-Islamic sentiments (both Pakistan's and India's own Muslim population), the new regime has demonstrated its commitment to the party's ideological vision of exclusionary nationalism through several political decisions and moves it has made since assuming office. Some of the interrelated themes of the BJP's exclusionary nationalism objectives may be delineated: to change the writing of Indian history and school textbooks through/by Sanskritic Hinduism at the ideational and institutional level; the abolition of Article 370 of the Indian Constitution (which grants special autonomous status to the Muslim-majority state of Jammu and Kashmir); a proposal for nationwide implementation of Article 48 of the Indian Constitution (which mandates the state to prohibit the slaughter of cows); the implementation of a uniform civil code (thereby doing away with Muslim personal law), etc.

In fact, the present policy of aligning with the rich and the powerful, instead of non-alignment, is in line with the conservative ideologues of Hindu supremacy, according to which, "India's success on the global stage is dependent upon the forging of a monolithic Hindu culture" (Ganguly, 2015: 9). The nationalism and national identity of the BJP is based on a sense of cultural or racial superiority, whereby *Hindutva* ideologues think (or hope) that other nations and regions will come eventually to recognize the superiority of Hindu ways of thinking and living.[3]

In consonance with their conservative *Hindutva* agenda, they would prefer to tolerate caste oppression. Hindu identity was defined "by those who were part of the national consciousness and drew on their own image of themselves resulting from an upper-caste Brahmin dominated identity" (Thapar, 1992: 85–86). Time and again, Rashtriya Swayamsevak Sangh (RSS)[4] has declared its antipathy towards affirmative action/reservation policy,[5] often terming it 'appeasement policy'. Therefore, given the history of Congress popularity with the socially disadvantaged, their opposition to reservation policy is both ideological and political. The most unrelenting and significant intervention into caste hierarchy or the critique of Hinduism has come from the Dalit intellectuals. Dalit writers, those who take upon the caste hierarchy system and oppressions by upper-caste Hindus, are often threatened and attacked for 'being anti-Hindu'. Passive-aggressive or victim-blaming tactics employed by the hegemonic discourse in perpetuating their dominance are obvious. Such a narrative attempts to impute all the community's misfortunes to others and ignores or disregards failings closer to home.

The RSS may be justified in accusing Congress or other political parties of 'appeasement' politics, but opposing affirmative action policy or conflating minority protection laws enshrined in the Constitution for repressed and vulnerable groups in the spirit of social justice with 'appeasement' is another thing. Such apathy and resentment towards affording certain protective provisions for minorities and marginalized in society is not only incongruent with international human rights laws but also shows a complete disdain towards the universal spirit of humanity. Interestingly, both the RSS and BJP and their supporters blame the Indian 'secular/liberal' public for being pro-Muslim and anti-Hindu. This argument is not only flawed but such framing of complex fissures within the democratic process in the simplistic Hindu–Muslim constructs eschews the space for any debate of problems faced by other marginalized sections in the country.

Harmony in the social sector, on the streets of India and in the lives of citizens is the single most essential requirement for economic growth and change. There is no place in the world for an intolerant nation. The attempt to forge a nation that is bound together on the basis of a common cultural heritage and one that privileges Hinduism by the majoritarian rhetoric has caused much anxiety amongst minority communities across India and has threatened the already depleted secular fabric of India. Homogenizing the republic based on a cultural or racial supremacist philosophy will be self-defeating for a country hoping to emerge onto the world stage in a leadership role. Insularity and parochialism will not only annihilate our domestic polity but could have disastrous ramifications for foreign policy. South Asia is home to many such failed states – states that chose to define themselves in terms of their majoritarian/dominant faiths. In a modern globalized interconnected world, almost every aspect of a country's internal politics impacts foreign policy. For example, how a country treats its minorities can significantly influence not only foreign policy but the very international system and regional dynamics as well (the Syria situation is an example). Exclusionary *Hindutva* domestic politics could not only invite external involvement and further escalation of tension and violence in the border regions, but could also negatively change the economic and trade relations with other important countries, especially with many in the Middle East.

## Neighbourhood/regional supremacy?

Interestingly, a cursory glance at India's foreign relations history, particularly with Asian countries, throws up a more strategic and even hegemonic type of approach. India applied an imperialist diplomacy in her relations with neighbours, albeit a rhetorical commitment to Third World solidarity, non-alignment, and liberal democratic principles. Scholars particularly attribute this character of the modern Indian state to its colonial past. India had not been fully successful in liberating its thought from the imperialist inheritance left behind by the British; and later, India set herself upon a hegemonic course to safeguard her security. Examples include the hegemonic diplomacy applied to Sri Lanka in the 1980s, whereby Sri Lanka accused India of trying to achieve her security interests through the weakening of Sri Lanka's stability, India's confrontational relations with Pakistan, and others. Bandu de Silva notes that Nehru displayed beneath his "outward tendency for liberalism, a hardcore legacy of imperialism" (Silva, 2015) as successor to the British Raj. As India claims a leadership position for herself, her South Asian neighbours accuse her of exercising hegemony.[6]

India's ancient cultural and historical links with other Asian countries as a tool for its foreign policy approach have been used by both Congress and the BJP. As a subvariant of soft power, 'cultural diplomacy' became popular later, but India had its encounter with cultural diplomacy long before the word was coined.[7] More recently, the Indian government has explicitly incorporated a 'cultural' element into its foreign policy. For example, the Indian Council for Cultural Relations has set up cultural centres in more than 18 countries. However, an emphasis on Indian cultural and civilizational values should not translate to hyper-nationalism. "The stronger India will be, the better it is for Bhutan and other SAARC nations" (*India Today*, 2014), Modi said in his address to the Bhutan parliament in June 2015. An aggressive posturing and patronizing stance in a quest for regional leadership only works well within an ideology of dominance and subordination. Nor is such a technique enough to navigate the complex neighbourhood. Given its ideological proclivities, it remains to be seen whether the BJP can tap these without emitting the odour of cultural superiority. In a similar but retrogressive positioning, India supported the Madhesi demand to declare Nepal as Hindu Rashtra, which needs to be incorporated into the newly drafted constitution of Nepal, according to the BJP and its family organs.

On the border issues, India cannot expect to hang on to erstwhile imperialistic claims and needs to seek a political solution. Securing a nation is a complex business. A country's security includes all aspects of development and rights. Almost every aspect of a country's foreign policy impacts the states. This is particularly true of border states. Therefore, it is important to appreciate that Indian states have a natural stake in the foreign policy of the country. The Indian Northeast's tragic engagement with violence has returned after the relative peace of a few years, as New Delhi replaces political leadership and responsibility with a short-term military response.[8] Like Kashmir, the Northeast is a telling narrative of political failure to complete the complex task of forming a cohesive independent country, from sewing up the petty egos of former royalties to deftly dealing with the grievances of divergent communities to form a liberal democracy. Triumphalist and confrontational moves with neighbours[9] can in no way be passed off as 'pragmatic foreign policy'. When gratuitous assertion of national masculinity leads to escalation of conflicts at the borders and directly impacts hundreds of thousands of civilians and families, it cannot be justified by the 'national interest' logic.

In recent times, India's loss of friendship in the neighbourhood has been a major concern for developing a more effective foreign policy. Rifts between India and Nepal, Bangladesh and Sri Lanka are largely perceived to be the handiwork of China's policy of wooing India's friends by economic dole and military support. It is observed that India is falling behind Chinese hegemonic moves to constrain India from holding onto its influence on its immediate South Asian neighbourhood. The curious case of Nepal declaring a new map that includes parts of Indian territory such as Lipulekh, Kalapani and Limpiyadhura is largely seen as a Chinese-backed creation of a boundary dispute with India. Similarly, Bangladesh's recent aversion to meeting the Indian high commissioner is seen as an attempt to woo the Bangladesh prime minister by making it a part of the Chinese Belt and Road project. India's bilateral ties with Sri Lanka too are not beyond ambiguity. Though Sri Lanka has signed a pact with India to develop the high-profile Colombo port project, it is only transactional without much long-term commitment. Even in the India and Bhutan relationship, the chink in the armour is a joint Bhutan–China army joint exercise near the disputed Doklam area. Similar such hiccups in India's relationship with its neighbours affect Indian interest in such a way that India's present policy formulations are not able to tackle the tricky situation emerging from the invisible hands of China in South Asia. A more direct setback came through Iran dropping India out of the transit and transport corridor at Chabahar port, dashing India's dream of establishing an alternative land route to Central Asia and beyond. All this is because of India's bumpy relations with China, which does not allow India its little manoeuvring space in various South Asian countries beyond. In particular, India's loss of allies in the neighbourhood is a consequence of India's unilateralism.

Therefore, the complex task of determining what constitutes 'national interest', and whether it really reflects the interests of the citizens, should be placed at the heart of a country's foreign policymaking process. The state has to find alternative ways to engage with and accommodate the interests of all stakeholders, particularly those directly affected by the actions and agreements/treaties the government signs. For example, all Northeast states have international borders; therefore, the area has special significance for Indian security and prosperity. Clearly the time has come for border states like Mizoram and Nagaland to also have a say in India's Myanmar policy, instead of merely having to bear its consequences. It is necessary not to define the nation's interests in chauvinist and very narrow terms. In foreign diplomacy affairs it is said that a smart diplomacy is one where a nation is able to defend its 'core interests' while it makes concessions on peripheral interests. However, the problem with the core interests approach is that it tends to be exclusionary and confrontational. China, as is well known, has a core interests-based foreign policy. Also, sacrificing periphery for the sake of core interests could be self-defeating in the long run. Instead, an ecosystem approach could be more appropriate and realistic in the case of India. This means that at the domestic level a discursive, interactive and explorative process should be involved so that there is meaningful dialogue and co-ordination between the centre, states, civil society, academic community, and discursive institutionalists on foreign policy issues. This may slow down decision making but its long-term impact would be beneficial for the country.

## Pragmatism and social justice do not have to be a trade-off

The international community perceives Modi to be a pragmatist, focused on economic growth and governance. Pragmatism[10] is the view that meaning or worth is determined by practical consequences. It is closely akin to utilitarianism, the belief that usefulness is the standard of what is good. To a pragmatist/utilitarian, if a technique or course of action has the desired effect, it is good. If it doesn't seem to work, it must be wrong. 'Doer', 'pro-business', 'tech-savvy' and 'most powerful PM' are some of the expressions regularly used to describe Prime Minister Modi. This successful projection of Modi as a business-friendly leader is also linked to the electoral mandate that the BJP commands in parliament. This has made thousands of fans, especially business leaders both at home and abroad, enthused. It was believed that numbers were enough to bring about changes and make things happen. His government is accused of intolerance, censoring critics, suppressing religious minorities, disregarding human rights, disdaining experts/science and undermining the judiciary. This has left both the Indian and the global human rights community and intellectuals anxious.

This equilibrium also presents challenges for India's foreign policy. Many human rights and religious-freedom sensitive countries will reframe their relationship with India in merely 'practical terms' of mutually beneficial economic cooperation. In fact, it has the potential to pigeonhole and reduce India's relation with the world to a bare minimum 'pragmatic ground' – too 'transactional' and less 'partnership'. For example, over the years the US and India shared values of secular democracies, and the multi-ethnic, multi-religious features of their civilizations have been cited as reasons for their relationship of 'mutual respect and benefit'. However, Modi's RSS background and his views of India as a Hindu *Rashtra* have made many people in India, particularly the minority communities and many people outside the country, apprehensive. According to Gurcharan Das, the polarizing figure of Modi leads to a "moral dilemma" between equally important values – a classic *dharma sankat*. In this, the electorates are faced with the risk of choosing between "India's precious secular traditions and collaborative traditions" *and* "good governance and prosperity" (Das, 2015). However, such blinkered binary understanding and framing not only fails to explain nuances of how the secular democratic processes should function, but it also ignores the fact that these two ideas are not necessarily mutually exclusive of each other. In fact, one is constitutive of the other. It is important to remember that the issue of prosperity/development is far more complex than simply economic growth. It also includes social, cultural and political well-being and harmonious co-existence of citizens. Development should include concerns of climate change as well as human resource management. Most importantly, it must take into active consideration people's grass roots institutions and organizations and must enlist their initiative and participation. In the context of India, the development agenda should be examined in connection with cultural pluralism and national identity.

Can Modi successfully mitigate the dilemma, and will pragmatism prevail over ethnic chauvinism? – pragmatism in the form of delivering on his good governance and development agenda, and thereby consolidating the future electoral plan for him and his party. Critics have questioned if Modi's visible 'pragmatic' orientation was just a smokescreen in order to win a broad electoral mandate, while essentially executing the *Hindutva*'s exclusionary vision of India. Modi's 'dilemma', therefore, is a political as much as it is a moral one. Ironically, pragmatism has roots in Darwinism and secular humanism. It is inherently relativistic, rejecting the notion of absolute right and wrong, good and evil, truth and error. Pragmatism ultimately defines truth as that which is useful, meaningful and helpful. Ideas that don't seem workable or relevant are rejected as false. In this spirit of pragmatism, Modi may well register his 'dissent' to the RSS ideologues and jumpstart the dialogue to reorient its ideology with the changing reality of modern India and the world. As Andersen and Berland wrote:

> In the long term, the RSS and the BJP will also need to grapple with a broader ideological issue: the future orientation of Hindu nationalism ... Modi has the potential to orient the BJP toward a more inclusive political message in a way that benefits all Indians.
>
> (Andersen and Berland, 2015)

## Majoritarian democracy and the credibility question

India presents itself to the world as a pluralist model of democracy. But in practice it has always remained a classical model of majoritarian democracy. 'Divided authority', 'decentralization' and 'open access' are some of the watchwords of a pluralist democracy, whereas a majoritarian democracy interprets government 'by the people' as government by the majority of the people. It attempts to approximate the people's role in direct democracy within the limitations of representative democracy. India has so far practised a majoritarian model of democracy both in its normative and structural sense. Being the majority with a head start in political and economic power, the Hindus upheld their cultural traditions as the standards, and Hindu-centrism is widespread. This kind of thinking is not exclusive to RSS and its affiliates only. The Indian state itself is structurally majoritarian. Our national life as well as our democracy discourse is so slanted towards this majoritarian model that most Indians (including individuals from minority communities) accept this as a given. Incidents of communal tension and violence take place only when some majoritarian hardliners target and terrorize the members of the minority communities for being the 'other'. Such majoritarian pervasiveness has led to the "creation of a governing culture where India's 'Hindu-ness' becomes a normal and matter-of-fact part of public life" (Kesavan, 2015).

This majoritarian contour also established the values and norms in India: what kind of beliefs an ideal Indian citizen should have; what to wear; what to eat; what kind of practices are not 'Indian' culture; what constitutes national interest; which race one should belong to or how one's physical features should look like; and so on. Legislation is passed to discriminate and to curtail minority/marginalized population groups. Interestingly, even the laws are slanted towards the dominant ideology –Article 48 of the Indian Constitution,[11] which is a directive that asks states to protect cows from slaughter, is a prime example. This is not the same as affirmative action; therefore it should be differentiated from the other specific laws that exist to protect vulnerable sections.[12] This 'majoritarian' model of Indian democracy is again institutionalized through its parliamentary system – representation is based on the state's size/population (West Bengal alone has 17 more MPs than all the eight Northeastern states put together). Among the various governmental systems, the US Senate, as is well known, has a membership which is not based on population – each state, large and small, populous and otherwise, has the same number of senators. Within a majoritarian state structure, limited parliamentary representation means electorally less significant or less threatening, ensuring little or no attention from the government at centre. Issues and dissent within the Northeast over the centre's foreign policy receive little play outside of the region.

Though the Indian state shares some of the characteristics of a *weak state* – government struggles to provide order to society, and will often resort to force in an effort to do so (ethno-religious and tribal factionalism predominates over nationalism), it is rightly categorized as a *modernizing state*. As a *modernizing state* (as opposed to a *modern state*), nationalism is often an instrument of Indian state power, and 'unruly' minorities are suppressed. It not only defines national security in terms of force, but it also routinely views non-state actors (especially foreign non-state actors) as a threat to national sovereignty, and may attempt to regulate, neutralize or ban/exclude them; and/or create their own 'non-state' lookalikes such as government-operated NGOs to further their state goals.[13] Commentators argue that non-state actors have less or restricted freedom of movement and expression in modernizing states than in *weak* and *developed states*.[14] It is not enough for democracy to be limited to the elections. It is necessary for India to remain a constitutional democracy.

Over the years, India has successfully promoted its democratic achievements abroad. In fact, presenting India to the world as a plural multi-cultural society is an important component of its foreign policy today. Several commentators have enumerated India's soft power.[15] Writing in 1990, Joseph Nye defined 'soft power'[16] (also called co-optive power) as the ability to shape the preferences of others through appeal and attraction. It is non-coercive and relies on culture, political values and foreign policies. Recently, the term has also been used in changing and influencing social and public opinion through relatively less transparent channels and lobbying through powerful political and non-political organizations. Not coincidentally, some scholars attribute India's increased 'soft power' push as a reaction to counter China's rise in Asia and international orders. Nicolas Blarel argues, "by publicizing the pluralist nature of its politics and society, India intends to prove it is a cooperating, stabilizing and exemplary rising power, in contrast to China's more aggressive, if not neo-colonial model" (Blarel, 2012: 32). Soft power rhetoric is used simply as a tool to create a congenial environment to promote other issues at stake. Blarel notes that references to Indian culture, to its diaspora, to its political values and to its economic development have mostly been rhetoric for image-polishing.

Later, in 2012, Nye explained that, with soft power, "the best propaganda is not propaganda", further explaining that during the Information Age, "credibility is the scarcest resource". He argued that 'smart' states can increase their credibility and soft power by their domestic and international performance. This begs the question: Is India a liberal, reformist, hospitable and credible nation? Or is it communal, intolerant, closed and unstable? A cursory glance at India's history of societal violence based on religion, caste, race and gender is telling. In the present context, this kind of threat to India's credibility on the international stage and to its domestic cohesiveness has been posed by what has come to be known as *Hindutva* syndrome. The Narendra Modi-led BJP government is facing a massive backlash for failing to act against what is widely seen as rising intolerance across the country. Recent attacks that have led to protests by the intelligentsia range from the lynching of a Muslim man on suspicions he ate beef to the killings of three rationalists by suspected Hindu religious hard-liners. In practice, India's soft power remains weak, therefore incapable of converting into 'smart' power. According to Rohan Mukherjee,

> the credibility of India's soft power lies in the coherence of its national identity, and India has not yet resolved the many contradictions in its self-image in a manner that might lend to the successful utilization of its latent soft power resources
>
> (Mukherjee, 2014: 47)

## Margins, diversity and foreign policy

In the era of globalization almost every international treaty signed by the government disproportionately affects the marginalized and the poor citizens. This is particularly true in the areas of climate change, health care, development and security. The Modi administration has focused on foreign policy to revive trade and investment, and called for international cooperation to counter terrorism treats and money laundering. However, it has not made any significant announcements suggesting greater commitment to protecting human rights. Human rights did not feature very strongly in public statements when Indian leaders met with counterparts from other countries, although they agreed to cooperate on regional issues. Domestic reforms and initiatives (labour reforms, infrastructure development, policy easing etc.) with a focus on stimulating foreign investment has little to do with the rights, development and security of the farmers, tribals, women, minorities and the poorest sections of the society. Industrialization and infrastructure construction have tended to disproportionately affect the most marginalized.

The recent discourse surrounding the new policy on land acquisition brings to light this trade-off.[17] Government cited the urgent need for GDP growth and building infrastructure while dropping the 'consent' and 'social impact' clauses in the Bill. It denounced the process of seeking consent as a barrier to prosperity. The then finance minister, Arun Jaitley, argued that participative processes have held back "hundreds of crores of projects". However, experts and activists in the field have been pointing out the deficiency in such an approach. Aruna Chandrasekhar argues, "the changes show a troubling shift in the perception of the relationship between business and human rights, which assumes that compensation is the only currency that matters".[18] However, in the absence of dialogue to address people's concerns, development projects are also likely to face lengthy litigation, protests and the same delays that the government wants to avoid. Also, by truncating the stakeholders in the policy process that seeks to mitigate issues/problems that involve them and their livelihoods, the state is left with a missing link in an otherwise integrated enterprise.

Involvement of the citizens and communities of border regions in the conceptualization and implementation of a proper border management policy is of great significance. Border regions need to be given special attention for a successful border management policy or international treaties signed by the government. An example is India's Look/Act Policy plan to corridorize the Northeastern region and create the possibility of trade in natural resources without any prior informed opinion and critique from people of the region. This leads us to surmise that India's trans-Asiatic engagement with South and Southeast Asia merely in security and economic terms creates a conflict between state sovereignty and the predicaments of an open liberalized economy with its direct effect on movements of ethno-sovereignty, development of the Northeast region and civil and political freedoms of individuals and groups. Overemphasis on liberalized economic policies without planned efforts aimed at securing the socio-economic welfare and common interests of the people at the grass-roots level has constrained local economies and subjected them to transnational policies of opening up and thereby giving up local, regional and cultural rights in the 'flow' of foreign policy.

Greater emphasis on the importance of and need for the marginalized's participation in the state's policy processes could lead to better peace and security for the people. At the same time, its exclusion from related policy processes jeopardizes its security in all areas. Any attempt by any state to construct a 'strong nation' based on a perceived majoritarian national self-image that excludes, suppresses and marginalizes its minorities is bound to fail. It will not only destroy its internal fabric and give rise to conflicts and threats, but also hamper any kind of development, security and social harmony (Chenoy, 2015). Any state that imposes its religious belief on statecraft and represses minorities alienates them into revolting. Moreover, policy that does not recognize minorities and give them equal citizenship rights is also linked to associating their minorities with other extremist groups outside the state. There is a connection between minority rights and international peace, security and human development. However, this critical aspect has not got enough attention from theorists and practitioners of foreign and security policy. If this is not recognized, the world will continue to be unsafe as more states will break up and more minorities revolt against states that deny them equal citizenship (Chenoy, 2015).

Nations' self-image and international relations debates are apparently confined to a 'power-against-power' strategy. This position would mean either a plan for the Ups to replace the Downs or a plan for the Downs to replace the Ups. A power-against-power approach is about politics of hegemony, confrontation and distrust, and thus marked by offensive and defensive postures.[19] Therefore, it is imperative to move towards a position of participation from the position of domination. However, participatory dialogues will be futile unless they are guided by a sense of respect for each other. For a participative public policy process, a respect for the relevance of minority rights and issues must be inculcated in the state's foreign policy. To this effect, we need a less violent and aggressive idea of nation and we need to revise and reorient our understanding of national interests, security and development which is at times narrow and exclusionary.

In recent times, India's insistence on what is termed the Citizenship Amendment Act, 2020 (CAA) to allow non-Muslim minorities from the neighbouring three countries of Pakistan, Afghanistan and Bangladesh to be granted Indian citizenship has created an unfavourable implication for India's foreign policy towards these three neighbouring countries. The implication is that India is projecting them as countries with a track record of religious persecution of their religious minorities, which creates a psychological divide with these countries, whose ripple effect can be felt elsewhere. India's relationship with Saudi Arabia became slightly turbulent and the Gulf countries in general started distancing themselves from India. The pandemic too became mixed up with a perception of India as anti-Muslim, resulting in a purge or a kind of forced exodus of the Indian workforce in countries like Kuwait, Brunei and Oman

How best can India build a framework to tackle such distancing by others for its alleged and perceived stance against Muslims? From a power-sharing participatory approach, diversity in all forms could have been a crucial human resource. There is an argument from biology which suggests that a minimum number of viable species is required to maintain a stable ecosystem. Here, diversity is recognized as an ecological resource. For example, cultural diversity in the population of a country results in a healthy diversity in the use of land and natural resources of all kinds (Bennett, 1975). Biological, philosophical, linguistic, gender, religious and cultural diversity are all important aspects of living in a wider and more adoptive society (Sangalli, 1996: 47). Had India followed this adoptionist policy both internally and externally, it would have better dealt with questions of perceived cultural difference with various countries in the Middle East and South Asia. Adopting a functionalist view, business groups and corporations have tried to turn around this 'problem' of diversity into a resource. Terms like 'human resources' and 'social capital' recognize the vast array of human skills needed to create functioning large-scale modern societies.[20] Similarly, countries like America and the UK have smartly used the skills and knowledge of minority and ethnic groups to improve their foreign relations and trade competitiveness.

Instead of viewing it as a problem to be overcome, India should embrace its cultural, religious, racial and ethnic diversity capital and use it as a strategic advantage for foreign policy purposes. For example, some states can play a crucial role in India's linkages with key countries. Indian boundaries are such that people speaking the same language and sharing the same culture and social traditions live on both sides of the borders. Many Indian states, particularly in India's Northeast, even in some states in the south, have huge Christian populations that have close religious ties with other Christian populations in many foreign countries such as the US, UK etc. India has so far given impetus to the Gita-Sanksrit-Yoga diplomacy abroad. It could also stress its rich Indo-Islamic tradition as has been exemplified in the Bhakti Movement etc. Similarly, in Kashmir, had India adopted a more resilient and accommodative understanding towards the case of Kashmir's autonomy instead of revoking its special status, there could have been lesser chance of skirmishes with China in Ladakh. India adopted a path of confrontation from a position of strength that culminated in a complex geopolitical way into an opportunity for China to meddle with India's Line of Actual Control with Tibet. For both global credibility and strategic partnerships with superpowers, India must respect human rights, especially of minorities. Kiran Karnik rightly observes that "immense diversity is India's special advantage. It is essential to sustain and encourage this and ensure that the push towards homogenization, to a single 'Indian' culture, is resisted" (Karnik, 2012).

## Methodological intervention

There is a need to interrogate received knowledge in foreign policy practice, a need to find alternative ways to conceptualize major ideas in the foreign policy field. Here, an analysis through the positions of margin could be helpful – which can be seen as a methodology for knowledge production. Such an intervention from the margins can bring to foreign policy the necessary checks and balances – making visible the erasures and silences around concepts such as culture, national interests, identity, and nation.[21] It can also highlight the uncertainties and dispossessions that foreign policy has rendered possible. Several postcolonial feminist scholars have also articulated this need for 'a new method of analysis' for international relations and world politics.[22] A methodological intervention in the foreign policy discourse will engender the articulation of marginalized voices and help interrogate the essential and exclusive identity constructions that usually underpin the imagining of nation and nationalisms and its related concepts of sovereignty, power and security.

The 'margins' critique thus needs to be understood against the general backdrop of this battle of narratives in which stories of (1) a 'strong nation' based on the myth of the racial superiority logic and (2) a secular democratic nation based on the myth of a plural, secular society of equality are critiqued by the narratives of the margins who have suffered from majoritarian domination and from the legacies of the Indian state hegemonies. The margins critique, thus, is not about differences of cultural values – this is not an incommensurability problem; rather, it needs to be understood in the context of race/caste/class relations in India. This is not to suggest that providing a counterpoint to the dominant foreign policy discourses will automatically change the world of policymaking. It means that the intervention from the margins will provide the required 'socialization' of the methodology. This socialization of methodology is a positive step towards the democratization of foreign policymaking.

The argument in favour of escaping critical review or a participative model in the name of policy autonomy and objectivity by resisting social interference is flawed. Participative process and review are likely to enhance the policy soundness or objectivity by resisting debilitating values and idiosyncrasies of policymakers and by encouraging facilitating values. In the absence of a community-wide vigilance, there is every possibility that the effects vitiating accounts based on the grand metanarratives of nation, nationalism and national interest might vitiate policy content too. Every discipline/methodology should have its own mechanism to encourage, incorporate facilitating values and resist univocal and exclusionary values. In fact, negotiation with the margins is a very effective tool of defying various kinds of centrism. Democracy is a truth-facilitator. It safeguards methodology by resisting distorted interpretations constructed by power in social sciences. The distance between the policymaker and the object of policy needs to be minimized to enable a dialogue between the policymaker and the object of policy. Dialogue is expected to sensitize the policymaker about her own biases and to strengthen her reflexivity. The margins are likely to offer valuable insight about the dimensions of social reality not exposed to the mainstream.

India's foreign policy needs to free itself from asymmetric relations of exigency, transaction and one upmanship, as such political and diplomatic ploys call for a greater aggressiveness in relation to comparatively weaker neighbours. Faced with a globally emerging strong country like China, India is now forced to follow a path of contingent alliances with powers like the US or Australia, which does not promise long-term stability for India in regional theatres. A good policy formulation free of the politics of brinkmanship and cold war is the need of the hour that can ensure India's peace and stability and shall allow India to rise on a growth path. A premature competition with China as a buffer or cushion for another major power like the US does not protect India's geopolitical interests and instead exposes it to incalculable risks that suddenly stress India's economy and polity in a manner of undesired and uncontrolled eventualities. The largest issue then is to deftly draw a balanced approach to acquire a stable place in the emerging global cold war and trade-related conflicts. India's foreign policy corps is certainly in a position to infuse lessons that are learnt by India in a situation of global uncertainty created by the pandemic and it is for sure that fine lines of policy formulation will become further refined and smarter.

## Acknowledgements

Chapter 3 was originally written by Sashinungla and Prasenjit Biswas and presented at conferences in Copenhagen and Kolkata, 2015. I accept full responsibility for all revisions made. I can sincerely hope that they retain their original spirit and energy, which flowed from our collective effort.

## Notes

1 For an excellent discussion of India's cultural pluralism and civilizational ethos, see Momin, 1996: 99–107. See also Figueira, 2015.
2 On 28 September 2015, a 50-year-old Muslim man, Mohammad Akhlaq, was beaten to death and his 22-year-old son severely injured in Uttar Pradesh's Dadri, after an announcement about the family consuming beef was allegedly made at a local temple. See Vatsa, 2015.
3 For an analysis of *Hindutva* triumphalism, see Guha, 2014.
4 Rashtriya Swayamsevak Sangh (RSS) is an Indian right-wing, Hindu nationalist paramilitary organization – the progenitor of Hindutva ('Hinduness') and the idea that India should be a 'Hindu nation'.
5 One of the principal exponents of Hindu nationalism, Madhav Golwalkar, in his book *Bunch of Thoughts* (1966), opposes reservations for Dalits and backwards. In September 2015, the then RSS chief Mohan Bhagwat called for a committee to be set up to suggest changes in the reservation policy.
6 For a discussion on India's role in South Asia, see Bhasin (2008).
7 For a detailed discussion of cultural diplomacy in the Indian context, see Pratap, 2015.
8 After pulling out of a 14-year long ceasefire with the government of India in April 2015, the Naga insurgent group NSCN-K shifted base to Myanmar, joined hands with other insurgent groups and formed the United Liberation Front of Western South East Asia (UNLFW), and turned its gun again on Indian Security Forces, killing 18 soldiers in an ambush in Manipur's Chandel district on June 4.

Immediately after that, the Special Action Group (SAG) retaliatory strikes at NSCN-K camps inside Myanmar threatened to sour India–Myanmar relations. Anyone with even the slightest know-how about the ethno-sovereignty movements in India's Northeast knows that there cannot be permanent peace in the Naga areas unless the major Naga insurgent factions are part of the peace process or any 'framework agreement'. It is clear Delhi made no effort to stop the NSCN-K from calling off the truce.

9 For a discussion of India's triumphalist approach, see Joseph, 2015.

10 Pragmatism as a philosophy was developed and popularized at the end of the last century by philosopher William James, along with such other noted intellectuals as John Dewey and George Santayana.

11 Maharashtra Animal Preservation Bill 1995 also bans import of beef and imposes five years' imprisonment in jail and a fine for sale and possession of beef.

12 Laws/statutes such as the Muslim personal law, Christian marriage act, Hindu succession act etc., specific to religions/communities, exist, and these laws are often discriminatory and exploitative, particularly towards women within the communities. But these do not impinge on the life of others outside the communities or are not uniformly applied to all individuals of other religions or communities. In this sense, Article 48 can be seen as an exemplar of the majoritarian model of democracy.

13 For a discussion on non-state actors in *modernizing states*, see National Intelligence Council, 2007.

14 For more discussions on non-state actors see Sen, 1999.

15 For discussions on Indian soft power, see Tharoor, 2008; Blarel, 2012; Mukherjee, 2014.

16 Joseph Nye coined the term in his book *Bound to Lead: The Changing Nature of American Power* (1990). He further developed the concept in his book *Soft Power: The Means to Success in World Politics* (2004).

17 Academics, rights activists and civil society groups have accused the BJP government of giving in to industry lobbies and wanting to pass a law that would allow the state to acquire land for a broad range of projects, including certain private industries, without seeking permission from land owners, most of whom are small farmers and tribal communities. Owners will be compensated, but will have no choice in the matter.

18 As quoted in Mohan, 2015.

19 For a discussion on power relations, see Warren, 1994.

20 Ferguson, 2000–2001.

21 See Said, 1984, 1993 for a discussion on culture, identity, erasures, memory, nation and the related issues.

22 See Agathangelou and Ling, 2004a, 2004b.

## References


Agathangelou, Anna and Ling, L.H.M. 2004a. 'The house of IR: From family power politics to the poesies of worldism', *International Studies Review* 6, No. 4, pp. 21–47.

Agathangelou, Anna and Ling, L.H.M. 2004b. 'Power, borders, security, wealth: Lessons of violence and desire from September 11', *International Studies Quarterly* 48, No. 3, pp. 517–538.

Andersen, Walter and Berland, Allison. 2015. 'Parivar gets a Modified lesson in pragmatism', *The Times of India*, 8 March.

Blarel, Nicolas. 2012. 'India: the next superpower?: India's soft power: from potential to reality?' IDEAS reports – special reports, Kitchen, Nicholas (ed.) SR010. LSE IDEAS, London School of Economics and Political Science, London, UK.

Bennett, Charles F. 1975. 'The advantages of cultural diversity', Paper presented at the symposium on *The Ecology of Conservation and Development in Central America and Panama*, sponsored by the Organization for Tropical Studies, San Jose, Costa Rica, in February, 1975.

Bhasin, Madhavi. 2008. 'India's Role in South Asia – Perceived or reluctant leadership'. Available at www.globalindiafoundation.org/MadhaviBhasin.pdf (accessed on 27 January 2016).

Chenoy, Anuradha M. 2015. 'Minority state in foreign policy'. Available at www.pressreader.com/india/the-new-indian-express/20150228/281870116893496 (accessed on 31 August 2020).

Das, Gurcharan. 2015. 'Why voters are poles apart on Narendra Modi', *Times of India*, 12 May.

Figueira, Dorothy M. 2015. *Aryans, Jews, Brahmins: Theorizing authority through myths of identity*, New Delhi: Navayana.

Ferguson, R. James. 2000–2001. 'Advanced international relations and advanced global politics 2', Department of International Relations, SHSS, Bond University.

Guha, R. 2014. 'Paranoia and triumphalism: Hindutva in history', *The Telegraph*, 12 July.

Ganguly, S. 2015. 'Hindu Nationalism and the Foreign Policy of India's Bharatiya Janata Party', *Transatlantic Academy Paper Series*, Washington, DC: Transatlantic Academy.

Golwalkar, Madhav. 1966. Bunch of thoughts, Gadag: Vikama Prakashan.

*India Today*. 2014. 'Modi addresses Bhutan's Parliament, says a stronger India better for Bhutan too', 12 June. Available at www.indiatoday.in/world/neighbours/story/narendra-modi-bhutan-parliament-full-speech-197051-2014-06-16

Joseph, Josy. 2015. 'Shun the triumphalism: Nation formation is a more complex job than chest-thumping about military might', *Times of India*, 12 June.

Karnik, Kiran. 2012. 'Ideas, freedom and diversity will ensure India gets its place in the bold new world', *The Economic Times*, 3 July.

Keeler, Vandan. 2015. 'Controversy is the middle name of culture minister', *The Times of India*, 19 September.

Kesavan, M. 2015. 'Hindus and others: The republic's common sense', *The Telegraph*, 21 August.

Malone, David and Mukherjee, Rohan. 2010. 'Polity, security, and foreign policy in contemporary India', in *South Asia's weak States: Understanding the regional insecurity predicament*, ed. T.V. Paul, Stanford: Stanford University Press, pp. 147–169.

Mohan, Rohini. 2015. 'Modi's seized earth campaign', *Foreign Policy*, 26 May. Available at http://foreignpolicy.com/2015/05/26/narendra-modi-land-law-acquisition-india/ (accessed on 17 September 2016)

Momin, A.R. 1996. 'Cultural pluralism, national identity and development', in *Interface of cultural identity and development*, ed. B. Saraswati, New Delhi: IGNCA and D.K. Printworld, pp. 99–107.

Mukherjee, Rohan. 2014. 'The false promise of India's soft power', *Geopolitics, History and International Relations* 6, No. 1, pp. 46–62.

National Intelligence Council. 2007. 'Non-state actors: Impact on international relations and implications for the United States', *Report Prepared under National Intelligence Officer for Economics and Global Issues*, DR-2007–16D, 23 August 2007.

Nye, Joseph. 1990. *Bound to lead: The changing nature of American power*, New York: Basic Books.

Nye, Joseph. 2004. *Soft power: The means to success in world politics*, New York: Public Affairs.

Nye, Joseph. 2012. 'China's soft power deficit: To catch up, its politics must unleash the many talents of its civil society', *The Wall Street Journal*, 8 May. Available at www.wsj.com/articles/SB10001424052702304451104577389923098678842 (accessed 17 September 2016).

Pratap, Bhanu. 2015. 'India's cultural diplomacy: Present dynamics, challenges and future prospects', *International Journal of Arts, Humanities and Management Studies* 1, No. 9, September, pp. 55–65.

Ramaseshan, Radhika. 2015. 'Shah on web with Savarkar', *The Telegraph*, 28 September.

Sangalli, Arturo. 1996. 'The importance of being diverse', *New Science* 151, No. 2043, p. 47.

Said, Edward. 1984. 'Reflections on exile', *Granta* 13, Autumn, pp. 159–172.

Sen, Amartya. 1999. 'Accessing human contribution', in *UNDP Human Development Report, 1999*, New York: Oxford University Press.

Sen, Siddartha. 1999. 'Some aspects of State-NGO relationships in India in the post-independence era', *Development and Change* 30, No. 2, pp. 327–355.

Silva, Bandu de. 2015. 'Emerging cultural emphasis in India's foreign policy under Modi: The signals from the first "reaching East" visits', *Colombo Telegraph*, 29 May. Available at www.colombotelegraph.com/index.php/emerging-cultural-emphasis-in-indias-foreign-policy-under-modi/ (accessed on 19 September 2016).

Said, Edward. 1993. *Culture and imperialism*, New York: Alfred Knopf.

Sagar, S. 2014. '"Jiski Lathi, Uski Bhains": The Hindu nationalist view of international politics', in *India's grand strategy: History, theory, cases*, eds. K. Bajpai, S. Basit and V. Krishnappa, London: Routledge, p. 237.

Schwartzberg, Joseph E. and Stoddard, Robert. 1995. 'Evolving ethnicity in South Asia with particular reference to India' (Geography Faculty Publications, 25). Available at https://digitalcommons.unl.edu/geographyfacpub/25

Thapar, Romila. 1992. *Interpreting early India*, Delhi: Oxford University Press.

Tharoor, Shashi. 2008. 'India as a soft power', *India International Centre Quarterly* 35, No. 1, pp. 32–45.

Vatsa, Aditi. 2015. 'Dadri: Mob kills man, injures son over "rumours" that they ate beef', *The Indian Express*, 14 October.

Warren, Karen J. 1994. 'Toward an ecofeminist peace politics', in *Ecological Feminism*, ed. Karen J. Warren, London: Routledge, pp. 179–199.

# 4 India's foreign aid policy

## Aid recipient and aid donor

*Jørgen Dige Pedersen*

### Introduction

In late October 2015 representatives of 54 African countries, including 41 heads of state, met at the 3rd India–Africa Summit in New Delhi. At the meeting India offered African countries US$10 billion over the next five years as concessional credit and grants worth $600 million in addition to 50,000 scholarships for African students and others schemes to support education (*Economic Times*, 29 October 2015). One could easily be forgiven for seeing this meeting as symbolizing India's rise in the global economy and its desire to make an impact on Africa, perhaps even as a challenger to China's rising position on the continent. More so as this was indeed the third and largest India–Africa summit meeting since the first one took place in New Delhi in 2008, followed by the second in Addis Ababa in 2011 and thus seems to represent a new and ambitious diplomatic initiative by India. It may also be seen as symbolizing India's transformation from being a poor recipient of external assistance from the Western world to a new and ambitious donor to needy countries of Africa.

While there is no doubt that the general impression of the significance of the meeting between India and Africa reflects much of the thinking in both New Delhi and in the various capitals of Africa, there is another supplementary (not alternative) interpretation. In this interpretation, the meeting is just another recent – and important – element in what has been a long story of collaboration between two of the world's poorest regions with a shared colonial history. The recent meeting thus brings memories of another – truly epoch-making – meeting, namely that of the Afro-Asian nations in New Delhi in 1947, just before the formal independence of India. That meeting was organized by the Indian National Congress, and it became the starting point of what later evolved into the Non-Aligned Movement and other similar attempts to organize a common front of developing nations in their struggle against the domination of the rich Western world led by Europe and the US. This movement also led India to offer various forms of assistance to African and Asian nations, as we shall see later. The transformation of India from aid recipient to aid donor thus has a much longer history than is usually recognized and for a long time the arguments for establishing aid programmes were rooted in arguments for solidarity among poor nations and common interest in economic advancement and reduction of the dependence on the rich world, as indicated by the term 'collective self-reliance' used in the 1970s to characterize India's early aid programmes.

From this introduction is clear that foreign aid has been part of India's foreign policy for quite some time. It has not always been recognized as such, however, and in recent times the fact that India is still a large, poor aid-receiving country has almost disappeared from the studies concerning India's foreign policy, as we shall see. There are two separate parts of the story of aid as part of India's foreign policy. On the one hand, India has always been a recipient of large quantities of foreign aid – indeed in cumulative terms the largest recipient of aid globally – and India has always needed to establish a policy towards the receipt of aid. Although not organizationally part of the agenda of the Ministry of External Affairs, the policy should be considered a key element in India's relationship with the wider world and indeed a part of its overall foreign policy. In most of India's existence as an independent state the search for foreign aid has been recognized as an important element in India's foreign policy or an economic imperative guiding the foreign policy, but more recently it seems to be assigned a minor role or simply neglected.[1] According to the recent literature, it seems as if the attraction of foreign aid has lost its importance for India, while aid provided by India has become much more important and normally finds mention in discussions on India's status as a rising power.

In the following I will provide an overview of India's policy as a recipient of foreign aid as well as a donor of aid in order to illustrate some of the complexities – even contradictions – involved in this unique double role for India. Both the provision of aid and the donation of aid are by their very nature intrusive activities that establish relations between internal actors and external agencies, thus crossing the borders between external and internal affairs. Ideally, aid should to some degree reflect domestic resource needs in recipient countries but, in addition, the donation of aid to foreign countries will often reflect domestic interests and needs in the donor country, directly through export of goods and services from donor to recipient, indirectly by simply improving the overall climate for positive relations between two countries.

First, however, a brief note on some problems and complexities involved in researching aid to and from India. The international donation of aid is a highly complex matter that goes far beyond that of a transfer of a sum of money. Aid normally involves the transfer of money across borders, but usually it also involves movements of people, of skills, ideas and culture, elements which are hard to measure and thus form a highly complex part of foreign policy both on the part of the donor and on the part of the recipient. In the case of India, even the movement of money is very hard to monitor. One reason is that what India regards as aid may not tally with what the dominant international definition – that of the OECD Development Assistance Committee (DAC) – includes in the aid calculations.[2] While no specific definition of aid has been given by the Indian authorities, it seems that loans on concessional terms from a wide variety of sources and outright grants from (foreign) governments and organizations are what is counted as foreign assistance. This may not be very different from the DAC definition, but when it comes to aid provided by India to other countries it is difficult to get a precise picture of what is considered as being aid or external assistance. This is further complicated by the absence (as yet) of a consolidated aid budget. The Ministry of External Affairs, the Ministry of Finance and the Reserve Bank of India in its balance of payment accounts publish figures for external aid that display wide discrepancies and seldom match for individual years (see Figure 4.1). In addition, figures are not published at regular intervals and in a consolidated manner that allows for detailed comparisons across time and space. The information available on India's own aid is thus scattered and hard to get a full picture of. Nevertheless, this paper will have to use whatever is available of data on India's aid, but the reader should be aware of the possible limitations and uncertainties in the interpretations of those data.

## Theories of foreign aid as foreign policy

Foreign aid initially surprised scholars working in the field of international politics. One of the first attempts to come to grips with this new, post-war phenomenon was by the founding father of modern Realist thinking in international relations, Hans Morgenthau. For him, foreign aid was indeed a 'baffling' new practice of foreign policy (Morgenthau 1962). Morgenthau saw aid as an activity that was intimately related to the overall foreign policy of the donor country. The motivations behind it may vary, from outright bribery or prestige-seeking to often misguided attempts to influence political and economic events in the recipient country, but always motivated by the political interests of the donor. Only humanitarian aid might possibly be regarded as having an apolitical character according to Morgenthau. In contrast to this unsentimental view, liberal thinkers have more often seen aid as a moral obligation and a solidarity act on the part of the rich countries to assist the development of poor countries (Lumsdaine 1993). Yet another school of thought is the radical so-called 'Aid as Imperialism' tradition named after Teresa Hayter's early analysis of World Bank aid (Hayter 1971). While in many ways similar to Realism in its view of international aid as the pursuance of donor interest, it differs because of its strong emphasis on the economic interests and motivations behind aid in addition to the political interests. The tradition also focuses more on the structural nature of North–South links that is being upheld through aid links. Most aid theory for obvious reasons deals exclusively with North–South relations, but there is one sub-species of the critical 'Aid as Imperialism' school that deals with the phenomenon of South–South aid, namely the sub-imperialism school. While it originally started in Latin

America, a prominent example of the application of the theory is Srikant Dutt (1984), who analysed the early pattern of India's relationship with the Third World and concluded that India's role in this relationship at the time could be classified as a sub-imperialist role and hence India should be seen as a proto- or second-tier imperialist country. This interpretation implied that, while India's policies generally were circumscribed by its relationship with the traditional imperialist powers (the North), it would itself act in a dominant and imperialist manner in its relations towards other developing nations.

While the political theories of aid represent a full spectrum of different views of the background, motives and impact of foreign aid, the economic theories tend to focus on the economic needs of developing nations that justify the receipt of aid from abroad. The most influential theory goes back to the discussion in Chenery and Strout (1966), where they set out their so-called 'two-gap theory'. The theory points to two key problems for developing nations, the lack of domestic investment resources and the lack of foreign exchange to procure much-needed imports. Aid provided from abroad could – in theory – contribute to filling both gaps, thereby helping the economic growth to a degree that eventually would make further aid superfluous. The theory has played a major role in the argumentation of both donors and recipients of foreign aid ever since. This economic view on foreign aid focused almost exclusively on the magnitude of the economic resources provided through aid, often in comparison with other resource flows like investments or foreign exchange earned through the export of goods and services. It has thus neglected the qualitative aspects of aid, including possible transfers of knowledge, ideas and culture embodied in aid activities. Similarly, political and economic dependency aspects involved in the aid relationship were ignored.

## India's role as a recipient of aid

By far the most important element in India's foreign policy related to the inflow and outflow of aid has been India's policy towards the receipt of foreign assistance in its efforts to achieve economic development through a strategy of state-directed economic planning. The overriding purpose of India's planning experience has been to achieve economic growth and economic self-reliance. The initial strategy during the planning efforts in the 1950s and 1960s was based on the development of a modern industrial sector, including heavy industry, and the construction of infrastructure necessary for economic progress. Most such activities were located in the public sector and during the first three five-year plans more than 90% of all incoming aid went to these purposes (Bhagwati and Desai 1970: 186). Aid from the USSR was particular important in this period. As aid was primarily regarded as a useful, indeed necessary, element for the Indian state's planning expenditure meant for industrialization following the logic of the two-gap theory, the negotiations over aid were done by the economic ministries and the Planning Commission with the Ministry of Finance's Department of Economic Affairs in the driver's seat. The Ministry of External Affairs has had relatively little direct involvement in this important part of India's relations with foreign governments and international organizations but indirectly it did through coordination with the economic ministries keep itself informed on aid relations. While no explicit policy for the receipt of foreign aid was formulated it is, nevertheless, easy to see that the economic policy pursued by India, in particular the emphasis on economic self-reliance, was closely associated with the overall foreign policy of non-alignment that allowed India to seek economic assistance from practically all available quarters, thus reducing reliance on any singular outside power. But the policy was not without tensions and contradictions. The key problem for any country receiving aid – as for India – was how to maximize the amount of (useful) aid while at the same time reduce as much as possible the dependency that almost by definition would accompany the receipt of aid. The hope was to use aid to promote a type of economic development that would result in a future situation where there would be no need for and no dependence on external assistance; cf. again the two-gap theory. More specifically, the following objectives can be inferred from India's experience with receiving aid over a long period:[3]

- To *receive maximum aid* on as lenient terms as possible. This has historically meant a preference for receiving grants rather than loans, although the receipt of grants can be seen as an acceptance of alms rather than the more equal partner-like quality of loans. The long-term goal, however, should be to make do without aid and achieve self-reliance in the provision of economic resources for development.
- To *minimize dependency* as much as possible. This could be done in many ways. The receipt of aid from many sources would reduce dependence on any individual aid provider. Multilateral aid from international organizations would generally be preferable to bilateral aid due to the reduced danger of dependency. Use of Indian personnel and Indian resources as much as possible (compared to the import of personnel and resources) would also be preferable.
- On the other hand, it would also be an objective to *receive as much as possible of technology* not available within India itself and this need had to be balanced against the other objectives of aid. The specific problem of tying of aid to particular suppliers – typically firms from the donor country – would pose particularly difficult problems in how to strike a balance between dependency and the maximum access to external resources.

Indira Gandhi once remarked that "This concept of ultimate self-reliance means that aid, which is an extraordinary form of transfer of resources, need not continue and that our own export earnings should meet our import requirements" (Gandhi 1966), supporting the overall aim of becoming independent from external assistance. This statement – however general in nature – fitted with the stated intentions in the various five-year development plans and with the logic of the two-gap model mentioned above, thus confirming the overall character of India's objectives.

In an early assessment of foreign aid to India, P.J. Eldridge noted that India had succeeded in largely determining the patterns and priorities of the assistance received from abroad (Eldridge 1969: Ch. 5). India had independently formulated her five-year plans and had been successful in persuading donors to provide finance for a sometimes significant part of the plans – basically a 'filling the gaps' approach. In terms of the desired quantum of aid, India had however been less successful, and one unforeseen implication of receiving aid, Eldridge noted, was that

> [a] continuous stream of advice, official and unofficial, is received by India on the conduct of her economic affairs. Her actions, statements and policies are subject to continuous and not always disinterested scrutiny, and she is obliged to make constant explanations and justifications for her policies and actions.
>
> (Eldridge 1969: 65)

These regular attempts by different donors to influence India's domestic economic policies clearly have had an effect. Especially in the early decades, it was interfering by the US that was most visible and was most debated publicly. While difficult to precisely pinpoint, there is little doubt that the receipt of aid under those circumstances had an impact on the ability of policymakers to chart their own independent course of action. The Indian prime minister, Jawarharlal Nehru, from early on had stated that India would not accept aid with 'strings attached' (=political conditions), but these high principles were difficult to uphold in reality. The most apparent example of pressure being applied to India came in the mid-1960s when the US administration in collaboration with the World Bank explicitly tried to change the direction of India's domestic economic policies in a liberalizing direction. The pressure came at a time when India was experiencing a deep economic crisis and when external aid was particularly needed, but the pressure nevertheless did not meet with much success (Lipton and Toye 1990: Ch.3; Pedersen 1993; Kirk 2011). Years later, in 1991, when India did change her economic strategy towards a more market-oriented strategy, this was seen by many as a result of the interaction with donor organizations, primarily the World Bank, which had employed – and probably influenced the thinking of – many prominent Indian economists who had returned to India as top-level influential bureaucrats (Pedersen 2000). There were other, most likely more important, reasons for the changes in economic policy, however, but the example illustrates that donor-recipient interactions in many different ways do influence the aid recipient and its policies. The organization of the donors into the Aid India Consortium in 1958 under the chairmanship of the World Bank had obviously also contributed to strengthening the collective influence that the donation of aid could provide to a united front of donors. Most observers of the aid relationship have noted that despite this India generally managed to be in the driver's seat in the sense of determining the distribution of aid for various purposes that were mostly in accordance with the plans laid by the Planning Commission (Veit 1976: 143; Lipton and Toye 1990; Kirk 2011). One issue that India from early on had to struggle with was the donor's tendency to tie their aid to purchases from donor country companies (Bhagwati and Desai 1970: 198–208), but little is known on the overall magnitude of this problem except that its occurrence has varied considerably over the years (Birla Institute of Scientific Research 1981: 50).

From the information available on the contribution of external aid to the financing of the Indian five-year plans (see Table 4.3 in Appendix), it seems likely that the influence of foreign donors was especially important before 1980. Foreign assistance financed close to one-third of plan outlays in the 1950s and 1960s but has subsequently been reduced to a level of less than 10%.[4] Before the 1990s, most foreign aid was used to finance projects administered by the central government (the Central Plan), but from the early 1990s, however, foreign aid has increasingly been directed towards projects and activities run by the various state governments (State Plans). In 1990–91, almost 70% of all external assistance went to projects administered by the central government. In 2004–05 that proportion had declined to 48% and the most recent figure available, for 2012–13, is down to 37%.[5] The growing importance of aid directed to state governments has come parallel to the growing political importance of state-based political parties for government formation in New Delhi and parallel to the increased importance of state governments in economic policymaking in the now more market-oriented Indian economy. For some states the foreign aid has financed around 20–30% of local development activities (Cox et al. 2002), thus raising the question of the possible influence of foreign aid-givers on policymaking in the states of India.

It was only after the turn of the century, however, that the Indian government in the Finance Minister's annual budget statement – probably encouraged by the rising level of foreign exchange reserves – formulated a new more restrictive policy towards the receipt of foreign aid. The exact wording of the statement released to the public after the speech is worth quoting:

> The finance ministry has decided to discontinue receiving aid from certain bilateral partners with smaller assistance packages so that their resources can be transferred to other developing countries in greater need of official development assistance.
>
> (quoted in *Times of India*, June 2, 2003)

Please note the officially stated reason: the expressed solidarity with other developing nations presumably in greater need of foreign aid than India at present. In the future, bilateral aid would only be accepted from G8 countries and from those donors who could provide more than US$25 million in aid per annum. Smaller amounts of aid could still be provided directly to non-state organizations, however.[6] As a result the number of aid donors was reduced

*Table 4.1* Aid to India – an overview

| *Aid utilization* | *Plans 1–3 (1951–66)* | *1970/71* | *1980/81* | *1990/91* | *2000/01* | *2019/20* |
|---|---|---|---|---|---|---|
| Total (Rs. billion) | 45.0 | 7.9 | 21.6 | 67.5 | 142.5 | 444.7 |
| *Percentage distribution* | | | | | | |
| Loans % | 61.3 | 83.3 | 81.7 | 92.0 | 94.9 | 99.6 |
| Grants % | 38.7* | 16.7 | 18.3 | 8.0 | 5.1 | 0.4 |
| *Percentage distribution* | | | | | | |
| Aid India Consortium members | - | 92.6 | 92.4 | 86.5 | 82.8 | 71.9 |
| -World Bank Group | 12.9 | 10.9 | 30.5 | 53.3 | 56.9 | 45.1 |
| -USA* | 26.7 | 40.0 | 3.8 | 0.8 | 0.6 | 0.0 |
| -UK | 6.5 | 9.9 | 9.7 | 2.7 | 2.2 | 0.0 |
| -Japan | 2.3 | 4.6 | 4.2 | 7.4 | 19.2 | 19.7 |
| -Germany | 2.3 | 7.2 | 6.6 | 6.3 | 2.7 | 1.8 |
| ADB | - | - | - | 3.2 | 18.5 | 19.5 |
| USSR/East Bloc/ Russia | 6.7 | 6.9 | 1.6 | 4.7 | 0.9 | 2.6 |
| Approximate number of bilateral donors**) | 20 | 19 | 15 | 18 | 9 | 4 |

Notes: * Inclusive of food aid repayable in rupees
** Some individual small donors are not listed separately in the source (but under 'Others')

Source: Government of India, *Economic Survey*, various years. Own calculation.

considerably (see Table 4.1), but the overall level of aid was hardly affected except in net terms for a few years after 2003 because of India's decision to repay outstanding loans to the governments whose aid it no longer deemed necessary.

From Table 4.1 the broad contours of India's experience with receiving aid can be briefly recapitulated. First of all, India has been successful in attracting a significant amount of aid. Not as much as hoped for, and not as much as could reasonably have been expected given the size of India and its level of poverty, but nevertheless substantial amounts. In the first 3–4 five-year plan periods foreign aid had indeed been a crucial element in financing India's strategy of industrialization (see Appendix Table 4.3), especially for the construction of steel mills, power projects, rail transportation and other forms of heavy industry and infrastructure construction.[7] Clearly this aid had involved a considerable degree of influence from foreign donors and especially the US government had tried to use its aid to gain influence on various Indian policies, but subsequently India had managed to diversify its sources of aid (and the US had decided effectively to terminate bilateral aid to India).

The Ministry of Finance had furthermore managed to exercise a substantial degree of control over the actual use of the aid provided, albeit in a constant discussion, sometimes a quarrelsome one, with donors eager to promote their own separate economic and political agendas. India had initially been able to take advantage of Cold War rivalries between East and West, getting important aid in strategic sectors from the USSR and Eastern Bloc countries, but also by using the threat of 'going to the Soviets' to get better conditions for aid to a variety of industrial projects eventually supported by the West (steel, oil, pharmaceuticals, etc.). After the 1970s, the Eastern bloc was increasingly less able or willing to help India and eventually the East–West aid competition almost disappeared. Instead, India has come to increasingly rely on aid from multilateral sources, in particular the World Bank. Multilateral aid in general is normally seen as being less intrusive for recipient countries and less infected by narrow commercial and political interests (Riddell 2007). This was not initially the case for the World Bank in India, however. The dominant position held by the World Bank and the viewpoint that the bank just acted as a kind of collective voice for dominant Western countries had made this aid very controversial in India and it took some time before India and the World Bank achieved a reasonable level of mutual understanding (Kirk 2011). Around the economic crisis and India's turn to a more market-oriented economic strategy in 1991, the World Bank did try to influence the turn of events through structural adjustment loans, but these efforts were extremely short-lived and can hardly be considered successful.[8] Nevertheless, India has in recent years come to rely more on 'non-Western' donors like Japan and the Asian Development Bank (ADB), possibly reflecting the fact that India has regarded these sources of aid as being more receptive to India's needs or just more understanding of India's aid priorities. Recent changes in India's own policies as a recipient has meant that 80–90% of all aid today comes from only three sources: the World Bank, the ADB and Japan. In theory, this could be seen as an increase in dependency but for India it probably indicates that aid has become an increasingly less important addition to its own resources, and one that should be managed as easily as possible. On the other hand, it must be acknowledged that even though India in relative terms has received a lesser amount of aid, aid flows have nevertheless in recent years stabilized, even increased slightly. In sum, India has neither become fully independent of aid, nor has it managed to achieve a surplus on its balance of trade that might have made aid redundant as anticipated by Indira Gandhi.

In 2014, India 'graduated' from the World Bank's facility for cheaper concessional loans, IDA (i.e. passed the average per capita income line for receiving IDA loans), but India has nevertheless managed to continue getting IDA loans for a transitional period up to and including 2017 (Ministry of Finance 2016). In 2020 it still continued to draw on IDA loans. A similar interest in obtaining continued aid from the World Bank group was displayed when Prime Minister Modi in 2014 requested support for some of his government's highly profiled initiatives (Swachh Bharat, Ganga Rejuvenation, Smart cities etc.).[9] These recent events indicate a continued strong interest from India to receive aid from the World Bank, and possibly also a strong interest from the Bank in continuing its long engagement with India (Kirk 2011).

India's long period as an aid recipient can according to this account be seen as a relatively successful story of a hard-headed India negotiating with international donors and managing to reduce its level of dependence on financial resources from abroad. It could not, however, avoid the fact that receiving aid also brought along a certain element of foreign influence, mostly on the domestic development strategy, and possibly also on India's foreign policy. India's criticisms of the dominance of Western powers in the decision-making processes of international economic institutions, e.g. the World Bank, has had to be modified somewhat by the need to be on friendly terms with the organization and possibly with its largest shareholders due to India's continued need for the Bank's financial resources.

**Box 4.1: Bilateral Aid: Denmark's experience in India**

Denmark started providing bilateral aid to India in 1963. As a share of total aid to India, Danish aid has always been small (less than 1%) but from the Danish side India was for many years a major recipient of aid. In 2005 official Danish aid to India was terminated and India had by then repaid its outstanding debt. The Danes decided as a reaction to India's nuclear tests of May 1998 to slowly phase out aid, but it was the Indian government that ultimately decided the timing.

The Danish experience with providing aid to India illustrates many of the above-mentioned characteristics of India's policy towards the receipt of foreign aid:

- The Danes experienced the Indian desire for central control over aid giving. The Ministry of Finance was regarded as a hard negotiator who was furthermore highly unwilling to discuss broader issues like human rights, democracy, good governance etc.
- Danish aid was made more concessional over time (from loans to grants).
- India was more interested in obtaining technical capabilities than in the limited financial assistance that a small donor could supply. The problem for India was how to balance this against the wish for untied aid. Aid tying was, however, reduced after 1989.
- India also expressed a strong wish to employ Indian experts and staff rather than relying on Danish experts. This was partly achieved but Danish experts were present to the end of the relationship.

Source: Folke and Heldgaard (2006)

## India as a donor of international aid

In 2003, simultaneous with the Finance Minister of India declaring that India would no longer need aid from small bilateral donors, a decision was taken to formally establish a separate India Development Initiative Fund (DN 2003; Price 2004). The Fund was, apparently, not only to be used to finance aid from India as it was later reported that some of the money allocated to the fund was being spend on a publicity campaign ('India Shining') in the run-up to the 2004 national election (Price 2004: 7). The new incoming government was also reportedly not very keen on continuing the initiative (ibid.: 5), but it resurfaced under the acronym IDEAS (Indian Development and Economic Assistance Scheme) and the money set aside would be used to subsidize EXIM Bank credit lines for selected developing nations.[10] The condition for using these credit lines was that 75% of the project-related supplies should be sourced from India – a clear example of aid-tying. In 2012, the government formally established a separate section, the Development Partnership Administration, within the Ministry of External Affairs to unify and to manage India's diverse aid programmes (Ministry of External Affairs, Annual Report 2012–13). The intention was for the section to handle the implementation and execution of all development projects financed by Indian lines of credit, but its capacity to do so is apparently not yet developed sufficiently for it to start operating. In addition, there may have been some resistance internally in the Ministry from the territorial divisions who used to manage the projects.[11]

These events are, however, only the latest in what is in reality a long history of India as a provider of aid to other developing nations. The first initiatives came as a result of India deciding to join the Commonwealth soon after Independence. Since 1950 India has participated as a donor in the Colombo Plan and later also in the Special Commonwealth African Assistance Plan (SCAAP). As a member of the UN, India has also provided funds for a number of different UN organizations, in particular the UNDP. Apart from monetary contributions, a large part of India's participation has been through technical training, mostly taking place in educational institutions in India. India's own bilateral aid programme was essentially kicked off with the establishment of the Indian Technical and Economic Cooperation Programme (ITEC) in 1964.[12] Under the programme, India has offered training at a wide variety of educational institutions as well as financing the deputation of Indian experts abroad. Over the years, the programme has expanded and has grown to provide training to nationals from more than 160 different countries (Ministry of External Affairs, *Annual Report 2015–16*). Most of the activities have focused on neighbouring countries, however. In a recent Annual Report from the Ministry of External Affairs, the programme is described thus: "ITEC programme is meant to support the political objectives of Indian diplomacy in developing countries and share Indian know-how, technology and expertise with these countries" (Ministry of External Affairs, *Annual Report 2004–05*: 131).The programme is thus an example of India's commitment to promoting South–South relations and at the same time contributing to the broader purpose of serving India's national interest.

As mentioned in the introduction to this chapter, it is not easy to provide a statistical overview of India's aid to other developing countries. Several Indian authorities do list the provision of loans and grants to foreign countries, but they are rarely combined with a list of contributions to relevant international organizations (UN organizations, regional development banks etc.) and it is not fully clear how export credits and commercial loans extended by the EXIM Bank and others should be included. To illustrate the variations in the estimates of aid from India according to the source (Reserve Bank of India (RBI), Ministry of External Affairs (MEA), Ministry of Finance (MoF)), see Figure 4.1. The figure shows the variation in aid data from different sources, but according to all sources aid from India expanded considerably up until around 2015. It can be remarked that during the Modi government overall aid seems to have stagnated or even declined. Estimates of Indian aid measured in relation to India's annual GNI find, however, that in those relative terms India's aid was until very recently slightly higher during the 1970s and early 1980s. Much of the increase in recent years is thus related to the growth of India's economy and probably most importantly its foreign exchange reserves (Fuchs and Vadlamanatti 2013: 112).

Leaving aside the ITEC programme, for the period up until 1998 it is possible to provide a systematic overview of (some of) India's aid activities.[13]

From Table 4.2 it is possible to discern some of the long-term trends in India's aid activities. Initially, India almost exclusively provided aid to countries in the South Asian region, and there were only three key countries in the region who received outright grants: Bhutan, Nepal and Bangladesh. Since the 1970s, aid to Bangladesh has been reduced and is now only given in the form of loans, while Nepal and Bhutan in the 1990s still enjoyed a privileged relationship with India. Outside South Asia, India has provided aid to South-East Asia (read: Vietnam) and also to African countries, in particular in the 1970s. Central Asian nations all started to receive aid from India during the 1990s, while only a few countries in the Western Hemisphere (Guyana, Nicaragua) on different occasions have received small amounts of aid. The 1990s seems to have been a decade of change with aid declining and being provided on harder terms as loans rather than as grants.

Developments in the 2000s are more difficult to survey due to the lack of consolidated data. India's aid to other countries has clearly increased considerably (cf. Figure 4.1), but the country-wise distribution is more difficult to get a full picture of due to lack of solid data. It is well-known that large amounts of aid have been provided to construction activities in Afghanistan and since the first Indo-African Summit in 2008, aid to African nations has experienced a large increase (Duclos 2012; Taylor 2012), the largest amounts being through the credit lines of the EXIM Bank. Many of the new initiatives are in the health and education sector and include support to building-up of continent-wide IT networks between educational institutions in Africa.

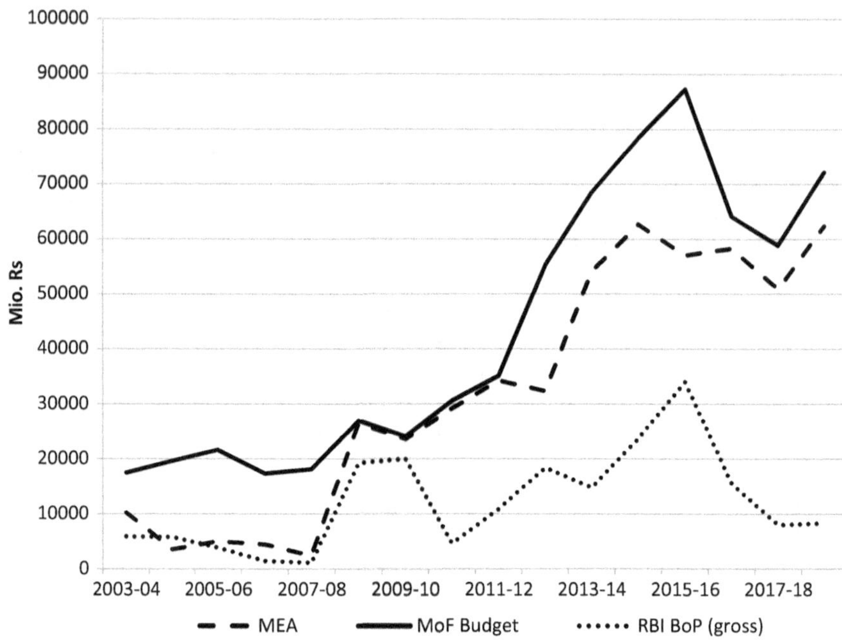


*Figure 4.1* Aid from India, 2003–2019

Sources: Websites of Ministry of External Affairs, Ministry of Finance and Reserve Bank of India.

From the data provided in the annual expenditure budgets published by the Ministry of Finance, it can be seen that India at least since 2009 has reverted to providing grants rather than loans, not counting credits from the EXIM Bank, however.[14] Close to 60% of the Indian grants for the period of 2009–16 were allocated to Bhutan, with aid to Afghanistan and to the small island republics of Seychelles, Mauritius and the Maldives becoming more important. Geostrategic considerations (competition with China) has probably played an important role in this (Choudhury and Nagda 2019). Aid to Africa has only constituted 5–6% of all grants in the recent period but the concessional credit lines administered by the EXIM Bank have primarily been directed to African countries (Saxena 2016).

India's membership of the BRICS group of countries has recently provided yet another method of providing aid in the form of loans to developing nations. In 2012, the BRICS group decided to establish an international development bank to fund infrastructure projects in developing countries, the New Development Bank (www.ndb.int/). In 2015 the bank formally began its operations. India has provided one-fifth of the share capital of the bank and has appointed its first president. It remains to be seen, of course, how the bank

*Table 4.2* Aid from India – the early phases

| *Rs. millions (current) aid utilized* | | *1951–66* | *1966–80* | *1980–90* | *1990–98* |
|---|---|---|---|---|---|
| | | *% distribution* | | | |
| **A. A. Loans** | | **33.4** | **36.4** | **39.6** | **63.2** |
| | *South Asia* | 33.4 | 26.2 | 23.5 | 34.2 |
| | -Bhutan | - | 2.9 | 13.0 | - |
| | -Nepal | 0.2 | 3.0 | 6.1 | 16.9 |
| | -Bangladesh | - | 12.9 | 1.9 | 5.5 |
| | -Burma/Myanmar | 33.2 | - | - | - |
| | -Sri Lanka | - | 6.5 | 2.3 | 10.8 |
| | -Afghanistan | - | 0.9 | - | - |
| | *Africa* | - | 1.3 | 6.2 | 3.9 |
| | *South East Asia* | - | 8.9 | 9.0 | 11.4 |
| | *Central Asia* | - | - | - | 13.2 |
| **B. B. Grants** | | **66.6** | **63.5** | **60.4** | **36.8** |
| | -Bhutan | 17.4 | 26.9 | 47.1 | 17.1 |
| | -Nepal | 49.1 | 18.3 | 12.4 | 19.4 |
| | -Bangladesh | - | 18.4 | 0.9 | 0.3 |
| | Others | - | - | - | - |
| Total aid (A+B) | - | 602.3 | 7104.5 | 10414.6 | 6795.2 |
| Average annual aid | - | 40.2 | 507.5 | 1041.5 | 849.4 |
| Number of recipient countries | | 3 | 9 | 16 | 17 |

Source: Reserve Bank of India, *Report on Currency and Finance*, various years. ITEC programme not included.

will operate in the long run and how the bank will operate in comparison with India's bilateral aid activities. It is inscribed in the statutes of the bank that "the proceeds of any loan … shall be used only for procurement in member countries of goods and services produced in member countries …". This formulation clearly indicates that the loan provided by the bank will be tied to procurement only from member countries. It will thus function as a kind of collective tying of the funds for the proposed projects in borrowing countries.

India's own policy for providing aid has displayed a wide variety of motives, both in terms of foreign policy concerns and in terms of commercial motivations. The substantial aid to the Himalayan neighbours should probably be seen as largely security motivated and as a continuation of the British policy of securing the borders of the Empire. It probably has also been influenced by ethnic solidarity and by true developmental concerns, as they easily go together with the security motives. For India, one security motive has been obvious since 1962: to secure itself against Chinese influence on the nations in the border region. Policies towards Sri Lanka and Bangladesh have fluctuated widely over the years, probably mostly as a result of domestic political changes in the two countries over the years and the constant concern over Indian dominance in the respective countries. Relations with African nations have also displayed some variation, although an element of stability in India's relation with the continent as such has come through India's membership since the early 1980s of collective African institutions like the African Development Fund and the African Development Bank. India has also cultivated close relations with the African Union and other pan-African institutions recently. Otherwise, India's relations with Africa may illustrate the gradual transition from aid seen in the context of South–South relations as evident during the 1970s (Vohra 1980), to aid seen more in the context of India as a rising power interested in expanding its political and economic influence while still maintaining elements of South–South solidarity; cf. the remarks in 2003 quoted above when India terminated bilateral aid programmes from smaller donors. India's activities as a donor of aid to developing nations have been administered by the Ministry of External Affairs (although always under the approval of the Ministry of Finance), and both in the past and in present times, they have been closely aligned with the overall foreign policy priorities. This has been clearly visible in India's aid policy towards Afghanistan.

**Box 4.2: India's Aid to Afghanistan**

India has a long history of providing technical assistance to Afghanistan, including training of Afghan nationals under the ITEC programme. Apart from a small amount of aid during the early 1980s, India only began a major aid engagement in Afghanistan after the fall of the Taliban regime in 2001. While India has always had some commercial interests in the country, it has clearly been the political and strategic interests that have led India to provide a large and diverse development assistance that has included a significant military element, primarily in the form of training and transport equipment. India has today activities in all Afghan provinces and has assisted in the construction of infrastructure, schools and educational institutions, health facilities, agricultural and industrial facilities and a host of other fields of activity, including the recently opened Parliament building. India's aid to Afghanistan is a prime illustration of the mixture of different motives in India's overall aid programme.

Sources: Banerjee (1982); Ministry of External Affairs (2004, 2009, 2019).

## Conclusion

This survey of the aspects of India's foreign policy that concerns the receipt and giving of international aid has demonstrated a number of interesting features. First of all, the fact of India having a double role as a recipient of aid and as a donor of aid is in itself relatively unique. It is also of interest to note that the balance between the two roles has shifted so that India now has an increasing number of clients for its own aid programmes while it receives aid from a decreasing number of donors. This can be seen as an indication of India's rise in the global system but with the caveat that India has not been able to move away from its role as an aid-receiving developing nation. The volume of aid received by India, today mostly in the form of loans, is still considerable and much larger than the aid it donates.[15]

As India's own aid activities have increased, the Indian government has had to formulate guidelines for the donation of aid. If one compares the aid-giving policies with India's own preferences for the aid it has received, there are glaring differences. As a recipient, India has preferred grants over loans due to the repayment burden, but as a donor it has preferred loans rather than grants, although this may have changed in recent years.[16] Similarly, although India has provided assistance through multilateral organizations, it has mostly preferred to hand out assistance bilaterally. And it has explicitly tied its own aid to supplies from India in stark contrast to its own long fight to avoid or minimize the tying of aid from foreign donors. In a sense, one could argue that India has in very large measure followed a practice of aid-giving that has been remarkably similar to that of the traditional Northern aid givers whom it had itself criticized so much. The aid aspect of India's foreign policy has thus become more and more contradictory as India has expanded its own aid activities.

Aid to India has on several occasions been used to influence the direction of India's economic policies. On macro-level policies the direction has mostly been in a liberalizing direction with donors trying (often in vain) to pressure the Indian authorities, but probably also to change development priorities, not least in the aid-receiving states.[17] Whether India's own aid activities have been used to influence the policies of recipient nations is harder to say, but there is little doubt that in particular in the South Asian region, India has used its financial muscles to further its own political and economic agendas. Relations with Nepal could probably provide several examples. When the IDEA Scheme was introduced in 2011, the purpose was stated clearly by the government: "The IDEA Scheme will promote India's political, economic and strategic interests besides building a positive image of India abroad" (Press Information Bureau 2011: 2). A final aspect of the interplay between internal and external forces in the development of India's aid policy concerns the role played by domestic interests. India has not had an influential domestic civil-society constituency advocating foreign aid, but it does have a domestic economic constituency in the form of the increasingly internationally active business class. The interests of both exporters and Indian firms investing abroad are clearly being served through the commercially oriented aid activities in Africa and elsewhere, especially when lines of credit and other forms of aid have been tied to supplies from India. It is not possible, however, to more concretely document the extent to which the Indian business class has sought to influence the aid policies, but in general there have always been cordial relations between the Ministry of External Affairs and Indian businessmen, who participate regularly in delegations visiting foreign countries. The Confederation of Indian Industry seems to have been particularly active in this regard. India's policies with regard to aid thus illustrate the increasing complexities of the foreign policy of an India that is both still a relatively poor developing nation and an upcoming power entering the world scene with new expanding interests, strategically, politically and economically.

## Notes

1 In Bandyopadhyay (1970, revised 1979), Appadorai (1981), Mansingh (1984) and Appadorai and Rajan (1985). The policy to attract foreign aid was seen as an important part of India's foreign policy. In contrast, Nayar and Paul (2003), Mohan (2003) and Ganguly (2015) hardly mention economic issues, not to speak of foreign aid. In recent works like Pant (2009), Malone (2011), Sidhu et al. (2013) and Ogden (2014), aid to India is only mentioned in passing and a recent much publicized attempt to formulate a new coherent vision for India's foreign policy simply ignores aid policy (Khilnani et al. 2012).

2 The DAC definition of aid requires that the money transferred should be targeted towards a well-defined 'development' purpose; it only counts official transfers; and the money should be given on concessional terms.

3 See Eldridge (1969: Ch.5), Bandyopadhyaya (1970, rev. 1979: 65–67) and Chakrabarti (1982: Ch.3) for accounts of the basic principles for India as an aid recipient.

4 As share of only public plan outlays figures are higher, but there is some variation in the figures provided in different sources, cf. Birla Institute of Scientific Research (1981: 9); Chakrabarti (1982: 48).

5 Scattered data on the statewise distribution of foreign aid is available on the website of the Ministry of Finance (External Assistance Brochure).

6 The policy guidelines were slightly revised in January 2005. See Ministry of Finance (2005).

7 The purposes for which aid was provided in this early period are listed in Eldridge (1969) and Bhagwati and Desai (1970).

8 There is a heated debate in India over the influence of the World Bank on the economic reform policies. Swami (1994) and Bhaduri and Nayyar (1996) see the influence as decisive, whereas Nayar (2001) and Panagariya (2008: 95) see the reforms as essentially domestic in origin. The period with a structural adjustment loan only lasted a few years.

9 See World Bank (2016: 5).

10 In his budget speech of 2003 the finance minister of the previous government had proposed discontinuing the practice of extending credit lines to other developing nations.

11 This can be inferred from the slightly changing description of the division of labour between the Development Partnership Administration and the territorial divisions. See Ministry of External Affairs, *Annual Report 2013–14* and following years.

12 The early story of India's aid relations with the Third World is narrated in Vohra (1980).
13 The Reserve Bank of India terminated their publication of the details of the aid programme after 1998.
14 This is based upon 'actual' budget figures for aid to different countries available only in the budgets from 2009–10 onwards. Scattered data on the distribution of aid during 2003–10 is available in the annual reports of the Ministry of External Affairs. The distribution broadly conforms to what is mentioned above for the most recent years.
15 In recent years when India's own aid activities have expanded, the foreign aid received is still 10–15 times larger.
16 Concessional credit lines extended through the EXIM Bank should be regarded as a loan component.
17 Cox et al. (2002) conclude that foreign aid has funded a large part of the development activities in social sectors. The priority given to these sectors has most likely been due to the influence of foreign donors.

## References


Appadorai, A. 1981. *The Domestic Roots of India's Foreign Policy 1947–1972*, Delhi: Oxford University Press.

Appadorai, A., and M.S. Rajan. 1985. *India's Foreign Policy and Relations*, New Delhi: South Asian Publishers.

Banerjee, Brojendra Nath. 1982. *India's Aid to Its Neighbouring Countries*, New Delhi: Select Books.

Bandyopadhyay, Jayantanuja. 1970, reprint 1979. *The Making of India's Foreign Policy: Determinants, Institutions, Processes and Personalities*, New Delhi: Allied Publishers.

Bhaduri, Amit, and Deepak Nayyar. 1996. *The Intelligent Person's Guide to Liberalization*, New Delhi: Penguin.

Bhagwati, Jagdish N., and Padma Desai. 1970. *India: Planning for Industrialization*, Delhi: Oxford University Press.

Birla Institute of Scientific Research. 1981. *Does Foreign Aid Help*?, New Delhi: Allied Publishers.

Chakrabarti, Radharaman. 1982. *The Political Economy of India's Foreign Policy*, Calcutta: K.P. Bagchi.

Chenery, Hollis B., and Alan M. Strout. 1966. "Foreign Assistance and Economic Development", *American Economic Review*, 56:4, 679–733.

Choudhury, Angshuman and Ashutosh Nagda. 2019. "How India Funds the World", Part I-II, *Economic and Political Weekly*, 54:22–23 (EPW Engage).

Cox, Aidan et al. 2002. *Do the Poor Matter Enough? A Comparative Study of European Aid for Poverty Reduction in India*, New Delhi: Concept Publishing Company.

DN. 2003. "Aid: Old Morality and New Realities", *Economic and Political Weekly*, 38:24, 2353.

Duclos, Vincent. 2012. "Building Capacities: The Resurgence of Indo-African Techno-economic Cooperation", *India Review*, 11:4, 209–225.

Dutt, Srikant. 1984. *India and the Third World. Altruism or Hegemony?*, London: Zed Press.

*Economic Times* (Mumbai). 2015, October 29. "Strengthening Ties: India to Offer Concessional Credit of $10 Billion to Africa, Says PM Modi", https://economictimes.indiatimes.com/news/economy/foreign-trade/strengthening-ties-india-to-offer-concessional-credit-of-10-billion-to-africa-says-pm-modi/articleshow/49578072.cms

Eldridge. P.J. 1969. *The Politics of Foreign Aid in India*, London: Weidenfeld & Nicolson.

Folke, Steen, and Jesper Heldgaard (eds.). 2006. *The Rich Mouse and the Poor Elephant. 45 Years of Danish Aid to India*, Viborg: Hovedland (in Danish).

Fuchs, Andreas, and Krishna Chaitanya Vadlamanatti. 2013. "The Needy Donor: An Empirical Analysis of India's Aid Motives", *World Development*, 44, 110–128.

Gandhi, Indira. 1966. "Extracts from speech given at the Economic Club of New York, March 30, 1966", reprinted in A. Appadorai (ed.), *Select Documents in India's Foreign Policy and Relations 1947–1972*, Volume II, Delhi. Oxford University Press 1985, 508–510.

Ganguly, Sumit. 2015. *Indian Foreign Policy*, New Delhi: Oxford University Press.

Government of India. (various years). *Economic Survey*, New Delhi.

Hayter, Terresa. 1971. *Aid as Imperialism*, Harmondsworth: Penguin Books.

Kirk, Jason A. 2011. *India and the World Bank: The Politics of Aid and Influence*, London: Anthem.

Khilnani, Sunil et al. 2012. *Non-Alignment 2.0: A Foreign and Strategic Policy for India in the Twenty First Century*, New Delhi: Centre for Policy Research.

Lipton, Michael, and John Toye. 1990. *Does Aid Work in India?*, London: Routledge.

Lumsdaine, David H. 1993. *Moral Vision in International Politics: The Foreign Aid Regime, 1949–1989*, Princeton: Princeton University Press.

Malone, David M. 2011. *Does the Elephant Dance? Contemporary Indian Foreign Policy*, New Delhi: Oxford University Press.

Mansingh, Surjit. 1984. *India's Search for Power: Indira Gandhi's Foreign Policy 1966–1982*, New Delhi: Sage.

Ministry of External Affairs (MEA). (various years). *Annual Report*, New Delhi.

Ministry of External Affairs (MEA). 2004. *Afghans First: India at Work in Afghanistan*, New Delhi.

Ministry of External Affairs (MEA). 2009. *India and Afghanistan. A Development Partnership*, New Delhi.

Ministry of External Affairs (MEA). 2019. *India-Afghanistan: A Historic and Time Tested Friendship*, New Delhi.

Ministry of Finance. 2005, January 4. *Guidelines for Development Co-operation with Bilateral Partners*, New Delhi.

Ministry of Finance. 2016. *Annual Report 2015–16*, New Delhi.

Mohan, C. Raja. 2003. *Crossing the Rubicon: The Shaping of India's New Foreign Policy*, New Delhi: Penguin.

Morgenthau, Hans. 1962. "A Political Theory of Foreign Aid", *American Political Science Review*, 56:2, 301–309.

Nayar, Baldev Raj. 2001. *Globalization and Nationalism*, New Delhi: Sage.

Nayar, Baldev Raj, and T.V. Paul. 2003. *India in the World Order*: Searching for Major-Power Status, Cambridge: Cambridge University Press.

Ogden, Chris. 2014. *Indian Foreign Policy*, Cambridge: Polity Press.

Panagariya, Arvind. 2008. *India: The Emerging Giant*, Oxford: Oxford University Press.

Pant, Harsh V. (ed.). 2009. *Indian Foreign Policy in a Unipolar World*, London: Routledge.

Pedersen, Jørgen Dige. 1993. "The Complexities of Conditionality: The Case of India", *European Journal of Development Research,* 5:1, 100–111.
Pedersen, Jørgen Dige. 2000. "Explaining Economic Liberalization in India: State and Society Perspectives", *World Development*, 28:2, 265–282.
Planning Commission. 2001. *Indian Planning Experience: A Statistical Profile*, New Delhi.
Press Information Bureau. 2011. *Extension of Indian Development and Economic Assistance (IDEA) Scheme*, New Delhi.
Price, Gareth. 2004. *India's aid dynamics: From recipient to donor?*, Asia Programme Working Paper, Chatham House.
Reserve Bank of India. (various years). *Report on Currency and Finance*, Mumbai.
Riddell, Roger C. 2007. *Does Foreign Aid Really Work?*, Oxford: Oxford University Press.
Saxena, Prabodh. 2016. "India's Credit Lines: Instruments of economic diplomacy", in Sachin Chaturvedi and Anthea Mulakala (eds.), *India's Approach to Development Cooperation*, London: Routledge, 60–78.
Sidhu, Waheguru Pal Singh et al. (eds). 2013. *Shaping the Emerging World: India and the Multilateral Order*, Washington: Brookings Institution Press.
Swami, Dalip S. 1994. *The Political Economy of Industrialisation*, New Delhi: Sage.
Taylor, Ian. 2012. "India's Rise in Africa", *International Affairs*, 88:4, 779–798.
*Times of India* (New Delhi). 2003, June 2. "India's Makeover: From Aid-taking to Aid-giving", https://timesofindia.indiatimes.com/india/Indias-makeover-From-aid-taking-to-aid-giving/articleshow/2333.cms
Veit, Lawrence A. 1976. *India's Second Revolution: The Dimensions of Development*, New York: McGraw Hill.
Vohra, Dewan C. 1980. *India's Aid Diplomacy in the Third World*, New Delhi: Vikas.
World Bank. 2016. *India Country Snapshot*, Washington.

## *Appendix*

*Table 4.3* External assistance in the financing of India's five-year plans

| *Plan period* | *% of plan outlay financed by external assistance* |
|---|---|
| First Plan (1951–56) | 9.6 |
| Second Plan (1956–61) | 23.7 |
| Third Plan (1961–66) | 28.3 |
| Fourth Plan (1969–74) | 12.9 |
| Fifth Plan (1974–79)* | 12.8 |
| Sixth Plan (1980–85)* | 7.7 |
| Seventh Plan (1985–90)* | 9.0 |
| Eight Plan (1992–97)* | 9.9 |
| Ninth Plan (1997–2002)* | 7.0 |

Note: *Latest estimates
Source: Planning Commission (2001).

# Part II

# Global ambitions, internal and regional constraints

# 5 Status of Malaysian-Indians in Malaysian social matrix

## Reconciling the juxtaposition of foreign policy and coalition politics in India[1]

*Tridib Chakraborti*

The federal structure of a country has been one of the most important factors that stipulate its foreign policy. Federalism remains a form of democratic political system and hence any federal government can hardly ignore the special interests of the constituent units while formulating its foreign policy. Federal governments usually divide the powers of a country between the centre and its constituent units. In most cases, the constitutions of federal governments bequeath the centre with most or all foreign policymaking powers and insignificant or none to the constituent units. However, recent trends clearly exhibit that the overall clench of the centre in this area is gradually shifting its stronghold because of the pertinence of various actors in the federal unions. These actors are variously called states, regions, provinces, cantons and so on. Generally, federalism is splotched by a constitutionally prescribed distribution of powers between two sets of players, one located at the central level and the other at the level of the federated components, i.e. states. Nevertheless, this power-sharing arrangement relates mainly to domestic matters, while decisions regarding foreign policy are usually exclusively confined to the federal government.

India is no exemption to this emerging trend in federal states. While the Constitution of India wholly authorizes the Union Government to outline and execute foreign policy, India, being a democratic polity, can hardly afford to ignore the special interests of its constituent units. In fact, several Indian states, because of their special local political concerns, have taken keen interest in foreign affairs and the Union Government has considered their aspirations. Therefore, whatever be the provisions of the Constitution regarding the powers of the federal government about foreign affairs, the proficient execution of foreign policy requires the willing cooperation of the states.

Since India achieved independence in 1947, the politics of centre-state relations has remained a powerful force in shaping India's foreign policy. After independence, the Indian National Congress was the only National Party that commanded the popularity and respect of the people. This party undoubtedly had a mass base in grassroots in India. It remained in power both at the centre as well as in many states right from 1947 to 1967 and had a monolithic character. In fact, the Congress as the single largest party formed the government and ruled India from 1952 to 1977 in the centre. However, that permutation and combination lost its strength with the emergence of regional parties and it gradually shifted the conversion of the dominant one-party system into a multi-party system. Thus, the culture of coalition politics evolved in the turf of the Indian political process. Generally, coalition government is a product of politics in a parliamentary democracy. It is a process due to the exigencies of a multi-party system in a democratic set-up. It is a form of government composed when no single party can secure majority on its own. Therefore, in a democracy, premised upon a majority party system, such a situation enables a number of minority parties to come together and join hands on a common platform by overcoming their broad differences to form a majority to run the government. In India coalitions of parties is extremely relevant. Thus, coalition is not merely the assembly of various political parties to capture power, because of the fragmentation of social interests at the grass-roots level (Chakrabarty 2008, 153).

With the dawn of coalition politics in India in the last few decades, the role of states in influencing and moulding India's foreign policy has assumed more prominence, particularly at a time when the central government has to depend on several regional leaders for its survival. Besides, the economic liberalization since the early 1990s has given the Indian states unforeseen opportunities to germinate an external wing. The mission of trade and investment has created the space of external orientation. This naturally generated an enhanced responsible and cooperative role of the states and transformed the entire gamut of power equation between the Union and the states, making the latter occasionally more assertive in policy formulation. On several occasions, the Union, in spite of being 'constitutionally strong', has become politically weak. In fact, the regional parties in India have an important role to play in an increasingly coalition-led central government. These regional parties are exercising a considerable influence over foreign policy formulation, especially with regard to India's foreign relations. In certain cases, they have even intervened on issues that previously would be considered the exclusive domain of the central government. For example, the assertive stance on the part of the West Bengal government over the Teesta Water-sharing Accord with Bangladesh has caused a major embarrassment to the Manmohan Singh government (2011) of the United Progressive Alliance (UPA) and even to the current Modi government (2017) of the National Democratic Alliance (NDA-II). Similarly, in the recent past, the Tamil Nadu Assembly unanimously passed a resolution seeking imposition of economic sanctions on Sri Lanka, or Dravida Munnetra Kazagham (DMK, a Tamil Nadu-based regional party) pulling out of the United Progressive Alliance-II (UPA-II) coalition over the Government of India's stance regarding a US-sponsored resolution on Sri Lanka in the UN Human Rights Council (2013). Moreover, other cases, such as the POSCO deal in Odisha, the issue of foreign direct investment in multi-band retail and the land acquisition constraint on the 'Make in India' initiative, are further examples of where a more competitive and accommodative federal arrangement had an impact on the foreign policy domain during the UPA and NDA periods. Besides, Jammu and Kashmir and Punjab have been asking the Union to take them on board while discussing water issues with Pakistan. Likewise, the proposal of the Union Home Ministry to set up a National Counter Terrorism Centre was opposed by several chief ministers with strong argument around the interpretation of federalism in the Indian Constitution. Also, the maltreatment of the Malaysian Indians, especially of the Hindu Rights Action Front (HINDRAF) leaders of Malaysia, and consequently the personal letter by Tamil Nadu's Chief Minister, M. Karunanidhi, to Indian Prime Minister Manmohan Singh in November 2007 to intervene in this matter, largely created severe commotion and political spite in the bilateral relations between India and Malaysia. Thus, a paradigm shift is taking place in the debates on what ought to be the role of the states in the making of India's foreign policy. This also raises the question as to whether the states acting as sub-national governments would provide a better option in negotiating and formulating Indian foreign policy and, furthermore, whether the states at all have recourse to any power to intervene on issues that are considered the exclusive domain of the central government.

## Heterogeneous character of Malaysian Indians

Malaysia is a veritable model of a heterogeneous, multi-ethnic and multi-religious country in Southeast Asia, with the Malays (Bumiputera (i.e. sons of the soil)), Chinese and Indians constituting the major ethnic groups. Of the total population in 2019 of nearly 32.6 million, 90.2% are citizens, of which the Malays and other indigenous groups constitute 69.3% (Malays and indigenous peoples, including Orang Asli, Dayak, Anak Negeri), the Chinese 22.8% and Indians 6.9%, with the remaining 1.0% constituted by others (Department of Statistics Malaysia 2019).

In terms of religion, about 60.4% of the population is Muslim, 19.2% Buddhist, 9.1% Christian and 6.3% Hindu. Besides this, within the country, Indians are the third-largest ethnic group. The group is heterogeneous in structure and is classified based on religion, language and place of origin. The overwhelming majority are Tamils, at 87.6% (Encyclopedia 2020). There were around 1.9 million people of South Asian origin in early 2019, most of whom share Tamil ancestry and profess the Hindu religion. Over the years, an 'Indian identity' was created over and above their primeval loyalties. The policy of the government to amalgamate them together as 'Indians', both for political and administrative purposes, has further reinforced this process. Nevertheless, during general elections, this Indian community has on many occasions played a striking balancing role in peninsular power and racial relations.

Over the years, due to the presence of composite identities affiliated to various sections of the population, the society has divided into major ethnic groups, based on respective racial, religious, linguistic and cultural identity. Furthermore, the Bumiputeras are themselves divided politically, thus prompting the support of the Chinese or the Indians as critical to any Malay faction not only in ensuring its survival as the dominant political force but also, ironically, for the sustenance of political dominance of the political process. Before the beginning of the NEP in 1970, the economic condition of Indians with reference to income position remained much higher than that of the Bumiputeras, though the Indians, in tune with their minority character, remain the third-largest ethnic group after the Malays and the Chinese, and have been playing the role of second fiddle in politics at large (Chakraborti 2002, 131). Unfortunately, with the beginning of the NEP, after the 1969 racial riots, the Indian community gradually became economically under-classed and, at present, it lags the Chinese and the native Malays in every socio-economic sphere. Moreover, as of 2010, the Indian people accounted for the lowest share of the nation's corporate wealth: 1.5% compared to 19.4% for the Malays and 38.5% for the Chinese. This under-class' economic position could be assessed against the backdrop of the NEP and the National Development Policy (NDP) commenced by the government since 1970, as well as through their participation in different parliamentary elections, which took place since 1959. During these years, the Indian community experienced various social, economic, trade, commerce and cultural predicaments, including economic and educational deprivation and lack of proper housing facilities, and thus countenanced soreness, suffering, humiliation, bigotry, incessant colonization, ethnic purge and sporadic genocide in their mundane activities.

A large proportion (63%) of Malaysian Indians work on plantations or as urban labourers for very low wages. Their presence on the rubber estates alone (51.2% in 1990) implies that members of the Indian community are still unable to break away from the stereotypes of rubber toppers and poor coolie labourers. Although Indians still dominate the estate sector, the 51.2% in 1990 demonstrated a fall from 75% in 1970. The Malay work force grew steadily and by early 1990 comprised 36.6% of the rubber estate labourers. Their numbers increased mainly due to high wages resulting from favourable rubber prices in the 1970s (Chakraborti 1996, 197). Moreover, the structure of estate labour is slowly changing due to the rural–urban drift among Indian labourers, who prefer to migrate to towns where wages are higher and job security better. This huge migration of Indian labourers originated in the wake of urbanization and industrialization programmes and simultaneous changes in land use in the 1970s. The fragmentation of the plantation sector between 1950 and 1967 because of British sales and ownership sub-divisions, due to uncertain ties in post-independence economic policies, severely affected the livelihood of the plantation workers, mainly Indians. The lack of promotion and incentives from the government to the plantation sector resulted in a severe decline in the rubber plantations, from 163,577 in 1979 to about 13,000 in 2004 (Department of Statistics Malaysia 1985, 196 and 2004, 24). Moreover, between the 20 years from 1980 to 2000, nearly 300,000

Indians were uprooted from the plantation sector. These evicted plantation workers and their families not only lost their jobs, but importantly housing, children centres, basic amenities and other facilities that they had enjoyed over decades (Nagaragan 2008, 277–278). Apart from this, the arrival of an estimated 500,000 Indonesian workers, mostly illegal migrant labourers who are willing to settle for lower pay without the legal safeguards and medical and housing benefits, mainly in the palm oil estates, has undoubtedly weakened the Indian position in the economic structure (*Far Eastern Economic Review* 1990, 18). Therefore, the vulnerable economic position of Indians as an ethnic community may be assessed against the backdrop of the economic policy as followed by the government since 1970 and how this policy gradually moved the Malaysian Indians from the top to the bottom of the economic ladder within society.

## Malaysian Indians' economic quandary: from independence to racial surge

The ethnic conflict between the politically dominant Malays and the economically dominant Chinese has overshadowed the socio-political situation of the Indians. After independence in 1957, due to their historical exclusion from full participation in the economic development of the country, a shared sense of relative deprivation rapidly emerged among the Malays.[2] By the mid-1960s, Malay feelings of being economically deprived had widened markedly, especially among the upwardly ambitious Malay civil servants and petty businessmen. The emerging Malay sentiment was that circumstances were not providing the opportunities and benefits to which Malays were justly entitled as Bumiputeras. An increasing number of Malays gradually became disenchanted with and blamed the Alliance government for not providing adequate assistance and opportunities to improve their life chances (Guan 2000, 16). While the Constitution, through Article 153, did stress that the socio-economic development of Malays was to be promoted, active government intervention in the economy to help the Malays was not effectively implemented. As a result, in early 1970 nearly two-thirds of the population (mostly Malays) were living under poverty, as manifested in the incidence of poverty.

The intricacy of the poverty dilemma, as illustrated in Table 5.1, clearly shows that the bulk of the poor consisted of Malays. During the years from 1957 to 1970, there was a reduction in the incidence of poverty among the Malays, though they remained at the bottom of the ladder. In 1970, 73.8% of the Malays were poor, compared to only 17.2% and 7.9% respectively of the Chinese and Indians. Besides this, poverty incidence was more serious in the rural (86.3%) than in the urban (13.7%) areas. Furthermore, in 1970, the average monthly per capita income of the Chinese community approximated M$ 68, whereas that of the Indians and the Malays approximated M$ 57 and M$ 34 dollars respectively (Bandyopadhyay 1990, 142).

With respect to average income, the inequalities were evident among the different communities in 1957 and 1970 and was where the position of Malays remained most grave.

Furthermore, through education and employment, mainly in the Federal Public Service, the Indian community was able to achieve inter-service mobility. By 1970, the ethnic composition of the higher civil service showed that Indians and others made up 1,245 out of 4,740, or 26.2%, of the total staff in the higher civil service, far in excess of their proportion in the population in 1970. The over-representation of the Indians in the higher civil service was even more dramatically demonstrated in certain technical and professional services.

Moreover, the mean household incomes of the Indians were much higher than the Malays in 1970. Furthermore, there was also a significant imbalance in terms of wealth (equity) ownership between the Malays and the Chinese. By 1970 the Malays owned only about 2.4% of the share capital, while the Chinese owned 27.2% and Indians 1.1%. This clearly reveals that, prior to the introduction of the NEP, the economic status of the Indians remained higher compared to Bumiputeras in the socio-economic composition.

## The New Economic Policy: the turf to marginalization of Indians

Prior to 1957, the economy was heavily dependent on primary products, specifically tin and rubber, to generate growth and employment. After the British left in 1957, initially the country pursued a development strategy under the advice of the International Bank for Reconstruction and Development (IBRD), and continued to develop its economy, based on five-year development plans, known as the Malaysia Plan, by investing in primary commodity exports with some diversification into the import-substitution industry and encouraging the investment of foreign capital in the country. To make such investment alluring, the government concentrated heavily on infrastructural projects (i.e. improved transport, land clearance schemes), subsidies or tariff protection schemes etc., and, as a result, the local industries were mere offshoots of industrial establishments in the developed economies, and foreign markets, foreign investments, foreign technology and foreign experts determined their growth. Such type of industrialization, however, did not transform the local economy enough, since it did not possess its own strength or momentum (Muzaffar 1993, 221). Besides this, different political parties based on ethnic lines dominated the entire economic operational process. The major political parties are the United Malay Nationalist Organization (UMNO), the Malaysian Communist Association (MCA), the Malaysian Indian Congress (MIC) and the Parti Islam (PAS). Although native Malays have bargained hard for a prerogative to political power, the parliamentary democracy has found it essential to form coalitions of parties instead of a single majority rule to neutralize ethnic tensions and avoid consequent legislative statements (Chakraborti 2002, 136). The result of this was that, prior to the 1970s, there was a serious economic imbalance in the areas of distribution of income, employment, ownership and control of economic activity, and the main obstruction was not the economic growth; however, the fact remains that the distribution of benefits was ill-managed, as a consequence of which the poor people, mainly the Malays, were getting poorer. Further, while the Constitution stressed that the socio-economic development of the Malays was to be promoted, active government intervention in the economy to help the Malays was not properly implemented. Thus, growing inequality in the distribution of wealth largely widened the gulf not only between rural and urban areas, but also between races, classes and racial groups. This resulted in an increase in inter-class and inter-ethnic tensions in the social structure. This growing weak economic condition of the Malays as well as the notable economic imbalance between the Malays and the Chinese was unsatisfactory to the Malays and strong criticism of the government's laissez-faire approach emerged. For the Malays, the continuation of the colonial laissez-faire economic policy by the Alliance government after independence had only ensured the growth of the Chinese economic interests but failed to improve the plight of the Malays and Indians. In the opinion of the Malays, the Alliance government was too friendly to Chinese interests. They called for more aggressive government interference to expedite the upward mobility of the Malays in education, employment and the economy to keep them abreast with the non-Malays.

What made the situation explosive was the fact that the frustration was almost equally rampant amongst the Chinese ethnic group. The Chinese community too felt that the government was doing too much for the Malays. From their perspective, the government was biased towards the Malays, and thus they became more vocal in criticizing the "Malay special rights" (Article 153 of the 1957 Constitution). This mutual mistrust among Malays and the Chinese community slowly developed a hatred mindset that reached its nadir following the outbreak of racial riots on 13 May 1969. This resulted in the government immediately declaring a state of emergency and suspending the newly elected parliament, and after a thorough examination it introduced the NEP in 1971. Between the violence of the May 1969 riots and the beginning of the NEP, a chain of major changes took place in the ascendance of Malaysia. In a sense, these changes were the consequences of the riots, and in sagacity, they were a prologue to a significant affirmative action programme under the direct leadership of Tun Abdul Razak, who succeeded Tunku Abdul Rahman as the new prime minister in September 1970. Tun Abdul Razak was instrumental in setting up two important institutions to meet the political and administrative needs of the time. One was called the *National Consultative Council* (NCC), which in a sense could be considered a 'substitute' to the suspended parliament though it was consultative (not legislative) in function. The other was the *National Operation Council* (NOC), which could be considered an 'additional executive branch of the government' (although one could argue that it was then more important and more effective than the cabinet). These two institutions – the 'consultative' NCC and the 'authoritarian' NOC – paved the way for an innovative (and 'affirmative') NEP (Abdullah 1997, 201). It was also realized by the government that political stability and national unity were dependent upon the elimination of poverty among the ethnic Malays who constituted the major electoral base of the government. This realization led the policymakers to introduce the NEP in 1971, which stressed that its ultimate and over-riding objective was to forge national unity, in the context of the Second Plan (1970–1975), as part of the 20-year Perspective Plan (1970−1990). While presenting the Second Plan in Parliament in July 1971, Prime Minister Tun Razak asserted that "it [NEP] was the last chance for the survival of the people and the country" (Vorys 1975, 406). It highlighted a two-pronged development programme. The first prong aimed at reducing and eventually eradicating poverty by raising income levels and increasing employment opportunities for all Malaysians, irrespective of race. The second prong aimed at accelerating the process of restructuring society to correct economic imbalances, to reduce and eventually eliminate the identification of race with economic functions (Government of Malaysia 1973, 1). However, the above objectives of the NEP were associated with the Malay nationalist economic agenda, and thus the NEP could be viewed as a fulfilment of the Malay nationalists' economic agenda (Shamsul 1997, 251). It was also discovered by the government that poor economic participation of the Bumiputeras in the ownership of shared capital remained an important cause of sporadic racial riots. Thus, in a pragmatic sense, the NEP placed more emphasis on the underplayed feature of 'Malay' economic advance, so that the other communities and mainly the Chinese could not monopolize economic power (Chakraborti 2002, 138).

The chief objective of social restructuring under the NEP demanded a rise in Bumiputera involvement in the ownership and management of the corporate sector of the economy from 2.4% in 1970 to 30% by 1990. The non-Malay (Chinese 27.2%, Indian 1.1% and nominee companies 6.0% in 1970) participation was to grow at the targeted rates of 12% per year to cover 40% of the share capital by 1990, and the share of foreign investors would fall from 63.3% to 30% during the same period (Chakraborti 1996, 199).

Although the NEP announced its aim of improving the economic position of the Malays, obviously, without jeopardizing the interest of other racial groups and foreigners, the fact remained that the shift in social reconstruction ostensibly had to be carried out at the expense of foreign enterprises. Moreover, these target areas could be achieved only through Article 153 of the 1957 Constitution, which was duly amended to introduce the quota system for Malays in institutions of higher learning. Clause 8(A) specifically provided for the reservation of places for Bumiputeras in any university, college and other educational institution; subsidies, land; issuing of permits or licences for operation of certain business etc.; and trade concessions (Smith 1992, 135).

To implement the target of the NEP intervention was necessary and the government established many state corporations, which were mainly classified into two categories. The first category was engaged in direct production, with an aim of increasing Malay employment and managerial skills, and the second category was state enterprise, and remained exclusively service oriented. Among the important measures taken by the government to realize the NEP objectives was the accelerated creation of a Malay (Bumiputera) Commercial and Industrial Community to upgrade or create specialized agencies for performing special functions. Additionally, the NEP sought to establish a skilled and educated Malay stratum by setting admission quotas in public educational institutions and, similarly, banned the establishment of Chinese private universities through legislation (Sivalingam 1988). In summary, then, the NEP did not apply equally towards the non-Malay community. The Chinese and the Indians felt that they were under-represented, and the policy was essentially giving preferential treatment to the majority ethnic group. The only positive development was that the MIC party established a 'Unit Trust' to encourage more Indians to hold shares in business. The overall impact of the economic policy since 1970 has remained contradictory, despite the apparently straightforward goals and principles of the NEP. Essentially, there has been a class-biased response, with the middle- and upper-income groups of all races benefiting at the expense of both the rural and urban poor (Smith 1992, 138–139). To carry out successfully the targets of the NEP, the government used four different five-year plans from the Second to the Fifth Plans; total allocation for both objectives, i.e. poverty eradication and restructuring the society, averaged more than 30%. It also clearly displayed that poverty eradication formed a large proportion of the allocation and the fact remains that the share of restructuring increased over time, particularly in the Fourth Plan. Thus, rapid economic growth was of paramount importance to realize the NEP's major objectives. This policy of the government could be considered as an active government intervention in the economy with the objective of improving the Bumiputera's economic participation and benefits.

## Implementation of the NEP

The NEP was an ambitious, though controversial, socio-economic restructuring affirmative action programme launched by the government in 1971. Its term ended in 1990. Although the NEP took on an economic shape, its undeclared objective was political – to produce national unity. To meet the NEP objectives, the policies of ethnic-Malay preference affected the Indian position more severely than that of the Chinese and the other ethnic groups.

In 1970, 47% of the Indians were engaged in agriculture, the overwhelming majority of whom (74%) were in plantation. The second area where the Indians were concentrated was in services, mainly in the lower grades and in impersonal services of all types, which provided employment to 24.8%. The third sphere was commerce (10.6%), confined almost wholly in petty trading.

The number of Indians and their contribution to the total share of employment in mining, manufacturing, construction, and banking were too insignificant to mention (Chakraborti 1996, 201). Similarly, in 1970, only 7.5% of Indians were found in administrative and managerial categories, and by 1990 the figure had decreased further to 4.0%. Further, in the field of clerical and related works, sales and related spheres, service and agriculture, the position of Indians had fallen by 1990 in comparison with 1970 (see Table 5.1 for details). This reduction in the percentage of Indians in public service was no doubt the result of a resolute effort by the government to upgrade the position of the Bumiputera within the societal fabric.

In addition to this, although the position of Indian registered professionals in 1990, in contrast to 1970, improved in numerical terms, their percentage in contrast to other ethnic groups declined from 23.3% to 13.2% in the same period (Government of Malaysia 1996, 84). In fact, the position of the Indians seemed to have been at least better than the Bumiputeras in 1970.

Furthermore, with reference to the enhancement of ownership of corporate equity of the Bumiputeras through the NEP, the figure increased from 2.4% in 1970 to 19.3% in 1990. Even though it still fell short of the NEP target of 30%, the Bumiputeras seemed to have made quite a significant progress in terms of ownership and control of capital, which resulted in the development a Malay business class over the 20 years, competing with and, at times, serving as partners of Chinese as well as foreign business. But this emerging class was largely limited to finance, property, and construction, was weak in manufacturing and generally dependent on state patronage. In contrast to the Malay position, the share of wealth held by ethnic Indians dwindled slightly from

*Table 5.1* Peninsular Malaysia: Employment by occupation and race, 1970 and 1990 (in %)

| *Occupation* | *Bumiputera* | | *Chinese* | | *Indians* | | *Others* | |
|---|---|---|---|---|---|---|---|---|
| | *1970* | *1990* | *1970* | *1990* | *1970* | *1990* | *1970* | *1990* |
| Professionals and technical | 47.2 | 60.5 | 37.7 | 29.1 | 12.7 | 7.7 | 2.4 | 2.7 |
| Administrative and managerial | 22.4 | 28.7 | 65.7 | 62.2 | 7.5 | 4.0 | 4.4 | 5.1 |
| Clerical and related workers | 33.4 | 52.4 | 51.0 | 38.6 | 14.3 | 8.6 | 1.3 | 5.4 |
| Sales and related workers | 23.9 | 29.9 | 64.7 | 58.4 | 11.0 | 6.8 | 0.4 | 4.9 |
| Service workers | 42.9 | 57.8 | 42.5 | 26.8 | 13.4 | 9.5 | 1.2 | 5.9 |
| Agricultural workers | 68.7 | 69.1 | 20.8 | 13.8 | 9.6 | 7.3 | 1.4 | 10.3 |
| Production, transport and other workers | 31.3 | 43.6 | 59.9 | 39.6 | 8.6 | 10.8 | 1.2 | 6.0 |
| *Total* | 51.8 | 56.9 | 36.6 | 33.7 | 10.6 | 8.7 | 1.0 | 0.7 |
| Ethnic proportions | 52.7 | 61.2 | 35.8 | 30.0 | 10.7 | 8.2 | 0.8 | 0.6 |

Source: Government of Malaysia (1996, 68).

*Table 5.2* Ownership of share capital (as par value) of limited companies 1970 and 1990 (in %)

| *Ownership* group | *1970* | *1990 (achievement)* |
|---|---|---|
| A. Bumiputera | 2.4 | 19.3 |
| - Bumiputera individuals and institutions | 1.6 | 14.2 |
| - Trust agencies | 0.8 | 5.1 |
| B. Non-Bumiputera | 28.3 | 46.8 |
| - Chinese | 27.2 | 45.5 |
| - Indians | 1.1 | 1.0 |
| - Others | - | 0.3 |
| C. Nominee companies | 6.0 | 8.5 |
| D. Foreigners | 63.3 | 25.4 |
| Total (A + B + C + D) | **100.0** | **100.0** |

Source: Gomez and Jomo (1997, 168).

1.1% to 1.0% between 1970 and 1990 (see Table 5.2 for details). Two-thirds of Indians remained trapped in poverty and the fruits of economic development did not reach the poorer sections of Indian society. Thus, the Indians have lost out, especially under the NEP – a reverse discrimination policy evolved in favour of the economically backward Malays and other indigenous peoples through an institutionalized system of hand-outs. Being non-Bumiputera, the Indians could not claim the NEP privileges, and they fell behind even as the economy prospered. In contrast, during the NEP period, not only was there remarkable economic growth and development of the country, but there was also improvement in the economic position of the Bumiputeras. Poverty eradication was successful under the NEP and fringing the Malay community into mainstream economic activities had been quite exceptional.

## The National Development Policy: the persistence in progression of marginalization of the Indians

The NDP succeeded the NEP in 1990. The NDP (1990–2000) included a revision of the previous formula for balancing growth with equity. For instance, this employed a shift in the focus of the anti-poverty strategy towards eradication of 'hardcore' poverty. This was expressed through a special programme, the Programme Pembangunan Rakyat Termiskin (PPRT), which created a register of hard-core poor households, offering them interest-free loans and targeting projects tailored to their needs. Attempts to restructure society also included employment generation and developing the Bumiputera Commercial and Industrial Community (BCIC), an agency mandated to increase the participation of the Bumiputera in the modern sectors of the economy. The NDP laid more stress on economic escalation and income creation, introducing greater reliance on the private sector as well as adopting the need for improvement in the skills base as a primary device for generating growth. Yet, notwithstanding these differences in policy objectives, the NDP preserved the essence of the NEP, namely, the pro-Bumiputera or 'ethnicity-oriented' form of economic policy.

With regard to the expectations for equity ownership, the relative failures under NEP were replicated under the NDP. The original NEP goal of a 30% equity ownership by the Bumiputera or their state-sponsored surrogates (the trust agencies) failed to reach its target, in spite of various Bumiputera institutions and trust agencies playing an important role in mobilizing Bumiputera resources and in the acquisition of effective equity ownership. However, the East Asian financial crisis in 1997 affected the restructuring of ownership and control of companies in the corporate sector. In absolute terms, Bumiputera ownership of share capital and proportion of corporate equity declined from 20.6% in 1995 to 19.1% in 1999. Similarly, non-Bumiputeras' share of corporate equity decreased from 43.4% in 1995 to 40.3% in 1999. Between them, the Chinese share of capital ownership declined from 40.9% in 1995 to 37.9% in 1999, while that of Indians remained at 1.5%.

Under the NEP, as through the NDP, the Indian community did not receive equitable admittance to economic opportunities, unlike the other ethnic groups in the country. The Indians belong to the poorest groups in the plantation villages and are among the urban poor. The socio-economic position of the Indians lags behind the other ethnic groups and inadequate policy attention has been accorded to this group in the government's development efforts. The high levels of poverty experienced by the Indian community resulted in their social and economic marginalization. It is to be noted here in this connection that during the period 1996–1999 compared to 1991–1995, the percentage of ownership of share capital of various communities (mainly Bumiputera and Chinese) had also come down, on account of the 1997 financial crisis (Chakraborti 2004, 217).

Like the years since 1970, it is clear from Table 5.3 that, although the position of Indian registered professionals in 2002, in comparison to 1990, improved in numerical terms, their percentage in comparison to other ethnic groups reduced quite marginally. This clearly exposed the weakness of the government's policy towards the Indians with reference to its declared policy of poverty eradication through the NEP and NDP. Thus, the NDP, in the Sixth and Seventh Plans for the period 1991–2000, designed to achieve the socio-economic uplift of the Bumiputera, as well as the MIC's efforts to classify the Indians as a separate ethnic grouping, seems to have made no headway. Being a minority, they neither have the numerical strength to exert any political influence nor do they enjoy any significant role in the national economic programme. It is to be noted here in this connection that in recent years (since 2003), the Bumiputeras' economic status has been improving due to the growth of Islamic finance in Malaysia. For Muslims, investment in share capital needs to be Syariah- compliant. Of the stocks listed on Bursa Malaysia in 2004, 83% were classified as Syariah-approved securities by the Syariah Advisory Council (Shafii et al. 2009, 400).

*Table 5.3* Malaysia's registered professionals[a] by ethnic group, 1970–2002

| *Year* | *Bumiputera* | | *Chinese* | | *Indians* | | *Others* | | *Total* | |
|---|---|---|---|---|---|---|---|---|---|---|
| | *No.* | *(%)* | *No.* | *(%)* | *No.* | *(%)* | *No.* | *(%)* | *No.* | *(%)* |
| 1990 | 11,753 | 29.0 | 22,641 | 55.9 | 6,363 | 13.2 | 750 | 1.9 | 40,507 | 100 |
| 1995 | 19,344 | 33.1 | 30,636 | 52.4 | 7,542 | 12.9 | 939 | 1.6 | 58,461 | 100 |
| 2000 | 29,376 | 35.5 | 42,243 | 51.1 | 9,739 | 11.8 | 1,286 | 1.6 | 82,644 | 100 |
| 2002 | 35,046 | 37.2 | 47,270 | 50.1 | 10,593 | 11.2 | 1,411 | 1.5 | 94,320 | 100 |
| **Increases and decreases** | | | | | | | | | | |
| 1970–2002 | 34,821 | 38.8 | 44,477 | 49.6 | 9,527 | 10.6 | 919 | 1.0 | 89,744 | 100 |
| 1980–2002 | 32,512 | 42.1 | 36,458 | 47.2 | 7,630 | 9.9 | 703 | 0.9 | 77,303 | 100 |
| 1990–2002 | 23,293 | 43.3 | 24,629 | 45.8 | 5,230 | 9.7 | 661 | 1.2 | 53,813 | 100 |
| 2000–2002 | 5,670 | 48.6 | 5,027 | 43.1 | 854 | 7.3 | 125 | 1.1 | 11,676 | 100 |

[a] Professional is defined as architect, accountant, engineer, dentist, doctor, lawyer, veterinary surgeon and surveyor.

Source: Jomo (2004).

## Overall splash of Malaysia's economic policy on the Indian community

The beginning of the NEP and NDP tended to focus on the socio-economic fissure between the Malays and other races. The importance of this gap, however, did nothing to contain the real problem of poverty among the others. It is true that the NEP and NDP were accountable for the economic achievement. But, as these programmes were successful in reducing poverty mainly amongst the Malays, the prospect of achieving inter-ethnic equation could not be fulfilled through them. This implied that the Malays should not have been deeply divided – be it socially, economically and politically. As poverty amongst the Malays has been successfully reduced under the NEP, intra-Malay inequality remained high throughout the NEP period and this remained a problematic and alarming fact. Hence, deeper social and political cleavages have evolved within the Malay community. The Bumiputeras, therefore, might no longer share a common economic and political interest amongst them as before. Thus, the idea of the NEP, which initially incorporated national ideals of equality and justice for Indians or otherwise, practically contradicted the national policy it promulgated. It implicitly established gradual economic domination by the Malays and created a new Malay middle class, grabbing a bigger slice of the pie (Chakraborti 1996, 202). On the other hand, the NEP and NDP considerably weakened the economic position of the Indians, but it is not beyond doubt that this clearly reflects a wilfully held and consciously employed discriminatory policy by the government against the Indian racial status.

Besides this, poverty among Indians in the urban sector also has its roots in the plantation economy from which many Indians originate. The plantation milieu is hardly conducive for attaining a decent education or acquiring critical skills that are needed in the modern sectors of the economy. Poverty becomes a way of life and when the plantation economy gives way to development projects, the estate labour force is displaced and migrates to the urban areas, joining the ranks of the urban poor who live in squatter areas. Presently, most of them are mainly confined to the '3D jobs', i.e. the difficult, dangerous and dirty jobs such as heavy machinery general workers, lorry, van and taxi drivers, security guards, toilet cleaners, garbage pickers, factory workers, contract unskilled general workers and private sector office boys etc. They are also denied rights of licence to food stalls, burger stalls and AIM business loans for scrap metal licences, franchise business etc., and this has practically marginalized the Indian community, rendering them socially helpless and wretched in the entire society.

Therefore, the economic development programme under the NEP and NDP of more than 30 years practically relegated the status of Indians and currently they appear as a genuine social saddle for the plural society. The Indians were economically weakened due to the one-track economic programme of the government. They were trapped in a horrible circle of poverty, which resulted in lack of employment, educational and other economic opportunities, and have therefore failed to contribute to the country's development process, be it in the educational, social or economic sectors. This weak economic position of the Indians has largely pushed the majority members of this community into dire distress. The major causes of their social ills are rural–urban migration, the impact of urbanization, high dropout rate from schools and fewer employment opportunities, as well as poverty. Besides this, the vulnerable economic position of the Indians is directly connected to their poor educational attainment. While other ethnic groups have benefited from education, the Indian community by and large due to educational under-achievement has lagged behind. Further, Indians are also seen to be affected by poor health and suffer diverse social dysfunctions. Alcohol and drug abuse as well as towering occurrence of domestic violence, suicide and child abuse have been found to be strangely high among the Indian community. The Indians are also grossly over-represented in serious crime and other anti-social activities.

## Weak leadership and electoral clout of Congress in coalition politics

Over the years, the weak community leadership and pitiable performance of the MIC as a community-based organization means it has failed to display its united strength and political clout in the coalition politics and remains a major weakness for the Indians. The prime failing of the MIC, which mostly represents the Indian community in the ruling Barisan Nasional party, has been the absence of capable leadership and political image. Internal feuds and power struggles among leaders, based on caste, culture, occupational and economic status, and on the Dravidian/Aryan and language-speaking divide, racists/bigots within the Tamil community, differentiation among the trade and the socio-economic classes, religious divide between Hindus and Muslims etc. have deeply compartmentalized and weakened the MIC's social mobility and political bargaining position within the Barisan Nasional, forcing them to accept the domination of the UMNO. The result is that, of late, the MIC has often been acting as a 'yes-man' within the Barisan Nasional and remains the weakest horse running on the power racing ground (Chakraborti 2002, 148–149). Over more than five decades, the position of Indians in Malaysia has undergone several fundamental changes. Since 1946, the Indians have had their own communal political party, the MIC. In conjunction with UMNO and the Malayan Chinese Association (MCA), the MIC formed the Alliance Party, which not only successfully led the independence movement in the federation (states) of Malaya but was also the governing party of that country. Since 1957, the country has faced 12 parliamentary elections, and in all these elections, the MIC have generally tended to vote in favour of the establishment, partly out of a cultural mindset which looks up to authority, and partly because, being poor, they are easily wooed on bread and butter issues (*Far Eastern Economic Review* 7 June 1990, 17).

The first parliamentary election took place in 1959. In this election, out of 104 parliamentary seats, the MIC contested only three seats and won all the constituencies, whereas UMNO contested 70 seats and won 52, and the MCA contested 31 seats and won only 19. Similarly, in subsequent elections the MIC contested between three and nine constituencies and finally won 2–9 seats,[3] and the contested seats of UMNO and MCA remained much higher and the results were quite positive. In the general election of 2018, the MCA contested seven seats and ultimately won one seat.

Since 1957, the Indians have represented only 8 to 10% of the total population, but their existence as a separate ethnic community has never been proportionately represented in their allotted number of seats. Although there was an increase in the number of seats from 1964 to 2013 from 104 to 222, this increase was nominal, i.e. from three seats in 1964 to nine seats in 2018. The loss of five seats in the 2013 election was due to the emergence of HINDRAF and dissatisfaction of the Indian community towards the MIC leadership, who failed to take a pro-Indian bargaining stand in Malaysian coalition politics. In summary, then, it can be contended that the Alliance partners in different parliamentary elections held since 1957 have never honoured the proportional representation formula towards the Indian community with reference to its population ratio. In fact, this disparity continues even today.

## A new turf of coalition politics re-surfaced

Before I discuss the history and impact of the Hindu Rights Action Front (HINDRAF) movement, which took place in 2007, I shall briefly analyse the changing dynamics of coalition politics in the 2018 general elections. Unlike 2013, the 2018 election results drastically changed the entire discourse of the political process, which is quite pertinent in the given perspective. Before the 2018 general elections, a political disagreement took place among the leadership of former Prime Minister Mahathir Mohamad with the opposition parties against his own past front Barisal Nasional. On 22 September 2015, under the leadership of Mahathir Mohamad, Pakatan Harapan (PH; Malay for 'alliance of Hope') was formed, consisting of the Democratic Action Party, People's Justice Party, National Trust Party and Malaysian United Indigenous Party. A political opposition coalition front was established in Malaysia against the former ruling Barisan Nasional coalition that had ruled the country since independence. After a lot of permutation and combination, after the May 2018 general elections, the PH coalition appointed Mahathir Mohamad as the new prime minister, while the president of Parti Keadilan Rakyat (PKR), or the People's Justice Party, Wan Azizah Wan Ismail, wife of Anwar Ibrahim, was appointed deputy prime minister. After the election result was announced, on 16 May 2018, the PKR leader Anwar Ibrahim, who had been convicted a first time in 1998 with the charge of suspicion of engaging in homosexual acts and then a second time with politically motivated charges of sexual misconduct and sodomy, and had been in prison since 2015, was swiftly released from jail due to the insistence of newly elected Prime Minister Mahathir Mohamad, on account of election strategy and political understanding, who reversed his earlier position and with the help of Malaysia's King, Sultan Muhammad V, officially pardoned Anwar's past charges and thereby transformed a political prisoner into a prime-minister-in-waiting.

In the general elections of 2018, there were three major fronts contesting in the election (Moniruzzaman and Farzana 2018, 209–210).

After the election results were announced, PH won with 113 seats, a simple majority, leaving Barisan Nasional behind with a wide margin at 79 seats. Following this understanding among the alliances, PH finally formed the government and Mahathir Mohamad became the first prime minister from PH, becoming the Head of State with two different banners. This new coalition front after 61 years dislodged the UMNO-Barisan Nasional front primarily on the grounds of their profoundly oppressive nature, entrenched incumbency, abandonment of multi-racial roots, growing use of the rhetoric of Islamic supremacy, political polarization, racial anger, economic vulnerability, nationalism and populism and domination of minority Chinese and Indian communities. The young urban voters of MIC, by turning against Barisan Nasional, thereby moved beyond the country's habitually race-based politics.

The catastrophic failures of the MIC and MCA in this election are multiple. The MCA's representation in parliament was reduced from seven to one and the MIC was bisected into two from four, which sounded the death knell of these parties. The total number of elected Members of Parliament (MPs) of Indian origin in the 2018 general election was 16, which was more than the post-2013 election figure of 11. Of these 16 MPs, only two are from the ethnic-based MIC which is part of the Barisan Nasional coalition and the other 14 MPs were from two political parties, namely the Democratic Action Party and PKR, each with seven Indian MPs, who joined in the PH coalition front of the new federal government. The major causes behind the upset of the MIC, as pointed out by Professor Datuk Denison Jayasooria, Institute of Ethnic Studies in Universiti Kebangsaan, Malaysia, are as follows (*Little India* 15 May 2018):

First, the MIC failed to adopt a rights-based approach to development and move away from a charity, welfare approach and hand-outs towards community empowerment and resilience; second, it failed to adopt a non-racial and non-ethnic approach and never went beyond ethnicity, gender, disability, class and caste status; third, the MIC was unable to set up a dedicated social inclusion unit by addressing social exclusion irrespective of ethnicity with specific targets to reach all disadvantaged communities (Babulal 2018); fourth, the MIC had weak leadership and failed to assert its bargaining position within the Barisan Nasional dominated by the UMNO party.

The core reasons behind the failure of Barisan Nasional and its partners MIC and MCA in the 2018 election were that it depended on recycled politicians instead of bringing in young blood. Furthermore, bread-and-butter issues, the rising cost of living, complaints over the 6% goods-and-services tax (GST), stagnant wages, higher fuel prices, an imbalance in development funding between the country's various states and disgust with former Prime Minister Najib Razak's corruption scandal were the major issues causing the vote to swing against the Barisan Nasional coalition front.

Therefore, in the last 30 years (from 1971–2000) under the NEP and the NDP programmes, the Indians have been left behind and "marginalized" by the "remarkable economic growth and rapid industrialization that has benefitted the wider Malaysian society at large … relegating the status of Malaysian Indians, who are largely from the 'working class', to one of a 'forgotten lot'".[4] Their weak economic condition (mainly in the plantation sector) has forced them to get involved in various anti-social activities and currently this is becoming an overall national predicament, especially after the riots of March 2001 at Petaling Jaya. The issue of continual racial discrimination over the years and weak MIC leadership has brought to the fore the emergence of the HINDRAF, which led a massive demonstration of more than 10,000 people in Kuala Lumpur in November 2007, largely targeted to draw the attention of the government to the plight of the Indian community, stemming from poor economic condition, religious discrimination, political marginalization and lack of education. The emergence of HINDRAF and its agitation against the government led to severe political unrest.

## The origin of HINDRAF movement

Over the years, the economic discrimination by the government towards Indians through the NEP and NDP (since 1970) largely shifted from an ethnic-elite teamwork mechanism to a Malay hegemonic system. This change of power equations within the Barisan Nasional and the weak political leadership and internal feud among the MIC within the coalition government failed to create substantial improvement in the economic condition of the Indians. Besides the economic and political factors, religious hounding has been an alarming means of marginalization for the people of the Indian ethnic community, mainly the Hindu Tamils. It has been reported that between 2004 and 2007, a massive number of Hindu temples were demolished (Ponnusamy 2009, 18). This lack of a homogeneous mindset on the part of the authorities in dealing with the issues of temple demolition, religious conversion etc., as well as the ignorant attitude of the MIC leadership, has led to massive uproar within the Indian community, resulting in the re-surfacing of the HINDRAF group on the map of the political system. This radical group (comprising roughly 30 Hindu NGOs, with its leaders mainly lawyers) was established in 2005 with the primary objective of fighting for Hindu rights, opposing the constitutional provision perpetuating Malay supremacy and special privileges through Article 153 of the Constitution, defending religious freedom, opposing demolition of Hindu temples, campaigning for abolition of Indian poverty, and investigating the deaths of Indians in police custody. The unrest and political grievances boiling amongst the Indian community for years against the authorities volcanically erupted on 25 November 2007, when around 50,000 people assembled under the streamer of the HINDRAF in the streets of Kuala Lumpur. For the first time in post-colonial history, such a gigantic crowd exhibited the portraits of Mahatma Gandhi and Nelson Mandela and expressed rebuke for the government's discriminative policies. Regrettably, the government reacted strongly against the protest, designated the protest leaders as terrorists and invoked punitive legal measures under the draconian Internal Security Act, normally associated with acts of terror and fanaticism, and arrested leaders like P. Uthayakumar, M. Manoharan, R. Kengatharan and V. Ganapathi Rao etc. under its provisions. Although the government crushed the HINDRAF movement forcefully, it eventually emerged as a powerful political voice (not as a political party) of the marginalized Indian community, exposing the ground reality of the country's 'multi-racial' and 'multi-cultural' image (Fong et al. 2012). This marginalization policy and its repressive action against the HINDRAF in 2007 prompted the Tamil community in the Indian state of Tamil Nadu to react very sharply and provide a pro-active response to the government on the issue, thereby crafting serious commotion within the existing coalition power structure of India. The request to interfere, through a letter to the Indian Prime Minister by Chief Minister M. Karunanidhi of DMK, to protect and safeguard the Tamil community raised important questions before the Indian government regarding its stand on the issue and whether the dynamics of coalition-cum-provincial politics were more supreme and profound when pitted against India's existing foreign policy towards Malaysia. In this context, the second part of the paper will examine how the internal minority problem of Indians has created domestic resentment among the Tamil people of India, analysing its spillover effects on the overall visage of Indian domestic and coalition politics.

***Impact on India's domestic and coalition politics***

These events had a spillover effect on Indian politics, when many protesters, including the leader of HINDRAF, P. Waythamoorthy, escaped state persecution and took shelter in Tamil Nadu. As a reaction to the Malaysian government's treatment of these leaders, Tamil Nadu's Chief Minister, M. Karunanidhi, sent a personal letter to the Indian prime minister on 27 November 2007, in which he wrote:

> I am very much pained at the way in which Tamils in Kuala Lumpur were treated by the police of the Malaysian Government on 25.11.2007. It is learnt that Tamils organized a protest rally in Kuala Lumpur against the marginalization of the ethnic Indian minority in Malaysia.
>
> (*Malaysian Bar* 2007)

In the same letter, he further mentioned that the government should be aware that Tamils constitute the largest percentage among the Indian minority in Malaysia and the peaceful protesters carried posters of Mahatma Gandhi. He also noted that the rally was organized for equal rights, but the police used water cannons and tear-gas to disperse the rally and detained over 240 ethnic Indians. Finally, he stressed the poverty among ethnic Indians and discrimination towards them, and mentioned that the people of Tamil Nadu in India were disturbed over the sufferings and happenings in Kuala Lumpur.

In response to this letter to the government as a coalition partner of the Union government, Malaysian Justice Minister Nazri Aziz, making a derisive statement, said, "His place is in Tamil Nadu, not Malaysia. He should worry about his own state. His own state has got problems. This has got nothing to do with him and lay off" (*The Economic Times* 30 November 2007). He further challenged the detractors and said: "The HINDRAF memorandum is also a matter of concern because its contents are seditious. We will act. These people must be responsible for their actions. Don't challenge the government" (Adigal 2007). He finally labelled the demonstrators as "penyangak" (thugs) and refused to apologize for doing so, and said:

> It's a mistake to make an apology to them. I cannot accept the action of 20,000 people who want to be involved in a simple action of submitting a memorandum. They can send one person or even 10. It's not the Indian community that's involved but only some samseng [gangsters].
>
> (Adigal 2007)

Another minister, Azmi Khalid, while endorsing Nazri Aziz's statement, said:

> The 20 per cent ethnic Indians outside the HINDRAF influence, skilled Malayalis from Kerala, Sikhs brought in as policemen, Sindhis who came

> as businessmen and Sri Lankan Tamils brought in as clerks, have all done much better. Why must they talk about being neglected?
>
> (Adigal 2007)

He then added that "India's 'honourable' MPs" should understand that tear-gas and watercannons, not live ammunition or lathi-charges were used (ibid.).

Likewise, Ahmad Shabery Cheek, Parliamentary Secretary in the Malaysian Foreign Ministry, while replying to the opposition leader Lim Kit Siang, who raised the issue of Mr. Karunanidhi's unhappiness in the Malaysian Parliament, said:

> Indians in Malaysia were better off than those in India, when seen in the perspective of the United Nations Millennium Development Goals. We have many Indian workers here, and their presence is a testimony that the situation in Malaysia is far better than [that] in India.
>
> (*The Hindu* 30 November 2007)

While replying to these offensive statements by the Malaysian ministers, Chief Minister M. Karunanidhi reacted very sharply and said: "It is my duty to defend Tamils", and "If there is any punishment for doing the duty, I am prepared to accept it", thereby making it amply clear that it was not his intention to criticize the Malaysian government, but that he was only urging Prime Minister Manmohan Singh to take steps to protect the Tamils in Malaysia: "It is my duty to bring it to the notice of the Prime Minister. I have carried it out on behalf of the people of Tamil Nadu", he said (*The Hindu* 30 November 2007). Not only that, Karunanidhi's daughter and Rajya Sabha member Kanimozhi, while reacting to the statement made by the Malaysian minister, said "the Malaysian minister's statement was unwarranted" as her father only expressed "pain" while writing to Prime Minister Manmohan Singh (*The Indian Express* 30 November 2007).

Unfortunately, these statements of the Malaysian ministers created a rumpus in both the Indian Houses of Parliament, where a large section of parliamentarians demanded the government's response, since the Indian government was somewhat quiet on this vital matter. While cutting across party lines, majority members from Tamil Nadu along with other political parties vehemently deplored the reported discrimination of ethnic Indians in Malaysia and demanded that New Delhi should address this issue instantly. Since the members urged the Union government to take steps to 'protect' the ethnic Indians in Malaysia, Speaker Somnath Chatterjee, sensitive of the diplomatic compassion involved in this matter, advised them against saying anything that would influence relations with the friendly country and said: "We are a very responsible democracy. We don't discuss … any other country in such a manner" (*The Economic Times* 30 November 2007). Some MPs in both the Houses even hoisted slogans against Malaysia, demanding a statement from the Indian External Affairs Minister, who was present in the House, and forced the speaker of Lok Sabha to adjourn the session temporarily (*The Economic Times* 30 November 2007). In the Rajya Sabha, the DMK MP, R. Shunmugasundaram, questioned the Malaysian minister's right to remark on a letter sent by a chief minister to the prime minister and said: "We cannot lose our self-respect to continue to have friendly relations with another country" (*The Hindu* 28 November 2007). Similarly, the former Tamil Nadu Chief Minister J. Jayalalitha, in another statement, termed the police attack on Tamils in Malaysia as barbaric and demanded that the centre should take immediate steps to get those lodged in prisons released (*The Sri Lanka Guardian* 30 November 2007). Fortunately, in retort to these reactions in the Rajya Sabha, the Deputy Chairman, K Rahman Khan, came out with an assurance that the government would definitely take note of it (*One India*, 1 December 2007).

Meanwhile, in both the Houses of Parliament, the members cutting across party lines severely retorted against the Malaysian minister's statement that snubbed Tamil Nadu Chief Minister M. Karunanidhi for taking up the matter with the Indian prime minister, and sought a written statement from the government. In reaction to this demand, the External Affairs Minister, Pranab Mukherjee, assured Parliament that the Indian government was "in touch with the Malaysian authorities" over the question of police action against people of Indian origin and that it remained deeply solicitous for the welfare of people of Indian origin living abroad, noting, however, that India "have friendly relations with Malaysia and we are in touch with the Malaysian authorities in the related matter" (*The Indian Express* 30 November 2007). Likewise, while a large section of the members of Rajya Sabha raised their voice against the Malaysian minister's derogatory statement against the Tamil Nadu chief minister and New Delhi's reaction to it, Pranab Mukherjee, in a suo motu statement made in the Rajya Sabha, said: "I am in touch with the Malaysian authorities and we will take it up" (*One India* 1 December 2007; Ministry of External Affairs 2007).

Besides this, outside the Parliament, different political parties raised their voice against this incident. Parties like the Pattali Makkal Katchi (PMK), a regional party in Tamil Nadu, the original Dravidian party Dravidar Kazhagam (DK), the Marumalarchi Dravida Munnetra Kazhagam (MDMK) etc. sternly condemned the "brutal" attack on Malaysian Tamils and utterly refused to accept the Malaysian government's position that no one should interfere in its internal affairs, calling upon the central government to press the Malaysian government to stop attacks on ethnic Tamils. An interesting point to be noted in this connection is that the reactions of the Tamil-led Tamil Nadu parties did not obtain a wholehearted support from other MPs from both the Houses. They raised the credentials of the HINDRAF movement in Malaysia. Dr. Subramaniam Swamy, in a debate organized by CNN-IBN, said: "It seems as if the parties have not really understood the problem at all. It is not a Tamil issue. The Tamil Muslims are not participating in the agitation", and accused Karunanidhi of being imprudent in making such a huge issue out of the subject. He also argued that the real issue had nothing to do with "ethnic Indians" since a group of Malay lawyers acted in the name of HINDRAF (Adigal 2007). Dr. Subramaniam Swamy further mentioned:

> They had filed a class action suit of USD 4 trillion against the UK and claimed they would send a petition to the British High Commissioner. The petition would ask Queen Elizabeth II to appoint a Counsel to represent the Indian community in the suit.
>
> (ibid.)

Finally, realizing the depth of the problem, Chief Minister M. Karunanidhi soft-pedalled the issue by mentioning that he only had performed his duty as a chief minister to request the prime minister to take action to mitigate the sufferings of Tamils in Malaysia, and said: "I don't want to reply to Aziz's remarks and to criticize the Malaysian government. I do not want to get into a tit-for-tat. It is my duty to defend Tamils". He then timidly added, "If there is any punishment for doing the duty, I am prepared to accept it" (Adigal 2007), and said he did not want to engage in verbal exchanges with the Malaysian minister.

Thus, it is evident that the Government of India became enmeshed in the issue when some HINDRAF leaders, including the head, P. Waythamoorthy, fled to Tamil Nadu to escape the Malaysian authorities. It was felt by many that these leaders somehow smeared a distorted and harsh image of the state of Malaysian Indians and thereby managed to stir the sentiments of the Indians. However, this issue placed the Congress Party, the big coalition partner of the UPA government, in a serious dilemma, since meddling in the issue could endanger its ties with Malaysia on the one hand, and remaining silent on the matter could expose it to the rage of its coalition partners and parts of Indian society, on the other. After a pragmatic inspection and objective analysis of the situation, the Indian government preferred to refrain from interfering in this matter and did not at all wish to jeopardize the existing cordial relations with Malaysia, since it remained an important radar of engagement with Southeast Asia as part of its 'Look East' policy. Besides this, the political, economic, trade and defence cooperation between Malaysia and India has increased since the 1990s. Bilateral trade rose to US$ 5.7 billion in 2006 from US$ 2.25 billion in 1998. Moreover, as facilitator of the India-ASEAN Free Trade Agreement negotiations, Malaysia played a key role in India's integration with the ASEAN economies. This way, it was felt that it would be economically and politically too pricey for India to sacrifice its relationship with Malaysia (Lahiri 2007).

## The fragile quandary of Indian coalition politics

In the last few decades, the emergence of strong regional parties in coalition politics has triggered severe crises in the Indian federal structure, often playing a decisive role in formulating India's foreign policy. There are number of cases where regional parties (which happen to be important coalition partners of the central government) have exerted pressure on the central government (larger party) to act, based on their regional political demands. The Sri Lanka issue, the Teesta Agreement, the demands of DMK, its coalition partner in 2007, regarding the maltreatment of the Indian diaspora in Malaysia, the nuclear agreement between India and the United States, the human rights issue of Sri Lanka, the POSCO deal in Odisha, the issue of foreign direct investment in multi-band retail and the land acquisition constraint on the 'Make in India' initiative etc. have time and again placed the UPA and NDA Indian governments in a tightrope walk and grave dilemma for balancing various sets of equations. With reference to this Malaysian Indian issue, the major dilemmas faced by India are as follows:

First, the centre–province power debate and its impact on Indian foreign policy: the central government depends largely on the political support of the regional parties to form the coalition government and in formulating both its domestic and foreign policies, since, nowadays, a one-party government at the centre remains a difficult proposition on account of the growing strength of various regional parties. Generally, in India, most of the political parties follow a similar type of foreign policy outlook, with minor ideological differences, which in other words means, barring occasional differences, there is commonality of their foreign policy agenda. In the case of the Malaysian Indians, the Tamil Nadu Chief Minister, M. Karunanidhi, of the DMK, expressed his concern more promptly than other regional parties, against the backdrop of regional politics, and thereby was not willing to lose any community-cum-political space to its other regional opponents.

The second dilemma has been the two external actors – the Malaysian Indians and the Malaysian government – which were fighting each other, on a majority–minority issue. Here the majority Malays by taking advantage of their larger population ratio and various other means tried to follow a discriminatory and marginalizing policy on the minority community of Indians. These adverse relations prompted severe internal tensions within the social fabric of Malaysia.

The third dilemma that the Indian government has been facing in recent years is its new emphasis towards the Indian diaspora. Following the Government of India's new economic policy NEP in July 1991 (not to be confused with Malaysia's NEP), the magnitude of the Indian diaspora, which appeared not only as a commanding economic community globally, but also as a budding front of resource-generation for development back in the mother country, has been pragmatically realized by the government (Ravi 2007). This diaspora community remains an important economic actor in India in four important segments – investments, foreign remittances, lobbying for India abroad and benevolent activities. Inspired by the Chinese model of internal economic development policy with the help of overseas Chinese, the Government of India, in order to activate these overseas resources, not only established a wing of the diaspora under the Ministry of External Affairs in recent years, but also strategically involved it by offering financial dispensation and tax exclusions for the promotion of overseas investment in the Indian economy. This resulted in the Indian Government interacting with the Indian diaspora on an annual basis through the celebration of 'Pravasi Bharatiya Divas' to attract its diaspora, including the Malaysian Indians. As a result, many of the provincial governments have been cultivating their wealthy overseas community to invest in their respective provinces for local economic development, chiefly from the United States, Britain, Australia, Southeast Asia and also from West Asian countries. This incentive for the overseas Indians naturally made them enjoy a more deep-rooted stake in their respective provinces and has often played a key role in formulating or influencing internal as well as foreign policies. The reaction of M. Karunanidhi amply focused the role played by the Indian diaspora in Malaysia since the 19th century, on multiple levels. So this attitude of betrayal of the Malaysian government, including the non-vocal mindset of the MIC party in the coalition government, seriously upset the DMK parties, leading it to over-react on this issue. Being a responsible representative of the Tamil community within Tamil Nadu and outside, M. Karunanidhi probably considered it his moral responsibly to look after the community interest first and foremost, without disturbing the investment flows from Malaysian Indians, for which he wrote the letter to the Indian prime minister expressing his deep concern (Jacob and Shekhar 2010, 157). These reciprocal interactions have naturally developed better bilateral economic interaction between them. Thus, all these facts created a new dilemma vis-à-vis the provincial governments, the central government and the Indian diaspora issue. Although the central government remains the prime player in devising the Indian diaspora policy, its final act on many occasions has been dependent on the provincial mindset.

The fourth dilemma has been the internal constraints of Indian foreign policymakers on how to augment its 'Look East' policy. In formulating India's 'Look East' policy, Malaysia has been an important bridging point. New Delhi's internal coalition constraints have made the Government of India face a two-way dilemma – on the one hand, how to sustain New Delhi's 'Look East' policy and make it more effective and, on the other, how to balance the provincial demands of the coalition partners in order to keep the alliance partner within the centre power structure intact. Thus, the growing involvement of regional political parties in the foreign policy formulation and implementation has appeared as a new dynamics of Indian coalition politics. Under such circumstances, three most pertinent and decisive questions come into prominence: whether provincial governments have an important say in foreign policy formulation, whether regional-cum-community interest has an important role in formulating the foreign policy, and whether India's foreign policy decisions are to be decentralized. The answers to these questions are very difficult to offer. It has been pragmatically comprehended by the Indian foreign policymakers that a fresh debate has evolved in the Indian political scenario related to the question of sovereignty of Malaysia, the national and diasporic economic interests of India and the community-loyal interests of Tamil Nadu. Therefore, it might be argued that encouraging closer links between Tamil Nadu and Malaysia, and giving the provincial government greater freedom in interactions and dealings with the foreign government to deal directly on economic cooperation, naturally jeopardizes its foreign policy behaviour and provides serious obeisance, inner-currents and flash points in the coalition politics of India. It is a fact that, in recent times, in the Indian coalition politics domain, the regional parties have tried to play a very decisive role in implementing foreign policy in the context of the existing federal system and political process. The Indian provinces and its leaders are becoming increasingly vocal with respect to foreign policy and international affairs and their views are beginning to have an impact on how the centre makes its foreign policy calculations (Jacob and Shekhar, 2010, 164). Day by day, this political command and coalition political pressure is increasing. It therefore challenges the Indian foreign policymakers' unilateral decision on formulating the foreign policy from within. It is thus imperative for the central and provincial governments to exert mutual pressure for devising a policy of greater rational interface and engagement in those foreign policy issues directly inter-connected with the provincial governments, and thereby avoid an unnecessary internal dilemma as faced by the central and the provincial governments with reference to this issue, against the backdrop of sustaining India's growing ascent in the emerging global order (Jacob and Shekhar 2010, 165–166).

## Conclusion

In summary, then, it is clear from the above analysis that, over the last four decades, economic governance in Malaysia has been marked by a high degree of centralized decision-making in policy formulation and implementation. During these years, development planning has maintained its core aims of boosting economic growth, largely by relying on foreign investment, as a primary goal for poverty reduction on the one hand, and social restructuring (and thus income redistribution) on the other. Both these factors have continued to embody the basic view for overcoming racial division and inequality, the perceived cause of the 1969 racial riots, which remained the principal challenges for Malaysia's development process. Over the years, it has been clearly revealed that the NEP and NDP were basically assenting action-based pro-Malay economic policies. During the implementation of the NEP and NDP, Malaysia achieved rapid economic growth, which significantly reduced poverty and brought the Bumiputeras into the economic mainstream. However, this sudden prominence of the Malays in the economy largely weakened another ethnic community, Indians, in the multi-racial societal patchwork. The NEP and NDP have reduced the Indian community's corporate equity share in terms of state assistance and access to economic benefits. Indeed, the poor of the Indian community seemed twice disadvantaged not only because of their lack of fortune but also because of their race. As a natural outcome, they have been marginalized and reduced to the status of an under-class in the socio-economic, educational, cultural and political spheres and remain at the bottom of the social pyramid. This position of the Indians may have stemmed from utter negligence rather than design, as the fruits of economic development have never been equally distributed among the different racial groups and, especially, these have failed to percolate to the poorer sections of the Indian community (Chakraborti 2002, 149). The poverty eradication programmes undertaken through the NEP and NDP, which were heavily biased towards the rural Bumiputera, need to be re-oriented to remove poverty, irrespective of race, unlike the past developmental policies. Thus, the contending versions of ethnic nationalism of the struggle in opposition to the majoritarian nationalism of the Bumiputera policy remain the most basic premises for Malaysia to strike stability and develop a formula for civic xenophobia in which the rights and status of all communities should be protected and permitted to burgeon.

In the final analysis, the Indian communities in Malaysia remain at a crossroads today. A community denied decades of official positive discrimination has turned Malaysia's ethnic Indians into a disgruntled under-class and left them in a parlous state. The Barisan Nasional government has not yet heard the cry of despair and hopelessness of the Malaysian Indians at their miserable alienation and marginalization from the mainstream of the development process. It should address this helpless predicament not as an isolated issue, but as a national problem within their social paradigm by abandoning the conventional minority–majority dichotomy. The UMNO-dominated Barisan Nasional should change their Bumiputera-centrist policy to prevent further major ethnic racial outbursts, as experienced in 1969 and 2001. The Petaling Jaya racial riot in March 2001 clearly exposed the delicate nature of intra-ethnic relations, and it points to a myriad of problems, which are deeply rooted in relentless poverty and social deprivation.

It is a fact that the Indians have contributed significantly to the development of their country of domicile. Over the decades, they have helped in reviving a vibrant democracy, creating a multi-cultural society and a sound economy. Despite such contributions, they are economically and politically disadvantaged in relation to the country's majority population. However, realizing the intensity of the implicit racial ethnic problems between Indians and other communities, the Barisan Nasional, for the first time since independence, declared through the Third Outline Perspective Plan (OPP3) on 3 April 2001 its commitment to a new perspective of equitable access to economic opportunities under the National Vision Policy. This is no doubt a major triumph of the Malaysian Indians in the mainstream developmental course of Malaysia since the racial riot of 1969.

Similarly, the Tamil Nadu government's reaction regarding the maltreatment of Malaysian Indians in Malaysia and the written request to the Indian prime minister to intervene in this matter created severe reactions in the Malaysian government. This community-focused request of the Tamil

Nadu Chief Minister, M. Karunanidhi, brought the Congress Party face-to-face with a two-pronged dilemma. If the Government of India directly meddled in the issue, it could endanger its existing ties with Malaysia, on the one hand, and if it is quiet on this problem, its coalition partner might shake the coalition's political understanding in the centre and thereby create internal crisis at the domestic level, on the other. While parliamentary elections remain a costly exercise in the Indian political process, the latter inevitably may not be a sensible option. The Government of India's overall response to Chief Minister M. Karunanidhi's letter of anxiety regarding the HINDRAF issue remained much more sensible than the incident of the arrest of the Indian IT professionals in Malaysia in 2003. Therefore, this issue can be termed as a case of cavernous concern or retort versus over-reaction and, finally, disperse its flavour according to the nature of power politics in due course.

## Notes

1 In preparing this article, I am grateful and indebted to my student, Dr. Mohor Chakraborty, for her research help.

2 A major leading feature of the Malaysian economy was the acute economic disparities between the Malays and the Chinese. With reference to ownership of capital, though the foreigners owned most of the private capital, the Chinese community mostly acted as the 'economic middleman' dominated by small and medium business and employment in most of the modern sectors and at nearly all occupational levels. The vast majority of Malays, in contrast, resided in the village areas and worked in the traditional agricultural sector. Relatively, then, the Chinese because of their well-off economic position were perceived by the Bumiputeras to be wealthy and in control of the economy.

3 Election data are collected by the author by using various election results, published in *The Straits Times*, *The Star* and *The New Straits Times*.

4 See homepage for Lim Kit Siang, http://limkitsiang.com/archive/2000/june00/lks0341.htm, p.1 (accessed on 22 June 2020).

## References

Abdullah, Firdaus Hj. "Affirmative Action Policy in Malaysia: To Restructure Society, to Eradicate Poverty", Ethnic Studies Report, Vol. XV, No. 2, July 1997.

Adigal, Natteri. "Should TN politicos protest Tamils mistreatment in Malaysia without knowing facts?", *Merinews*, 2 December 2007.

Babulal, Veena. "Malaysian Indians have dropped MIC, opt for multiracial parties", 15 May 2018, *The New Straits Times*, see www.nst.com.my/news/politics/2018/05/369691/malaysian-indians-have-dropped-mic-opt-multiracial-parties (accessed on 12 June 2020).

Bandyopadhyay, Kalyani. *Political Economy of Non–alignment: Indonesia and Malaysia*, New Delhi: South Asian Publishers, 1990.

Chakrabarty, Bidyut. *Indian Politics and Society Since Independence: Events, Processes and Ideology*, New York: Routledge, 2008.

Chakraborti, Tridib. "Minority Underclassed: Negating a Sociological Truism in Malaysia", in *Indian Diaspora in Asian and Pacific Regions: Culture, People, Interactions*, edited by Ghosh, Lipi and Chatterjee, Ramkrishna. Jaipur and New Delhi: Rawat Publications, 2004.

Chakraborti, Tridib. "Malaysian Indians: A Study in Marginalization", in *Human Rights: Theory and Practice*, edited by Chatterjee, Debi, Sucheta, Ghosh and Sumita, Se. New Delhi: South Asian Publishers, 2002.

Chakraborti, Tridib. "The New Economic Policy of Malaysia: Its Impact on the Malaysian Indians", *Jadavpur Journal of International Relations*, Vol. 2, Department of International Relations, Jadavpur University, Calcutta, 1996.

Department of Statistics Malaysia, 2019, see www.dosm.gov.my/v1/index.php?r=column/cthemeByCat&cat=155&bul_id=aWJZRkJ4UEdKcUZpT2tVT090Snpydz09&menu_id=L0pheU43NWJwRWVSZklWdzQ4TlhUUT09 (accessed on 10 July 2020).

Department of Statistics Malaysia, *Monthly Rubber Statistics Malaysia*, May 2004.

Department of Statistics Malaysia, *Handbook of Rubber Statistics*, 1985.

Encyclopedia, "Malaysian Indians", 2020, see www.encyclopedia.com/humanities/encyclopedias-almanacs-transcripts-and-maps/malaysian-indians (accessed on 10 July 2020).

*Far Eastern Economic Review*, 7 June 1990.

Fong, Yang Lai and Ishak, Md. Sidin Ahmak. "Framing Interethnic Conflict in Malaysia: A Comparative Analysis of Newspaper Coverage on the Hindu Rights Action Force (Hindraf)", *International Journal of Communication*, Vol. 6, 2012.

Gomez, E.T. and Jomo, K.S. *Malaysia's Political Economy: Politics, Patronage and Profits*, Cambridge: Cambridge University Press, 1997.

Government of Malaysia. *Mid-Term Review of the Second Malaysia Plan: 1971–75*, Kuala Lumpur: Government Printer, 1973.

Government of Malaysia. *Seventh Malaysia Plan 1996–2000*, Kuala Lumpur: Government Press, 1996.

Guan, Lee Hock. "Ethnic Relations in Peninsular Malaysia: The Cultural and Economic Dimensions", *Social and Cultural Issues*, Singapore: Institute of Southeast Asian Studies, no. 1, 2000.

Jacob, Jabin T. and Shekhar, Vibhanshu. "Provincial Interests and Foreign Policy: Indian Provinces' Responses to the Malaysian and Kenyan Ethnic Crises", in *Shaping India's Foreign Policy People, Politics and Places*, edited by Mattoo, Amitabh and Jacob, Happymon, New Delhi: Har-Anand Publications, 2010.

Jomo, J.S. "The New Economic Policy and Interethnic Relations in Malaysia", *Identities, Conflict and Cohesion Programme*, Paper No.7, September 2004, United Nations Research Institute for Social Development, p.16, see www.unrisd.org/80256B3C005BCCF9%2F(httpAuxPages)%2FA20E9AD6E5BA919780256B6D0057896B%2F%24file%2Fjomo.pdf (accessed on 25 April 2020).

Lahiri, Dilip. "Malaysian Indian Community: Victim of 'Bumiputera' Policy", *ORF Issue Brief*, February 2008, no.12, p.7, see www.orfonline.org/cms/export/orfonline/modules/issuebrief/attachments/malaysia_1203067850658.pdf (accessed on 28 June 2020).

Malaysian Bar. "Letter from the Tamil Nadu Chief Minister to the Indian Prime Minister", 29 November 2007, see www.malaysianbar.org.my/letters_others/letter_from_tamil_nadu_chief_minister_to_the_indian_prime_minister.html (accessed on 25 June 2020).

Ministry of External Affairs, Government of India, "Suo Motu Statement by the Minister of External Affairs, Shri Pranab Mukherjee in Rajya Sabha regarding 'HINDRAF Demonstration in Malaysia'", 30 November 2007, see https://mea.gov.in/press-releases.htm?dtl/3370/Suo_Motu_Statement_by_the_Minister_of_External_Affairs_Shri_Pranab_Mukherjee_in_Rajya_Sabha_regarding_HINDRAF_Demonstration_in_Malaysia_on_30112007 (accessed on 26 June 2020).

Moniruzzaman, M. and Farzana, Kazi Fahmida. "Malaysia's 14th General Election: End of an Epoch, and Beginning of a New?", *Intellectual Discourse*, Vol. 26, no. 1, 2018, pp. 209–210.

Muzaffar, Chandra. "Political Marginalization in Malaysia", in *Indian Communities in Southeast Asia*, edited by Sandhu, K.S. and Mani, A, Singapore: Institute of Southeast Asian Studies, 1993.

Nagaragan, S. "Indians in Malaysia: Towards Vision 2020", in *Rising India and Indian Communities in East Asia*, edited by Kesavapany, K., Mani, A. and Ramasamy, P., Singapore: Institute of Southeast Asian Studies, 2008.

*One India*. "India to take up with Malaysia statement against Karunanidhi: Pranab", 1 December 2007, see http://news.oneindia.in/2007/12/01/india-to-take-up-with-malaysia-statement-against-karunanidhi-pranab-1196465643.html (accessed on 26 June 2020).

Ponnusamy, Waytha Moorthy. *Malaysian Indian Minority and Human Rights Violations Annual Report 2008*, Presented at the Global Organization of People of Indian Origin (GOPIO) and Pravasi Bharathiya Divas International Conference at Chennai, India, 7–9 January 2009, see www.indianmalaysian.com/MalaysianIndianReport.pdf (accessed on 24 June 2020).

Ravi, Vayalar. "Indian Americans can invest more in India", *Sify News*, 24 September 2007.

Shafii, Zurina, Abiddin, Norhasni Zainal and Ahmad, Abdul Razaq. "Ethnic Heterogeneity in the Malaysian Economy: A Special Reference to the Ethnic Group Participation in Financial Planning Activities", *The Journal of International Social Research*, Vol. 2/8, Summer 2009.

Shamsul, A.B. "The Economic Dimension of Malay Nationalism: The Socio-Historical Roots of the New Economic Policy and Its Contemporary Implications", *The Developing Economies*, Vol. XXXV, no. 3, 1997.

Sivalingam, G. "The New Economic Policy and the Differential Economic Performance of the Races in West Malaysia", in *Economic Performance in Malaysia: The Insiders View*, edited by Manning, Nash, New York: World Peace Academy, 1988.

Smith, David Drakakis. *Pacific Asia*, London: Routledge, 1992.

*The Economic Times (Kolkata)*. "Uproar on Malaysian leader's remarks", 30 November 2007, see https://economictimes.indiatimes.com/news/politics-and-nation/uproar-on-malaysian-leaders-remarks/articleshow/2583413.cms?from=mdr (accessed on 26 June 2020).

*The Hindu (Chennai)*. "Kurananidhi writes to Manmohan", 28 November 2007, see www.thehindu.com/todays-paper/Karunanidhi-writes-to-Manmohan/article14884181.ece (accessed on 26 June 2020).

*The Hindu (Chennai)*. "I did not criticize Malaysian Government", 30 November 2007, see www.thehindu.com/todays-paper/ldquoI-did-not-criticise-Malaysian-Governmentrdquo/article14885523.ece (accessed on 29 June 2020).

*The Indian Express*. "Govt in touch with Malayisa: Pranab", 30 November 2007, see http://archive.indianexpress.com/news/govt-in-touch-with-malaysia-pranab/245542/ (accessed on 26 June 2020).

*The Sri Lanka Guardian*. "Former CM Jayalalitha slams attacks on Malay Tamils", 30 November, 2007, see www.srilankaguardian.org/2007/11/former-cm-jayalalitha-slams-attacks-on.html (accessed on 26 June 2020).

Vorys, Karl Von. *Democracy without Consensus*, Princeton New Jersey: University Press, 1975.

# 6 Towards an Eastern South Asian community

## Regional and sub-regional cooperation as a viable foreign policy initiative

*Riddhi Bhattacharya*

Foreign policy of any nation does not function in a vacuum. It is a product of the prevailing international environment and the country's indices in terms of its geostrategic location, economic health, military strength and domestic stability. In the countries of South Asia,[1] regional and sub-regional cooperative policy essentially remains a foreign policy issue and thus an issue in elite politics. Issues of regional cooperation are beyond the immediate concern of mass citizens and do not involve large numbers of people. South Asian mass publics are thus generally uninformed and unconcerned about regional cooperation. Moreover, in the minds of South Asian people, consciousness of the nation remains infinitely stronger than a sense of South Asian community. What is useful for the progress of regional cooperation in South Asia is the development of multiple loyalties and identities – both national and regional – among South Asian citizens. Moreover, South Asia is known to constitute one of the "critical regions" or "security complexes" in the world, primarily due to the fact that most of the South Asian states are engrossed in varying degrees of inter-state disputes and conflicts. While the British imperial rule brought the South Asian countries within a common colonial system, it simultaneously sowed several seeds of discord that continue to plague inter-state relations in the area even today. The final hasty retreat of the British Raj and the ensuing bitterness generated between the ruling elites of the two major South Asian states, India and Pakistan, gravely disrupted the traditional complementarities and cohesion. After the end of the Cold War the fulcrum of global geopolitics shifted in large part to Asia, which embraced the process of regional and sub-regional cooperation as a mechanism to deal with the new international order. Thus, South Asia too can use this trend effectively to deal with its many developmental issues.

The present article argues that, by exploring meaningful cooperation, the under- developed sub region of Eastern South Asia can embark on a path towards development and progress, and ultimately this will help in creating a wider Eastern South Asian community.

## Regionalism and sub regionalism

The concept of security is undergoing a change in this uni-polar world today and in foreign policy goal in most countries with human security and cooperative security is considered more important than a state-centric concept of security. Human security is especially relevant for post-colonial regions like South Asia, including India, where states are still grappling with post-industrial political-institutional issues of nation-state formation that the developed countries have successfully dealt with in their long political evolution. The inadequacy of the traditional conception of security has been addressed by the development of such terms as "economic security", "food security", "energy and resource security" and "environmental security". Some countries have officially adopted these concepts as part of their national security agenda. There is as yet no consensus definition of "non-traditional security". Economic development, social stability, provision of food, energy and other resources, environmental protection, the protection of unique cultures, individuals' freedom and freedom from hunger – these are all parts of non-traditional security. It may be argued that for analytical purposes it is more useful to examine each of these types of security issue separately rather than subsuming them under the general concept of "non-traditional security". However, this fails to recognize the importance of the social and historical context in which "non-traditional security" has been proposed in opposition to or in contrast to "traditional security". The Human Security Index suggested by Kanti Bajpai[2] with qualitative and quantitative inputs is a step towards greater conceptualization of human security.

The inexorable march of the market into a developing region like South Asia has also presented new challenges to human security in the region, reflected in the foreign policy that each of these countries has adopted. The post-Cold War concerns with human security are not part of the predominantly realist official discourse of foreign policy in this region. But now it is high time to adopt a cooperative security mechanism for sustainable development of this region. Neoliberal economic globalization with its emphasis on trade liberalization and international financial deregulation, in conjunction with a related dramatic increase in trans-boundary activities, has begun to challenge the central role of the nation state in political and social affairs. Nation states and their governments have simply started searching for more cooperative means to address some of the difficulties arising from globalization. In this context, regional and sub-regional spaces and regional institutions have begun to serve as increasingly important intermediate levels in the emerging multilayered structure of governance. Furthermore, regionalism and sub regionalism and globalization are complementary to each other. Technologies related to globalization also enable the coordination of large-scale regional processes, and in many cases regional configurations have been an effective mechanism for administering global norms such as notions of universal trade rules or technical standards, and human and cooperative security.

After the end of the Cold War the fulcrum of global geopolitics shifted in large part to Asia, which embraced the process of regional and sub-regional cooperation as a mechanism to deal with the new international order. Though regionalism is hardly a post-Cold War phenomenon, it is still possible to discern two big waves of regionalism. According to Jens-Uwe Wunderlich,[3] there are two big waves of regionalism. The first wave was visible between the late 1940s and 1960s and was dominated by the European experience. Several factors, such as exhaustion from war, US hegemony and its role in the reconstruction of Western Europe, Cold War politics, regional security interdependencies and a general questioning of the role of sovereignty, all converged to make regional cooperation in West Europe a reality. There were attempts at region-building outside Europe as well, the most successful being ASEAN (Association for South East Asian Nations), established in 1967. It was all these empirical developments together that created an entirely new focus in international relations theory – the study of regional cooperation and regionalism.

Thus, to understand "regionalism", one has to understand "region". A region is generally known as a cluster of geographically proximate countries that share common historical bonds, cultural and social identities and economic, political and strategic interests, with a desire to live in harmony and cooperation. Moreover, this set of countries should be sufficiently enlightened so as to understand the significance of placing cooperation above conflict in the conduct of inter-state relations. This should also be bolstered by a collective desire to come together on a common plank to create some lasting mechanism for regional cooperation. Other definitions of region include a geographical area with particular landforms, resources and natural features. Economically, it means a unit with common trade patterns, transportation routes and markets. Politically it signifies an area with a common political experience and, culturally, an entity with a shared history.

Whatever may be the "regionness" of a region, it should be bound together with meaningful cooperation. "Regional cooperation" is a term coined not too long ago to denote joint action and interaction by geographically contiguous countries with common cultural identities to address complex goals such as reducing poverty, promoting peace and security and achieving sustainable development. In reality, though, such processes of interaction between people have been carried out from time immemorial and in fact the creation of modern nation states has only disrupted this process. The need for increased economic cooperation has been a dominant feature of the global economy ever since the emergence of the European Economic Community (EEC) in the late 1940s and ASEAN in the late 1960s. In the 1990s the rationale for cooperation was further strengthened with the formation of trading blocs like the European Union (EU) and the North American Free Trade Area (NAFTA). In their book *Microregionalism and World Order*, Shaun Breslin and Glenn D. Hook[4] state that regionalism refers to the conscious, deliberate and purposive attempts made by national states to create formal mechanisms for dealing with common transnational issues. Such regionalism may well be a response to economic factors and may even have been promoted by non-state actors, but the regional project is defined as one, which is promoted by governments and proceeds through intergovernmental interaction. In this sense, it is "top-down" in terms of governments implementing policies which impact on the economy and society. Hence, regionalization refers to processes that, rather than resulting from predetermined plans of national or sub-national governments, primarily emerge from the actions of non-state actors. These cross-national processes can be initiated by non-governmental organizations (NGOs) and other actors. With the end of the Cold War and the trend towards economic globalization as well as the increasing complexity of international relations, the concept "region" risks becoming an empty idea. Raimo Vayrynen[5] says that our regional images are often based on unexamined and outdated meta-geographical conceptions of the world – a perspective dubbed "the jigsaw puzzle view" that assumes that discrete, sharply bounded static continental units fit together in an unambiguous way. Yet the world is not structured in such a neat manner; on the contrary, regions disappear and reappear as they are transformed by various economic, political and cultural factors. Often those engaged in defining the concept "region" are content to list physical, political and economic criteria. But now these definitions have undergone change. In the post-Cold War era more importance is given to the functional aspect than to the physical aspect. Vayrynen thus concludes that, in the study of regions, the key dimensions centre around the division of the world by levels of analysis and by the physical/functional distinction. Physical regions refer to territorial, military and economic spaces controlled primarily by states, but functional regions are defined by non-territorial factors such as culture and the market, which are often the purview of non-state actors. In the global system, economic regions are defined by transnational capitalist processes, environmental regions by the interplay between human actions and the biosphere; and cultural regions by identity community. Regionalism both revived and changed dramatically in the 1980s and gained strength in the 1990s. Regionalism today is emerging as a potent force in the globalizing process and is thus an important consideration in framing foreign policy.

Endemic conflicts between the various South Asian countries have made many scholars doubt whether this is a "region" or not. From the standpoint that a region is a cluster of geographically close states with common culture and heritage, there is no doubt about the *regionness* of South Asia. As a term, "South Asia" has been in use only for the past few decades or so. It is the "Indian sub-continent" that has been in longer use. The political division of the Indian sub-continent brought about at the time of the British withdrawal in 1947 gave rise to the use of the term South Asia for the "Indian sub-continent". The American area studies programme popularized the use of the term South Asia, and the emergence of Bangladesh in 1971, from what was hitherto East Pakistan, reinforced this usage. One can say that the concept of *South Asia* is a colonial contribution.[6] Regionalism in South Asia is a recent phenomenon in comparison to many other regions of the world. The establishment of SAARC[7] is a significant development in the process of South Asian regional cooperation. During the last 28 years of its existence, SAARC has been finding ways and means to foster development and cooperation in the region. It has also "widened" as well as "deepened". Widened, as its membership has increased from seven to eight, and as many as six observers have been attending its summits. It has deepened as its institutional network and activities have increased. There is also an agreement on trade liberalization and the formation of a free trade area. However, despite all these achievements, the regionalization process has not taken roots in the region. The region has been a serious constraint to the smooth functioning of SAARC. The member states' initiatives are constrained due to lack of funds and commitments. They have not yet agreed to the idea of visa-free entry of people to the region. The eradication of poverty and child labour, women's empowerment, social equality etc. are nothing more than slogans. Most of the actions and activities are restricted to the holding of conferences, seminars, workshops and short training programmes. Most importantly, SAARC suffers from a severe resource crisis. Unless the organization is successful in mobilizing funds and technical know-how from outside sources, most of its projects cannot be implemented and, thus, its relevance would remain limited. There has been a lack of enthusiasm and interest among the people and their leaders in the region in Track I initiatives, or official-level diplomacy, which is heavily formal, procedural and complex. On the other hand, Track II initiatives, or "beyond the state" diplomacy, has been widely recognized as more likely to lead to better steps in confidence building towards the reconstruction of South Asia as a community. In understanding people-to-people cooperation and interactions towards making a community, as a proxy for necessary state-to-state cooperation, one needs to focus on at least three types of issues: integrative factors, constraining factors and possible areas of non-governmental interventions. It seems that a credible modified structure for sub-regional growth remains beyond the imagination of South Asian leaders, who are quite simply trapped in their inability to develop policies, prisoners of their own political trappings. This region lacks the political will to convert the huge geography and population into a thriving market, serious policy coordination to maximize the complementary gains, infrastructural facilities to exploit the latent potentials and the will to make use of socio-cultural similarities for collective enhancement in the quality of life of their citizens. This is because, historically, South Asia was one political entity with many decentralized structures. Each sub region had its own shade of culture. This unity in diversity continued even after colonization by Britain. However, some kind of standardization, particularly in legal and administrative frameworks, tied together the diverse units during the British era. When colonial rule ended, those diverse units got truncated, leaving behind not only unprecedented ethnic flows of population across the borders, but also a permanent source of ethno-religious discord. Colonial rulers had largely created the South Asian states by executive orders. The burden of resolving the unresolved and bitter territorial or border disputes fell on subsequent national elites. The concept of nationhood was often negotiated by colonial powers and materialized in truncated forms. In many cases the creation of a state went against territorial, ethnic, religious or cultural traditions. Very often, national governments were imposed on a society, which was itself divided by the gap between traditional beliefs and modern attitudes, and by sectoral differences, religious beliefs or differential access to power. The state, in order to assert its domination, most often became bureaucratic and coercive and became entrenched well before a coherent idea of nationhood could develop. There are also at least two nations (Pakistan and Bangladesh) in the region that experienced "neocolonialism" and "internal colonialism" and therefore have a bitter past. The internal difficulties faced by most South Asian governments have contributed to deterioration in law and order, increasing ethnic and sectarian conflict, the theocratization of societies, degradation of the environment, rampant corruption, massive violation of human rights and the marginalization of the poor and the weak. Given the regional politico-economic divide, substantial cooperation in the region cannot be achieved overnight.

Despite many problems and challenges, SAARC is a positive development for the regional integration process of South Asia. It provides identity and status to the smaller countries. It is a forum where all nations of the region can put their minds together to resolve their common problems, share their ideas and develop a consensus. In the end, it is true to say that the ultimate target of SAARC economic cooperation is an integrated South Asian economy, in a step-by-step manner to implement the shared aspirations of 1,800 million South Asians for a more prosperous region. The action to achieve this goal has been more in form than substance. Moreover, unless the above-mentioned challenges and constraints faced by the member states, in particular the normalization of Indo–Pak relations, are not settled, SAARC cannot make any substantial contribution to improving cross-border connectivity, boosting trade among member countries and strengthening the regional economic cooperation process of the region. Thus one may say that regionalism in South Asia is still evolving, but that meaningful cooperation is possible in the Eastern part of the South Asia sub region and, instead of having a statist approach to foreign policy, it is high time for a regional cooperative venture to lead to sustainable development in the Northeastern part of India.

A dominant trend in contemporary international relations and foreign policy in many countries of the world along with regionalism is sub regionalism. The enduring pursuit of regionalism and sub regionalism has an underpinning thrust on peace, security and development through exploration, identification and gradual intensification of trade, economic and cultural ties among the geographically contiguous areas. The novelty of the idea of a subregional economic zone with its promise of benefits for the participants has caught the imagination of many around the world, including in South Asia. In the globalized world a new wave of awareness is sweeping through the Asian countries. It is about their perception of priority in international relations. All the countries of Asia had hitherto been looking up to the nations on the other side of the Atlantic Ocean for inspiration, guidance and knowledge, as well as all kinds of assistance and partnership. For business, they have forever been counting on the countries of Europe and North America for a market. The West on their part would consider the East as the ultimate receiver of anything it had on offer for the trusting East. However, of late, the age-old perception of the Asian countries has been undergoing changes. They are now looking more towards the East for leadership, experience, inspiration and partnership. This new phenomenon is often described as *sub-regional cooperation* or a *growth triangle.* It is also referred to as a *growth zone* or *sub-regional economic zone* (SREZ) and sometimes also *Natural Economic Territories* (NET). This is one of the most recent features in the political economy of Asia and the Pacific region where there is cooperation in parts of separate national economies in territorially defined sub-regional zones. A proper definition of "growth triangle" or "sub-regional cooperation" is very difficult to arrive at. It can be described as arrangements through which three or perhaps more geographically close regions of member countries come together to derive economic benefits through complementarities. It is believed that sub-regional cooperation can result in poverty reduction and equitable development. Further economic integration can lead to fuller and more stable employment through export growth. Many neighbouring countries share common resources for their livelihood. In addition to economic benefits, sustained cooperation among neighbouring countries builds trust and helps in minimizing conflicts, which in turn could translate into a reduced cost of maintaining borders. Mohammad Humayun Kabir, of the Bangladesh Institute of International and Strategic Studies, believes that, while regionalism is based on the political concept of geographically proximate nation states coming together with the objective of forging cooperation in jointly identified areas for their mutual benefits, growth triangles or sub-regional cooperation are localized arrangements and procedures with limited objectives to achieve. He further adds, "Indeed a growth triangle may be termed as a controlled experiment in regional cooperation, representing a new approach to regional development strategy".

Yet, despite the growing number of formal sub-regional projects and informal sub-regionalizing processes, sub regionalism remains understudied. Perhaps more correctly, while political and economic geographers and urban planners have long recognized the importance of sub regionalism, it has yet to receive significant attention in the politics and international relations disciplines. The underlying assumption is that sub regionalism and other forms of regionalism should not be viewed as contending forces. These localized areas of economically integrative activities have in some cases been given popular geometric designation depending on the number of participant states: triangle, quadrilateral, even hexagonal. However, analyst Glenn Hook believes that sub regionalism[8] is distinct from regionalism (which is promoted by the big powers) and sub state regionalism (promoted by national and sub-national actors). He calls "growth triangles" "sub sub-regionalism" or "micro-regionalism". In their book *Microregionalism and World Order*, Shaun Breslin and Glenn D. Hook[9] state that "micro-regionalism" is a particular form of regionalism, driven by economic forces, production and finance, that does not acknowledge formal borders and so micro-regionalism places an emphasis on the creation of transnational economic spaces which result from "the deliberate or indeliberate action of other actors which at least initially may foster a relocation of authority from the political to the economic realm". But for our purpose we will use the term "sub-regional cooperation" instead of "micro-regionalism".

According to Samir Amin,[10] the historical development of capitalism has been to gradually move from the local level to the global and at each step to create new polarizing tendencies. To be able to improve their economic position, peripheral countries have had to delink themselves from the global system and adopt alternative countervailing strategies, one of which is sub regionalization.

Five critical factors have been identified as prerequisite for establishing a successful growth zone, viz[11]:

- economic complementarities
- geographical proximity
- integrated infrastructure
- political will
- participation of masses
    1) Economic complementarities – When countries intend to cooperate under a sub-regional set-up, they must have something to offer their partners in the group, be it product, services, capital or even transit facilities for land-locked countries. Complementarities could also occur in the areas of production, available resources, technology and skills, as well as in the areas of specialization of labour forces, in service rendering and even in geographical locations. Thus complementarities arise in large part from the differentials in factor endowments. Moreover, complementarities may have varied forms. For instance, countries producing the same products might still be interested in trading the items. Complementarities might not necessarily be existing or visible all the time and could even be latent, or might well surface once economic cooperation takes off the ground.
    2) Geographical proximity – Geographical proximity or contiguity is another important factor for countries intending to cooperate with one another, in order for transactions to be cost effective. Countries with geographical proximity could establish a multi-modal system of transportation within the region to facilitate exchanges of goods, services and even ideas without any hassle. The cost of such exchanges would definitely be lower than the cost of similar exchanges between

countries that are distantly placed. The proximity factor would lead to increased interaction amongst the people of the countries, which would in turn lead to a more intense cooperation. It is also possible that geographically proximate neighbours inherit proximate languages, common culture and similar history. Such similarities and commonalities induce neighbouring countries to seek solutions to their common problems through closer cooperation underpinned by common history, culture and ethnic links. In the case of economic exchanges such cooperation might often be continuation of many existing informal economic links, which might only need to be formalized within the growth zones in order to give them an impetus through the backing of the public policy.

3) Integrated infrastructure – Integration of infrastructure is extremely important. If participating countries integrate their transport and communication then exchanges of goods and services will be easier. Moreover, transportation cost will also be cut down to a certain extent.
4) Political will – Although formal intergovernmental agreements are not critically important for growth zones, political will or commitment on the part of the governments of constituent countries is an important determining factor for the success of sub-regional cooperation. Such agreements are important in terms of the essential policy framework as well as institutional support to effectively operationalize the growth zone. Moreover, the private sector has to be the main actor in such a growth zone. However, with or without formal intergovernmental agreements, there is a need for policy coordination, on a more limited scale than what is required for trading blocs or customs unions.
5) Participation of masses – The success of a sub-regional cooperation is based on the ease of the projects and their implementation, which can be very well facilitated if the ordinary people, NGOs and the media are involved.

The conceptual foundation of an SREZ, NET or sub-regional cooperation posits that the factors of production – capital, land, labour, resources, technology, national territory – are important. According to thinker MD Nuruzzaman,[12] growth triangles are all about the intensification of economic cooperation on a limited geographical scale to attract foreign investments and thus boost export promotion. They are based on localized economic zones where geographically contiguous countries with different economic sizes, socio-cultural patterns and political systems seek to integrate parts of their territories for mutual gains. A set of complex key factors – the most prominent being foreign direct investment, complementarities in production systems, export-oriented development strategies and differences in factor costs – facilitates the emergence of growth triangles. Other thinkers, however, believe that sub-regional patterns enlarge the concept of proximity to encompass factors other than geographic distance. Indeed, historical legacies and economic forces can provide the propellant for migration of industries, employment creation and spillovers to other areas. In Asia, SREZs have gained currency as a mode of international economic cooperation. SREZs represent an attempt by neighbour countries to initiate deeper economic cooperation at a sub-regional level, a mechanism that has proven expedient when integration of entire economies and regions proves limited and fraught with difficulties. Through SREZs, governments of neighbour countries work together to make a particular transnational but contiguous area, also known as growth polygons, attractive platforms for enhanced economic activity. Jointly they design incentives – in the form of policies that are more liberal than national policies, the coordination of such policies, and the provision of essential infrastructure – to attract investments into the polygons. Particularly, ASEAN governments have embraced the SREZ concept as a way of promoting regional integration without having to change national trade policies. SREZs can also serve as testing grounds for policies that imply political risk for possible national implementation.

Some analysts believe that sub regionalism might be perceived as an emerging layer of economic governance between the nation state and the global economy – a mechanism through which the domestic meets the international and the global. Sub regions might, then, emerge as new sites of competency and potential authority that could complement the role of the nation state. If they succeed in promoting development and growth, then the legitimacy and authority of the participating national governments may be enhanced by participation in sub-regionalist projects. Alternatively, sub regionalism might be seen as a challenge to the existing "Westphalian" authority of national governments and nation states.[13] For example, in Europe, the expansion and consolidation of the EU might lead to the creation of new layers of governance below the national level and across national borders. Sub regionalism might simply be the right size and level of economic governance as states lose power "upwards" to the "super-region", and "downwards" to the global economy.

A foreign policy discussion of the implications of an SREZ for the foreign relations of national actors must begin with national interest.[14] It can be stated as a given that the strategy of SREZ building is one of an array of policies adopted in East Asia and ASEAN to maximize export-led industry in the interest of sustaining rapid economic growth. What distinguishes this strategy from wholly domestic policies designed to further the same interest is the requirement of formal or informal intergovernmental agreements to foster enterprise through liberalization of legal and political restrictions inhabiting "natural" economic integration in contiguous state territories in order to share the factors of production. As one Thai analyst has noted, "a country's industrial policy has now become an important variable in foreign policy analysis". A foreign policy supporting the development of SREZs can be pursued as long as it does not conflict with or undermine other policies deemed more effective or threaten interests viewed as more vital. The hierarchy of interests and the selection of policies to promote interests will vary from state to state.

The need for sub-regional cooperation is even more important today than before. This is because, in addition to their role in furthering economic interests, SREZs are also useful in improving relations for the national actors and enhancing the cooperative environment for bilateral and multilateral relations in general. Although SREZs are not a necessary part of cooperative relations between national actors, once they have been established their failure or dismantlement would have a negative impact on the cooperative relations. Beyond their chartered local and limited interests SREZs have some importance in fostering and spurring larger and even more significant regional integrative activities and institutions. Thus, in the book *South Asian Growth Quadrangle: Framework for Multifaceted Cooperation*, writers Muchkund Dubey, Lok Raj Baral and Rehman Shoban write that there are certain advantages in a sub-regional grouping. These are as follows:

1) Political risks are localized and failures too are comparatively smaller than a regional grouping where national interests can get hurt. "Even countries having difficulties in overcoming their mutual political and general economic problems can effectively cooperate within the framework of growth triangles".[15]
2) Major changes in the policy framework of a country do not need to be made in a growth triangle. Sub-regional cooperation can be established at a relatively low cost and within a short time.
3) The domestic market is usually not threatened by a growth triangle, as most of its produce is export oriented.
4) If the participants in a sub-regional cooperation happen to be members of a regional grouping, and if some of them are least-developed countries, then this cooperative framework can be the most effective means of ensuring equitable benefits to the latter category of members.
5) Regional cooperation can very well become the preliminary stage before entering into regional integration agreements.
6) Sub-regional cooperative endeavours are generally non exclusionary in nature as they do not compete with the larger regional arrangement of which they are members.
7) Growth triangles can be helpful in maintaining and strengthening the competitiveness of the economies of the partner countries. There is transfer of skill and technology from the more developed to the less developed partners and the upgrading of the skills of the local labour force in both categories of countries.
8) Sub-regional cooperation often helps in developing backward and forward linkages in the national economy, thereby acting as a catalyst for triggering development in other parts of the economy.

According to James H. Mittelman,[16] sub-regional cooperation can be equated with "transformative regionalism", that is a counterthrust to neo-liberal restructuring. While only embryonic, it is partly a defensive reaction mounted by those left out of the mosaic of globalization, particularly in zones outside the macro regions. The political and economic programme is not unlike that of the development of integration model: close political cooperation at the beginning not the end of the project; equity and balance in relations between member states including redistribution formulas; and increased trade based on regional industrial planning. Though a weakened actor, the state must be an active agent in transforming integration, its main roles being to rationalize production, build infrastructure and promote exchange. Stressing self-organization, the alternative formulation calls for regionalism that flows from the bottom upward and is linked to new forms of cultural identity – the women's movement, environmentalists, pro-democracy forces etc. At the end of the day, the possibilities and limitations of transformative regionalism rest on the strength of its links to civil society. Creative potential for bringing about sustainable growth and democracy lies in popular support and a sense of involvement of multiple strata of the population. The most prominent example of this is the establishment of MERCOSUR (Southern Common Market) in Latin America, which created a new form of regionalism. This cooperation has sparked a major surge in international trade.

## Sub-regional cooperation in Eastern South Asia

The idea of establishing a growth zone in South Asia and more particularly in Eastern South Asia originated from the need to exploit the huge under-utilized resources of the region. This was prompted by the lack of visible success of the formal regional grouping – SAARC – to move the wheel of cooperation forward at a reasonable pace and meet the collective needs of its members. Many countries of this sub region therefore were exploring possibilities in other regional and sub-regional configurations that were beyond the SAARC ambit. Some of these even included countries that are outside the South Asian region: BIMSTEC (Bay of Bengal Initiative for Multi-Sectoral Economic Cooperation) and the Indian Ocean Rim Cooperation could be cited amongst such groups as examples. The irreversible process of globalization has confronted the developing countries with many daunting challenges. The flow of development assistance is stagnating and is being increasingly linked to the promotion of trade objectives of the donor countries. This has triggered an intense competition for foreign direct investment among developing countries. Under the Uruguay round, rules governing intellectual property rights, subsidies, countervailing duties, trade-related investment and environment and health issues would eventually be the same for industrial and developing countries. Therefore, the basic challenge before South Asian countries in this new regime is how to raise efficiency and international competitiveness of their economies and implement "pro-poor" growth strategy to tackle pervasive poverty. One of the ways of meeting this challenge is to overcome regional apprehensions and constraints and move towards sub-regional cooperation in investment and economic integration, which will pave the way for the most efficient use of the region's resources through additional economies of scale, value addition, employment and diffusion of technology. There is a prevailing view that the South Asian countries can also prosper by replicating the East Asian and ASEAN experiences of sub-regional cooperation where there are many successful sub-regional cooperative ventures.

By Eastern South Asia is meant the sovereign nations of Bangladesh, Nepal, Bhutan and the Northeastern states of India (i.e. the seven hill sisters – Assam, Tripura, Meghalaya, Nagaland, Mizoram, Arunachal Pradesh and Manipur) and the states of West Bengal and Sikkim. This sub region lies roughly between 27°9' and 20°5' north latitude and 86°35' and 92°30' east longitude, has a total area of 688,600 square kilometres and a population of about 300 million, with average annual income of a little above 300 dollars per capita. South Asia is one of the poorest regions of the world. With 22 per cent of the world's population and with high density, this sub region is plagued by high levels of illiteracy, prevalence of poor health conditions and, above all, a poor degree of gross national product. Historically, the region has been the profitable hinterland for several colonial powers, which perhaps remained as major reasons for backwardness in all sectors from education to health, from agriculture to industries etc. On the other side of the coin, the potentials in the sub region are not too bad. In fact, the region is rich in terms of natural resources, which, if harnessed appropriately, could perhaps change the entire scenario. This sub region shares one of most fertile river basins in the world, the Ganges–Meghna–Brahmaputra basin, and is also blessed with natural endowments like the hydropower potential of Nepal and Bhutan, the coal resources of West Bengal and the hydrocarbon reserves of Bangladesh, Assam and Tripura, which make this sub region one of the great store houses of potentially cheap energy. Additionally, there are large non-energy mineral deposits, forest resources, livestock and marine resources and a useful network of port cities in Chittagong, Mongla, Calcutta and Haldia. Moreover, the people of this sub region, both poor and non-poor, make a huge workforce of hard-working and disciplined workers at relatively low wages. Given an opportunity to be productively employed, with suitable investment in their skill formation, this workforce will be a major competitive advantage of the region.[17] The rice fields of the Ganga–Brahmaputra–Meghna basin also constitute one of the largest granaries of the world. With appropriate investments in improving agricultural productivity, and efficient water management, this granary can comfortably feed the large workforce of the region at reasonable prices. Since the early 1990s, the countries of the sub region have also been implementing broad-ranging market-oriented reforms. These have created a sound environment for accelerated investment over a broad front. Thus, all the essential ingredients are available here and now to transform one of the poorest sub regions in the world into a leading sub region of dynamic economic growth. The region not only shares the geographical features of mountains, jungles and rivers and landlockedness in the case of Nepal, Bhutan and India's Northeast, but also the ecological hazards emanating from floods and environmental degradation. The historical linkages, geographic proximity and ecological unity of the sub region-Bangladesh and Northeast India are partners in a historical civilization, they form part of the same ecological sub system, and share the great rivers of Ganges, Brahmaputra and Meghna. The cultural pattern and practices of the Indian states – particularly West Bengal and Assam – bordering Bangladesh are very similar. This is unsurprising as in colonial India these areas were organized in a single administrative unit. Prior to the partition of British India in 1947, the different parts of northeast South Asia were more or less linked up through 5,000 miles of inland waterways and a few thousand kilometres of railways. The inland waterways provided an extensive transportation network for the movement of goods and peoples. From Calcutta via the Brahmaputra River, there were regular steamer services up to Assam through Bangladesh. The West Bengal province of India and East Bengal (now Bangladesh) were also integrated by road and rail communications. The two wars between India and Pakistan over Kashmir in 1948 and 1965, however, led to a major disruption of the communication networks in northeast South Asia as the Pakistan government forbade rail communication and imposed restrictions on inland waterways' transportation between East Pakistan and contiguous parts of India. Only in 1947 were they politically separated on a permanent basis. Still, the cultural, historical and colonial affinity remains as a useful factor that can be exploited to forge intensive cooperation on a localized basis.

In addition to the above, this region constitutes a very dynamic potential particularly because it lies at the crossroads between the very dynamic regions of East and Southeast Asia on the one hand and South Asia on the other, the latter extending into Central Asia, West Asia and Europe. The region could use its strategic location within Asia to build links with other regions and could gain immensely from such cooperation. The potential of the backward eastern zone of South Asia coming together, bound by shared natural inheritance, strategic access to Myanmar and beyond to South East Asia and China, provides the underlying premise to the potential of ESAS as a growth zone. The integration of South Asia with East Asia can never fully consolidate itself unless the backward region of South Asia is sufficiently energized to emerge as a dynamic growth zone.

Despite the opportunities, progress in achieving sub-regional cooperation in South Asia has been at best very modest due to a host of economic and political factors. The political environment needs to be improved by the regional governments and political leaders for a meaningful sub-regional cooperation. Political fragility makes it difficult for governments to take initiative where opposition parties can exploit. The governments, private sector, academia, professionals and social sector organizations have to work in unison. In order to move towards successful integration, sequencing of actions is crucially important. The South Asian region should develop its own short-, medium- and long-term strategy for economic integration. It is important that each stage is implemented effectively before moving on to the next in order to build a sound foundation for progress. In this context the development of the EU may be studied, which is considered to be the most advanced model for regional grouping. The European integration evolved over four stages: first, a preferential free trade regime where member countries reduced or eliminated tariff and non-tariff barriers amongst themselves. Second, a customs union created a common external tariff so that import duties were the same for each member country. Economic union was the third stage, which further integrated the market, eventually leading to a single market. The final step was a monetary union in which the national currencies of the member countries were replaced by a single currency. South Asian countries need to address the following key issues, however, in order to move towards successful cooperation. Trade reform and facilitations require complementary policies such as a regulatory framework, improved governance, stable law and order, reduced corruption, upgrading of infrastructure and improvement in the overall investment climate. To achieve these, South Asian governments and the private sectors have to work together. In South Asia the potential gains are expected to be much more as the system is shackled by excessive paperwork, discretionary powers of the bureaucrats and various bottlenecks.

## Towards meaningful cooperation

The ruling class in New Delhi should have a clear vision of the development of an Eastern South Asian community if it wants development of the Northeastern states, and thus needs to adopt regional and sub-regional cooperation in India's foreign policy. The Eastern South Asian community "personality" broadly depends on three interlinked economic and political factors: first, the character of economic transactions such as formal and informal trade relationships and whether there has been an honest attempt at reducing trade imbalances; second, how leaders feel about the outstanding regional problems, especially bilateral ones, such as the Indo-Pakistan conflict, India–Bangladesh border disputes, and those leaders' efforts to minimize these tensions; and third, the level of consciousness among citizens of the region towards the status of human rights in the region and, specifically, how they feel about states, which, at times, instead of promoting freedoms, curb them.

The 2017 Dokalam Standoff[18] added certain complications in the way of cooperation for this region. Bhutan, which had always shared a cordial relation with India, is experiencing certain changes in its domestic political landscape. The pro-democratic movement in Bhutan often witnesses anti-India rhetoric with a leaning towards China, and as always Nepali political parties using anti-India sentiment to garner electoral benefits has created a setback to itinerant and local traders. In fact, there has been cooperation and integration in this sub region since time immemorial through cross movement of people, trade, commerce, pilgrimage and a host of other activities. But gradually the mobility and fluidity in this sub region reduced, first due to certain circumstances in many countries of the region, then colonialism, and lastly due to the creation of post-colonial modern nation states, partition and the creation of borders. The makers and enforcers of boundaries use maps today to define human reality inside of national territory. As a result, everything in the world has acquired a national identity. We see the boundaries of national states so often that they almost appear to be a natural feature of the globe; however, they can be further away from reality. State-authorized mapping is now so common that most governments do not regulate map-making, but almost everyone draws official lines on maps by habit anyway. Indeed, this dynamic is so pervasive that few people ever even think about it, yet it has covered the planet with the nation states' territorial authority. As a result, we are now accustomed to seeing maps that nationalize topography by erasing spaces on the edge of a nation's identity. In India, this includes several major spaces – areas in Nepal, Bhutan and Bangladesh – which have become mostly blank spaces in the country's national view of South Asia.

Development of regional identity and loyalty is possible through concrete achievements by SAARC that can create solidarity among South Asian people. SAARC has not been successful in fashioning cooperative relations between South Asian countries as the strategies for conflict resolution have been premised on the use of force. However, SAARC can be useful in formulating strategies based upon the human security approach wherein the security of one state is not the cause of insecurity for its neighbours. Development of regional identity and loyalty is possible through concrete achievements by SAARC that create solidarity among South Asian people. Lack of political will is considered to be the major hindrance to the success of regional integration. The tension between India and Pakistan, the distorted perception of national interest and the dictates of so-called security, and to a lesser degree the distrust of India by her smaller neighbours and their chronic and huge trade imbalance with India, have created an atmosphere which is not very conducive to regional cooperation. Bias against regional partners is perhaps inborn in the government machineries of the region, which have to far monopolized the decision making and literally kept the public sector alienated from mainstream economic participation. Another important missing ingredient is a shared perception of common benefit – all the members must feel they are sharing the costs and benefits of the cooperation equitably. India's economic preponderance and comparative advantage in a wide range of products has resulted in asymmetric trade relations with her neighbours, hindering regional integration. India accounts for more than 80 per cent of South Asia's combined GDP, population and trade. Therefore, as the predominant economic force, India must respond through proactive leadership and demonstrate early harvest and goodwill to encourage the smaller partners and to dispel historical suspicions. If, for example, we examine the Indo-Bangladesh relationship, we can readily identify several economic issues that are hindering closer cooperation.

SAARC as a regional intergovernmental organization is very unique as far as regional conflicts are concerned. The regional states do not have a common approach to resolving inter-state disputes in the region. India emphasizes bilateralism and also rejects the role of extra-regional powers in resolving regional disputes. Other regional states, on the other hand, do not reject the role of extra-regional powers. It seems that the South Asian countries have not been able to develop clear perspectives on domestic and regional issues. Their domestic problems have often shaped their attitude towards SAARC. It seems that, due to certain preconceived notions, SAARC has not been viewed as an independent variable. Other reasons pertain to a lack of convergence of political security of the member states, as well as the absence of a perceived threat to their vital interest from common enemy factors, which contributed towards the viability of other regional groupings such as the EU and ASEAN.

This sub region is witnessing great shifts in its domestic and external relations. The border issues between West Bengal and Bangladesh, the blow-hot-blow-cold relation between India and Nepal and the large looming Chinese presence in this region are definitely issues that often hinder the cementing of sub-regional ties. The ever-changing border claims of China over Indian territory and growing tensions from 2014 onwards in the constant skirmishes on both sides of the Indo-China border, along with the growing closeness between Nepal and China since 2019, act as a deterrent to cooperation. It is the view taken here that the policymakers in this sub region of Eastern South Asia ignore the historical linkages of this sub region and that is why this sub region has been artificially cut off, making it an isolated and neglected region. While British imperial rule brought the South Asian countries within a common colonial system, it simultaneously sowed several seeds of discord that continue to plague even today. The final hasty retreat of the British Raj and the ensuing bitterness generated between the ruling elites of the newly emerged states gravely disrupted the traditional complementarities and cohesion. Moreover, there is a lack of a strong historical perspective while dealing with this sub region and the various problems that plague it are due to this failed historical sense. Historical insights inform decision making, voting and the making of judgements within and about public life. This sub region would have been better governed and administered if a better understanding of the past were available to both decision makers and the public. International political thinkers and policymakers often ignore historical realities. I believe that sub-regional cooperation was already practised here from ancient times, and that what is required here is re-linking that old historical linkage to really move the wheel of cooperation forward and address the issue of under-development and poverty, which are the major problems of this sub region. The success of sub-regional cooperation is conditioned by its own peculiarities. Sincere and transparent efforts to incorporate alienated communities through cultivation of ethnic, religious, cultural and civil society networks may produce good dividends. In designing proper development strategy for the frontiers, provincial scholarships as well as social scientists and historians can contribute to chalking out appropriate strategy through their peculiar local experiences and insights. Soliciting the participation of local communities or civil society in creating policy strategy may be helpful. Wide publicity of the merits of trade, tourism and economic cooperation is imperative to enable different communities to prepare for such opportunities. Giving autonomy to and planning with the provinces will help the process of sub-regional cooperation in Eastern South Asia move forward.

## Notes

1 By South Asia is meant the sovereign nations of India, Pakistan, Afghanistan, Bangladesh, Nepal, Bhutan, Maldives and Sri Lanka.
2 Bajpai K (2000), "Human Security: Concept and Measurement", *Kroc Institute Occasional Paper*, No. 19, August.
3 Wunderlich J (2007), *Regionalism, Globalisation and International Order: Europe and South East Asia*, Ashgate Publishing: Hampshire, England.
4 Breslin S and Hook GD (2002), *Microregionalism and World Order*, Palgrave Macmillan: New York.
5 Vayrynen R (2003), "Regionalism: Old and New", *International Studies Review*, Vol. 5, No. 1, pp.25–51.
6 "South Asia as a Region", SD Muni, www.southasianmedia.net.
7 South Asian Association for Regional Cooperation.
8 Hook GD and Kearns I (1999), *Sub-Regionalism and World Order*, Macmillan: London.
9 Breslin S and Hook GD, op cit.
10 Amin S (1999) "Regionalization in Response to Polarization", in *Globalism and the New Regionalism*, edited by Bjorn Hettne, Andras Sapir and Osvaldo Sunkel, New York, St. Martin's Press.
11 "Growth Zones in South Asia: What Can We Learn from South East Asia?", Dhaka, Centre for Policy Dialogue, Report No. 20, January 2000.
12 Nuruzzaman MD (1999), " SAARC and Sub-regional Co-operation: Domestic Politics and Foreign Policies in South Asia", *Contemporary South Asia*, Vol. 8, No. 3, pp.311–322.
13 Breslin S and Hook GD, op cit.
14 Weatherbee DF (1995), "The Foreign Policy Dimensions of Subregional Economic Zones", *Contemporary South East Asia*, Vol. 16, No. 4, pp.421–432.
15 Dubey et al. (1992), *South Asian Growth Quadrangle. Framework for Multifaceted Cooperation*, Macmillan India Ltd: New Delhi, p.2.
16 Mittelman JH (1999), "Rethinking the 'New Regionalism', in the Context of Globalization", *Global Governance*, Vol. 2, No. 2, pp.189–213.
17 Speech by Yoshihiro Iwasaki, Director, Programs Department (West), Asian Development Bank, in the First Private Sector Forum on South Asian Sub-regional Economic Cooperation, 28–29 November, 2000. Calcutta.
18 June 2017–August 2017 there was a military border standoff between The People's Liberation Army and Indian Armed Forces when the former tried to construct a road in the trijunction of Sikkim, Bhutan and TAR (Tibet Autonomous Region).

# 7 The elephant and the panda – India and China

## Global allies and regional competitors

*Johannes Dragsbæk Schmidt*

Home to 2.4 billion people, India and China represent the largest and fastest growing economies the world has ever seen. The two countries have for a long sustained period been labelled the world's office platform and factory outlet, respectively, although GDP growth fluctuated recently as a direct result of the global financial crisis and the Covid-19 pandemic and new priorities of the Chinese government. India's growth has been based on services in software and information technology while China has concentrated on manufacturing and logistics. This has all changed now with a self-confident China aiming to become a global standard setter and advanced industrial superpower while India in 2018 became the world's fastest growing economy. Both countries consist of mega markets for global cost reduction and are increasingly seen by the Eurocentric 'masters of the universe' as an existential threat to Western dominance of the global hierarchical order (Schmidt and Hersh 2019). As a combined impact on the global economy, they represented 21 percent of the world's Gross Domestic Product (GDP) in 2019 (*Nikkei Asian Review*, 25 January 2020). In 2060 these two economies will account for 35 percent of global gross domestic product, nearing the US and European nations' combined share (ibid). This indicates a steady rise in India's and China's share of global GDP with important implications for changes in the composition of the global economy and potential spill-over effects for global governance and international order.

Seen in perspective and in contrast to other smaller growth economies, the high economic surge in India and China has far-reaching implications. This is the case not only for global living standards and poverty reduction but also for competitiveness and distribution of income in the rest of the world. Although both entities have lifted millions out of poverty and huge middle classes have emerged, it is also striking that during the past decades the two economies added more than 500 million new workers to their combined labour markets – a number which was slightly greater than the total Western labour force – thus pushing global productive capacity to skyrocket. Most of these additional workers found manufacturing employment with wage levels below that of their North American and Western European counterparts. In

2008, their salary was only 1/20, or even less, of that of the Western workers doing the same work (Haizhou 2008); this has doubled several times and in 2020 rising wages in China have skyrocketed the buying power of the consumer class. A pattern which India is copying though with a longer timeline ahead. The question of course is whether these achievements are connected to a globalization dividend under the geo-economic regime in the form of a relatively open trading system, financialization, outsourcing and Foreign Direct Investment (FDI), or whether there are other explanations such as the developmentalist role of the state. No matter what the answer is, India and China's growth seems to be exceptional in the history of economic development, but it should also be noted that they show some of the world's highest income disparities, polarization and in the case of India extraordinary levels of poverty (Schmidt 2020).

Although the development models differ fundamentally, they also share several similarities. They have different political systems, with a democratic parliamentary system in India and an authoritarian one-party system in China. India has a better developed and more transparent financial sector, while China has, largely, opened its economy to foreign trade and FDI. Chinese reforms started in 1978, almost 15 years before India (Eichengreen et al. 2010). The dependency levels of the two countries on export orientation differ sharply: China's export share in 2004 was around 40 percent, corresponding to over two and a half times that of India's, but since 2018 this has been levelling down so that both countries now have approximately 20 percent export share to GDP.

Strategically, however, they both share a gradualist approach to economic reform and have not allowed the institutionalized regulatory control to be discarded. In fact, despite all the hype about globalization, privatization and liberalization, the experiences of both economies challenge the core assumptions of neoliberalism:

1. It is incorrect to project the two countries' economic growth as the result of liberalization alone. It was essentially more the impact of industrial policy restructuring and local entrepreneurial classes that determined the outcome.
2. Both countries retained the power to control the flow of foreign investment.
3. It may not be accurate to describe China's success as the result of combining the neoliberal economic solution with political authoritarianism, while the balance is kept in India by strong vested capitalist groups and organized labour.
4. India's experience suggests that the relaxation of rules on foreign investment must be addressed at the same time as the issue of poverty reduction.
5. Neoliberal prescriptions have been resisted by both states and sufficient regulatory space has been kept (Sornarajah 2010, 162–163).

The impact of these economies on the hierarchical structure of global capitalism and governance, especially China, has seen a tectonic shift from geo-economics to geo-politics in command of the world system. In very short time, from 2016 to 2020, the US–China decoupling and strategic rivalry has replaced previous business logics, 'free trade' and multilateralism, creating a precarious situation for the North and South Block where India's ministries of finance, defence and external affairs – and the Prime Minister's Office – are located. These events and the health, economic and social impact of the Covid-19 pandemic are rearranging the outlook of the post-pandemic foreign policy choices of the Bharatiya Janata Party (BJP)-led government in Delhi. However, let us take one step back in trying to understand and explain the tensions involved in the return of India and China as major powers on the world scene.

Seen in historical perspective, China and India's growth story may not be defined as catching-up but rather as a comeback. After long periods of self-centred development, they are gradually reinserting their economies to the former dominant status they had in the world before the 18th century, when they represented approximately half of the world's GDP (Maddison 2001 cf. Figure 7.1; Frank 1998). In contrast, mainstream explanations rely

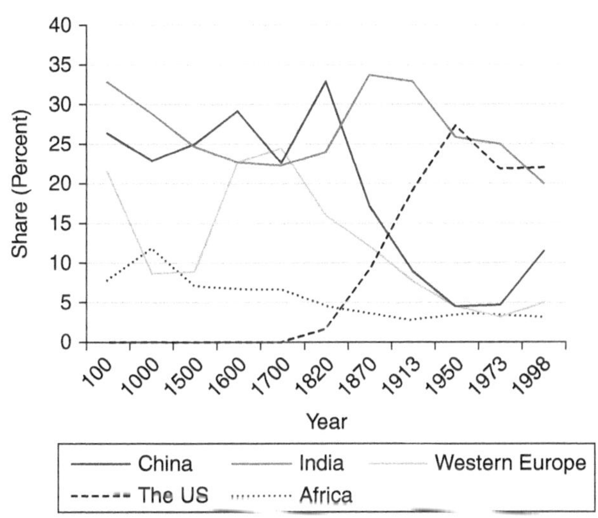


*Figure 7.1* World GDP Shares

Figure 7.1 Seen in historical perspective, China's and India's growth story may not be defined as catching-up but rather as a comeback. After long periods of self-centred development, they are gradually reinserting their economies to the former dominant status they had in the world before the 18th century, when they represented approximately half of the world's GDP.

Source: Computed from Maddison 2001; cf. Mudambi 2010: 257.

on Eurocentric ideology when they characterize this comeback as 'emerging markets' or something new or unusual (Schmidt and Hersh 2018, 2019).

From a 'comprehensive security' perspective,[1] the self-perception among the political class in Delhi and Beijing ultimately not only emphasizes their position as great powers but essentially reinserts their role as global leaders in determining international affairs in the near future (Radtke 2003, 499). This compelling evolution nurtures the scenario of a completely different vision of the future world order. Some commentators note that the beginning of the 21st century will be remembered for the rapid decline of the United States' unilateralism and the 're-emergence' of a multipolar world where India and China restored Delhi's and Beijing's rightful places first as regional then as global players with huge implications for security and the economy worldwide.

If these tendencies continue, it ultimately spells the end of three to four centuries of global domination of the Atlantic powers. How such a process will evolve is one of the most important future questions for the world system. Although suffering from 'imperial overstretch', the United States remains the ultimate hegemonic military superpower, but its options are becoming more and more limited both geo-economically and geo-politically, and Washington's room of manoeuvre appears to be shrinking due to the shift in economic gravity and the concomitant challenges from Asia (Schmidt 2014a).

The intertwined geo-political and geo-economic security and foreign policy strategies and visions of India and China show an interesting overlap in terms of both being re-emerging giant economies and exemplar attempts challenging Western dominance through the establishment of alternative political and economic institutions such as the BRICS alliance (Brazil, Russia, India, China and South Africa).[2]

Both entities have seen fundamental foreign policy changes in the past two decades. Especially after the dissolution of Soviet-type socialism and the end of the Cold War, a new more pragmatic, gradualist and experimental type of foreign policy emerged, including a renewed attempt to upgrade bilateral relations although with important setbacks as well. Two-way trade increased from $270 million in 1990 to more than $68 billion in 2012, and China was, in 2018, the largest trading partner of India. Albeit the relationship is also characterized by low levels of FDI, which makes it precarious, still it denotes a closer political economic embracement. Trade between the countries touched historic heights despite bilateral tensions over a number of issues including the China–Pakistan Economic Corridor, Beijing blocking India's entry into the Nuclear Suppliers Group, the military stand-off at Doklam lasting 73 days (*Times of India* 7 March 2018) and the recent incident at the Galwan Walley face-off in Ladakh in June 2020 with casualties on both sides.

On official occasions like the BRICS summit in Brasília in April 2009, India's prime minister, Manmohan Singh, declared, "India and China are not in competition" and "There is enough economic space for us both". China's president, Hu Jintao, said the same (The Economist 2010). At the BRICS 2014 summit in Fortaleza in Brazil, the new leaders of India and China, Prime

Minister Modi and President Xi, spoke about "shared interests and common concerns" and gave a clear impression about collaboration and synergies even in security matters, exemplified by China's invitation for India to join the Shanghai Cooperation Organisation (SCO) (Ramachandaran 2014).[3] Later, the two countries reaffirmed the "series of consensus" reached by Prime Minister Narendra Modi and Chinese President Xi Jinping at their meetings in Astana (June 2017), Wuhan (April 2018) and Chennai (October 2019), which committed the two countries to a cooperative relationship.

It seems that PM Modi in the beginning of his premiership abandoned the traditional realist approach towards China by loosening up and expanding the engagement, emphasizing the mutual cultural heritage and Buddhism instead of anti-colonialism and Third Worldism, and at the same time not hiding his government's simultaneous attempt to create strategic partnerships with other countries like Japan and the US (Mohan 2015a). Recent events also show that Delhi emphasized enhanced diplomatic friendship in bilateral relations with China at Mamallapuram summit in 2019. The question is whether these are more than the public statements and can be validated.

The future Indian–Chinese relationship is a work in progress. The outcome will affect the entire world. This is inescapable, but the problem needs to be approached in an analytical and non-deterministic manner. It ought to be the guiding principle behind the study of development and international political economy generally. This applies even more to the subject at hand while observing the potential titanic movement in the world system and what appears to be a fundamental change in foreign policy patterns.

One of the main drivers in foreign policy is related to energy scarcity. There have been attempts at coordinating Chinese and Indian arrangements for Middle Eastern and African oil, and the term 'Chindia' has been coined to project a vision of cooperation and collaboration between the two countries. Not only oil, natural gas and other energy sources like access to coal are increasingly confronting policy and decision-makers with hard choices, and also hydropower and water appears to play an increasingly significant role in this context. Therefore, foreign policy, energy security, geo-politics and geo-economics have become intermeshed and appear less separated than before.

This contribution explores the comparative political economic relations between India and China in a critical political economy framework focusing on bilateral, regional and strategic foreign policy ties. It discusses the intertwined geo-political and geo-economic foreign policy alignments at the global level, where both countries seemingly have opposed Western dominance in climate change policy, world trade policies and to a certain extent in security. However, disagreement persists on unresolved problems in terms of attracting FDI while access to energy shows an asymmetric pattern of cooperation, conflict and competition. When it comes to the regional Asian setting, the policy convergence increasingly being pursued with the other BRICS countries is also embedded in a complex theatre of mixed relations and competition for influence and security. While India may enjoy a dominant position in South Asia – albeit with varying success – China has a more complicated relationship with its Northeast Asian and Southeast Asian neighbours. Both countries have mixed relationships with Central Asia or what India regards as West Asia since Iran and Afghanistan belong to what Delhi perceives as its interest sphere (Schmidt 2014a).

## Conceptual framework

Neorealist perspectives proclaim that structural change at the regional level is more volatile than at the global level. Seen in this light, Asia appears to be undergoing a comprehensive and dangerous structural transformation, equal to what Europe underwent in the first half of the 20th century. This change consists of movement of states on their power cycles, generally accompanied by change in their foreign policy roles (Doran, 1991). Historically, such change was non-linear and unpredictable (Kumar 2003, 114). To elaborate this kind of change, it is necessary to distinguish between 'power' and 'role' as done by Doran when he notes that "Role exists only if legitimized through systemic acceptance, whereas power expresses itself through unilateral action and as control" (Doran 2003, 15). However, this type of thinking is based on state-centric realism, which does not give an adequate picture of the complexities involved. The neorealist perspective is ahistorical and dictates that by focusing on the 'essentials', such as the role of the state, sovereignty and 'balance of power', the future will always be like the past. This way it reflects the status quo and the interests of the current hegemon – not emancipation or potential social change and no real reflection of the interface between domestic social factors and foreign policy.

The objective here is to go beyond the mainstream neorealist and liberal theories by offering a critical comparative political economy approach to foreign policy based on a subjective approach focusing on actual empirical evidence, with an explicit theoretical and normative commitment.

Foreign policy decisions are made by agency but always within a set of structural constraints. Critical accounts of foreign policy pursue a holistic view of politics and avoid the pitfall of seeing politics as only involving governments and state actors. It is furthermore necessary to understand the constitutive nature of knowledge and theoretical assumptions and question whether it serves particular purposes and interests (Cox 1981, 128); this way, there is no value-free or neutral understanding of foreign policy, or any other social scientific research problem for that matter. Critical comparative political economy leaves room for alternative ideas and visions and includes a developmental and socioeconomic perspective on foreign policy; policymakers are constrained by societal contexts, but they also do make decisions and are able to establish elaborate critique and policies against the current (Williams 2005; Hay 2002). This type of approach opens up for a holistic, ideational 'state-society complex' conceptualization including other relational and ideational interests and private, corporate, military and civil society, which potentially may impact foreign policy outcomes (Cox 1987).

This is neatly illustrated in China, where the strategic political decision was taken by Beijing "to integrate China into the global political economy. This has 'allowed' Chinese sovereignty, in the economic sphere at least, to become 'perforated', and thus increasing the number of actors in the policy spheres" (Breslin 2002, 34; cf. Schmidt 2008, 26). When it comes to the important question about who defines 'national interest', it seems fairly obvious that in both countries a number of epistemic actors and social and economic interests and actors perform an increasingly important role and influence, although financial and productive capital remain in a dominant position in terms of direct and indirect influence on strategic security and external relations. The Sino–Indian foreign policy relationship and security sphere is also being increasingly penetrated by non-traditional security issues related to climate, environment and energy, internal divisions with external links in the blurred lines of the policy sphere, and as result the distinction between inside and outside becomes more and more difficult to distinguish. This new foreign and security pattern must be understood in an internal–external dynamic perspective because it is not only formal and informal domestic epistemic actors but also international epistemic communities, institutions and power projections that influence foreign policy decisions either through advice, norm setting or pushing new rules which may or may not enter foreign policymakers' and ultimately the domestic agenda.

Traditionally, 'foreign policy' and 'national interest' have been treated like a 'black box' dictated by the ruling elite's perception of who is the enemy. However, with the emergence of powerful entrenched interests, think tanks and external institutions using all kinds of leverage to influence a country's decision-making structure, it seems that in both countries foreign policy and even national security itself is becoming affected by a greater variety of actors and, this way, foreign policy "is partly self-determined and partly other determined" (Norbu 2005, 105; Mohan 2009, 157). Ideology must also be taken into consideration not only in democracies like India, where Hindu nationalism, for instance, has shaped an anti-Muslim and anti-foreign agenda, but also in one-party China, where "official policymakers and interest groups that strive to influence foreign policy formulation all interpret China's national interests based on their own, sometimes narrowly defined perspectives and preferences" (Jakobson and Knox, 2010, 47). It is furthermore important to stress that the BJP continues to dominate India's realist lobby with reference to specific chosen "historical and contemporary geo-strategic threats, but also continues to build strong support for India's nuclear deterrence by reconstructing certain postcolonial insecurities" (Das, 2003, 80). However, it would be wrong to simply categorize the BJP as sole promoter of realism, as these sentiments are also much entrenched by lobbyists and perceived 'neutral' observers and commentators associated with the Congress party. In fact, India's foreign policy establishment consists of a number of competing views

(Schmidt 2014b) and what Mohan (2009,158) describes as "the existence of tiny, informal and consequential networks spanning the full spectrum of the Indian elite opinion and acting as the vanguard of India's new foreign policy", but corporate interests have also become "important determinants of India's foreign policy options" (Baru 2009, 277). This is also the case in China where the distinction between shaping and implementing foreign policy is sometimes elusive and, in fact, there are different views of policy formulation. The impact of new foreign policy actors in China has led to a fractured authority, varying views of how China should internationalize and demands that China defends its core interests. These new impediments are changing the nature of Chinese foreign policy formulation and the way in which China will interact with the outside world (Jakobson and Knox 2010).

However, these interpretations may have changed recently with the growing pressure from the US–China trade war and the scenario of decoupling and emergence of a tripolar world economy – one centred on China, the EU and the US, respectively. Strongman politics, protectionism and nationalism seem to be the new politics of the world polity, signalling a move away from what some have termed a rule-based world order. India's PM Modi's much-vaulted slogan 'Make in India', which was recently changed to 'Self-reliant India Mission', and China's 'Made in China 2025' illustrate the changing international environment sliding towards more self-reliance and domestic affairs. It also neatly illuminates the interface of internal and external factors determining foreign policy. Indeed, one may argue that India is obsessed with China while the opposite is not always the case. Not only because of the increased China–US rivalry but partly because China's attempts towards reconciliation and cooperation with India have time and again been met with antagonism and in some extreme cases with Sinophobia.

These perspectives lead to several interlinked issues of strategic importance. What explains the fact that both countries share mutual interests in several global policy areas while the same areas retain a degree of rivalry and competition at the regional level? What is India's reaction to China having a hands-off leadership role when it comes to economic investment and respect for sovereignty?

## Bilateral relations

Apparently both countries have today replaced previous foreign policy preferences of non-alignment with a more pragmatic and non-ideological approach, or what some observers call "multi-alignment with all" (Mohan 2015b). Both countries endorse the capitalist market and free trade, despite state-managed policies continuing, although India has average tariff levels that are more than twice as high as in China. The unresolved (border) problems remain an issue but, at the same time, there seems to be a pragmatic move away from geo-political anxieties and uncertainties to a more geo-economically based convergence in both bilateral and multilateral foreign policy relations and even development models. Recently though there have been several eruptions of what might escalate into military conflict.

India's foreign policy gradually changed from a socialist to a capitalist vision, which came with a shift away from conservatism, nationalism and politics to letting economics dominate and finally a change away from being anti-Western leader of the Third World to becoming a foreign policy actor in its own right (Mohan 2006). Likewise, China's foreign policy also moved away from overtly relying on Maoist ideology to a situation today where the relationship with the United States overshadows all other relations. Nevertheless, bilateral links between India and China have improved and new alliances have been sought through diplomatic and economic rapprochement. This also implies less concern about national sovereignty – the traditional hard core of approaches dealing with 'balance of power' – towards a more pragmatic relationship where geo-economic matters, until recently, have played an increasing role.

The trade imbalance in China's advantage causes some tensions. Chinese non-tariff barriers are only a small part of this. The problem is India's uncompetitive manufacturing sector. The deficit problem is more complicated because trade primarily takes place via sea-lanes, while cross-border trade remains underutilized due to perceived security threats, difficult geography and reluctance by Delhi to implement policies and support land-based trading. India has sought to diversify its trade basket, but raw materials and other low-end commodities still make up the bulk of its exports to China. In contrast, manufactured goods, from trinkets to turbines, are exported from China into India. India–China bilateral trade reached $84.44 billion in 2017, a historic milestone. It included an astonishing 40 percent increase in India's exports to China (*Times of India* 7 March 2018).

The two countries continue to face impediments in moving from bilateral trade to mutual investment, although, according to a consulting firm, "there are about 150 Indian companies operating in China compared with 40 Chinese companies doing business in India" (Huang 2010, 122). This has changed dramatically since Chinese investment in India increased to $8 billion in 2017 from $1.6 billion in 2014. Alibaba has invested in PayTM, Snapdeal and Zomato. In the next three years, during the Modi regime, investment grew five-fold to $8 billion. This makes the Chinese presence in the Indian market very prominent where four out of the top five brands are Chinese (Gatewayhouse 2020).

In this context, it is interesting to note the increasing economic cooperation and exchange between cities and private companies through the liaison and critical role of consulates.

> The regions of the Yangtze River Delta and the Pearl River Delta of China have had significant cooperation with Indian enterprises, a result

> that can be attributed to the efforts of the Indian consulates in Shanghai and Guangzhou. Investments by Chinese enterprises such as Huawei Corporation and Zhong Xing Telecommunication Equipment Company Limited (ZTE) in Maharashtra and Bangalore were also made possible by the Chinese consulate in Mumbai.
>
> (Ni 2010, 148)

Also, the BCIM economic corridor initiative (Bangladesh, China, India and Myanmar), with railways, highways, personnel and information flows, tourism, energy links and people-to-people contacts, has contributed to almost $1 billion in trade between India and China. However, recently, India skipped the Chinese-initiated 'Belt and Road' global investment programme, and that had severe repercussions for the BCIM corridor initiative as well.

Nevertheless, bilateral relations continue to be upgraded but cannot acquire a real strategic dimension if the border disputes remain unresolved. The Sino–Indian entities as regional Asian giants appear fated to become economic and possibly political competitors, although at the same time there is a pragmatic wish for increasing cooperation from both government and the private sector. Despite their mutual good wishes about partnership, there are still unsettled issues given the countries' old enmities, complicated neighbourly relations in South and Southeast Asia, a nuclear détente, and two of the world's biggest armies with almost 3.5 million troops. According to neorealist thinking (Frankel 2011), China is seen as aiming to dominate Asia, and once it becomes the world's largest economy, it will be in an advantageous position to twist its neighbours' arms even further. However, seen through more pragmatic liberal lenses, there are more areas of mutual interest and cooperation, especially in economic affairs, than traditional security approaches can comprehend.

Despite these contradictions, and important interruptions along the border, steady rapprochement between the political elites in Delhi and Beijing gradually matured and stronger bilateral confidence-building measures in 2010 did show political will to enhance cooperation and even regularize military ties. This involved navy and army exercises and a memorandum of understanding signed with a whole variety of military exchanges and measures including regular 'strategic dialogues' about the border issues (Godwin 2011, 121). These measures signified a more coherent effort to accomplish and rely on a geo-economic approach, which would allow more space for non-state entities in the conduct of economic and political exchanges between the two countries.

Recently, though, there have been several eruptions of what might escalate into military conflict. For the first time since 1967 there were clashes between unarmed soldiers in Himalayan Galwan Valley in June and later a stand-off along the Line of Actual Control in Ladakh. This has turned public opinion in India virulently anti-China and the Modi government has banned 118 Chinese apps and Huawei and FZ from establishing the 5G internet structure due to security concerns. India's sanctions against China and closer ties to the US could either result in a serious conflict (Kapur 2020), or, as a recent joint statement underscores, the two countries will continue to uphold the "series of consensus" reached at the leadership level – where a key template is their common conviction that China and India are not competitive rivals or each other's threats, but cooperation partners and each other's developmental opportunities. As one key observer notes,

> The biggest gain is that a war has been averted and a new phase of constructive engagement of China with a sense of realism becomes possible. This is a moment of truth to rethink the entire foreign policy trajectory the government followed in the recent years.
>
> (Bhadrakumar 2020a)

Furthermore,

> Fundamentally, India needs to come to terms with China's rise and should have the composure and maturity to regard it as an inexorable historical process. The country is caught in a time warp – entrapped between an irascible parliament on one side and an ill-informed nation on the other side. Our zero-sum mindset has done colossal damage. We must jettison it forever and refocus on constructively engaging China so as to take advantage of that country's meteoric rise for our country's development, which is the number one priority today.
>
> (Bhadrakumar 2020a)

The only winner of a conflict between the two Asian giants is the United States of America, who will use all means to confront any challenge to US hegemony and unilateral dominance. As one commentator puts it: "India should be extremely wary of getting entangled in the US–China tensions" (Bhadrakumar 2020b).

## Global allies or foes

Recent global diplomacy has shown important signs of an emerging alliance between India and China as well as other so-called emerging economies like Brazil, Russia and South Africa. The breakthrough came at the World Trade Organization (WTO) ministerial meeting in Mexico in 2003. Under the motto 'no deal is better than a bad deal', the global South walked out followed by the G22 and, in turn, the G77. For the first time,

> Western divide and rule did not work, nor did it work during the following years with the repeated attempts to revive the Doha round and the exhortations of Western negotiators. This signalled a new diplomatic weight and cohesion of the global South under the leadership of India and China.
>
> (Kremer, van Lieshout and Went 2009, 30)

The Sino–Indian alliance repeated itself at the Doha negotiations in Geneva where India's trade minister, Kamal Nath, accused the United States of putting the livelihoods of a billion of the world's poorest people against "commercial interests" as each country blamed the other for the acrimonious collapse of world trade negotiations. China, too, joined the frenzy of finger pointing, weighing in to support India. The Chinese news agency, Xinhua, referred to the "selfishness and short-sighted behaviour" of wealthy nations for bringing down the negotiations at the 11th hour (Stewart 2008). The alliance between India and China and other BRICS countries was critical in challenging the traditional structure of power within the WTO and transformed the Doha Round of trade negotiations into a battle drawn along North–South lines (Scott 2017).

Although both countries have a vital interest in trading with each other and cooperating by taking advantage of a liberalized global trade and development agenda, it is interesting to note that under the current WTO regime, India and China cannot pursue a development-oriented agenda through industrial policy, domestic protection and preferential treatment (Trachtman 2010). There has been a continuing agreement against the imposition of labour and environmental standards and a clear no from the Western countries to liberalizing agriculture.

The Obama administration sought to create bilateral agreements – the transpacific and transatlantic treaties, TPP and TTIP, that were supposed to organize business activity under one monumental umbrella of new rules beyond the WTO regime. It was a conscious move from Washington to isolate especially China and to a lesser degree Russia and India, and a deliberate policy aiming at maintaining American hegemony. Today, with the decoupling and disruption of the international trade regime by the Trump government, by utilizing a transactional approach, Washington aims to decouple the Atlantic economies from China by using tariffs and protectionist policies to ban Chinese technology and finance from the American market. This is a fundamental shift in the US–China relationship and will have great consequences for India as well. There is partisan consensus in Washington to get tough on China while Beijing asserts sovereignty and thereby override the quest towards multilateralism and 'free trade' (Rachman 2020). This obviously puts India in a difficult situation and leaves its foreign policy choices in a vacuum, which might potentially challenge its dictum on 'strategic autonomy'.

Nevertheless, the trends toward mutual self-interest has also been clear in climate change negotiation, where Delhi and Beijing share a common mistrust towards the Western agenda. This Sino–Indian unity emerged at the United Nations Climate meeting in Copenhagen in December 2008, where the world's biggest and fourth biggest emitters of carbon gas rejected American-led demands for them to undertake tougher anti-warming measures (The Economist 2010). There has been a continuing resistance against the imposition of carbon emission caps, tax and tradable permits but this changed with the signing of the Paris climate agreement in 2016 and both countries are committed to reducing emissions and to increasing production and consumption of non-fossil fuels.

Sino–Indian cooperation is evident not only in trade and climate change but also in security-related issues, for instance US policy towards Iran and Afghanistan. The US is panicking that India might bolt away just as a window of opportunity has opened to tether it to the Quad stable (thanks to the stand-off in Ladakh), which has been a key objective of the US regional strategies against China in the Asia-Pacific. India and China also shared a common approach with regard to the global financial crisis, where there have been examples of a common platform and partnership through the SCO, which is being used to coordinate policies in all areas covering security, energy, climate and other important areas that essentially confront Western hegemony. The two entities share a wish to reform what is perceived as an undemocratic global governance system and go up against the unilateral American-dominated security order and the use of exclusive military power in the Balkans and the Middle East. Both Delhi and Beijing directly and indirectly support Russia in the case of Ukraine and Moscow's annexation of Crimea, and together in BRICS they share a wish to create a multipolar system with alternative parallel international financial institutions, rules and norms.

Gradually the BRICS nations are moving away from using the euro and the dollar to settle international accounts and recently they initiated the establishment of a New Development Bank (NDB) with an announced capital structure of $100 billion, equal to approximately half of the World Bank. The new Contingency Reserve Arrangement (CRA) adds another $100 billion and these institutions may either break the monopoly of the World Bank and IMF or at least be parallel structures competing with established multilateral institutions dominated by the EU and the US. These initiatives must be seen in conjunction with (1) the establishment of an Asian Infrastructure Investment Bank, AIIB (an alternative to the Japanese and American dominated Asian Development Bank, ADB); and (2)

> the consolidation of the Chiang Mai Initiative Multilateralization (CMIM) and the associated Asian Multilateral Research Organization (AMRO) among the Association of Southeast Asian Nations (ASEAN) + 3 (China, Japan and the Republic of Korea). The CMIM is now a $240 billion financing facility to help member countries deal with balance of payments difficulties. This is like the $100 billion CRA set up by BRICS. AMRO has evolved into a mechanism for macroeconomic surveillance of member countries and provides a benchmark for their economic health and performance. This would enable sound lending policies and may very well be linked in future to the AIIB. The CMIM and the AMRO thus provide building blocks which could serve as the template for the NDB, the CRA and the AIIB.
>
> (Saran 2014; cf. Schmidt 2015, 135)

According to another notable source, the dollar is in for a 35 percent drop against other major currencies (Landsman 2020), whatever the impact on the role of the euro and the renminbi.

These initiatives through alliances by convenience against the 'West' have a clear connection with the impact of the rise of China and to a lesser degree India on global governance structures and institutions. China in particular is attempting to reinvent the rules, the norms and the regulations of global governance, by utilizing a combination of soft diplomacy and hard foreign policies in protecting its national interest. As mentioned in a much-celebrated book *The Beijing Consensus*:

> China's rise is already reshaping the international order by introducing a new physics of development and power (...). It replaces the widely-discredited Washington Consensus, an economic theory made famous in the 1990s for its prescriptive Washington-knows-best approach to telling other nations how to run themselves.
>
> (Ramo 2004, 2–4)

The Washington Consensus was a hallmark of 'end of history' arrogance. It left a trail of destroyed economies and bad feelings around the globe. China's new development approach is driven by a pragmatic desire to promote high-quality growth, and critically speaking,

> it turns traditional ideas like privatization and free trade on their heads. It is flexible enough that it is barely classifiable as a doctrine. It does not believe in uniform solutions for every situation. It is defined by a ruthless willingness to innovate and experiment, by a lively defence of national borders and interests, and by the increasingly thoughtful accumulation of tools of asymmetric power projection. It is pragmatic and ideological at the same time, a reflection of an ancient Chinese philosophical outlook that makes little distinction between theory and practice.
>
> (Ramo 2004, 4)

China is using 'soft power' remedies to nurture alliances with developing countries to solidify its position in the WTO, flex its muscles on the world stage and act as a counterbalance to US power. This evolution is spearheaded by the impact of the global financial crisis, which resulted in an "observable swing to nationalist and protectionist measures" in the Western hemisphere (Schmidt 2010, 24), which is gradually moving into China bashing.

While India has been slower to capture the recent weakness of the EU and the US because of the financial crisis and the threats of decoupling, there are signs of increasing foreign policy convergence in alliance with China and the BRICS nations to stand up to pressures by Washington. The question is whether India is joining the bandwagon or prefers the status quo. It seems that as long as

> India–China–America is constrained by the strategic triangular relationship it remains to be seen what impact it will have on the evolving world order. So far, there seems to be agreement to manage India and China's integration into the world system as smoothly and peacefully as possible. Furthermore, the cornerstone of enhancing strategic triangularity is the bilateral rapprochement between India and China in trade and security, which is growing rapidly and in vital ways although not without obstacles, as well.
>
> (Schmidt 2014a, 217)

This notwithstanding, and more fundamentally, the growing 'Asianess' of India's and China's trade is seen as the way forward to create an Asian regional multilateral platform, excluding the United States. This has created new apprehensiveness among anti-Chinese segments in Delhi and Washington, and more rivalry at the regional levels in Asia may be coming soon.

The nexus between the two entities will evolve accordingly with respect to their willingness to cooperate in the regional context but competition in all areas from the maritime to the outer space to resource scarcity shows that the outcome is still unpredictable. In Myanmar, for instance, the competition for influence is open and vigorous, and in this case, there is a potential rivalry and competition for resources and influence on the newly emerging democratization process (Schmidt 2014b).

It is within this context of competing regionalisms that the question about energy security enters the equation in terms of keeping up the supply and demand, concentrating on own production and resources, and diversification of imports and transportation. Problems of diversification of energy sources for India arise from the political volatility, geo-politics involved and the fact that, in many cases, it puts India in direct competition with China as the new energy source destination, which further adds more complexities to an existing competitive and often conflicting India–China relationship (Sharma 2020). These are issues involving high risks, enormous amounts of capital and not least geo-strategic security-related issues regarding instability, conflict, and partnerships with friendly actors.

In the present phase of capitalism, where military might is not the only means of leverage,[4] both India and China are pursuing their foreign energy security policies in close state-business alliances (Mohan 2009, 130; Kitano 2011, 47). It is interesting to note that political control of transnational oil conglomerates is more important in the case of India than China. In some cases, the two entities cooperate, which may also include private companies, and in others they compete (Sharma 2019). Of outmost importance is the fact that China occupies a permanent seat on the United Nations Security

Council (UNSC). This can almost be considered a comparative advantage as it generates a lot of clout, goodwill and power when the UNSC is engaged in foreign policy issues where access to energy and other resources like water and hydropower are involved.

Of course, this raises the question about India's potential for obtaining a seat on the UNSC. Chinese approval will not only depend on India allowing China to become a member of the South Asian Association for Regional Cooperation (SAARC). This is obviously not a sufficient condition since China's position on this issue appears ambiguous. During one of Prime Minister Narendra Modi's visits to Beijing, in June 2015, a joint statement read that China "understands and supports India's aspiration to play a greater role in the United Nations including in the Security Council" (Kaura 2015).[5] Related to this, and as previously mentioned, the ties of both countries to the United States affect their bilateral relationship. Consequently, the rapprochement between Delhi and Washington through the civil nuclear initiative keeps on dividing India and China and also impacts at least indirectly their ability to cooperate rather than compete over energy resources. This issue is also linked to Chinese moves to improve relations with and provide military assistance and official development assistance (ODA) to Myanmar, Pakistan, Bangladesh, Sri Lanka and Nepal, and the attempt to establish diplomatic and trade relations with Bhutan, which worries Delhi.

On the other hand, India's 'Look East' policy may be perceived by Beijing as rivalling China's interest (Glosny 2010, 127), and especially its military relations with both Japan and Vietnam and incursion into the 'troubled waters' of the South China Sea may worry China's energy and national aspirations in the area. Current disagreements between Japan, the US and China are linked closely to oil resources in disputed areas of the South and East China Sea. India's decision to send warships to Vietnam and Prime Minister Modi's Act East policy signal a continuation of the older Look East policy based on the intertwined geo-political China concerns and geo-economic energy security concerns. The South China Sea was already in 2004 declared to be part of India's extended neighbourhood and this should be seen as a complex response to China's encroachment in South Asia, the Indian Ocean and also the close ties between Beijing and Pakistan. As a footnote, India's position towards the Japan–China dispute is in line with its customary approach to all of its offshore territorial disputes. China previously offered to jointly exploit the energy resources in the area (Tønneson and Kolås 2006, 36), but Japan and the Southeast Asian states refused.

However, both sides seem to accept the presence of each other in what they consider their interest sphere, and concentrate on economic exchanges, trade and cooperation. There is considerable scope for cooperation between India and China in accessing and ensuring energy security (Huda 2020). There is also ample evidence of competition where China has more leverage than India, and finally there is potential conflicts related to the South China Sea and also the lack of real support from China towards India's wish to obtain a permanent seat on the UNSC.

## Concluding remarks

Seen with neorealist eyes, the bilateral relationship between India and China is characterized by an unequal trading regime and the two countries appear to be playing a chess game of containment and encirclement – where China supports Pakistan and tries to penetrate the Himalayan states of Nepal, Kashmir and Bhutan, while India in principle and symbolically supports Tibetan independence and acts in a protectionist way to keep Chinese encroachment at bay.

However, whether the glass is half empty or half full, this picture also aims to be a self-fulfilling prophecy as it is a way to counter those social and political forces who wish for a more balanced, cooperative and peaceful relationship and who see signs of rapprochement and collaboration not present before. The question is whether the political classes are ready to enmesh in a real strategic partnership and can bring the global alignment and solidarity from the BRICS alliance to bilateral and regional levels. The relationship between India and China has paramount importance in this regard and, "although the five BRICS countries do not share a clear and coherent foreign policy and also rely on different values there is a clear convergence on key issues related to 'multilateralism, anti-hegemonic actions and democratizing global governance'" (Harden 2014, 14; cf. Schmidt 2015, 135).

At the global level, there seems to be alignment in terms of cooperation in climate, trade negotiations and security-related issues, in some cases in tandem with Brazil, Russia and South Africa. Both countries share a profound interest as partners in strengthening a multipolar world and reforming the Bretton Woods system. The BRICS organization is also one of the main reasons why the Western developed countries are rapidly losing global market shares in exports and it remains a major challenge to the EU's and US' industrial competitiveness.

However, Indo–Sino foreign policy unity has not been pronounced when it comes to energy competition and this has been illuminated in the regional settings, but again not entirely. Numerous examples show it is possible to adapt to each other's needs and find new solutions like the creation of a new 'Asian security grid', and this presents a unique opportunity for Sino–Indian cooperation in the realm of energy security and climate change (Siddiqi 2011). BRICS, the SCO and bilateral agreements illustrate a keen interest in collaborating, especially in high-risk countries and vulnerable regions like the Middle East and Central Asia.

This is exactly why the comparison between India and China is so illuminating. China's main obsession is economic growth and the enhancement of the basic needs of poor people and the attempt to create equalities between social and spatial entities. With the BJP-led government and especially Prime Minister Narendra Modi's emphasis on a move away from non-alignment towards multi-alignment and the establishing of strategic alliances (Mohan 2015b) – in BRICS and the SCO but also with Japan and the United States – there can be no doubt about the precedence of geo-economics in both India and China's overall foreign policies, while political conditionalities are of less importance or even irrelevant. It is still not uninteresting to note the overlapping interests between the two entities in terms of focus on development first and mercantilism as a strategy to rise in the world system, very well illustrated by the overall comparative advantage of the BRICS group and PM Modi's approach, which relies on what Indian observers call 'uber-pragmatism with business acumen' (Khandekar 2014, 2), trying to take advantage of the relatively liberal level playing field in global trade (Schmidt 2015, 136).

One important thing needs to be understood: the relationship between India and China is changing and will remain so both in the not so distant future and also in the longer term. These countries are *re-emerging* to their natural status as world and regional powers and their relationship will determine the future in both geo-politics and geo-economics globally. The most important question is whether Delhi and Beijing are ready to dissolve or at least de-emphasize territorial nationalism and thereby increase security at home and in the region. India's first prime minister, Jawaharlal Nehru, envisioned a China and India unified by a common history of exploitation by the West – a vision that he called 'Asianism', while the Chinese premier talked about how "Our two people's common interests in their struggle against imperialism outweigh by far all the differences between our two countries. We have a major responsibility for Sino-Indian friendship (…)" (Malone and Mukherjee 2010, 139). So, historically speaking, history is not without precedent. This is poetically illustrated by Liang Qichao, welcoming Tagore to China in 1924 (Mishra 2012, 218):

> Our old brother [India], 'affectionate and missing' for more than a thousand years is now coming to call on his little brother [China]. We, the two brothers, have both gone through so many miseries that our hair has gone grey and when we gaze at each other after drying our tears we still seem to be sleeping and dreaming. The sight of our older brother suddenly brings to our minds all the bitterness we have gone through for all the years.

## Notes

1 Comprehensive security refers to analysis about security that consciously avoids references to hypothetical enemies to facilitate dialogue (Radtke 2003, 502) and is focusing on both individuals and sub-state communities as well as national, regional and international issues. It also includes linkages between domestic and external security, and other forms of security including non-traditional issues with the latter being emphasized at the expense of traditional conceptions of national security.

2 The term 'BRICS' first appeared in a 2001 Goldman Sachs research team report that identified the most important emerging market countries for their clients. The BRICS countries represent one-quarter of the world's land mass across four continents and 42 per cent of the world population with a combined GDP of 24 trillion dollars in 2014.

3 At the 2014 meeting in Fortaleza, the BRICS decided to lay the contours of an alternative global order by establishing a strategic dimension to the alliance by decisions to set up a New Development Bank (NDB) and emergency fund, the Contingency Reserve Arrangement (CRA), to counter existing Western-dominated Bretton Woods institutions.

4 Naturally, the military-industrial complex in the United States to a large extent determines the importance of militarism in the world economy as a state capacity.

5 Although China has never supported or opposed India's bid for a permanent seat on the UNSC, Beijing's reluctance is related to its ties to Pakistan which would be jeopardized, and another factor is related to India's warm relations with Japan, an old foe of China (Kaura 2015).

## References


Baru, Sanjaya, The Influence of Business and Media on Indian Foreign Policy, *Indian Review*, Vol. 8, No. 3, 2009.

Bhadrakumar, M. K., An India-China reset is still possible, https://indianpunchline.com/an-india-china-reset-is-still-possible/, 12 September 2020a.

Bhadrakumar, M. K., Shutting the door to China is self-defeating, https://indianpunchline.com/shutting-the-door-to-china-is-self-defeating/, 1 August 2020b.

Breslin, Shaun, IR, Area Studies and IPE: Rethinking the Study of China's International Relations, Centre for the Study of Globalisation and Regionalisation (CSGR), University of Warwick, 2002. Accessed 17 July 2011 at www2.warwick.ac.uk/fac/soc/csgr/research/workingpapers/2002/wp9402.pdf/

Cox, Robert, Production, Power, and World Order: Social Forces in the Making of History. New York: Columbia University Press, 1987.

Cox, Robert, Social Forces, States and World Orders: Beyond International Relations Theory, *Millennium: Journal of International Studies*, Vol. 10, 1981.

Das, Runa, Postcolonial (In)securities, the BJP and the Politics of Hindutva: Broadening the Security Paradigm Between the Realist and Anti-nuclear/Peace Groups in India, *Third World Quarterly*, Vol. 24, No.1, 2003.

Doran, Charles F., Systems in Crisis: New Imperatives of High Politics at Century's End. Cambridge: Cambridge University Press, 1991.

Doran, Charles F., Economics, Philosophy of History, and the 'Single Dynamic' of Power Cycle Theory: Expectations, Competition, and Statecraft, *International Political Science Review*, Vol. 24, No. 1, 13–49, 2003.

Economist, A Himalayan rivalry. Asia's Two Giants are Still Unsure What to Make of Each Other. But As They Grow, They Are Coming Closer – for Good and Bad, 19 August 2010. Accessed 19 August 2019 at www.economist.com/node/16843717?story_id=16843717

Eichengreen, Barry, Poonam Gupta and Rajiv Kumar (Eds), *Emerging Giants. China and India in the World Economy*, Oxford Scholarship Online: September 2010.

Frank, Andre Gunder, ReOrient: Global Economy in the Asian Age. University of California Press, Berkely & Los Angeles, 1998.

Frankel, Francine R, The Breakthrough of China–India Strategic Rivalry in Asia and the Indian Ocean, *Journal of International Affairs*, Spring/Summer, Vol. 64, No. 2, 2011.

Gatewayhouse, Chinese Investments in India, report no. 3, map no. 10, 1 February 2020. www.gatewayhouse.in/wp-content/uploads/2020/07/Chinese-Investments_2020-Final.pdf

Godwin, Paul H. B., Security Policy and China's Defense Modernization, in Allen Carlson and Ren Xiao (Eds), New Frontiers in China's Foreign Relations, Lanham, Maryland: Lexington Books, 2011.

Glosny, Michael A., China and the BRICs: A Real (but Limited) Partnership in a Unipolar World, *Polity*, Vol. 42, No. 1, 2010.

Haizhou, Huang, Go Deep Into the Nature of Sub-prime Mortgage Crisis. Paper for the Symposium on Building the Financial System of the 21st century: An Agenda for China and the United States, Shanghai 5–7 September 2008.

Harden, Bryant Edward, The Diplomatic Ambitions of the BRIC States: Challenging the Hegemony of the West, *Journal of International Relations and Foreign Policy*, Vol. 2, No. 2, 2014.

Hay, Colin, Political Analysis: A Critical Introduction. Basingstoke: Palgrave, 2002.

Huang, Yasheg, The Myth of Economic Complementarity in Sino-Indian Relations, *Journal of International Affairs*, Vol. 64, No. 2, 2010.

Huda, Mirza Sadaquat, Energy Cooperation in South Asia Utilizing Natural Resources for Peace and Sustainable Development. London and New York: Routledge, 2020.

Jakobson, Linda and Dean Knox, New Foreign Policy Actors in China, SIPRI Policy Paper No. 26, Stockholm, Sweden, 2010.

Kapur, Devesh, India and China Are Edging Towards a Serious Conflict, Financial Times, 14 September 2020.

Kaura, Vinay, China on India's UNSC Bid: Neither Yes Nor No, The Diplomat, 3 June 2015. Accessed 23 July 2015 at http://thediplomat.com/2015/06/china-on-indias-unsc-bid-neither-yes-nor-no/

Khandekar, Gauri, Modi's Foreign Policy Mantra: Geoeconomics, Regional Hegemony, Global Aspirations, Agora, Asia-Europe, nr. 17, November 2014.

Kitano, Mitsuru, China's Foreign Strategy, *Asia-Pacific Review*, Vol. 18, No. 2, 2011.

Kremer, Monique, Peter van Lieshout and Robert Went, Towards Development Policies Based on Lesson Learning: An Introduction, in Monique Kremer, Peter van Lieshout and Robert Went (Eds), Doing Good or Doing Better: Development Policies in a Globalizing World, The Hague/Amsterdam: Amsterdam University Press, 2009.

Kumar, Sushil, Power Cycle Analysis of India, China, and Pakistan in Regional and Global Politics, *International Political Science Review*, Vol. 24, No. 113, 2003.

Landsman, Stephanie, A Dollar Crash Is Virtually Inevitable, Asia Expert Stephen Roach Warns, CNBS, 15 June 2020. Accessed 20 June 2020 at www.cnbc.com/2020/06/15/dollar-crash-is-almost-inevitable-asia-expert-stephen-roach-warns.html

Maddison, Angus, The World Economy: A Millennial Perspective. Paris: OECD Publishing, 2001.

Malone, David and Rohan Mukherjee, India and China: Conflict and Cooperation, *Survival*, Vol. 52, No. 1, 2010.

Mishra, Pankaj, From the Ruins of Empire: The revolt Against the West and the Remaking of Asia. London: Penguin Books, 2012.

Mohan, Raja C., Beyond the Boundary, Indian Express, 11 May 2015a. Accessed 22 July 2015 at http://indianexpress.com/profile/columnist/c-raja-mohan/

Mohan, Raja C., Chinese Takeaway: Modi's Geopolitics, Indian Express, 7 July 2015b. Accessed 17 June 2019 at http://indianexpress.com/article/opinion/columns/chinese-takeaway-modis-geopolitics/

Mohan, Raja C., Energy Security and Indian Foreign Policy, in Ligia Noronha and Anant Sudarshan (Eds), India's Energy Security, London: Routledge, 2009.

Mohan, Raja C., India's New Foreign Policy Strategy, paper presented at a Seminar in Beijing by China Reform Forum and the Carnegie Endowment for International Peace, Beijing, 26 May 2006.

Mudambi, Ram, The Re-emergence of the Old World: MNCs and the Emerging Economies of China and India, *Journal of International Business Studies*, Vol. 41, No. 3, 2010.

Ni, Pengfei, Cities as the New Engine for Sino-Indian Cooperation, *Journal of International Affairs*, Vol. 64, No. 2, 2010.

Nikkei Asian Review, China and India to Make Up One-third of Global GDP in 2060: JCER, 25 January 2020.

Norbu, Dawa, After Nationalism? Elite Beliefs, State Interests, and International Politics, in Kanti Bajpai and Siddhart Mallavarapu (Eds), International Relations in India. Theorising the Region and Nation, Hyderabad, India: Orient Longman, 2005.

Rachman, Gideon, US-China Decoupling Has Only Just Begun, Financial Times, 18 August 2020.

Radtke, Kurt, Sino-Indian Relations: Security, Dilemma, Ideological Polarization, or Cooperation Based on 'Comprehensive Security'? *Perspectives on Global Development and Technology*, Vol. 2, No. 3–4, 2003.

Ramachandaran, Shastri, BRICS Forges Ahead With Two New Power Drivers – India and China, International Press Service News Agency, 17 July 2014. Accessed 27 September 2014 at www.ipsnews.net/2014/07/brics-forges-ahead-with-two-new-power-drivers-india-and-china/

Ramo, Joshua Cooper, The Beijing Consensus, London: The Foreign Policy Centre, 2004.

Saran, Shyam, BRICS – The End of Western Dominance of the Global Financial and Economic Order, IPS News, 24 July 2014. Accessed 7 May 2015 at www.ipsnews.net/2014/07/brics-the-end-of-western-dominance-of-the-global-financial-and-economic-order/

Schmidt, Johannes Dragsbæk, India and China in Comparative Perspective: Emerging Asian and Global Powers, in Kim Young-Chan Kim (ed.), China–India Relations: Geo-political Competition, Economic Cooperation, Cultural Exchange and Business Ties, Cham, Switzerland: Springer, 2020.

Schmidt, Johannes Dragsbæk, India's Rise, the European Union and the BRICS. An Uneasy Relation, in Marek Rewizorski (ed.), The European Union and the BRICS: Complex Relations in the Era of Global Governance, Berlin: Springer, 2015.

Schmidt, Johannes Dragsbæk, The Asia-Pacific Strategic Triangle: Unentangling the India, China, US Relations on Conflict and Security in South Asia, *Journal of Asian Security and International Affairs*, Vol. 1, No. 2, 2014a.

Schmidt, Johannes Dragsbæk, India China Encroachment and Positioning in Southeast Asia, in Jakub Zajączkowski, Jivanta Schottli and Manish Thapa (Eds), India in the Contemporary World: Polity, Economy and International Relations, Delhi: Routledge, 2014b.

Schmidt, Johannes Dragsbæk, A Cacophony of Crises: Systemic Failure and Reasserting People's Rights, *Human Geography*, Vol. 3, No. 1, 2010.

Schmidt, Johannes Dragsbæk, China's Soft Power Diplomacy in Southeast Asia, *Journal of Asian Studies*, Vol. 26, No. 1, 2008.

Schmidt, Johannes Dragsbæk and Jacques Hersh, Eurocentrism and Imperialism, in Zak Cope and Immanuel Ness (Eds), The Palgrave Encyclopedia of Imperialism and Anti-Imperialism, London and New York: Palgrave Macmillan, 2019.

Schmidt, Johannes Dragsbæk and Jacques Hersh, Economic History and the 'East Wind': Challenges to Eurocentrism, *Monthly Review*, Vol. 69, No. 9, 2018.

Scott, James, The Future of Agricultural Governance in the World Trade Organization, *International Affairs*, Vol. 93, No. 5, 2017.

Sharma, Ashok, India's Quest for Energy Security, The Daily Pioneer, 23 February 2020. Accessed 8 April 2020 at www.dailypioneer.com/2020/sunday-edition/india---s-quest-for-energy-security.html

Sharma, Ashok, India's Pursuit of Energy Security: Domestic Measures, Foreign Policy and Geopolitics. New York: Sage, 2019.

Siddiqi, Toufiq, China and India: More Cooperation than Competition in Energy and Climate Change, *Journal of International Affairs*, Vol. 64, No. 2, 2011.

Sornarajah, Muthucumaraswamy, India, China and Foreign Investment, in Muthucumaraswamy Sornarajah and Jiangyu Wang (Eds), China, India and the International Economic Order, Cambridge University Press, 2010, Cambridge and New York.

Stewart, Heather, Doha: India Accuses US of Sacrificing World's Poor at Trade Talks, The Guardian, 31 July 2008.

Times of India, India–China Bilateral Trade Hits Historic High of US 84.44 Bln in 2017, 7 March 2018.

Trachtman, Joel P., The WTO and Development Policy in China and India, in Muthucumaraswamy Sornarajah and Jiangyu Wang (Eds), China, India and the International Economic Order, Cambridge University Press, 2010, Cambridge and New York.

Tønneson, Stein and Åshild Kolås, Energy Security in Asia: China, India, Oil and Peace, Oslo: PRIO, 2006.

Williams, Paul, British Foreign Policy Under New Labour 1997–2005. Basingstoke: Palgrave, 2005.

# Part III

# Identity, migration and structural dimensions

# 8 Party politics and its influence over foreign policymaking in India

*Aleksandra Jaskólska*

## Introduction

The main aim of this study is to analyse party politics and its influence over foreign policymaking in India, with a special emphasis on the growing role of regional parties. To understand this process it is crucial to define and classify the party systems and describe their role in framing the country's foreign policy. The evolution of the Indian party system was one of the key factors which allowed regional parties to have a bigger influence over foreign policy decision-making. The Indian party system has evolved from a dominant party system to a multiparty system. The description of the legal framework of foreign policymaking helps in the analysis of the regional parties' attitudes towards foreign policymaking. The regional parties chosen for a case study are All India Trinamool Congress (TMC)[1] from West Bengal, Dravida Munnetra Kazhagam (DMK) and All India Anna Dravida Munnetra Kazhagam (AIADMK) from Tamil Nadu, Biju Janata Dal (BJD) from Odisha, Shiromani Akali Dal (SAD) from Punjab and Telugu Desam Party (TDP) from Andhra Pradesh.

## Party system classification

It is important to define the party system and to classify party systems before going on to a discussion of Indian party politics and its influence on foreign policymaking. According to one analyst,

> Parties make for a system, then, only when they are parts (in the plural) and a party system is precisely the system of interactions resulting from inter-party competition. That is, the system in question bears on the relatedness of parties to each other, on how each party is a function of the other parties and reacts, competitively or otherwise, to the other parties.
>
> (Sartori, 1976, 44)

The initial classification of party systems relied on quantitative measures of size and relative size. First, Duverger's distinction between two-party and multiparty systems was one of the most important analyses of the system (Duverger, 1954). Blondel also proposed four categories (based more on vote shares than seat shares): two-party systems (two-party share of 90% or more), three-party or two-and-a half-party systems (two-party vote share between 75 and 80%), multiparty systems with a dominant party (dominant party obtaining about 40% of the votes and about twice as much as the second party), and multiparty systems without a dominant party (Blondel, 1968). The classification of party systems according to Sartori is based on the number of parties vying to gain power. During the 1990s, Ware provided a schema which returned to using quantitative measures (Ware, 1996). According to Faurby, it is also important to underline that the number of parties does matter and is important for the way the system works. However, regular counting is not enough because not all the parties are equally important. Nevertheless, the numerical criteria cannot be used in isolation. Besides the number of parties, their ideological distances are very crucial for the party system. Two types of party systems can be distinguished: moderate pluralism and polarized pluralism (Faurby, 1979).

Many scholars, including Faurby, believe that the form of the government and the party system play their role in framing a country's foreign policy. The party system can influence foreign policymaking in particular communities, which evolve the system of activities for changing the behaviour of other states and for adjusting their own activities to the international environment (Modelski, 1962). In multiparty democratic systems like India, coalition governments often have to sort out conflicting viewpoints and interests. This may lead to avoidance or postponement of crucial decision-making on foreign policy. Political leadership also plays an influential role in framing the country's foreign policy (particularly in India). The role of the leadership depends largely on the party system. Government structure and societal realities constrain the qualities of a leader; however, during crisis time the leader often shows the path to the government and society. As Rosenau et al. write,

> A leader's belief about the nature of international arena and the goals that ought to be pursued therein, his or her peculiar intellectual strengths and weakness for analysing information and making decisions, his or her past background and the extent of its relevance to the requirements of the role, his or her emotional needs and most of other personality traits – these are but a few of the idiosyncratic factors that can influence the planning and execution of foreign policy.
>
> (Rosenau et al., 1976)

## National versus state parties in India

The Election Commission of India recognizes two types of parties: national parties and state parties, often called regional parties, though here both terms are used (Chhibber and Nooruddin, 1999). According to the Election

Commission of India,[2] a party is recognized as a national party if it manages to get a minimum 6% of the valid votes registered in any four or more states during the Lok Sabha (lower house of Indian Parliament) elections or the assembly elections in the respective states. Furthermore, the party has to win at least four seats in the Lok Sabha from a single state or more than one state. If that does not happen, it has to aim at getting at least 2% seats in the Lok Sabha (which means 11 out of the existing 543 seats). These 11 members should be elected from at least three different states.

A state political party, according to the Election Commission, should fulfill the following criteria to be recognized: the party has to get at least 6% of the total votes given in that state during the general elections or the assembly elections and the party should win at least two seats in the Legislative Assembly; or the party has to win at least 3% of the total seats in the state Legislative Assembly or a minimum three seats in the Assembly, whichever is more.[3] Most regional political parties have grown in the last three decades and have started to play a crucial role in state politics. Regional parties began to challenge Congress successfully at the state level from the 1960s onwards. This resulted in a greater number of non-Congress governments at the state level but did not make a significant difference to majorities at national level. It is only in the 1990s that the full significance of the regional parties for national politics became apparent. The inability of a national party to win a clear majority meant that regional parties became important partners in coalitions and electoral alliances. The strength of the regional parties also explained why national parties could not win majorities in the Lok Sabha (Chiriyankandath, 1996). In the first elections to the lower house of the Indian parliament (after India gained independence) in 1951/52, regional parties won 35 seats (out of 489), in 1957 – 34 (out of 494), in 1962 – 13 (out of 494), in 1967 – 36 (out of 520), in 1972 – 51 (out of 518) and in 1977 – 51 (out of 542). In the 1980 elections the number of seats for regional parties declined to 36 (out of 542), in 1984 they increased to 76 (out of 533), in 1989 they won 45 (out of 545) and in 1991 – 56 (out of 545). The elections in 1996 were crucial for the evolution of the Indian party system. The regional parties got the biggest number of seats in history, 137 (out of 545). In 1998, the number of seats for the regional parties increased to 161 (out of 545) and in 1999 to 188 (out of 545). In 2004, 159 (out of 543), and in 2009, 146 (out of 543) were won by the regional parties collectively. In the 2014 elections, state parties got 176 seats (out of 543) and in 2019 – 156 (out of 543) (Jaskólska, 2018).

## Evolution of the Indian party system

The evolution of the party system since India's independence can be divided into four stages: 1947–1967, domination of the Indian National Congress; 1967–1989, consolidation of the opposition and the emergence of a multi-party system; 1989–1998, a time of change; 1998–nowadays, formation of the coalition system. Congress was a dominant party due to the lack of similar potential in any other Indian party. The only party that could endanger Congress was the Muslim League, but after 1947 it disappeared from the political scene. After the death of the longtime leader of Congress, Jawaharlal Nehru (1964), the Indian National Congress began to be divided. When in 1966 Nehru's daughter, Indira Gandhi, became the new leader of Congress, unrest within the party began to grow. In 1969, Congress split into the Congress (R) faction under the leadership of Indira Gandhi and the Congress (O) faction (Wyatt, 1999). At that time also, the anti-Congress parties grew in strength. The change in the party system emphasized the end of the dominant party system in India. The emergence of the Janata Party, the party in opposition to Congress (Socialist Party, Bharatiya Lok Dal, Bharatiya Jan Sang, Congress (O)), won the elections in 1977 and changed the Indian political scene. Congress dominated and won every election till 1977 when the Janata Party got nearly 300 seats. Regional parties like Akali Dal (from Punjab) and DMK (from Tamil Nadu) were partners in the Janata Party government. This was the first time that regional parties shared power at the national level (Singh 2001). The 1977 elections not only sped up the demise of the Congress system but also inaugurated a new era of partnership between the all-India parties and the regional parties (Tully, 2007). The dominant party system could be replaced by a two-party system. However, it soon turned out that it was impossible. The Janata Party was too weak. The coalition was unstable and because of the earlier elections in 1980, Congress returned to power (Das, 2007). The weakening Congress was given an appearance of rude political health by a landslide result in the 1984 general elections but the sympathy vote in the wake of Indira Gandhi's assassination disguised its organisational fragility (Hewitt, 1989). India in 1989 entered into a phase of change. Analysts like Yogendra Yadav called the situation a "post Congress polity", which means that the Congress no longer dominated the political scene in India. The Bharatiya Janata Party (BJP[4]) and other parties (regional parties) became a challenger to Congress (Yadav et al., 2008). Congress began to lose support in the late 1980s. Muslims as a community felt less endangered than they had during the immediate decades after 1947 and decided to move away politically from supporting the Congress and seek the support of other parties. Business groups, the middle class, merchants and small entrepreneurs were also against state control over the economy, and the upper-middle class was against the Congress because its bureaucracy and socialist approach to economic development discouraged them (Tharoor, 2007). A large part of the middle class turned to the BJP. "Non-Congressism" brought many regional parties together in the National Front (NF) formed in 1988. The year 1989 witnessed the end of the Congress domination in Indian politics, which was unable in later years to rebuild its influence in the Indian political scene. The BJP emerged as the largest opposition party but its support was regionally limited and it could not make a convincing claim to be a national party. The political scene was very unstable during the following decade and a half. The V.P. Singh government survived only for 11 months (December 1989 to November 1990).

This NF coalition was led by the Janata Dal and included four regional parties. The BJP and the Left Front supported it from the outside. Learning from the Janata Party experience, it did not try to unify very different parties but put together a coalition of distinct parties based on a common manifesto. It brought in explicitly regional parties like the DMK, Telugu Desam Party (TDP) and Asom Gana Parishad (AGP), and the Left parties, unlike the late 1960s/1970s coalition experiments (Gowda and Sridharan, 2007). Then Chandra Shekhar succeeded as prime minister (November 1990 to June 1991) by breaking with the Janata Dal Party in November 1990 and forming his own Janata Dal-Socialist Party. With the support of Rahul Gandhi's Congress (I) Party, he was able to replace V.P. Singh. After Congress (I) withdrew its support he resigned. In June 1991, Congress came back to power initially with a minority government being formed by Prime Minister Narasimha Rao, who maintained his position for a full term, until 1996. Since 1996, however, regional parties have become indispensable in the formation of government at the national level. They have been important partners in the coalitions that came to power after 1996. Besides, the numerical strength of the regional parties has considerably increased, with a sizable vote share being captured by regional parties. Finally, regional parties have emerged in a large number of states. Atal Behari Vajpayee, leader of the BJP, was the leader of a coalition which gained power only for two weeks (16 May–1 June 1996). The next government, headed by Deve Gowda, remained in power from June 1996 to April 1997. A nine-party-led United Front (UF) minority coalition government was formed. Crucial outside support was provided by the Congress and most Left parties. The UF was a territorial coalition but had ideological coherence in terms of secularism, as its component parties and outside supporters were ideologically opposed to the Hindu nationalist BJP. The Congress withdrew support in April 1997, forcing a change of prime minister, and then again withdrew support in November 1997, precipitating early elections in February 1998 (Chandra, 2004). The experiment of the UF government first underscored the centrality of regional parties to national politics. This gave rise to the impression that regional parties were occupying the "third" space within Indian politics, outside of Congress and the BJP. I.K. Gujral, who was foreign minister in Deve Gowda's government, became the next prime minister (April 1997 to March 1998). In March 1998, an 11-party BJP-led minority coalition government based on a coalition consisting of 13 pre-electoral members (including three Independents) and one post-electoral member of the government, and 10 post-electoral supporters and three pre-electoral allies who opted out of the government, assumed power for a year (Zajączkowski, 2007). In October 1999, the 12-party BJP-led National Democratic Alliance (NDA) won a decisive victory and formed a minority coalition along with post-electoral allies, despite some NDA constituents opting to support from the outside. In May 2004, the nine-party Congress-led United Progressive Alliance (UPA) formed a minority coalition government with the external support of the four Left parties and two others, plus the external support of two pre-electoral allies who opted to stay out (Chandra, 2004). UPA ruled India for two full terms from 2004 until 2014. For the first time Congress was forced to create such a big coalition, beginning a new era for the party (Dixit, 2005). The Indian political system went through a big transformation, from a dominant party to a multiparty system, which perhaps was more reflective of a fragmented polity. The number of political parties since the first elections in 1952 has increased several dozen times. Since 2004, many researchers, including D.L. Sheth, have acknowledged that the Indian party system is based on a two-party coalition system (Sheth, 2004). In the last parliamentary elections, which were held in April and May 2014, the BJP won enough seats to rule the country alone (for the first time since 1984) as the other main national party, Congress, was badly defeated, leading to some commentators arguing that the era of coalition politics in India was over. In my opinion, it is too early to predict that. Significantly, even with a majority of its own, the BJP has decided to continue with its pre-electoral coalition, the NDA. In any case, though recently held elections in 2014 have brought into power a more stable NDA under the BJP, which has achieved a majority on its own, it still has to depend on the local parties for the passage of bills in the Rajya Sabha, the upper house of the Parliament, as the NDA does not have a majority in the upper house. The main national parties also have to depend on local/regional parties in different state-level and local elections, especially in areas where they are not powerful enough (Jaskólska, 2016). In 2019 BJP as a leader of NDA again won the Lok Sabha election with a majority, but in the Rajya Sabha the situation is the same as in the previous term.

## Institutional and legal framework of foreign policymaking

Formal institutions which have influence on the foreign policy of India include, among others, the prime minister, the Ministry of External Affairs, parliament and the political parties (Kohli, 1991). The Indian parliament tends to discuss only on issues and matters of great national significance like the possibility of war and crises at regional or international level or epochal policymaking changes. The government does not need to ask the parliament for approval of agreements and treaties. Members of parliament can request the prime minister or the foreign minister to give a statement regarding any international issue having influence on the foreign policy. Opposition parties can bring a no-confidence motion against the prime minister on any serious issues related to the country's foreign policy. The first prime minister of independent India, Jawaharlal Nehru, faced his first no-confidence motion after the war with China in 1962. In 2005, the Left parties withdrew support for the Manmohan Singh government on the issue of the India–US Civil Nuclear Deal (Ollapally and Rajagopalan, 2011). In 2013, the DMK pulled out of the Congress-led UPA coalition in protest against the government's position on a United Nations resolution on Sri Lanka's civil war with the separatist Tamil Tigers. The parliament can also have influence on the foreign policymaking of the country through various parliamentary committees. The Estimate Committee and the Public Accounts Committee, for instance, exercise influence over foreign policy through their control of finance to the Ministry of External Affairs. In 1960–1961, the Estimate Committee recommended reorganization of the Foreign Office and the missions abroad. The Consultative Committee of Parliament on External Affairs holds regular discussions on various aspects of the country's foreign policy, even though its conclusions or recommendations are not binding on the government. M.C. Chagla, the Minister of External Affairs in Indira Gandhi's cabinet, once observed that "The Consultative Committee is more of an agency for getting policies accepted and muting criticism than for influencing foreign policy" (Chagla, 2000). Overall, parliament provides free rein to the executive to formulate and implement the foreign policy. The respective governments also most often take the prudent approach of showing sensitivity to the opinions generated through parliamentary debates.

The Vajpayee government's refusal to join the US-led war in Iraq in 2003, for instance, was a result of the parliament's intervention, with the general opinion being against such participation. The cabinet in a parliamentary form of government should play an important role in creating foreign policy. In India, however, this principle works only in theory, as in practice generally the Prime Minister's office (PMO), especially under powerful occupants like Jawaharlal Nehru, Indira Gandhi, Rajiv Gandhi and Narasimha Rao, makes decisions mostly alone. The situation has changed significantly since the era of the coalition system. A.B. Vajpayee, for instance, enjoyed great autonomy of decision-making in the government of Moraraji Desai (in 1977–1979) in which he was the foreign minister. Similarly, Indra Kumar Gujaral could decide on the shape of India's foreign policy as foreign minister in V.P. Singh's cabinet (1989–1990), and in H.D. Deve Gowda's government (1996–1997), I.K. Gujaral replaced Deve Gowda as the prime minister for a very short period during the reign of the UF. Soon, he returned to serve as foreign minister in the government of Narasimha Rao. He no longer had as much autonomy as before, especially when it came to policy towards the United States, China and Pakistan (Zajączkowski, 2008).

The Ministry of External Affairs plays an important role in formulating and implementing the foreign policy of India. The Ministry provides infrastructure and necessary information and presents the recommendations and analysis that are necessary for decision-making. Until 1964 there was also a position of Secretary-General, who was an advisor to the minister of foreign affairs. This function was very useful to Nehru, who was not only the prime minister but also the foreign minister. The post of Secretary-General was necessary to coordinate the implementation of foreign policy utilizing several related departments immediately after independence. After Nehru's death, his successor, Lal Bahadur Shastri, decided to abolish this post. The Indian Ministry of External Affairs also has special units which have an impact on foreign policy, such as the Historical Division, the Policy Planning and Review Division and the Policy Advisory Committee. When Rajiv Gandhi became prime minister, Indian Foreign Service members began to play a greater role in formulating and implementing foreign policy. Prime Minister Atal Bihari Vajpayee created the post of National Security Advisor, who worked closely with the Ministry of Foreign Affairs, Ministry of Defence and Internal Affairs (Dugis, 2008–2009). The formal institutions that have influence on the foreign policy of India are still evolving and their coordination is often dependent on the personality of the persons holding ministerial posts.

The Indian party system has been through enormous change, from a dominant party system to a multiparty system. This process has clearly affected the foreign policymaking of India. The stages of evolution of the party system since India's independence can be compared to the phases of India's foreign policy. The formal institutions have not changed much since independence, yet the decision-making process is much more complex now than it was 50–60 years ago. Changes in the Indian party system are very dynamic (Zajączkowski, 2015). India will be facing new challenges in the coming years.

## Regional parties' attitude towards foreign policymaking

To understand the regional parties' attitude towards foreign policymaking it is crucial to analyse their influence on India's relations with neighbouring countries and on economic policy (especially towards foreign direct investment). Some of the regional parties focus mostly on their relations with their neighbours, others on attracting foreign direct investment. The parties chosen as case studies are the All India Trinamool Congress (TMC) from West Bengal, Dravida Munnetra Kazhagam (DMK) and All India Anna Dravida Munnetra Kazhagam (AIADMK) from Tamil Nadu, Biju Janata Dal (BJD) from Odisha, Shiromani Akali Dal (SAD) from Punjab and Telugu Desam Party (TDP) from Andhra Pradesh.

### *Relations with neighbouring countries*

For TMC, because of the geographic location of West Bengal, stable relations with Bangladesh and the Himalayan neighbours of Nepal and Bhutan are crucial. The dynamics of electoral politics, however, often lead it to criticize or oppose federal level decision-making over crucial issues in the region. In September 2011 when TMC was part of UPA, Mamata Banerjee refused to join Prime Minister Manmohan Singh in his trip to Bangladesh at the last minute due to disagreement regarding the Teesta River accord. M. Singh decided to visit Bangladesh without the support of the TMC leader. As a result, India and Bangladesh failed to sign an accord on sharing of the Teesta River water (Twining, 2015). There was also no deal granting India overland access across Bangladesh to its land-locked north-eastern states. Bangladesh expressed its "frustration and dissatisfaction" over the TMC leader's "sudden u-turn", which it said had kept the two countries from signing two very crucial deals (*BBC News*, 2011). The way the TMC's decision could have a major impact upon the federal government's decision-making was an indication of the growing influence enjoyed by the regional parties over crucial areas in governmental decision-making, even in so-called key areas supposed to be under exclusive central control like foreign affairs. In 2015, the chief minister of West Bengal decided to change her stance and support Prime Minister Narendra Modi during his trip to Bangladesh and subsequently agreed to the territorial settlement of the existing enclaves. Mamata Banerjee's decision to support Modi in his negotiation with Bangladesh was perhaps based on more regional and local political considerations. In June 2015, she joined Modi in his trip to Dhaka. India and Bangladesh signed an agreement to simplify their 4,000-km-long border and clarify the identities of 52,000 living in enclaves for over four decades after the neighbours first tried to untangle complex territorial rights. Of course, N. Modi had a very important role in signing the agreement, but it is important to underline the crucial role of Mamata Banerjee and the role that a regional player like TMC could play as a regional party in deciding crucial issues related to Indian foreign policymaking in specific regional contexts. Dhaka's Foreign Minister Abul Hassan Mahmood Ali described the deal, which has since been updated, as "a historic milestone in the relationship between the two neighbouring south Asian countries" (Chatterji et al., 2016). However, due to the lack of agreement between the central government and state governments on the division of the Teesta River waters, Prime Minister Modi failed to sign the agreement with Bangladesh, negotiated since the mid-1990s (Ganguly, 2018). Sheikh Hasina's government has been criticized once again by the opposition led by Khaed Zia of the Bangladesh Nationalist Party. In April 2017, Bangladeshi Prime Minister Sheikh Hasina was in New Delhi on an official visit. She met with Prime Minister Narendra Modi and TMC leader M. Banerjee. However, despite the negotiations, the meeting did not bring any effects on the signing of the agreement on the division of the Teesta River waters. M. Banerjee did not change her mind on the percentage of water distribution, which is unacceptable to Bangladesh. The TMC leader proposed dividing the waters of the Torsa, Sankosh and Raidak rivers during the meeting, but Sheikh Hasina did not want to discuss it until the agreement on the waters of the Teesta River was signed (Bagchi, 2017). In November 2019, Minister of Home Affairs Amit Shah met with Bangladeshi Prime Minister Sheikh Hasina in Calcutta. The meeting was also attended by M. Banerjee. The pretext for the meeting was the India–Bangladesh cricket match. The meeting did not bring a breakthrough in the negotiation of the division of the Teesta River waters. The position of M. Banerjee remains unacceptable to Bangladesh.

The other example of increasing involvement of local political parties in influencing the foreign policymaking process comes from the southern state of Tamil Nadu. DMK and AIADMK prioritized India's bilateral relations with Sri Lanka and its impact upon the large Tamil diaspora in that country.

One aspect of that was the tacit (and sometimes open protest) over the issue of discrimination and atrocities committed by the Sri Lankan state on the local Tamils. There was little local support for the Indian Peace Keeping Force (IPKF), which was sent to Sri Lanka by the Indian government following the Rajiv Gandhi–Jayewardene Peace Agreement of 1987. The IPKF, in fact, was withdrawn from Sri Lanka after the Congress lost the elections in 1989–1990 as the DMK played a major role in the new coalition government. There was often tacit and open popular support for the Sri Lankan Tamils' demand for a separate homeland or the "Tamil Eelam", though popular support for the terror organizations like the Liberation Tigers of Tamil Eelam (LTTE) dissipated with the discovery of their involvement in the assassination of Rajiv Gandhi in 1991 (Ghosh, 1999). The civil war and crushing of the LTTE in the 1990s and the numerous complaints of human rights violations committed by the Sinhalese forces, however, continued to keep the case of the Sri Lankan Tamils a popular issue in Tamil Nadu politics. Both Tamil parties have been demanding that India vote in favour of the US-sponsored United Nations resolution on Sri Lanka's civil war with the separatist Tamil Tigers which ended in 2009. Karunanidhi and Jayalalithaa also demanded amendments in the resolution by adding words like "Eelam" and "genocide" (Mishra and Miklian, 2016). Under pressure from the Tamil parties, India voted in favour of the resolution in 2012 and 2013, but did not insist on changing the text of it. It was a change in India's strategy, because before India usually did not vote in country-specific resolutions. DMK and AIADMK also demanded that the Indian prime minister should not take part in the Commonwealth Heads of Government Meeting (CHOGM) in Colombo in 2013 (*Times of India*, 2013). The Ministry of External Affairs and the prime minister's advisers believed it was necessary to attend the meeting. They made numerous arguments, including the fear that Sri Lanka would be more vulnerable to Chinese influence without Indian support. Furthermore, they expressed concern that not attending the meeting would negatively affect relations with the government in Colombo, which would make it difficult for India to ensure the security of Sri Lanka's Tamil minority. However, due to pressure from the Tamil parties, especially DMK, which threatened to withdraw from the UPA coalition, Prime Minister M. Singh did not participate in CHOGM (Pattanaik, 2014). Nevertheless, DMK in 2013 pulled out of the Congress-led UPA coalition. The DMK leader explained that the Indian government did not do enough to fight for justice for the Tamil minority in Sri Lanka. The DMK had 18 seats in the Lok Sabha and five ministers in the UPA cabinet. The ruling UPA coalition was already in a minority, but the crucial external support of regional powerhouses the Bahujan Samaj Party and the Samajwadi Party meant it was not in danger of collapse and so managed to survive (Malik and Malik, 2014). In another vote in the UN which took place in 2014, India abstained from voting, returning to its previous tactics in such cases. At that time, the DMK was not part of the UPA and the stability of the coalition did not depend on its support (Blarel, 2019). It is worth noting that the post-2014 Tamil parties still use the events of 2009 to gain support among voters in Tamil Nadu and influence politics on a central level. Party members and leaders blame each other for not doing enough for the Tamil minority in Sri Lanka during the civil war and after the war was over. Both parties are still monitoring the situation in Sri Lanka. The leader of DMK, M.K. Stalin, expressed his concern that, in 2019, during the celebration of the independence of Sri Lanka, the national anthem was sung only in Sinhala. It was a custom that it was also sung in Tamil. The DMK leader requested Prime Minister N. Modi and Minister of Foreign Affairs S. Jaishankar to intervene in this matter to the President of Sri Lanka, Gottabay Rajapaksa (Manikandan, 2019).

SAD is involved in numerous initiatives which aim to improve relations with Pakistan. SAD focuses on building relationships with the Pakistani Punjab.[5] The Indian Punjab and the Pakistani Punjab have a regulated border with no issues of water division, which helps in building stable and long-term cooperation. Unfortunately, unsolved conflict in Kashmir from time to time stops the implementation of joint initiatives and has a negative impact on relations between the two Punjabs (Ayres, 2005). However, SAD members strive to overcome these difficulties and influence the central government's policy to establish as good relations with Pakistan as possible. Chief Minister of India's Punjab, Prakash Singh Badal (SAD leader), in 1999, during Prime Minister Vajpayee's trip to Pakistan, coordinated negotiations to improve trade and the maintenance of Sikh temples in Pakistan. In 2004, next Chief Minister Amarindar Singh announced the establishment of the World Punjabi Centre in Patiala, whose aim was to promote trade between the Punjabs. In the same year, The All-Punjab Games were held, attended by over 700 athletes from Indian and Pakistani Punjab (Ayres, 2005). The next competition was supposed to be held in 2005 in Pakistani Punjab, but was cancelled due to the Kashmir earthquake (Muradlidhar Reddy, 2005). Amarinder Singh collaborated with his Pakistani counterpart Chaudhry Pervaiz Elahi. Thanks to their efforts and the support of the central government, in 2006 the Amritsar–Nankana Sahib bus route started operating (Kormoll, 2019). When Parkash Singh Badal became chief minister for a second time he continued the policy of his predecessor. Badal's deputy, Sukhbir Badal, was in Pakistan in 2012 and discussed issues related to economic cooperation between the two Punjabs. The most important result of the meeting was the establishment of a joint Business Council, whose task was to establish common industrial zones, organize joint business conferences and intensify economic cooperation. Also in 2012, a new checkpoint Weighth-Attari was opened. It enabled cultural promotion, intensification of scientific and economic cooperation and the signing of further agreements to facilitate cross-border trade (Maini, 2012). A year after the start of the checkpoint, exports to Pakistan increased to USD 1.84 billion, an increase of 19%, and imports from Pakistan amounted to USD 523 million, an increase of 28%. Total trade was USD 2.4 billion, an increase of 21%. The director of the India–Pakistan Chamber of Commerce and Industry (IPCCI), S.M. Munir, has repeatedly emphasized the importance of Punjab for relations between

India and Pakistan and the intensification of economic cooperation. IPCCI is lobbying for the reopening of all border crossings that operated before 1965 (Maini, 2017). IPCCI's demand had SAD support.

### *Attracting foreign direct investment*

According to the Department for Promotion of Industry and Internal Trade (DPIIT), the value of foreign direct investment in West Bengal in 2000–2019 was USD 58.5 million. The state is the largest vegetable producer, but it still needs large amounts of investment and know-how. Other sectors in which West Bengal is at the forefront are leather manufacturing, finishing, tea production, steel ore mining, metallurgy and textiles. This means that in these sectors, West Bengal is particularly interested in attracting investors. West Bengal, which was previously seen only as the cultural capital of India by investors, has become the preferred investment destination in the last decade. With over 100 million inhabitants and over 300 million in East and Northeast India, the state is an ideal investment destination for companies that want to establish themselves not only in this part of India but also in Southeast Asia. The state has improved its infrastructure, proposed clearer regulations and offers more skilled workers. In addition, the attractiveness for investors of West Bengal and the Northeast states will increase due to the planned opening of the deep port in Tripura and the Amritsar–Kolkata Industrial Corridor, which is part of the infrastructure development programme in East India (Eastern Dedicated Freight Corridor) (*Business Today*, 2019). Since 2011, the chief minister of West Bengal, TMC leader M. Banerjee, has made official trips to Great Britain, Germany, Italy and Singapore in search of foreign direct investment. The goal of TMC is to promote the image of the state as an investment centre (Sengupta, 2018). Despite this, in September 2012, Mamata Banerjee urged the UPA government not to open the retail market sector to foreign direct investment. Prime Minister Manmohan Singh refused to change his decision, which led to the withdrawal of TMC from the UPA II coalition in September 2012 (Sharma, 2012). The loss of the largest coalition partner resulted in the UPA government losing a majority in Lok Sabha and becoming a minority government. The opposition took advantage of this moment and, during a special session of parliament, demanded a vote of confidence for the UPA government. The UPA government remained in power thanks to the support of two regional parties from outside the coalition: the Bahujan Samaj Party (BSP) and Samajwadi Party (SP).[6] In 2016, M. Banerjee was against the opening of the pharmaceutical and agricultural sectors to foreign direct investment. The TMC leader stressed that she is not against the idea of foreign direct investment, but fears that foreign companies will dominate Indian brands, which will not stand up to the competition. However, in 2017, the TMC leader announced a new economic policy aimed at attracting more foreign direct investment. Mamata Banerjee repeatedly emphasized that the organization of economic summits and other initiatives to encourage companies from outside India to invest is a very important part of the state government's policy. An example is the Bengal Global Business Summit organized since 2015.[7] TMC also promotes the creation of technology parks to attract investors. Currently existing parks in Panagarh, Goaltore, Vidyasagar and Haringhata had to be modernized. West Bengal Industrial Development Corporation (WBIDC) obtained additional funds to send and receive economic missions.[8] WBIDC is also expected to work more closely with the Federation of Indian Chambers of Commerce and Industry and the Associated Chambers of Commerce of India, which will attract larger investments to West Bengal. Another change is that WBIDC representatives are to report directly to the chief minister of West Bengal, the TMC leader. It is important to underline that Chinese companies are an important partner for West Bengal. Mamata Banerjee hosted an economic mission from China in 2015, and the finance minister of West Bengal visited China in the same year. The TMC leader has been receiving invitations from the Chinese side since 2016, but the Ministry of External Affairs did not give her clearance (Das, 2018a). The trip was supposed to take place in 2017, but due to the dispute over the Doklam plateau, the visit was cancelled. In 2018, M. Banerjee cancelled her trip to China just hours before her scheduled departure. China issued another invitation to the prime minister of West Bengal. However, the visit did not take place (Das, 2018b).

According to the Department for Promotion of Industry and Internal Trade (DPIIT), the value of Andhra Pradesh's foreign direct investment in 2000–2019 was USD 18.98 billion. The key sectors in which the state attracts investments are IT, drug production, silk production, agriculture, fishing and mining (Andhra Pradesh has India's largest natural gas reserves). TDP leader Chandrababu Naidu was one of the first chief ministers to use opportunities given by the central government to attract more foreign direct investment. The TDP leader emphasizes that the priority is the economic development of the state, which is directly related to attracting new domestic and foreign investors. The party assumes significant expenses in the state budget for the development of infrastructure and technology parks, and plans to create new special economic zones (Tiwari, 2018). An important part of the strategy is also the development of the so-called IT Corridors, between the cities of Hyderabad and Bangalore among others, which will affect the development of cities such as Kurnool and Anantapur. TDP also proposes the development of the textile sector (Prakasam, Guntur and Krishna), cement plants and ironworks (YSR Kadapa, Kurnool and Anantpur), the automotive industry (Krishna) and the production of solar panels (Anantpur, Chitoor and Kurnool). In the years 1995–2004, Naidu participated six times in the Economic Forum in Davos. Bill Clinton, Bill Gates and many others visited Andhra Pradesh. The TDP leader managed to create a so-called Cyber City in Hyderabad, where Microsoft was one of the first investors (Baru, 2002). In addition, he obtained funding and loans for state development from international institutions like the World Bank (Wyatt, 2017). In 2015 and 2016,

Naidu once again took part in the Davos Economic Forum. His son Nara Lokesh in 2015 made an unofficial trip to the US to obtain support and funds for TDP from the Indian diaspora. During *Make in India Week* in 2016 in Mumbai, Chandrababu Naidu presented investment opportunities that will be devoted to newly emerging technology parks, especially in the food processing sector. Naidu stressed that Andhra Pradesh has an advantage over many states in India due to a very well-developed infrastructure (road, rail, energy transmission) and a long coastline. Also in 2016, during a visit to the World Economic Forum in China, Chandrababu Naidu signed an agreement on a Chinese investment worth USD 1.5 billion in a fertilizer factory. In addition, Andhra Pradesh has signed a Memorandum of Understanding (MoU) for cooperation with Sichuan Province on cooperation in the pharmaceutical sector. In 2019, the state of Andhra Pradesh signed an MoU with Asia Pulp & Paper worth USD 3.5 billion. The state of Andhra Pradesh represented the Andhra Pradesh Economic Development Board, which is responsible for coordinating the state's economic growth through trade, foreign direct investment and strategic partnerships (*Outlook India*, 2019). Chandrababu Naidu, as prime minister of Andhra Pradesh, managed to take advantage of the changes resulting from economic liberalization to build his strong position and strengthen the TDP. For a very large group of voters, the economic development of the state has become inextricably linked with his person.

According to the DPIIT, the value of direct foreign investment in Odisha in 2000–2019 was USD 589 million. The state is a leader in the production of minerals and other fossil resources. The aluminium production sector, iron ore mining and the steel industry are crucial sectors for development of the state. Paradip is the second largest port in India in terms of transshipment capacity. The state capital, Bhubaneswar, was ranked first in the Smart City Challenge ranking. The state was the first to open the so-called Single Window for Investor Facilitation and Tracking (GO SWIFZT), which enables efficient service and assistance for investors. However, the beginning of foreign direct investment was difficult. In 2000, the BJD leader, Chief Minister of Odisha Naveen Patnaik, approved the level of 100% foreign investment in the mining sector. Odisha, which at the time was one of the least developed states but rich in minerals, came under the spotlight of several foreign investors, including South Korean POSCO and British Vedanta. In 2005, both companies signed letters of intent with the government of Odisha, represented by N. Patnaik, POSCO for USD 12 billion investment in the aluminium sector and Vedanta for USD 2.1 billion investment in the steel sector. The amount declared by POSCO was then the largest investment in the history of India. However, none of the investments could start due to the complications regulating the foreign investment policy. TDP wanted to cooperate with the central government to make changes in law to acquire land and to create the necessary infrastructure to ensure a regular supply for investments (Park, 2011). However, the process of negotiation was stopped by the Forest Rights Act in 2007, which made it impossible to make changes due to a breach of environmental regulations. The

Supreme Court of India initially backed the POSCO and Vedanta investment, but the Ministry of Environment issued a ban on further work on the project, based on a report it had received from a special working group set up to investigate the situation in Odisha (*Indian Express*, 2012). Due to the inability to implement investments, investors began to withdraw from the state (Koo and Davis, 2012). The Odisha government demanded the central government send a special group to investigate the case for a second time. The group gave a positive recommendation in 2011 (*Hindustan Times*, 2016). Conflict over the POSCO and Vedanta investment caused the state government to launch a *Save Orissa* campaign (*Hindustan Times*, 2010). N. Patnaik has accused the central government of policies designed to obstruct the state government's attempts to industrialize the state and create new jobs. In addition, he argued that central government (Indian National Congress), through its policy, sought to regain support from its traditional electorate, the tribal people who, due to investment, usually had to leave land on which they had lived for generations. According to the BJD, Congress only pretended to be concerned about environmental protection. Congress was seeking to discredit the actions of the state government in obtaining foreign investments such as POSCO and Vedanta. N. Patnaik emphasized that, in the neighbouring state of Andhra Pradesh, Congress supported foreign investment despite similar concerns about the protection of human rights and the environment. The state of Andhra Pradesh was then ruled by parties that supported Congress at the central level. In 2014, eight years after signing the letter of intent, both projects met all the conditions necessary to start the investment. But the execution of the projects was once again delayed by legal complexities and protests. Unfortunately, in 2017, POSCO and Vedanta decided to withdraw from their investment plan in Odisha. BJD is constantly promoting the state through various initiatives, one of which is *Made in Odisha*, which aims to attract domestic and foreign investors. The party promotes the aluminium sector and steel production. The BJD leader also allocated funds for the expansion of technology parks in Sambalpur, Rourkela, Cuttack and Koraput. In addition, BJD is planning investments in technology corridors and in the promotion of the film industry (Millennium City of Cuttack). Despite the state promotion programme, N. Patnaik also actively participates in central government events such as *Make in India Week* in 2016 in Mumbai. The TDP leader presented a Vision 2025 for Odisha's Industrial Development. He emphasized that, in order to achieve the assumptions of the plan for 2025, it is necessary to attract foreign direct investment and to open technology parks. Therefore, the state government fully supports the liberalization of the foreign direct investment sector.[9]

## Conclusion

The Indian party system has changed from a dominant party system to a multiparty system. The evolution of the Indian party system has had a significant impact upon India's foreign policymaking. Coalition governments were forced to sort out conflicting viewpoints and interests. Of course, this led to postponement and delay of the decision-making process related to foreign policy. To an extent, it requires greater convergence between policymaking at local and federal levels. However, that process would be a long-term one, with national parties increasingly having to create an inclusive agenda with regional parties through regular consultations and consensus building. The turning point in the evolution of the Indian party system was the end of the 1990s, when the coalition period in Indian politics started. The Indian National Congress was not able to win enough seats to form a government without needing to form a coalition. Congress' biggest rival, the Bharatiya Janata Party, was growing in power and finally won an election at the end of the 1990s but was also forced to form a coalition. The regional parties became very important players within the Indian political system. In 2014 and 2019 the BJP won enough seats to create a government but its decision to create an NDA government reflected the fact that the regional parties still play a very important role in the Indian party system. The empowerment of regional parties was reflected not only in their increasing presence within the corridors of power in New Delhi but also in their impact on the framing of crucial policy issues at the federal level inclusive of foreign policymaking. The regional parties extend a broad range of regionalist arguments. These surround invocations of regional pride and marks of regional identity. Regional arguments involve demands pertaining to regional culture, history and language. The demands for formation of a state or the inclusion of certain territories into a state are potent weapons of mobilization. For some of the regional parties, foreign policy was not a crucial part of their agenda but for some parties, particularly those located in border states or proximate to international borders, such as the TMC from West Bengal, SAD from Punjab or DMK and the AIADMK in Tamil Nadu and SAD in Punjab, the regional aspects of foreign policy were crucial as these often had local and regional impact. Trinamool Congress decided not to support Congress in its policy towards Bangladesh and later pulled out of the Congress-led UPA coalition. DMK decided to leave UPA because of its perceived insensitivity towards the Tamils in Sri Lanka. SAD from Punjab in the future may play a key role in India's cooperation with Pakistan if relations between states normalize. Other regional parties focused on economic policy, especially on attracting foreign direct investment, like TDP from Andhra Pradesh and BJD from Odisha. TDP is a success story of a regional party which managed to use the opportunity given by the central government to create a more autonomous economic policy. The case of POSCO and Vedanta illustrates how failure of the central government to cooperate with the state government can lead to investment losses. The central government did not have good relations with BJD and Patnaik, which translated into a lack of support for investments in the state. Odisha's example proves that parties that oppose the central government are discriminated against despite the fact that both the state government and the central government declare their support for attracting foreign direct investment. The regional parties' activities prove that party politics play an important role in foreign policymaking in India.

## Notes

1 Trinamool Congress has been recognized as a national party since September 2016 because it became recognized as a state party in West Bengal, Manipur, Tripura and Arunachal Pradesh. But in my paper I will focus on the Trinamool Congress' attitude towards foreign policymaking before September 2016.
2 The Election Symbols (Reservation and Allotment) Order, 1968, http://legislative.gov.in/sites/default/files/%286%29%20THE%20ELECTION%20SYMBOLS%20%20%28RESERVATION%20AND%20ALLOTMENT%29%20ORDER%2C%201968.pdf
3 The Election Symbols (Reservation and Allotment) Order, 1968, http://legislative.gov.in/sites/default/files/%286%29%20THE%20ELECTION%20SYMBOLS%20%20%28RESERVATION%20AND%20ALLOTMENT%29%20ORDER%2C%201968.pdf
4 In 1980 the Bharatiya Janata Party was created, which later grew into the biggest rival of the Congress.
5 Punjab was divided during partition in 1947. The mostly Muslim western part became part of Pakistan and the mostly Hindu and Sikh eastern part became part of India.
6 SP initially declared its opposition to opening retail trade to FDI (Malik and Malik, 2014).
7 See: https://bengalglobalsummit.com/ (access: 20.11.2018).
8 *West Bengal Industrial Development Corporation:* www.wbidc.com/ (access: 15.01.2020).
9 *Vision 2025 for Odisha's Industrial Development*, Invest Odisha: https://investodisha.gov.in/investible-projects/ (access: 12.03.2019).

## References

Ayres, A. (2005): "The two Punjabs: A cultural path to peace in South Asia?", *World Policy Journal,* no. 4.

Bagchi, I. (2017, April 11): *Bangladesh PM Sheikh Hasina rejects Mamata's plan, wants only Teesta*, "The Economic Times", https://bit.ly/3qLVTJy (access: 15.12.2019).

Baru, Sanjay. (2002): "Strategic consequences of India's economic performance", *Economic and Political Weekly*, no. 26.

*BBC News*. (2011, September 6): "Indian PM Singh ends Bangladesh trip without key deals", www.bbc.com/news/world-south-asia-14799350 (access: 24.11.2016).

Blarel, Nicolas. (2019): "Coalition politics and the making of Indian foreign policy: A new research program", *India Review*, no. 5.

Blondel, J. (1968): "Party systems and patterns of government in Western democracies", *Canadian Journal of Political Science*, no. 1/2.

*Business Today*. (2019, February 5): "West Bengal's untold story: An investment destination growing in stature, and significance", www.businesstoday.in/impact-feature/corporate/west-bengal-untold-story-an-investment-destination-growing-in-stature-and-significance/story/316813.html (access: 24.02.2020).

Chagla, M.C. (2000): Roses in December, an Autobiography, Bharatiya Vidya Bhavan, New Delhi.

Chandra, Kanchan. (2004): Why Ethnic Parties Succeed: Patronage and Ethnic Head Counts in India, Cambridge University Press, Cambridge.

Chatterji, R., Chaudhury, Basu R. and Banerjee, Basu P. (2016): "India-Bangladesh Connectivity: A year after Modi's visit", *Observer Research Foundation*, www.orfonline.org/wp-content/uploads/2016/06/ORF_SpecialReport_14.pdf (access: 28.11.2016).

Chhibber, Pradeep and Nooruddin, Irfan. (1999): "Party Competition and Fragmentation in Indian Elections: 1957–1998", in Ramashray, Roy and Wallace, Paul (eds.), Indian Politics and 1998 Election, Sage, New Delhi.

Chiriyankandath, J. (1996): "The 1996 Indian general election", *Royal Institute of International Affairs Briefing Paper,* no. 31.

Das, Gurcharan. (2007): India Unbound, Penguin Books, New Delhi.

Das, M. (2018a, June 19): "All eyes on China's reachout to Mamata Banerjee", *The Economic Times*, https://bit.ly/3gB2XE1 (access: 23.03.2018).

Das, M. (2018b, June 23): "Mamata Banerjee cancels her visit to China, says Chinese side could not confirm meetings", *The Economic Times*, https://bit.ly/3m62fQn (access 23.03.2020).

Dixit, J.N. (2005): Indian Foreign Service, Konark Publishers, New Delhi.

Dugis, V. (2008–2009): "Domestic political structure and public influence on foreign policy, a basic model", *Jurnal Global dan Strategis*, no. 2.

Duverger, M. (1954): Political Parties: Their Organization and Activity in the Modern State, Wiley, New York.

Faurby, I. (1979): "Party system and foreign policy in Denmark", *Cooperation and Conflict*, no. 4.

Ganguly, Sumit. (2018, March 8): "Modi's foreign policy revolution? In India, radical change is hard to come by", *Foreign Affairs*, www.foreignaffairs.com/articles/india/2018-03-08/modis-foreign-policy-revolution?cid=nlc-fa_fatoday-20180308 (access 8.03.2018).

Ghosh, P.A. (1999): Ethnic Conflict in Sri Lanka and Role of Indian Peace Keeping Force (IPKF), APH Publishing, New Delhi.

Gowda, Rajeev and Sridharan. (2007): "Political Parties and Democracy in India", in Ganguly, Sumit, Diamond, Larry and Plattner, Marc F. (eds.), The State of India's Democracy, Johns Hopkins University Press, Baltimore.

Hewitt, V. (1989): "The Congress Party system is dead: Long live the party system and Democratic India?", *Journal of Commonwealth and Comparative Politics*, no. 2.

*Hindustan Times*. (2010, September 4): "BJD rallies for Vedanta", www.hindustantimes.com/india/bjd-rallies-for-vedanta/story-iOavbHZ7KmrtIuVhhd7VJK.html (access: 22.06.2017).

*Hindustan Times*. (2016, December 24): "Govt fast-tracks plan to revamp urban infra, NDA-ruled states to benefit", www.hindustantimes.com/india-news/govt-fast-tracks-plan-to-revamp-urban-infra-nda-ruled-states-to-benefit/story-cjQyB5nLiVr0QRNCY7ptgJ.html (access: 22.06.2017).

*Indian Express*. (2012, August 27): "Odisha top destination for FDI in India", http://archive.indianexpress.com/news/odisha-top-destination-for-fdi-inindia/993878/ (access: 26.06.2017).

*Indian Express*. (2016, June 24): "Will oppose FDI, as it will kill Indian brands: Mamata Banerjee", https://indianexpress.com/article/india/india-news-india/will-oppose-fdi-as-it-will-kill-indian-brands-west-bengal-cm-mamata-banerjee-2872269/ (access: 23.01.2020).

Jaskólska, Aleksandra. (2016): "Influence of the party system on the foreign policy", Proceedings of 4th UBT Annual International Conference on Business, Technology and Innovation.

Jaskólska, Aleksandra. (2018): "Liberalna teoria polityki zagranicznej – studium przypadku partii regionalnych w Indiach", *Stosunki Międzynarodowe*, no. 4.

Kohli, Atul. (1991): Democracy and Discontent: India's Growing Crisis of Governability, Cambridge University Press, New York.

Koo, C. and Davis, J.T. (2012): "A study of disputes between POSCO and local communities on POSCO's steel mill development in India", *International Journal of Urban Sciences*, no. 3.

Kormoll, Raphaela Tabea. (2019): Practicing the International: India-Pakistan Relations in the Punjab Borderland. PhD thesis, Durham University, http://etheses.dur.ac.uk/13511/

Maini, T.S. (2012): "The two Punjabs one step more towards closer cooperation?", *East Asia Forum*, www.eastasiaforum.org/2012/11/14/the-two-punjabs-one-step-more-toward-closer-cooperation/ (access: 12.09.2019).

Maini, T.S. (2017, March 28): "The state of Indian federalism after the BJP's election victories", *The Diplomat*, https://thediplomat.com/2017/03/the-state-of-indian-federalism-after-the-bjps-election-victories/ (access: 12.09.2018).

Malik, F.A. and Malik, B.A. (2014): "Politics of coalition in India", *Journal of Power, Politics & Governance*, no. 2, pp. 1–11.

Manikandan, M. (2019, December 28): "DMK, PMK slam Lanka govt over decision to suspend playing of national anthem in Tamil", *Hindustan Times*, www.hindustantimes.com/india-news/dmk-pmk-slam-lanka-govt-over-decision-to-suspend-playing-of-national-anthem-in-tamil/story-fqgtKXA8wrPzLCmblxSumL.html (access: 15.01.2020).

Mishra, A. and Miklian, J. (2016): "The evolving domestic drivers of Indian foreign policy", *Norwegian Peacebuilding Resource Centre.*

Modelski, George. (1962): A Theory of Foreign Policy, Praeger, New York.

Ollapally, Deepa and Rajagopalan, Rajesh. (2011): "The pragmatic challenge to Indian foreign policy", *The Washington Quarterly*, no. 2.

*Outlook India*. (2019, January 9): "Andhra Pradesh gets India's largest FDI at $ 3.5 billion", www.outlookindia.com/website/story/india-news-andhra-pradesh-gets-indias-largest-fdi-at-35-billion/323257 (access: 23.02.2020).

Park, J. (2011): "Korean FDI in India: Perspectives on POSCO-India Project", *Transnational Corporations Review*, no. 2.

Pattanaik, S.S. (2014): "The Tamil Nadu factor in post-war Sri Lanka: Perspectives of Tamils and Muslims", *Strategic Analysis*, no. 5.Rosenau, J.N., Thompson, K.W. and Boyd, G. (eds.). (1976): World Politics: An Introduction, Free Press, New York.

Sartori, G. (1976): Parties and Party Systems. A Framework for Analysis, vol. I, Cambridge University Press, Cambridge.

Sengupta, S. (2018, November 26): "Didi's policy soars Bengal FDI fortune", *The Pioneer*, www.dailypioneer.com/2018/india/didi---s-policy-soars-bengal-fdi-fortune.html (access: 24.02.2020).

Sharma, R. (2012, September 24): "Mamata divorces UPA – but economic reforms may come of age", *The Diplomat*, https://thediplomat.com/2012/09/mamata-divorces-upa-but-economic-reforms-may-come-of-age/ (access: 24.02.2019).
Sheth, D.L. (2004): "The Crisis of Political Authority", in Vora, R. and Palshikar, S. (eds.), Indian Democracy: Meanings and Practices, Sage, New Delhi.
Singh, M.P. (2001): "India's national front and United Front coalition governments: A phase in federalized governance", *Asian Survey*, no. 2.
Tharoor, Shashi. (2007): India, from Midnight to the Millennium and Beyond, Penguin Books, New Delhi.
*Times of India*. (2013, March 25): "DMK, AIADMK want India to skip Commonwealth meet in Colombo", http://timesofindia.indiatimes.com/india/DMK-AIADMK-want-India-to-skip-Commonwealth-meet-in-Colombo/articleshow/19192257.cms (access: 12.03.2018).
Tiwari, R.K. (2018): Political Parties, Party Manifestos and Elections in India, 1909–2014, Routledge, Abingdon, New York.
Tully, Mark. (2007): India's Unending Journey, Rider, Kent.
Twining, D. (2015): "India's foreign policy toward East Asia and the neighborhood under Modi: Implications for Europe", *NFG Policy Paper*, no. 10.
Ware, A. (1996): Political Parties and Party Systems, Oxford University Press, New York.
Wyatt, A. (1999): "The fragmentation of political parties and the quality of Indian democracy", prepared for the ECPR Workshop: *Democracy in the Third World – What Should be Done?*, Mannheim.
Wyatt, A. (2017): "Paradiplomacy of India's chief ministers", *India Review*, no. 1.
Yadav, Yogendra, Shastri, Sandeep and Suri, K.C. (2008): State of Democracy in South Asia, Oxford University Press, New Delhi.
Zajączkowski, Jakub. (2007): "Ewolucja i wyzwania system politycznego w Indiach", *Krakowskie Studia Międzynarodowe*, no. 1.
Zajączkowski, Jakub. (2008): Indie w stosunkach międzynarodowych, Scholar, Warszawa.
Zajączkowski, Jakub. (2015): "Wybory parlamentarne w Indiach w 2014 r.: znaczenie dla polityki wewnętrznej i zagranicznej", *Stosunki Międzynarodowe*, no. 1.

## Bibliography

Ayres, A. (2017): Our Time Has Come: How India Is Making Its Place in the World, Oxford University Press, Oxford.
Bakshi, S.R., Sharma, S. Ram and Gajnani, S. (1998): Parkash Singh Badal: Chief Minister of Punjab, APH Publishing, New Delhi.
Bhattacharyya, H. and König, L. (eds.) (2015): Globalisation and Governance in India: New Challenges to Society and Institutions, Routledge, New York.
Bhuyan, Dasarathi. (2009): "Election politics and voting behaviour of Odisha: A study of fourteenth assembly election", *The Indian Journal of Political Science*, no. 1.
Brass, Paul. (1991): Ethnicity and Nationalism: Theory and Comparison, Sage, New Delhi.
Burakowski, Adam and Iwanek, Krzysztof. (2013): Indie. Od kolonii do mocarstwa 1857–2013, PWN, Warszawa.
Ganguly, Sumit and Pardesi, Majeet S. (2009): "Explaining sixty years of India's foreign policy", *India Review*, no. 1.

Hall, Ian. (2015): "Is a 'Modi doctrine' emerging in Indian foreign policy?", *Australian Journal of International Affairs*, no. 3.

Hall, Ian. (2019): Modi and the Reinvention of Indian Foreign Policy, Bristol University Press.

Hermann, Margaret, G. (1976): Circumstances under Which Leader Personality Will Affect Foreign Policy: Some Propositions, Free Press, New York.

Kolappan, B. (2018, August 18): "What next for the DMK after Karunanidhi", *The Hindu*, www.thehindu.com/news/national/tamil-nadu/what-next-for-the-dmk-after-karunanidhi/article24726900.ece (access: 23.01.2020).

Kothari, Rajni. (1970): Politics in India, Orient Blackswan, New Delhi.

Kugiel, Partyk. (2017): India's Soft Power: A New Foreign Policy Strategy, Routledge, London and New York.

Kumar, A. (2019): Electoral Politics in Punjab: Factors and Phases, Routledge India, New Delhi.

Pant, Harsh V. (2009): "Indian foreign policy challenges: Substantive uncertainties and institutional infirmities", *Asian Affairs*, no. 1.

Pant, Harsh V. (2016): Indian Foreign Policy: An Overview, Manchester University Press, Manchester.

Pant, Harsh V. (2019): India's Foreign Policy: Theory and Praxis, Cambridge University Press, Cambridge.

Pradhan, A. (2009): Naveen Patnaik, the Chief Minister of Orissa, Mintech Publications, New Delhi.

Prasad, Rajendra. (2004): Emergence of Telugu Desam: And an Overview of Political Movements in Andhra, Master Minds, Hyderabad.

Rajan, R. (2015): "Make in India, largely for India", *Indian Journal of Industrial Relations,* no. 2.

Ralhan, O.P. (1997): Shiromani Akali Dal, Anmol Publications, New Delhi.

Ramaswamy, V. (2017): Historical Dictionary of the Tamils, Rowman & Littlefield, Lanham, MD.

Ravishankar, S. (2018): Karunanidhi: A Life in Politics, Harper Collins Publishers India, New Delhi.

Reddi, A. Easwara and Sundar Ram, D. (eds.). (1994): State Politics in India: Reflections on Andhra Pradesh, M.D. Publications Pvt. Ltd., New Delhi.

Singh, B. (2016): "India's neighbourhood policy: Geopolitical fault line of its Nepal policy in the post-2015 constitution", *Journal of International and Area Studies*, no. 1.

Sridharan, E. (2018): "Coalition Congruence in India's Federal System", in Albala, A. and Maria Reniu, J. (eds.), Coalition Politics and Federalism, Springer, Berlin, Heidelberg, New York.

Subramanyam, P. (2007): "Regional Political Party in Andhra Pradesh: Telugu Desam – A Study", in Bhuyam, D. (eds.), Role of Regional Political Parties in India, Mittal Publications, New Delhi.

Tandon, Aakriti. (2016): "India's foreign policy priorities and the emergence of a Modi doctrine", *Strategic Analysis*, no. 5.

Wolpert, Stanley. (2000): A New History of India, Oxford University Press, Oxford.

Wyatt, A. (2010): Party System Change in South India: Political Entrepreneurs, Patterns and Processes, Routledge, New York.

Wyatt, A. (2015): "Tamil Nadu: Strategic Interaction and Alliance Choices", in Wallace, P. (eds.), India's 2014 Elections: A Modi-led BJP Sweep, Sage, New Delhi.

Zajączkowski, Jakub, Schottli, Jivnta and Thapa, Manidh (eds.). (2014): India in the Contemporary World: Economy, Polity, International Relations, Routledge, New Delhi, London, New York.

Zarhani, S. Hossein. (2018): Governance and Development in India: A Comparative Study on Andhra Pradesh and Bihar after Liberalization, Routledge Advances in South Asian Studies, Routledge, New York.

# 9 Differentiated citizenship

## Multiculturalism, secularism and Indian foreign policy

*Catarina Kinnvall and Ted Svensson*

### Introduction

In winning the elections in 2014 and 2019, a government dominated by the Bharatiya Janata Party (BJP) and headed by Prime Minister Narendra Modi has established itself as a dominant force in India. Contrary to expectations that India would not again, for a long time, be ruled by a single dominant party, the BJP – propped up by its intimate relations to the wider Hindu nationalist movement – has twice succeeded in gaining a majority in the Lok Sabha, the lower house of Parliament, with Modi being the first leader since 1979 to secure a single-party majority in back-to-back elections. This has not only taken India one step closer towards a majoritarian democracy, but has been accompanied by repression, violence and illiberalism, thus intensifying fears of India turning into an authoritarian state. Such developments have impacted on a range of domestic and foreign policy related changes, as one of the main tasks of the Modi-ruled government has been to enhance and change the image of India at home and abroad. A positive image has been a key ingredient for India's foreign policy makers in their attempts to make India an important player on the global stage, but it is also an image that is not possible to divorce from assertions of Hindu national identity. That foreign policy is related to national identity is nothing new and has, in the case of India, not been confined to the consecutively elected BJP-headed governments. Rather, national identity images are often at the core of foreign policy clashes between adversaries and have become a common presence in much diplomatic discourse.

Such foreign policy clashes have become particularly visible during the last few years. For instance, in December 2019, India and Japan were scheduled to hold a prime ministerial summit meeting in Guwahati. However, due to the protests in Assam over the issue of the Citizenship (Amendment) Act (CAA), the meeting had to be cancelled. Moreover, owing to the controversies related to the nature of the CAA, Bangladesh's Foreign Minister, A. K. Abdul Momen, also decided to call off his upcoming visit to India. Meanwhile, in Washington DC, India's Foreign Minister S. Jaishankar was slated to meet the Foreign Relations Committee of the United States' (US)

House of Representatives. However, citing the presence of Pramila Jayapal, a well-known critic of India on Kashmir, Jaishankar decided not to attend the meeting. India and its foreign minister came under a lot of criticism for not participating in the meeting. Besides, as the US approaches presidential elections in November 2020, managing the India–US strategic relationship also remains a challenge (Gurjar 2019). India's economic slowdown and a perceived majoritarian political turn have made it difficult for pro-India voices in the US to support the CAA, even if this has not entirely prevented Hindu nationalist diasporic groups from showing their support for Modi's policies (Bhattacharjee & Ulmer 2020).

These events bring together a number of public narratives that we wish to explore in this chapter. The *first* has to do with the relationship between policies at home and images abroad. This narrative concerns a shifting world order in which India has been perceived and perceives itself to be 'rising' and to represent the world's largest democracy, while also having to justify recent policies on citizenship and Kashmir, long-standing internal practices of violent suppression of secessionist movements, extensive human rights violations linked to caste-based discrimination and what, by now, resembles a civil war against the Maoists in Central and Eastern India. To what extent can this contradictory imagery be read as a form of ontological anxiety – regarding such things as integrity, unity and uniformity – in which the search for secure national boundaries assumes existential dimensions? This narrative takes as its point of departure the persistent residues of colonial state practices as these are related to current Hindu nationalist identity constructions and post-colonial anxieties.

The *second* narrative refers to ideas about a global Indian community. Here the focus is on the Indian diaspora where Hindu nationalists have a long history of devising a religion-specific nationalist agenda in order to reach out to the Hindu community abroad. As a narrative it is focused on the entwinement of foreign policy and national identity, especially as related to the debate on the desired relation between religion and secularism. How can we understand such entwinement as having its origins in cultural and religious concerns about Hindu identity and to what extent are notions of a shared 'Hinduness' rather than 'Indianness' acting as a guide to foreign policy? A *third* narrative concerns the place of India in regional affairs, which involves such matters as its relations to neighbouring states, projections of regional hegemony and leadership, and conceptions of India as a Hindu state that embodies and extends the lineage of a grand civilization. This narrative is specifically framed in terms of India's ambivalent relationship to Pakistan, its tendency to project blame for terrorist acts outwards and onto actors operating from neighbouring states and the territorial anxieties that arise along its borders with Bangladesh and Nepal. Proceeding from these, one must ask: how do imaginings of India's role as a regional pivot shape and affect foreign policy?

A *fourth* and final narrative has to do with the gendered aspects of the nationalist religion-specific agenda, as both 'mother' and 'father' have been attached to conceptions of India, at home and abroad. These effects emerge from a Hindu nationalism torn between tradition and an economic liberalism fused with realist power politics. What can a gendered reading of nationalist identity construction tell us about the governing of identity as a constitutive part of Indian foreign policy? Together, these public narratives highlight four features of Indian foreign policy: 1) the relationship between policies at home and images abroad; 2) the entwinement of foreign policy and national identity; 3) the extent to which 'Hinduness' rather than 'Indianness' has acted as a guide for foreign policy; and 4) the ways in which the capitalization of unease, fear and resentment – so-called emotional governance – have impacted on the formation of foreign policy. Even though, in the case of India, there has often been a discrepancy between influential notions of nationhood and the actual content of its foreign policy (Mehta 2009; Pant 2009), our argument in this chapter is that the latter, at present, is increasingly imbued with connotations drawn from the dominant party's ideational underpinnings, i.e. its Hindu nationalist tenets.

## Narratives of Indian exceptionalism

In recent years there have been a number of attempts made in international relations (IR) theory to de-essentialize ideas and concepts, such as 'foreign policy'. Hence, foreign policy analysis has gone from being preoccupied with rationalist orientations of pre-established states to being concerned with the discourses of danger that serve to discipline and thus constitute the state. In postcolonial terms it means to question the taken-for-granted desirability of the nation-state and its associated claims of self-governance, autonomy, self-respect and justice (Kinnvall & Svensson 2015), thus interrogating a Euro- and Anglocentric worldview where certain concepts – such as reason, progress and individualism – have assumed universal status (Bhabha 1990). The implications for nationhood, in India and elsewhere, have been well described by Reicher and Hopkins (2001: 51), who claim that 'if national mobilization depends upon national identity, then establishing identity depends upon embedding it within an essentializing historical narrative'.

It is within these essentializing narratives that Indian foreign policy must be approached in terms of a shifting world order. Under successive Congress-led governments, Indian foreign policy became concerned with non-alignment and strategic autonomy as cornerstones of the Nehruvian tradition of international relations. These were guided by a post-independence tendency to pursue secular redistributive and populist policies – not only domestically but also internationally, not least to counter the Eurocentrism involved in the legacy of the British Empire. To imagine another nation, as Chatterjee (1993) once suggested, a nation freed from the many imperialisms of the past, could mainly be done through the emphasis on 'Indianness' to guide policies at home and abroad. During the last two decades, such egalitarian and identity-based concerns have often been downplayed in favour of a foreign policy bureaucracy driven by economic growth and the preservation of national security. Due to this, India's foreign policy during Modi's tenure has been described as characterized by pragmatism rather than confrontation (see Hall 2015; Chatterjee Miller & Sullivan de Estrada 2017), which is a depiction that can be questioned – especially after the abrogation of Article 370 in August 2019, which eradicated the autonomy of Jammu and Kashmir and imposed a complete military lockdown.

The key traits of such alleged pragmatism have been identified as a focus on 'economic development, enhanced regionalism, improved security and greater "soft power"', which, at first glance, makes it congruent with foreign policy work of previous governments (Hall 2015: 250; see also Hall 2019a: 17; Basrur 2017). It is hence a pragmatism that is oriented towards transforming India into a global power (Hagerty 2014: 295) without it abandoning its insistence on the inviolability of sovereignty and non-intervention (Hansel & Möller 2015: 79; Hall 2013) and its commitment to the notion of strategic autonomy (Brewster 2015: 225; Pant & Super 2015). India has, accordingly, demonstrated limited desire to take on the role of realizing and maintaining global order (Narlikar 2013: 598), which is reflected in its curtailed commitment to democracy promotion in its immediate region (Stuenkel 2013: 347–348; Mehta 2011).

Until the re-election of the BJP and Modi in 2019, most observers seemed to be of the impression that the Indian prime minister – despite being guided by a Hindu nationalist imagining of India's place in the world (Hall 2019a) – had conducted himself with remarkable circumspection in the face of these seemingly set parameters, reassuring Muslims and other minorities about their place in Indian society, avoiding loaded or ambivalent language and stressing the building of bridges with Pakistan. However, this was overturned when India launched an attack at Balakot, inside Pakistani territory, in September 2019. The attack was a response to the killing of 40 members of the Indian paramilitary Central Reserve Police Force by the Pakistan-based Jaish-e-Mohammed militant group at Pulwama in Jammu and Kashmir. This is likely to reflect a doctrinal shift in the way India will handle what is regarded as 'Pakistan-sponsored' terror in the future (see Katju 2020). The clashes between Indian and Chinese soldiers in June 2020, on a ridge adjacent to the Line of Actual Control in Ladakh, similarly indicate such a shift towards a more belligerent propensity.

Hence, the more 'proactive' foreign policy strategy described by the then Indian Foreign Secretary S. Jaishankar in 2015 as constituting five 'innovations' in terms of statecraft – i.e. narratives, lexicon and imagery, soft power, the Indian diaspora, and the link between foreign policy and national development (Parameswaran 2015) – may be undergoing a significant change. The narrative dimension, Jaishankar proposed, could be found in efforts to link India's past sacrifices in the two World Wars to peacekeeping operations as well as to its endeavour to obtain a permanent position on the UN Security Council. The new lexicon and imagery refer to changes in policy, such as the

'Act East' policy or the image as a 'first responder' in humanitarian assistance and disaster relief. The use of a soft power approach highlights the country's culture and heritage – the International Day of Yoga, for example – while the Indian diaspora was to be mobilized and a more explicit link between diplomacy and international development efforts was to take place through various initiatives, such as the 'Make in India' enterprise. The seemingly new doctrine that is emerging is likely to be at odds with this 'proactive' strategy, even if framed in a similar narrative language. For instance, India's unilateral action to revoke the special status of Jammu and Kashmir was narrated by Modi as a grand strategy to usher in peace and development in the restive state (Mir 2020). Rather than bringing about peace and development, however, what has ensued is escalating tension and military confrontation between India and the region's other nuclear powers.

The above narrative about peace and development cannot be disconnected from the narrative of India as 'rising' and as the 'world's largest democracy' – a narrative that tends to correspond with domestic renderings of Indian exceptionalism. As part of this narrative, it is necessary to recognize how Indian foreign policy concerns and activities are shaped both by notions of India's exceptional place among 'great powers' (Mehta 2009: 224–225) and of equalling a grand civilization with deep historical roots (Chacko 2014: 329). Recurrent projections of 'India's responsibility and innate peacefulness' abound, in part as a way of making India distinct from Pakistan (*ibid.* 339–340). Reading this narrative from a postcolonial perspective, however, it soon becomes clear how it relies upon ideas of a uniform (Hindu) nationalist identity, an identity that is constantly being hampered by sub-national and ethnic attempts to challenge the idea of a strong, integral and totalizing nation-state.

Hence, the postcolonial narration of India as the world's largest democracy is open to critique due to India's problems with fulfilling and acting on this status in a uniform manner, i.e. across its entire territory and in relation to all its citizens. India's failed efforts to counter separatist challenges in Kashmir and in the North-East, its violent and inefficient suppression of Maoist militancy in Central and Eastern India and the widespread caste-based discrimination against *Dalits* in particular also impact on its foreign policy undertakings and on the way that it is viewed by other states and their citizens. In Kashmir, for example, the use of exceptional practices has for a long time generated 'an everyday experience of embattlement, of living life under occupation and under siege' for many Kashmiris (Hoffman & Duschinski 2014: 503). The revocation of Article 370 and Article 35A, followed by the domicile law in March 2020 which opens up for non-Kashmiris to buy land, were motivated by the BJP-led government as bringing about 'equality and dignity for all' (Al Jazeera 2020). However, the domicile law can be read as an attempt to change the ethnic composition to disadvantage India's Muslim minority by encouraging more Hindus to settle in the region.

In the case of counterinsurgency towards Maoist insurgents, there is a dual depoliticization at work in which the Indian state either portrays insurgents and their supporters as 'criminals in need of punishment or as poor *adivasis* ["tribals"] whom the state must care for and control using developmental measures' (Kennedy & Purushotam 2012: 857). Roy and Kumar Singh describe the application of extraordinary measures in certain parts of India as generating a 'regime of impunity [...] through a process of delay, deferral and denial of justice by the state' (2015: 321). Taken together, the Indian state's activities in regions where its monopoly of violence and its intactness as a nation-state are challenged have brought about entrenched grievances and far-reaching denigration of human rights, which tend to prolong, rather than end, these conflicts (Pogodda & Huber 2014: 447–448; see also Parashar 2019).

Using postcolonial analysis, it would not be erroneous to talk about internal colonization in such instances, within which nationalist practices act as privileging structures for domestic governance and control, all of which then become translated into foreign policy issues. Also, in all instances where India is engaged in challenges to its territorial hold and presence, we can see how a certain 'cartographic anxiety' informs state behaviour (see Krishna 1996: 194–195). Such territorial anxieties inform foreign policy in three ways (Mehta 2009: 216): it induces India to conceive of its place in South Asia in terms of 'pre-eminence', it brings about obstacles for India to negotiate territorial matters with neighbouring states – with one exception, namely the successful exchange of landlocked enclaves with Bangladesh, as discussed below – and it results in an unrealized yearning for cohesive identity. Hence the narrative of India as the world's largest democracy is challenged by India's evident history of violent imposition of rule, which often leads to the interruption and hollowing out of democratic practices, and of its incapacity to rule in certain parts of its territory. Others have similarly argued that India's potential rise towards becoming a responsible great power is hampered by existing domestic-level problems that tend to negatively affect how it is conceived abroad – which is ultimately changing the character of what has been described as 'brand India' or even 'brand Modi' (see Narlikar 2011; Gurjar 2019; Gupta 2020).

This narrative provides further evidence of how the postcolonial is reimagined through nationalist policies in which the internal other is often dealt with as if it was external – or to put it in the words of foreign policy – in which some of the legacies of colonial policies co-construct domestic and foreign policy. Here the 'Indian' notion of secularism has played an important part for *Hindutva*[1] politics and for transforming the term 'Hindu' into a set, monolithic category and a trump-card identity that overrides other identity constructions. Those who fall outside of and contest this idea of the majority family of Hindus are thus viewed as 'foreigners' or as imperfect patriots. Hindu nationalism, by clearly identifying and projecting unwanted traits of the self onto the other, has been and continues to be successful in its attempts to build majoritarian religious nationalism, a trend exacerbated by recent developments (Adeney 2015; Sud 2019). The traumatic experiences of the partitioning of British India in 1947 affected and deepened feelings of distrust between Hindus and Muslims. Such feelings have been further exacerbated due to the continuous conflictual relation between India and Pakistan. In many ways one can argue that the Partition has worked as a 'chosen trauma' (Volkan 1997; Kinnvall 2006; Svensson 2020) that is constantly referred to and validated in new contexts such as communal riots, the 1992 destruction of the Babri Masjid, the Kargil conflict in 1999, the 2002 Gujarat massacre, the Mumbai attacks in 2008 and the Supreme Court's decision in 2019 to allow the construction of a Ram temple in Ayodhya. To these examples can be added the annulment of Jammu and Kashmir's special status, the Balakot attack and the controversial changes made to India's citizenship legislation – an issue to which we turn more fully below.

## At home while abroad: narratives about the Indian diaspora and national identity

Such chosen traumas or glories have been particularly visible among the Hindu diaspora. With the shrinking of space and time, there is a revival of the local in the global context – not least perceptible among Hindu diaspora communities. At the same time, transnational migration also sparks intense emotions, including fear, nostalgia, anguish, exile, trauma and a sense of loss – i.e. a longing for the homeland on the one hand, and a need to adjust, assimilate or integrate and connect globally, on the other. This has had an impact on successive generations due to narratives told by individuals and parents in the family and in communities (Safran *et al.* 2009). Diasporas thus challenge traditional conceptions of territoriality and ingrained ideas of what is inside and what is outside a state at the same time as they both affect and are affected by transnational homeland organizations aiming to mobilize those living abroad while also influencing public opinion. This type of transnational action needs to be accounted for, not only in terms of nationalist organizations but also in terms of religious or other movements (Jaffrelot & Therwath 2007; Kinnvall & Svensson 2010).

The term diaspora is not unproblematic, however, as it may run the risk of homogenizing a diverse set of populations, thus disregarding internal inconsistencies and fundamental disagreement. The Hindu diaspora is no different in this regard as *Hindutva* leaders must insist on normalizing the particular cultural condition of being diasporic while downplaying divisions on the basis of caste, ethnicity, gender or religious intensity. Moreover, among certain individuals and communities, a sustained diasporic identity can result in civic and cultural estrangement, thereby exacerbating recourse to fragments of identity from a perceived place of acceptance and honour, an archaic homeland, increasingly romanticized and essentialized as the succeeding generations are born from the original diasporic families (Kinnvall & Nesbitt-Larking 2011; Pradhan and Mohapatra 2020). This is a particularly important point to make when discussing the Hindu diaspora as many of them indeed do belong to this so-called 'post-diasporic' generation (Kinnvall & Nesbitt-Larking 2011).

Indeed, for many of these young people, their relationship to India has been mainly through their parents' homeland affiliation and through return visits. According to Duval (2004), any conceptualization of return visits requires a deeper understanding of how individuals position themselves within the context of two localities where one refers to an external homeland, while the other refers to the current place or country of residence. The space created within such positioning is what Brah has termed 'diaspora space', as 'a point of confluence of economic, political, cultural, and psychic processes' (Brah 1996: 208). Prime Minister Modi has been careful to cultivate this diasporic space by providing a number of political, economic, cultural and not least psychological reassurances of homeland care.

Upon winning the 2014 election, the Indian Prime Minister spent the years leading up to the next election garnering the support and energy from Indian diaspora communities around the world. With the aim to turn every Indian into an ambassador, he made a number of passionate speeches in public places worldwide, such as New York Madison Square Garden, the Allphones Arena in Sydney and the Wembley Stadium in Britain. The message was clear in his repeated appeals to the diaspora community to contribute money, time and technical expertise to his signature programmes, including cleaning up the river Ganges, making India garbage free and building rural toilets. He also called upon Indians abroad to visit India every year and to boost the tourism industry (Lakshmi 2015). 'We are changing the contours of diplomacy and looking at new ways of strengthening India's interests abroad', said Ram Madhav, General Secretary of the ruling BJP; and, '[t]hey [the members of the Indian diaspora] can be India's voice even while being loyal citizens in those countries. That is the long-term goal behind the diaspora diplomacy' (Lakshmi 2015). The Modi government also decided to provide single identity cards to make it simpler for the diaspora to connect with the homeland, secure lifelong Indian visas and avoid checks at local police stations during visits, and also made it possible for Indians abroad to own land and for Indian citizens living abroad to vote in Indian elections. The rally at the NRG Stadium in Houston in September 2019, dubbed 'Howdy, Modi', can thus be viewed as an effective campaign rally, allowing Modi to be seen back home in a positive light, thereby consolidating his position as the most dominant Indian politician of his era.

Many have argued that India now has a prime minister who is more in tune with global diplomacy than his predecessors as he has been trying to court global investors, arguing that 'our regulatory regime is much more transparent, responsive and stable' (Pant 2015). The aim seems to be to effectively connect India's past with the nation's future. His outreach to the Indian diaspora is here viewed as key to his approach in foreign affairs, giving the diaspora a stake in the Indian economic regeneration. Indian expatriates were also among the staunchest supporters of his election campaign in 2014 and the remittances have been estimated to equal 80 billion US dollars a year, or approximately 3.5 per cent of India's GDP (The Economic Times 2018). India's booming high-tech industry has also benefitted enormously from the success of Indians in Silicon Valley, including those who have returned to India (*ibid.*). The 2019 election campaign saw an increase in election spending of almost 2 billion US dollars, with a significant amount originating from the Hindu diaspora (Hall 2019b). However, the new citizenship law that affords special treatment to non-Muslim religious groups fleeing persecution from three Muslim neighbouring countries has also created protests among a smaller section of Hindu diaspora communities. This has led the BJP to launch a social media push with the diaspora, circulating testimonies from 'persecuted minorities in Pakistan' who could benefit from the amended citizenship law (Bhattacharjee and Ulmer 2020).

These are but a few examples of how the current regime is making attempts to connect its policies at home to images of India abroad. *Hindutva* ideology and organizations have also become increasingly visible in many diaspora South Asian communities since the early 1990s. The *Rashtriya Swayamsevak Sangh* (RSS – the Association of National Volunteers) has established itself in some 150 countries, including sixty *shakhas* (branches) in the UK, while the *Vishwa Hindu Parishad* (VHP or World Council of Hindus) has become the central organization claiming to represent the entire Hindu world and a *Hindutva* world-view (Bhatt 2000, Mukta 2000). The RSS also operates under the label *Hindu Swayamsevak Sangh* (HSS – the Hindu Volunteer Corps) in the UK, US, Canada, the Netherlands, Trinidad and Hong Kong. In May 1990, the Hindu Student Council (HSC) was formed, and today it claims some fifty branches in universities throughout the US and Canada (Kurien 2007; Hindustudentcouncil.org 2020). The Council runs the Global Hindu Electronic Network (GHENT), which connects together more than a thousand Hindu websites, and supports the activist group American Hindus against Defamation – a group that protests against misuse and commercialization of Hindu deities (Kurien 2007). The HSS *shakhas* are evidence of the transnational reach of the Indian model of the RSS in the diaspora. The *Sangh Parivar* (the family of organizations created by the RSS) has transformed the movement into a network of transnational Hinduism by reproducing most of its structure abroad, and affiliates in both India and abroad swear allegiance to the same executive power.

There is also a strong educational aspect of the Hindutva transnational movement that is directly related to policies at home. In the VHP, young Hindus in the West have found an organization that is able to explain the Hindu catechism clearly. It has even sought to effect the rewriting of history textbooks, as was the case in California in 2005 (Jaffrelot 2010). The spread of Hinduism in the West is thus radically contrasted with the proselytizing activities of Islam and Christianity; '[i]n the Hindutva view, Hinduism does not convert others; instead, others are spontaneously turning towards Hinduism' (Bhatt 2000: 572). There is, as Swain (2015; see also Swain 2020) maintains,

> an intimate symbiotic relationship between the Hindu diaspora and Hindu extremism in India. The Hindu diaspora wants to undermine the

> secular and inclusive character of India and instead promote the notion of a "Hindu Rashtra". As long as Modi's Hindu nationalist credentials are intact, he will continue to be a rock star among his frenzied Hindu diaspora fans.
>
> (Swain 2015)

This emphasis on *Hinduness* rather than *Indianness* – both in relation to Muslim others and as a guide to foreign policy – is not only prevalent within the diasporic community, however, but is equally visible in India's relations to its neighbours, especially if read in a postcolonial vein.

## Narratives about India's place in regional affairs

It is noteworthy how India, in its immediate region, has struggled with being considered a 'benign hegemon' rather than a 'regional bully' (Hall 2012: 1096). This has, among other things, impacted on India's possibilities to portray itself as a regional leader and to be able to act on behalf of other South Asian states in global governance settings (Vieira & Alden 2011) – although it has, in most external impressions of it, shed the identity of being seen 'as a lumbering leviathan, severely constrained by extreme poverty and low growth rates' (Narlikar 2007: 984). Hence, the regional imbalances and state-level mistrusts in South Asia, and in particular the persistent antagonism between India and Pakistan, act as obstacles to Indian initiatives to, in a more global context, be regarded as representing the entire region. Instead, we find that India, in its function as an inadequate and reluctant regional pivot, continuously has to negotiate its place in a region that is characterized by highly conflictual state relations, the transnational expanse of numerous collective identity claims and state territories that represent liminal and thus contested border zones. Hence, the bulk of security threats that India is facing are not foremost global in character but stem from South Asia and, in particular, from the persistent oscillation and tension between autocratic and democratic tendencies in the region (Mehta 2011). The instability of the region is heightened by a lack of regional coordination, as attested to by the circumscribed role of the South Asian Association for Regional Cooperation (SAARC).

It might with accuracy be said that the conflict between India and Pakistan constitutes an 'enduring rivalry' – with a manifest dissonance between their respective concerns regarding 'regional preponderance' and 'territorial claims' – and as such it represents a 'particularly *dangerous* form of inter-state' dispute (Ahmad & Ebert 2015: 49–50; emphasis in original). A post-colonial reading would, however, suggest that much of the rivalry is impelled by incongruent conceptions of statehood and nationhood, and hence open to re-imaginings by the very actors involved. Both India and Pakistan came into being as sovereign states in August 1947 when British India was divided on the basis of the two-nation theory that conceived of Hindus and Muslims as belonging to distinct and irreconcilable nations. At the time, the notion of religious-based nationalism as the principal ground for postcolonial state-making in the region was foremost advanced by the Muslim League. Today, Hindu nationalists, who at the time were marginal and mainly irrelevant to decisions concerning a present and future India, cohere with this view of a unique nationhood for and of Hindus at the same time as they lament the betrayal of India's secular-minded 'freedom fighters' when accepting a partitioning of *Akhand Bharat* ('Greater India'). These ideas inform present-day diplomatic and strategic engagements with Pakistan.

It is evident that India evinces a strong predisposition to associate terrorism and 'asymmetric warfare' with agents based in Pakistan (Ogden 2013), and that this, at times, is being linked to perceptions of Indian Muslims as potential collaborators and as espousing Muslim rather than Indian nationhood (Svensson 2009). It is, in addition, apparent that India is constrained by the fact that it is difficult to assess and predict political developments in Pakistan, which reduces it to having 'an essentially reactive role' to events in the neighbouring state and severely undermines India's ability to engage in constructive diplomatic transactions (Grare 2014). Considering the future probability of acts of terror that have been devised by actors based in Pakistan, it is clear that India stands before a strategic dilemma regarding how to prevent and respond to these (Perkovich & Dalton 2015: 23). In the past, and perhaps most clearly in the case of the Mumbai attacks in 2008, India has decided to principally act in a restrained manner and through diplomatic engagements with Pakistan in order to avoid an intensification of existing tensions (*ibid.*). However, the Balakot attack proved this perceived restrainment policy wrong and instead attested to what an assertive BJP and a reactionary Modi at the helm were prepared to do. As the Foreign Secretary at the time, Vijay Gokhale, expressed it, 'in the face of imminent danger, a pre-emptive strike became absolutely necessary' (see Katju 2020). In this narrative battle, India's borders must be protected from the neighbour's 'terrorism and tyranny' (Sud 2019). Here India is portrayed as a 'righteous nation that will defend its borders against Muslim-majority countries, while magnanimously offering shelter to "*sharanarthis*", i.e. refugees looking for *sharan* or protection', through its new citizenship law (*ibid.*).

A counter-image to India's relation to Pakistan is that of exchanging landlocked enclaves with Bangladesh, previously a longstanding anathema for the BJP as it would amount to the severance and forsaking of intrinsic constituents of a 'Hindu homeland' (Jones 2009: 379). For the BJP it would mean an abrupt cessation of efforts to make these 'border spaces [...] part of national territory' (Dunn and Cons 2014: 95) and risk negatively impacting on the party's tough stance on illegal immigration from Bangladesh. The enclaves and their character as the nation's frontiers have been referred to as 'symbols of an incomplete and ongoing Partition', a partition that by outfits of the Hindu Right, including the BJP, is often spoken of as illegitimate and aberrant (Cons 2012: 528, 553–554). It was thus remarkable that India and Bangladesh, in August 2015, finally agreed to exchange the 162 enclaves that since 1949, when the Princely State of Cooch Behar became part of India, had existed in a stateless condition, with little or no presence of state representatives (Jones 2009). Another puzzling facet, considering that the agreement was effectuated while the BJP was the dominant party, is how it – in addition to a mutual transfer of territory – entailed a commitment to incrementally provide citizenship to the inhabitants of the enclaves (Shewly 2015: 14). It is notable that almost all of the enclave inhabitants, who numbered approximately 55,000 in total, 'decided to stay where they were and opted for a change in their citizenship' (Ferdoush 2019: 83). The exchange of enclaves, in other words, represented a rare antonym to India's usual insistence on territorial integrity.

The decision to commit to the exchange of enclaves does not become less perplexing if placed next to the aforementioned changes to legislation that sets the parameters for Indian citizenship. The Citizenship (Amendment) Bill was approved by the Rajya Sabha in December 2019. The new – highly controversial and widely contested – Citizenship (Amendment) Act (CAA) prescribes that persons deemed to belong to religious minorities in three of India's neighbouring states, i.e. Afghanistan, Bangladesh and Pakistan, will be exempt from having the designation 'illegal immigrant' ascribed to them and will be allowed to apply for naturalized citizenship after having resided or worked in India for six years. The CAA not only effectuates a situation where Muslims from these neighbouring states are treated differently than Hindus, Sikhs, Buddhists, Jains, Parsis and Christians, it also renders members of these religious minorities 'candidates for fast-tracked citizenship' (Gopal Jayal 2019: 35–36). The result is 'a pronounced deviation from the [earlier] religion-neutral conception of citizenship' (*ibid.*) – one that foremost negatively affects Muslims in Indian states bordering Bangladesh. It is evident that the CAA is largely the outgrowth of the BJP's promises – made as part of its drive to secure electoral support and to buttress its majoritarian aspiration – 'to "free" the state [of Assam] from illegal Bangladeshi migrants' and to concurrently afford 'Indian citizenship to all Bangladeshi Hindu immigrants' (*ibid.* 37).

It might, finally, be noted that the relations between India and Nepal have undergone significant change in the last few years. In the wake of the promulgation of a new constitution in Nepal in September 2015, a decisive step away from India's former 'open-borders policy' (see Mehta 2011: 104) occurred. In response to its ratification, a blockade of border crossings to India was imposed by parties and organizations, representing the Madhesi and Tharu communities, that conceived of the constitution as defective in terms of their guaranteed parliamentary representation and the federal structure that it laid the groundwork for. The Madhesis are often referred to as being of Indian origin and connected to India through cultural and linguistic traits (Cherian 2015) and the blockade – which happened right after the devastating earthquakes that took place in April and May 2015 – both reinforced an impression of Nepal's overreliance on India and increased public 'support to elites that favoured an anti-India sentiment' (Bhatnagar and Ahmed 2020: 9). The outcome was not only a growing 'anti-India public opinion', however; it also led to a deepening of Nepal's ties to and cooperation with China (*ibid.*; see also Hall 2019a: 123). While the background to a majority endorsement of the constitution in Nepal was marked by eleven years of civil war between 1996 and 2007, the undoing of monarchic rule, earlier failures to agree on a democratic constitution and a highly contested election result in November 2013, India's adverse and unenthusiastic reaction to it was described as 'panicked' and as equalling a 'hardline position' (Muni 2015: 18–19). From an Indian perspective, the new constitution failed to enact a sufficiently inclusive order and it was feared that the disturbances that arose in the border region might spill over into India (*ibid.* 17). The developments in 2015 represented a stark contrast to Modi's visit to Nepal in 2014 when he was invited to speak in the parliament and articulated hopes that the controversial India–Nepal Treaty of Peace and Friendship would be revisited (Cherian 2015; see also Tripathi 2019). The case of Nepal, with its turbulent recent trajectory from being a Hindu monarchy to a democratic state with an influential Maoist movement, hence represents an imbroglio for the presentation of Modi as a harbinger and guarantor of accommodative foreign policy change.

## Narratives about gendered national identity

The image of Modi as the founder of a 'new India', as a man of progress, development and anti-corruption market-oriented policies, represents both the male Hindu warrior and the saviour of 'Mother India' (Wilson 2013). Externally this new India will not be pushed around on the global stage, while internally it will be protected from the 'pseudo-secularism' espoused by the Congress Party and from the appeasement of minority groups. In this regard, Modi provides a cohesive narrative to a masculine state that is able to assert itself both internally and externally. His open rejection of the English-speaking elite in India becomes a way to improve Hindu pride as a response to ostensible Western dominance and resentment towards the upper classes. This masculinist state does not, however, only exert itself upwards and outwards, but also downwards towards the most marginalized groups in the Indian society, Dalit and Muslim women. Hence, Dalit women are repeatedly targets of sexual violence whenever their communities are challenging oppression and exploitation. Recent liberal policies, says Kabir (2014), have intensified Brahminical-patriarchal ideas of the Hindu Right, in which Dalit women and girls have no value, leaving Dalits and other exploited people even more vulnerable. Less than one per cent of the rape cases of Dalit women lead to conviction (*ibid.*).

Muslim women, in comparison, often become pawns in competing narratives of the secular state and religion. Hence, Muslim women constitute a highly politicized group in the Indian context by being subsumed and then made visible in the debate about minority rights versus minority appeasement, personal law versus uniform laws, secularism versus communalism and modernity versus communitarian traditions (Hasan 2000). The recent criminalization of the 'triple talaq' – through which a man can divorce his wife by uttering the word 'talaq' three times – in 2019 under the Muslim Women (Protection of Rights on Marriage) Act can be viewed as specifically targeting Muslim men (Krishnan 2019). Although the criminalization was supported also by Muslim women's rights organizations, it can be seen as yet another instance of Muslim women's rights becoming politicized in the battle between constitutional rights and religious customs. Supporters of the practice argue that the issue has deliberately been made controversial by Modi's BJP, saying that it is an attack by Hindu nationalists on Islamic faith and practice with the aim of homogenizing India.

Modi's claim that the criminalization of the triple talaq is an attempt to 'save the Muslim women' (from dangerous Muslim men) cannot be viewed apart from the Hindu Right's economic and social agendas, however, or from the idea of a Hindu masculinist state. Narratives of the Hindutva state, Wilson *et al.* (2018: 2) argue, have constructed women 'according to their social location as subjects and bodies to be protected, exploited, placed under surveillance, morally and socially policed or targeted by organised and state-sponsored violence'. The repeal of Article 370 can also be read in this light, in which the Indian state embodies and adopts the guise of a dominating masculinist nation-state and where Kashmir's feminized body and the domestication of dissent on the Kashmir question have normalized and legitimized state violence and the state's obsessive claims to possess Kashmir (Kaul 2018). The role of gender has thus been crucial to this masculinist sovereign state as it aims to protect Mother India from internal and external threats. Narrating 'the Nation as Mother' is connected to ideas about the birth of the nation, the real *Bharat* (India), a female that should be freed from external onslaughts by external others (e.g. Muslim, Christian or even Western others). This Hindu state, or *Hindu Rashtra*, can be conceived of as a gendered space of protection in both spatial and temporal forms; an authentic space that existed before the 'invasion' of the Muslims and before the colonization of the British (Sarkar 1999; Kinnvall 2006, 2019).

The victory of the BJP in the last two general elections under the leadership of Modi has spurred a number of inquiries into how this gendered space has worked to institutionalize gendered insecurities in BJP-dominated states. The violent targeting of minority women together with intensified surveillance and control over all women, including so-called 'moral policing' of young bodies and relationships, have happened alongside a rising tide of attacks on religious minorities (especially Muslims) and Dalits by Hindu far-right militias, vigilantes and mobs promoted and legitimized by the state (Wilson 2013; Kabeer 2014; Wilson *et al.* 2018). This surveillance of women's bodies is particularly noticeable in the 'love jihad' campaigns run by Hindu right-wing groups against what they say is a Muslim conspiracy to convert Hindu girls to Islam (Dixit 2014; Sarkar 2018). Such conspiracy theories are closely tied to narratives about a gendered Hindu nation and the threat of Muslims.

Using the revolution in communication, the *Sangh Parivar* has been able to manipulate language, symbols and ideas to control and change the mind of a section of the people with the intention of capturing political power. Such 'emotional governance' (Richards 2013) shapes the climate on both a national and international level by affecting the 'tone of the emotional public sphere' (*ibid.*). Recreating a past in terms of a singular and often linear reading of the nation, history, culture and people is a good example of this governing process. Hence the current leaders deploy a discourse which seeks to capture and organize the unease, fear and resentment that is felt among some parts of the Indian public, cleverly playing upon the 'risky' status of Indian Muslims to the Indian homeland (Kinnvall 2019). This seems to be particularly appealing to those segments of the male Indian society who are anxious about the future of India and discontent with liberal policies that advance the power of women and marginalized groups (Srivastava 2015). Modi has successfully utilized this connection between masculinity and anxiety by promising to restore Indian pride and bring order to the chaos of modern India. But he is also able to make emotional appeals to his 'humble background': 'I understand you because I am from among you', Modi told a rally in Gujarat (*India Today* 2014), thus playing into the concerns of a frustrated middle class. However, Modi's particular kind of emotional governance is also rooted in the resentment and anger directed towards the local political elite and the Westernization of society, as well as towards changed gender roles.

In this sense, a government who is facing increasing political pressure from anti-Islam political actors – as has been the case in India – can attempt to capitalize on these actors' rhetoric and depict particular groups of minorities as a security threat. A number of salient issues have emerged in India since Modi came to power that reinforce such readings. In late 2014, for example, Sadhi Niranjan Jyoti, a junior minister in Modi's government, stated publicly that Indians should 'decide whether you want a government of those born of Ram, or those born illegitimately' (Barry 2014). Although Modi distanced himself from her statement, he also sought to excuse her on the basis of her rural origins (Parth 2014). Shortly after assuming office, Modi also appointed a historian of mixed reputation, Yellapragada Sudershan Rao, as the new director of the prestigious and influential Indian Council of Historical Research. Among a number of controversial views, Rao holds that the two Hindu religious epics, the Ramayana and the Mahabharata, should be considered accurate accounts of India's past. Nationalist historians, Vijetha (2012) argues, have also sought to eliminate any critical examination of the epics from the university syllabus, with some success. These developments culminated in the decision by the Supreme Court in November 2019 to allow for the construction of a Ram temple on the site of the demolished Babri Masjid (Subramanian 2020; Varadarajan 2020). The persistence of Modi and the BJP-led government to change public narratives in a desired direction is evident in the new management techniques of the current government concerned with redefining the masculinist state on the international arena.

This state is believed to conform to and protect what is thought to be its feminine core – thus disregarding the multitude of internal voices not currently included in this master narrative.

## In conclusion

Narratives are most powerful when they provide paradigmatic truths, i.e. when they become perceived as natural, essential and given. As Patterson and Monroe (1998) have argued, such narratives constrain action as they create and maintain assumptions of what is thought to be canonical, ordinary and right in a specific context. The more institutionalized a narrative becomes, the more likely it is to remain unquestioned. Narratives are thus always about power in relation to political action or inaction, belonging and legitimacy. They are ultimately political as they 'affect our perceptions of political reality, which in turn affect our actions in response to or in anticipation of political events', implying that 'narrative plays a critical role in the construction of political behavior' (*ibid.* 315–316). The narratives discussed in this chapter all share a number of characteristics in relation to how Hindu nationalist behaviour affects Indian foreign policy.

They clearly show how it is almost impossible to conceive of Indian policies at home without taking into consideration the effects and images they create abroad. The idea that India is rising and that it concomitantly is the world's largest democracy is a powerful narrative image that shadows a number of repressive policies at home while enhancing a territorial anxiety that spawns a desire to clearly define and ascertain state borders. It is also an image that is promoted through a Hindu diaspora coming to terms with its insecurities and longings for an imagined past and future. It, in addition, becomes a powerful tool in India's positing of exceptionalism *vis-à-vis* its neighbours at the same time as it conceals its masculinist features.

Narratives about diaspora and national identity display a similar function. Such narratives are formed by a postcolonial anxiety that can only secure itself through exclusive national identity constructions. India is not only the largest democracy in the world, but also a democracy that has secured its internal and external borders through homogenizing what it means to be an Indian at home and abroad. By reducing threats to the nation as emanating from the outside, predominantly from Pakistan, there is an attenuated need for India to deal with inequalities and injustices within. Here the protection of Mother India then becomes a protection of only a subset of the domestic population, thereby ignoring the many voices that are viewed as sympathizers of the outside.

This is at the core of the narratives of India's place in regional affairs in which there is a tension between notions of a Greater India and of unquestionable regional primacy, on the one hand, and a respect for notions of non-intervention and sovereignty, on the other. However, each instance of territorial dispute between India and its neighbours actuates concerns regarding the perceived inviolability of Mother India. Such gendered perceptions display the emphasis on *Hinduness* rather than *Indianness* as a guide to Indian foreign policy and display the many ways in which Hindu nationalists have been able to capitalize on the unease, fear and resentment of Indian foreign policy. Emotional governance is thus at the heart of Hindu identity politics at home and abroad. Here India as the largest democracy is to act as a role model for the world, for its neighbours and for the diaspora, at the same time as it provides emotional justification of and appeal to a singular national identity that can oppress its internal others and, especially, its minority women. Emotions and foreign policy are hence closely intertwined and are most visible through national gendered identity constructions that aim to reconstruct a civilizational Hindu narrative at the expense of other competing narratives.

A civilizational narrative that tends to privilege discourses on religious rights – and particular Hindu and Muslim rights – is likely to ignore other right claims, such as those based on caste, class, ethnicity and gender, for instance. However, it is also likely to reproduce a governing process that makes religious groups appear natural, authentic and essential – thus ignoring religious diversity as well as those other groups who exist outside this narrative.

## Note

1 The term was used in V.D. Savarkar's work *Hindutva: Who is a Hindu?* (1923), where he argued that the Aryans who settled in India at the beginning of history constituted a nation now embodied in the Hindus. Their *Hindutva*, Savarkar claimed, rested on three pillars: geographical unity, racial features and a common culture.

## References

Adeney, Katharine, 2015. 'A Move to Majoritarian Nationalism? Challenges of Representation in South Asia'. *Representation*, vol. 51, no. 1, pp. 7–21.

Ahmad, Ishtiaq and Ebert, Hannes, 2015. 'Breaking the Equilibrium? New Leaders and Old Structures in the India-Pakistan Rivalry'. *Asian Affairs: An American Review*, vol. 42, no. 1, pp. 46–75.

Al Jazeera, 2020. 'Kashmir Muslims Fear Demographic Shift as Thousands Get Residency', *Al Jazeera*, 28 June 2020. Accessed at: www.aljazeera.com/news/2020/6/28/kashmir-muslims-fear-demographic-shift-as-thousands-get-residency

Barry, E., 2014. 'Indian Official's Firing Sought over Remarks'. *The New York Times*, 3 December 2014.

Basrur, Rajesh, 2017. 'Modi's Foreign Policy Fundamentals: A Trajectory Unchanged'. *International Affairs*, vol. 93, no. 1, pp. 7–26.

Bhabha, Homi, 1990. *Nation and Narration*. London: Routledge.

Bhatnagar, Stuti and Ahmed, Zahid Shahab, 2020. 'Geopolitics of Landlocked States in South Asia: A Comparative Analysis of Afghanistan and Nepal'. *Australian Journal of International Affairs* (online first).

Bhatt, Chetan, 2000. 'Dharmo rakshati rakshitah: Hindutva movements in the UK'. *Ethnic and Racial Studies*, vol. 23, no. 3, pp. 559–593.

Bhattacharjee, Nivedita and Ulmer, Alexandra, 2020. 'Four Months after "Howdy Modi", Some Indians Abroad Protest over Citizenship Law', *Reuters*, 27 January 2020.

Brah, Avtar, 1996. *Cartographies of Diaspora: Contesting Identities.* London: Routledge.

Brewster, David, 2015. 'Indian Strategic Thinking about the Indian Ocean: Striving Towards Strategic Leadership'. *India Review*, vol. 14, no. 2, pp. 221–237.

Chacko, Priya, 2014. 'A New "Special Relationship?": Power Transitions, Ontological Security, and India-US Relations'. *International Studies Perspective*, vol. 15, no. 13, pp. 329–346.

Chatterjee, Partha, 1993. *The Nation and Its Fragments: Colonial and Postcolonial Histories.* Princeton: Princeton University Press.

Chatterjee Miller, Manjari and Sullivan de Estrada, Kate, 2017. 'Pragmatism in Indian Foreign Policy: How Ideas Constrain Modi'. *International Affairs*, vol. 93, no. 1, pp. 27–49.

Cherian, John, 2015. 'Strained Ties'. *Frontline*, vol. 32, no. 22. Accessed at: https://frontline.thehindu.com/world-affairs/strained-ties/article7809710.ece

Cons, Jason, 2012. 'Histories of Belonging(s): Narrating Territory, Possession, and Dispossession at the India-Bangladesh Border'. *Modern Asian Studies*, vol. 46, no. 3, pp. 527–558.

Cullen Dunn, Elizabeth and Cons, Jason, 2014. 'Aleatory Sovereignty and the Rule of Sensitive Spaces'. *Antipode*, vol. 46, no. 1, pp. 92–109.

Dixit, Neha, 2014. 'Love Jihad': War on Romance in India: Hindu Right-wing Groups Run Campaigns Against What They Say Is Muslim Conspiracy to Convert Hindu Girls into Islam'. *Al-Jazeera*, 14 October 2014.

Duval, D.T., 2004. 'Linking Return Visits and Return Migration among Commonwealth Eastern Caribbean migrants in Toronto'. *Global Networks*, vol. 4, no. 1, pp. 51–67.

Ferdoush, Md Azmeary, 2019. 'Acts of Belonging: The Choice of Citizenship in the Former Border Enclaves of Bangladesh and India'. *Political Geography*, vol. 70, pp. 83–91.

Gopal Jayal, Niraja, 2019. 'Reconfiguring Citizenship in Contemporary India'. *South Asia: Journal of South Asian Studies*, vol. 42, no. 1, pp. 33–50.

Grare, Frederic, 2014. 'India-Pakistan Relations: Does Modi Matter?' *The Washington Quarterly*, vol. 37, no. 4, pp. 101–114.

Gupta, Shekhar, 2020. 'The World Has a Message for Modi: Brand India Is Severely Damaged'. *The Print*, 25 January 2020.

Gurjar, Sankalp, 2019. 'Three Challenges for India's Foreign Policy in 2020'. *Deccan Herald*, 31 December 2019.

Hagerty, Devin T., 2014. 'India's Evolving Nuclear Posture'. *Nonproliferation Review*, vol. 21, nos. 3–4, pp. 295–315.

Hall, Ian, 2012. 'India's New Public Diplomacy: Soft Power and the Limits of Government Action'. *Asian Survey*, vol. 52, no. 6, pp. 1089–1110.

Hall, Ian, 2013. 'Tilting at Windmills? The Indian Debate over the Responsibility to Protect after UNSC Resolution 1973'. *Global Responsibility to Protect*, vol. 5, no. 1, pp. 84–108.

Hall, Ian, 2015. 'Is a "Modi Doctrine" Emerging in Indian Foreign Policy?' *Australian Journal of International Affairs*, vol. 69, no. 3, pp. 247–252.

Hall, Ian, 2019a. *Modi and the Reinvention of Indian Foreign Policy*. Bristol: Bristol University Press.

Hall, Ian, 2019b. 'Howdy Modi in Houston: Why India's Narendra Modi Puts So Much Effort into Wooing the Diaspora'. *The Conversation*, 23 September 2019.

Hansel, Mischa and Möller, Miriam, 2015. 'Indian Foreign Policy and International Humanitarian Norms: A Role-Theoretical Analysis'. *Asian Politics & Policy*, vol. 7, no. 1, pp. 79–104.

Hasan Zoya, 2000. 'Religion and Politics in a Secular State: Law, Community and Gender', in Z. Hasan (ed.) *Politics and the State in India*. New Delhi and London: Sage, pp. 269–289.

Hoffman, Bruce and Duschinski, Haley, 2014. 'Contestations over Law, Power and Representation in Kashmir Valley'. *Interventions*, vol. 16, no. 4, pp. 501–530.

India Today, 2014. 'Narendra Modi's Meerut Rally Speech on Feb 2, 2014: Full Text'. *India Today*, 14 February 2014.

Jaffrelot, C., 2010. *Religion, Caste and Politics in India*. Delhi: Primus Books.

Jaffrelot, C. and Therwath, I., 2007. 'The Sangh Parivar and the Hindu Diaspora in the West: What Kind of "Long-Distance Nationalism"?' *International Political Sociology* vol. 1, pp. 278–295.

Jones, Reece, 2009. 'Sovereignty and Statelessness in the Border Enclaves of India and Bangladesh'. *Political Geography*, vol. 28, no. 6, pp. 373–381.

Kabeer, Naila, 2014. 'Grief and Rage in India: Making Violence Against Women History'. *Open Democracy Net*, 12 June 2014.

Katju, Vivek, 2020. 'After Pulwama, India Effected a Doctrinal Shift'. *Hindustan Times*, 13 February 2020.

Kaul, Nitasha, 2018. 'India's Obsession with Kashmir: Democracy, Gender, (Anti) nationalism'. *Feminist Review*, vol. 119, pp. 38–44.

Kennedy, John and Purushotam, Sunil, 2012. 'Beyond Naxalbari: A Comparative Analysis of Maoist Insurgency and Counterinsurgency in Independent India'. *Comparative Studies in Society and History*, vol. 54, no. 4, pp. 832–862.

Kinnvall, Catarina, 2006. *Globalization and Religious Nationalism in India: The Search for Ontological Security*. London: Routledge.

Kinnvall, Catarina, 2019. 'Populism, Ontological Insecurity and Hindutva: Modi and the Masculinization of Indian Politics'. *Cambridge Review of International Affairs*, vol. 32, no. 3, pp. 283–302.

Kinnvall, Catarina and Nesbitt-Larking, Paul, 2011. *The Political Psychology of Globalization: Muslims in the West*. Oxford: Oxford University Press.

Kinnvall, Catarina and Svensson, Ted, 2010. 'Hindu Nationalism, Diaspora Politics and Nation-Building in India'. *Australian Journal of International Relations,* vol. 64, no. 3, pp. 274–292.

Kinnvall, Catarina and Svensson, Ted, eds., 2015. *Governing Borders and Security: The Politics of Connectivity and Dispersal*. London: Routledge.

Krishna, Sankaran, 1996. 'Cartographic Anxiety: Mapping the Body Politic in India', in Shapiro, Michael J. and Alker, Hayward R. (eds.) *Challenging Boundaries: Global Flows, Territorial Identities*. Minneapolis: University of Minnesota Press, pp. 193–214.

Krishnan, Murali, 2019. 'Triple Talaq: Instant Divorce Ban Draws Mixed Reactions in India'. *Deutche Welle*, 31 July 2019.

Kurien, Prema, 2007. *A Place at the Multicultural Table: The Development of an American Hinduism*. New Brunswick: Rutgers University Press.

Lakshmi, Rama, 2015. 'Narendra Modi Urges the Indian Diaspora to Become an Extension of Foreign Policy'. *The Guardian*, 2 March 2015.

Mehta, Pratab Bhanu, 2009. 'Still Under Nehru's Shadow? The Absence of Foreign Policy Frameworks in India'. *India Review*, vol. 8, no. 3, pp. 209–233.

Mehta, Pratab Bhanu, 2011. 'Reluctant India'. *Journal of Democracy*, vol. 22, no. 4, pp. 97–109.

Mir, Tariq, 2020. 'What Was the Deadly India-China Border Clash Really About?' Al Jazeera, 5 July 2020.

Mukta, Parita, 2000. 'The Public Face of Hindu Nationalism'. *Ethnic and Racial Studies*, vol. 23, no. 3, pp. 442–466.

Muni, S.D., 2015. 'Nepal's New Constitution: Towards Progress or Chaos?' *Economic and Political Weekly*, vol. 50, no. 40, pp. 15–19.

Narlikar, Amrita, 2007. 'All That Glitters Is Not Gold: India's Rise to Power'. *Third World Quarterly*, vol. 28, no. 5, pp. 983–996.

Narlikar, Amrita, 2011. 'Is India a Responsible Great Power?' *Third World Quarterly*, vol. 32, no. 9, pp. 1607–1621.

Narlikar, Amrita, 2013. 'India Rising: Responsible to Whom?' *International Affairs*, vol. 89, no. 3, pp. 595–614.

Ogden, Chris, 2013. 'Tracing the Pakistan-Terrorism Nexus in Indian Security Perspectives: From 1947 to 26/11'. *India Quarterly*, vol. 69, no. 1, pp. 35–50.

Pant, Harsh V. and Super, Julie M., 2015. 'India's "Non-Alignment" Conundrum: A Twentieth-Century Policy in a Changing World'. *International Affairs*, vol. 91, no. 4, pp. 747–764.

Pant, Harsh V., 2009. 'A Rising India's Search for Foreign Policy'. *Orbis*, vol. 53, no. 2, pp. 250–264.

Pant, Harsh V., 2015. 'How Modi Is Transforming India's Foreign Policy'. *DailyO*. www.dailyo.in/politics/narendra-modi-france-germany-angela-merkel-canada-congress-make-in-india-rafale/story/1/3262.html

Parashar, Swati, 2019. 'Colonial Legacies, Armed Revolts and State Violence: The Maoist Movement in India'. *Third World Quarterly*, vol. 40, no. 2, pp. 337–354.

Parth, M.N., 2014. 'India's Narendra Modi Apologizes for Official's Remarks on Non-Hindus'. *The Los Angeles Times*, 5 December 2014.

Patterson, M. and Monroe, K., 1998. 'Narrative in Political Science'. *Annual Review of Political Science* vol. 1, pp. 315–331.

Pradhan, Ramakrushna and Mohapatra, Atanu, 2019. 'India's Diaspora Policy: Evidence of Soft Power Diplomacy under Modi'. *South Asian Diaspora*, vol. 12, no. 2, pp. 145–161.

Perkovich, George and Dalton, Toby, 2015. 'Modi's Strategic Choice: How to Respond to Terrorism from Pakistan'. *The Washington Quarterly*, vol. 38, no. 1, pp. 23–45.

Pogodda, Sandra and Huber, Daniela, 2014. 'India's Peacebuilding Between Rights and Needs: Transformation of Local Conflict Spheres in Bihar, North-East India and Jammu and Kashmir?' *International Peacekeeping*, vol. 21, no. 4, pp. 443–463.

Parameswaran, Prashanth, 2015. 'A "New Proactive" Indian Foreign Policy under Modi?' *The Diplomat*, 21 July 2015.

Reicher, Stephen and Hopkins, Nick, 2001. *Self and Nation: Categorization, Contestation and Mobilization*. London: Sage.

Richards, Barry, 2013. 'Extreme Nationalism and the Hatred of the Liberal State', in N. Demertzis (ed.) *Emotions in Politics: The Affect Dimension in Political Tension*. Basingstoke: Palgrave, pp. 124–142.

Roy, Anupama and Kumar Singh, Ujjwal, 2015. 'The Masculinist Security State and Anti-terror Law Regimes in India'. *Asian Studies Review*, vol. 39, no. 2, pp. 305–323.

Safran, William, Kumar Sahoo, Ajaya and Lal, B.V. (eds.), 2009. *Transnational Migrations: The Indian Diaspora*. London: Routledge.
Sarkar, Tanika, 1999. 'The Gender Predicament of the Hindu Right', in K.N. Panikkar (ed.) *The Concerned Indian's Guide to Communalism*. New Delhi: Penguin, pp. 131–159.
Sarkar, Tanika, 2018. 'Is Love Without Borders Possible?' *Feminist Review* vol. 119, pp. 7–20.
Savarkar, Vinayak Darmodar, 1923. 'Hindutva: Who is a Hindu?', an ideological pamphlet.
Shewly, Hosna J., 2015. 'Citizenship, Abandonment and Resistance in the India-Bangladesh Borderland'. *Geoforum*, vol. 67, pp. 14–23.
Srivastava, Sanjay, 2015. 'Modi-Masculinity: Media, Manhood, and "Traditions" in a Time of Consumerism'. *Television & New Media*, vol. 16, no. 4, pp. 331–338.
Stuenkel, Oliver, 2013. 'Rising Powers and the Future of Democracy Promotion: The Cases of Brazil and India'. *Third World Quarterly*, vol. 34, no. 2, pp. 339–355.
Sud, Nikita, 2019. 'Textbook Authoritarianism Is Played out in India'. *The Wire*, 30 December 2019.
Subramanian, Samanth, 2020. 'How Hindu Supremacists Are Tearing India Apart', *The Guardian*, 20 February 2020.
Swain, Ashok, 2015. 'Why Are So Many in the Hindu Diaspora Completely Taken with Modi?' Scroll.in, 17 November 2015. Accessed at: https://scroll.in/article/768946/why-are-so-many-in-the-hindu-diaspora-completely-taken-with-modi
Swain Ashok, 2020. 'India Must Stop Spreading Hindu Nationalism to its Global Diaspora'. *Asian Review*, 2 June 2020.
Svensson, Ted, 2009. 'Frontiers of Blame: India's "War on Terror"'. *Critical Studies on Terrorism*, vol. 2, no. 1, pp. 27–44.
Svensson, Ted, 2020. 'Curating the Partition: Dissonant Heritage and Indian Nation Building'. *International Journal of Heritage Studies* (online first).
The Economic Times, 2018. 'India to Retain Top Positions in Remittances with $80 billion: World Bank', *The Economic Times*, 8 December 2018. Accessed at: https://economictimes.indiatimes.com/nri/forex-and-remittance/india-to-retain-top-position-in-remittances-with-80-billion-world-bank/articleshow/66998062.cms
Tripathi, Dhananjay, 2019. 'Influence of Borders on Bilateral Ties in South Asia: A Study of Contemporary India-Nepal Relations'. *International Studies*, vol. 56, nos. 2–3, pp. 186–200.
Varadarajan, Siddharth, 2020. 'Demolition Men Do Not Build Nations, They Destroy Them'. *The Wire*, 5 August 2020.
Vieira, Marco Antonio and Alden, Christopher, 2011. '*India, Brazil, and South Africa (IBSA): South–South Cooperation and the Paradox of Regional Leadership'. Global Governance*, vol. 17, no. 4, pp. 507–528.
Volkan, Vamik, 1997. *Bloodlines: From Ethnic Pride to Ethnic Terrorism*. Boulder: Westview Press.
Vijetha, S.N., 2012. "Historians Protest as Delhi University Purges Ramayana Essay from Syllabus". *The Hindu*, 19 January 2012.
Wilson, Amrit, 2013. 'Gender Violence, Narendra Modi and the Indian Election'. *Open Democracy Net*. www.opendemocracy.net/5050/amrit-wilson/gender violence narendra modi and indian elections.
Wilson, Kalpana, Ung Loh, Jennifer and Navtej Purewal, 2018. 'Gender, Violence and the Neoliberal State'. *Feminist Review*, vol. 119, pp. 1–6.

# 10 From periphery to the centre

## Subnationalism and federal foreign policies within a state nation

*Shantanu Chakrabarti and Johannes Dragsbæk Schmidt*

### Introduction

The process of 'glocalization' is often defined as an interactive process of globalization, which through the due process of several permutations and combinations, creates several interactive categories by combining with local factors. Among several aspects of public policymaking, the glocalization process has also affected foreign policymaking, making it more inclusive in character. The theoretical exclusivity of sovereignty enjoyed by the state over foreign policymaking has been questioned, both academically and in reality, leading to several fallouts. This has particular implications for federally organized state structures, particularly in developing/underdeveloped parts of the world where state building continues to be an ongoing process, leading to a blurred or often underdefined categorization of sovereign authority and exclusivity, leaving room for contestations. In the post-Cold War period, one important trend that is becoming particularly discernible in this context is the process and manner in which the component units within the Indian federation are articulating new options and in the process challenging and opposing 'official' foreign policy options of the Indian state. While input from local constituent units of a state in determining the direction of foreign policymaking has not been altogether absent before, its rising incidence in global affairs has been marked since the ending of the Cold War during the 1990s. Citing several instances of such local initiatives in foreign policymaking, one analyst notes that such "international activities of non-central governments create a multilayered diplomacy that binds local governments and the governments of sovereign states. Moreover, it creates a triangular relationship connecting the non-central government, the central government and foreign governments" (Kumar 2004, 17).

### India as a 'state nation'

The post-Cold War Indian foreign policymaking process has been facing stiff challenges from within and without. This has been illuminated by a growing literature heavily influenced by postmodern theories covering a wide spectrum ranging from debates over the nature of the Indian state to dynamics of indigenous policymaking. One analyst, for instance, traces the evolution of the 'encountered state' with its concomitant bureaucratic dominance over policymaking in India since Nehruvian times through a process of "encountering rather than believing in the official imagination of nationhood, through recognizing the sights and sounds of the state rather than 'buying into' its mythologies, that the nation-state is formed and reproduced" (Roy 2007, 15). In that sense, 'robustly multinational' countries like India have also been projected by social scientists like Juan Linz and Alfred Stepan as 'state nations' rather than as nation states. As the proponents explain:

> 'State-nation' policies stand for a political-institutional approach that respects and protects multiple but complementary socio-cultural identities. 'State-nation' policies recognize the legitimate public and even political expression of active socio-cultural cleavages, and they include mechanisms to accommodate competing or conflicting claims without imposing or privileging in a discriminatory way any one claim.
>
> (Stepan et al. 2010, 53)

Implicit in such assumptions is that any political mechanism which can keep a check on the assertion of centripetal power in the underdeveloped and developing societies that are multiethnic in nature is a good option for retaining and maintaining a democratic order in such vulnerable societies. The federal option for India, in this connection, is continuously advocated as vital for retaining stability. It is, however, often forgotten that, in the global literature, it was only during the last decades of the last century that diversity – particularity, identity issues, minority cultures, collective rights, locality and regions and so on – came to be recognized (Bhattacharyya 2015, 214). In this connection, one scholar has recently argued in favour of a conceptual distinction between diversity-claims and equality-claims in order to reflect critically on the relation between federalism and democracy in India. In his opinion, federalism and democracy suggest two different problematics, but in India democracy has often played second fiddle to the claims of diversity, resulting in India's success as a federation which has not been paralleled by its record as a democracy in terms of its equality functions (Bhattacharyya 2015).

## Foreign policymaking in the federal context

To what extent do such academic debates and discussions have any relevance for a nation's foreign policymaking? To an extent, old interpretations related to Indian foreign policymaking would tend to highlight political personalities cutting across the political spectrum (like Nehru, India Gandhi, Manmohan Singh, AB Bajpayee and recently, Narendra Modi) (Lie and Perwita 2019) and the idiosyncratic factors, while pointing out that India has not developed institutions that can effectively mobilize popular support for specific foreign policy positions. Consequently, the chief executive, who has the added burden of approximating what domestic groups want and balancing his or her perception of domestic political concerns with other foreign policy interests, has largely shaped foreign policy (Andersen 1983, 45). The solution, as suggested by one scholar, may lie in India's adopting a decentralized structure of 'Jeffersonian' federalism at the state and federal levels with directly elected executives providing both coherence and balance by displacing the juggling of interest groups and party factions (Chaudhuri 1993, 461).

Too much focus on personalities or the quasi-federal nature of the Indian state, however, has often led to the ignoring of the imperative of domestic contestation and debates in matters related to the external sector (Chaudhuri 2012, 110). Recent research has revealed how, even under Jawaharlal Nehru (referred to by one of his political opponents as a Gentle Colossus!), various options were debated and analysed by people within the government as well as discussed by the civil society. That trend has continued and a decentralization process in core areas of policymaking has gradually become visible despite centripetal pressures being exerted by the bureaucratic structure of India's governance model. To quote Amartya Sen in this context, "simultaneous flourishing of many different convictions and viewpoints in India has drawn substantially on the acceptance – explicitly or by implication – of heterodoxy and dialogue. The reach of Indian heterodoxy is remarkably extensive and ubiquitous" (Sen 2005, ix). In terms of a problem-solving approach, one analyst notes that

> [t]he rise of sub-national forces and interest groups and the eclipse of any serious balancing of executive-legislative powers are all evidence that its parliamentary-federal system of government is adrift. A more decentralized and more truly federal structure would be more likely to create appropriate buffers to allow regional problems to be resolved regionally.
>
> (Kumar 2004, 25)

In the economic paradigm of liberalization and decentralization undertaken since the 1990s, proper coordination between the centre and the constituent states within the federation has become vital. It has been noted that the federal states also have wide authority on vital sectors that have significance for India's investment climate, like power, agriculture, land, domestic investment and the police (Chari 2014, 3). There is a greater acceptance on the part of the centre of this approach towards greater decentralization and delegation of policymaking as revealed through the dismantling of the Planning Commission and the initial policy focus emanating from the newly created Niti Ayong. As Swenden notes:

> Liberalization and structural adjustment came to replace the centrally planned economy, but with it came a clear signal that the states would gain more autonomy in running their own affairs, including industrial

> policy and foreign investment. Furthermore, the regulatory retrenchment of the centre in industrial policy and its cut-back in welfare expenditure weakened its regulatory and financial capacity to discipline the states.
>
> (Swenden 2016, 503)

## Post-2014 developments

The decentralization aspect of foreign policymaking is also in the process of being institutionalized through the formation in 2014 of a new division named 'States Division' within the Indian Ministry of External Affairs (MEA) under a new Joint Secretary. In the context of its formation, the Minister of State in the Ministry commented while answering a question in the Lok Sabha that "The functions of the States Division are to coordinate facilitation of efforts of states in promoting their exports, tourism and attract more overseas investment and expertise" (Ministry of External Affairs 2016). Significantly, the focus is on facilitating the process of economic and trade partnership and opening up new windows for investment opportunities, a process that has received support from all ends of the Indian political spectrum, with minor differences and exceptions. The new division, however, is not expected to coordinate on policymaking on strategic and bilateral issues. It was reported, for instance, that the new division will not deal with policy disagreements of the kind seen between the centre and Tamil Nadu over the Tamil issue in Sri Lanka and with West Bengal over the Teesta accord with Bangladesh (Haidar 2014).

The new forces shaping public opinion and influencing foreign policy are not limited to the national theatre. Nor is the 'federalization' of policymaking something new. In the context of globalization theory and its focus on weakening of Westphalian and legalistic sovereignty of the state, analysts have claimed that

> [i]n democratic rising powers in particular, this entails a weakening of the central executive organs in the state and a diffusion of power to a range of subnational actors. Thereby, soft sovereignty acts as a catalyst for transnational grievances such as ethnic solidarity, environmental, or economic concerns transgressing national boundaries in a given region, and further undermines interdependence and possibly even international legal and Westphalian sovereignty.
>
> (Plagemann and Destradi 2015, 731)

The 'distorted' nature of the Indian federation has been a long-standing issue of dispute between the central and the state governments in terms of finance sharing or delegation of authority. The failure of any major political party to win a straight majority at the central level has led to the formation of coalition governments at the centre since 1991. This period has also witnessed the rise of several regional parties often organized based on caste/kinship ties or having a firm regional base. Differences over interpretation of allocation of authority and power distribution between the local/regional parties dominating over the majority of the constituent states and the centre, being ruled by either of the two major national parties (Indian National Congress or the Bharatiya Janata Party (BJP)) through increasingly weak coalition governments, often formed through alliances with the same regional/local parties, have been an important feature of Indian politics. The 2014 elections and, subsequently, the 2019 elections, however, reversed this trend and brought to power the BJP under Modi's leadership with absolute majority. It is significant to note that, in spite of having a majority on its own, the BJP has decided to continue the National Democratic Alliance (NDA) consisting of its erstwhile coalition partners. Moreover, as indicated in the introduction, the BJP's attempts to expand its base in new areas particularly in South India and in Eastern and Northeastern states, and even in Jammu and Kashmir, has led to the party making efforts to forge alliance with local parties and political formations and trying to co-opt local leadership within its party structure. Often, the party has had to dilute its core ideology based on Hindutva while trying to emerge as an 'umbrella-like' organization covering the Dravidian states in South India, a Muslim majority Jammu and Kashmir (broken into federal units in 2019 through Parliamentary legislation) and the largely Christian and animist Northeast India. Thus, regional parties and local pressure groups do continue to play a major role in influencing the Indian state's decision-making process.

Consensus building in a diverse country like India is, however, not an easy task and such differences are now being spelled out through publicly articulated differences/standoffs putting into question the traditional belief that there exists a broad consensus among Indian political formations over matters related to foreign policy. Such active participation by the subnational governments has increased over time even if it lacks *de jure* status or endorsement on the part of the central government. As Plagemann and Destradi note:

> Although most current federal systems – including India – do not envisage any role in foreign policy for their member states, these have de facto become prominent players during the past decade. Hence, it is less on legal grounds than those in practical terms that subnational governments become involved in foreign policy.
>
> (Plagemann and Destradi 2015, 731)

This sounds strange as in fact, currently, there are only three constituent states located within 'interior' India – Haryana, Chhattisgarh, Madhya Pradesh and Jharkhand – which do not share borders with either a country or international waters (Mishra and Miklian 2016, 3). The majority of the Indian constituent states have to grapple with the issues and problems of border sharing almost on a daily basis in a region that is strategically regarded as very volatile. These include 'border issues' like illegal migration, illegal human trafficking (particularly of vulnerable sections like women and children) and smuggling of essential commodities, cattle as well as narcotics and weapons. Differences over policy issues and border management, in fact, lead to almost daily complaints over the functioning of the centrally controlled paramilitary Border Security Force personnel at local levels and a lack of sensitivity on the part of policymakers at the central level.

Though the elections in 2014 brought into power a more stable National Democratic Alliance (NDA) under the BJP, which has achieved a majority on its own, it still has to depend on the local parties for passage of bills in the Rajya Sabha, the upper house of the Parliament, as the NDA does not have a majority in the upper house.

Nor have such conflicts been recent news. During 1987, for instance, friction was generated between the central and the constituent government of Tamil Nadu over the issue of the Indian government's decision to send the Indian Peace Keeping Force to Sri Lanka. Recent examples include the differences between the West Bengal government and New Delhi *vis a vis* policymaking towards Bangladesh, particularly on the issue of making fresh agreements over water sharing of the Teesta river, and land border demarcation.

To an extent, such frictions result from the continuous spillover of domestic issues and because of intra-regional linkages in terms of ethnic and religious connections cutting across state borders in South Asia. However, such frictions over official decisions can have harmful effects for the image of India in the global sphere, which might lead to lowering the Nation Brands Index placement, adversely affecting its power projections and ability to attract investment, tourism and trade. Such frictions often arise from lack of proper coordination and information sharing at the policymaking stage. Like other forms of domestic planning and implementation of policies, foreign policymaking in India has also been affected by centripetal tendencies and overt bureaucratization. Decision-making tends to be a concentrated and limited process with the consequence being intimated to the constituent units and agencies. In the case of foreign policymaking, there have been cases of decisions, already arrived at, being conveyed to the constituent units at the last moment without proper consultation and setting up of channels of coordinated action and discussion. While this is in contrast to the changing nature of policymaking in most parts of the democratic world, such types of old policymaking are also no longer possible in a political climate within the country which is showing increasing centrifugal tendencies at various spatial levels with greater intensity of political socialization. Nevertheless, federalization of policymaking need not be only conflict prone in nature. A better coordinated federal approach would lead to well-coordinated and consensual policymaking rather than frictions and frustration and thus may potentially increase the coherence and probability of a more unified outcome that meets the intended objectives. As has been argued, coalition politics since the 1990s that provide regional and local parties greater access to the centre along with its concomitant process of decision-making have led to the subnational grievances on foreign and security policies and regional interdependencies are being articulated at the centre to an extent unseen (Plagemann and Destradi 2015, 735).

## Understanding federalization of foreign policy: some theoretical interpretations

In most countries around the world foreign policy is influenced by domestic affairs and in many cases complex issues related to identity and subnational categories. These entities may be articulated through a plethora of social and political actors, institutions and ideational categories such as cultural or gendered entities encapsulating direct and indirect pressures on the conduct of foreign relations. In some cases, this influence is caused by engagement by subnational units such as federal states and other agents exerting various degrees of control over cross-border issues related to transnational actions and policies like environment, control, resistance and diplomacy over natural resources, and in other instances economic issues.

The process that is often termed 'glocalization', a combination of localist tendencies along with globalization, is increasingly challenging the authority of the centre within federal set-ups. While reducing distance and enhancing contact, this process has also generated conflicts related to ethnicity, kinship, caste and religion, with ramifications for the ideology and polity at federal and central levels. One attempt to explain this pattern has been John Kincaid's term "constituent diplomacy" (Kincaid 1990, 1991). The basic tenet of this concept is that subnational units (states, provinces and other localities) undertake activities that cross international borders and that these activities act as constituent units of federal politics and are in fact co-sovereigns and not subnational units. Another related question raised by several scholars is whether globalization is draining away the lifeblood of the nation-state, its sovereignty. Jenkins (2003), for instance, in his analysis of the World Trade Organization's and World Bank's influence and exchanges with local states and a variety of cases shows convincingly that Rudolph and Rudolph's concept of "shared and negotiated sovereignty" (Rudolph and Rudolph 2010) between centre and states may be a better term to explain the balancing act of federalism and foreign relations when related to transnational economic issues (Jenkins 2003). Whether this idea about divided sovereignty and 'non-nation-state rule' underestimates the increasingly important role played by coalition governments in federal politics and foreign relations may hypothetically overrule the central level. These debates are also related to the discussion about 'asymmetric federalism' (Khan 2014) and whether rising powers make use of 'soft sovereignty' gaining and losing power and authority due to the double-bound impact of international actors and institutions and norms and regulations on the one hand, and, on the other hand, subnational transnational actors from below (Plagemann and Destradi 2015).

Borders and hinterlands define the interactive interplay between the constituent state and neighbour's political configurations and the political cultural matrix surrounding the centrifugal actors and institutions attempting to re-establish a new spatial, social and geopolitical outcome. Regional parties at the federal level increasingly play an important role at the centre and attempt to influence and direct foreign policy as a way to accommodate federal, regional and sometimes chauvinist interests. In other instances, foreign policy is directly being conducted by federal states with important consequences for security, peace and India's foreign policy towards conflict in the immediate neighbourhood. This has been the consequence of the change from dominant-party to multi-party politics and the emergence of regional and state-level parties and coalition governments at both central and local level, which took place in the 1990s.

India's borders to China, Pakistan, Nepal, Bhutan, Myanmar, Bangladesh and Sri Lanka affect neighbouring states and there has been a long tradition of state governments' involvement in international affairs (Appadorai 1981). The common subcontinental history and shared ethnic and cultural linkages were not snapped by post-decolonization state building and reconstructions. Hence, domestic problems tend to spill over and cause wider regional and even Asian disruptions. For much of post-independence, regional conflicts have been caused by the concerned constituent states taking the main lead and then drawing in the centre. The conflict in Goa in 1961, the problems in East Pakistan and the creation of Bangladesh in 1971–72, and the two-decade long Tamil–Sinhalese conflict in Sri Lanka all demonstrate the significant role of the constituent states in developing a local problem into a national agenda for action.

The relations between the centre and the constituent states have also not always been cordial and smooth. There have been instances when the centrifugal pull has threatened the state of the union, as stipulated in the Constitution of India where the founding fathers deliberately avoided the word federal. Tensions between the central and the state governments have led to bloodshed and conflict and even in some instances demands for separate statehood and in other cases cross-border actions, with both internal and external implications. Adoption of a more nuanced and collaborative approach towards decentralized policymaking could be one possible approach to end such conflicts. Foreign policymaking need not be an exception. Creation of institutionalized mechanisms like the new States Division within the MEA is a positive step towards that direction. Another example is the Modi government's establishment of 'cooperative-competitive federalism', which is supposed to create and promote more collaboration through shared decision-making in which each actor (the centre and the states collectively) exercises a mutual veto (power sharing). As mentioned by Sharma and Swenden, goods and services tax (GST) is one of the few policy domains in which the principle of collaboration has been implemented (Sharma and Swenden 2018, 56), though the inability of the centre to pay the compensation arrears to the states as originally promised in view of the economic decline as a result of the Covid-19 pandemic has resulted in tensions and open protests by most of the states where the opposition is in power (The Hindu Businessline 2020).

## Leverage on foreign policy

With reference to the BJP's election slogan 'Team India', this institution was an attempt to recognize the fact that local states have a legitimate role to play in the conduct of foreign policymaking. In this way the Modi government's initiatives to forge cooperation between the subnational levels of local states and the central government were a consequence of the fact that subnational governments have had a huge and determining impact on India's policies over the years, particularly towards its South Asian neighbours. This is particularly reflected in India's relations with Bangladesh and Sri Lanka. During 1987, for instance, friction was generated between the central and the constituent government of Tamil Nadu over the issue of the Indian government's decision to send the Indian Peace Keeping Force to Sri Lanka. Local and central government differences also came out during the Indian government's attempts to corner Sri Lanka over the issue of human rights violations or the visit of the former Sri Lankan president Mahinda Rajapakshe. Similarly, differences between the West Bengal government and New Delhi *vis a vis* policymaking towards Bangladesh, particularly on the issue of making fresh agreements over water sharing of the Teesta river, and land border demarcation, have continued to generate problems (Kumar 2004).

More recently, another example of such federalization of foreign policymaking is being reflected through articulation of the demand for more inclusive foreign policymaking through greater involvement of the Northeastern states in India. Though the primary focus is on the urgent need for a robust national doctrine that could guide the Northeastern states in tackling pressing issues and also helping them boost their economy by accessing opportunities beyond borders, there is also revelation as to how the border states like Tripura have tried out little-known unconventional policies *vis a vis* its external neighbourhood to check cross-border infiltration of illegal migrants and terrorists (Bhaumik 2016).

The Teesta river, one of the fifty-four rivers shared by Bangladesh and India, is another case in point where the West Bengali government overruled the central Sing-led government. New Delhi and Dhaka had agreed on a fifty-fifty sharing agreement over the river's resources but this was never signed due to opposition from the West Bengal Chief Minister Mamata Banerjee.

In 2016, Telangana established a Ministry of External Affairs and declared that it needed an independent foreign policy in order to promote the state abroad for business, foreign investment, tourism, and not least to deal with the pending issue of migration. The local government referred to Punjab and Kerala with their separate policy entities dealing with migration as an example to follow. As one observer (Jacob 2016) notes, this was an attempt to put "the periphery at the centre", but the fact that the Modi government has not managed to facilitate greater connection between New Delhi and local state capitals by institutionalizing the role of states remains a major challenge. As Jacob stresses:

> Unfortunately, the performance of the Modi government on this front has not been entirely satisfactory, either institutionally or politically. Not only has the present government not tried to bring about a broad-based institutional framework to accommodate states' legitimate foreign policy interests, it has weakened existing institutions such as the ISC and NDC. Taking states and their legitimate interests into account also requires a great deal of consensus building by the central government. The Modi government's outreach to states is more for the purposes of economic policy facilitation rather than foreign policy consultation.
>
> (Jacob 2016, 19)

These observations leave a puzzle since the de facto federalization of foreign policy is taking place and may even accelerate since the centre cannot generate coherent and fast-enough responses to the urgent problems, especially in those states bordering fragile or even conflict-prone neighbours. The constitutional status privileged to some states in some cases gives a larger role to the local state's chief minister in India's foreign policymaking, and the political weight of a state leader, which may also count in foreign policy decision-making, though indirectly.

Mattoo and Jacob attribute the weakening of central control over foreign policy to the following four factors:

- Some states, such as Jammu and Kashmir, enjoy a special constitutional status that may enhance their political leaders' influence on foreign policy.
- Certain state leaders have the political clout to informally shape foreign policymaking.
- Central coalition governments have empowered state governments and leaders to have a greater say on foreign policy because such coalitions are composed of regional parties, many of them located in a single state.
- Finally, although the constitution has not undergone change, the forces of globalization have created new practices and possibilities that have already given the states a greater role and will continue to do so in the future (Mattoo and Jacob 2009, 175).

In relation to these observations, it is interesting to note that the Constitution of India does not mention the word federalism and it is very clear regarding foreign policy as the jurisdiction of the unitary central state; however, as can be seen there are exceptions in the Northeast and in Jammu and Kashmir. As Asthana and Jacob mention:

> States in India, especially those with international borders, are emerging as significant players in the conduct of India's foreign, economic and strategic policy. However, given the absence of any legal and constitutional basis for this role, contingent factors such as coalition structures tend to influence the ability of the subnational actors to impact policy outcomes.
>
> (Asthana and Jacob 2017, 336)

## Paradiplomacy in the Indian context

This type of paradiplomacy or "constituent diplomacy" (Kincaid 1990, 1991) was already launched during the 2014 election by Narendra Modi, the prime ministerial candidate of the BJP, who was calling for a greater role for states in India's economic diplomacy largely based on his own experiences as chief minister of the state of Gujarat from 2002 to 2014. This type of parallel diplomacy or quasi foreign policy has positive as well as negative sides.

The concept itself diminishes the distinction between domestic and external affairs and focuses on the need for local government to engage in global competition. From this perspective, there is a strong functional logic in local government's external projection, which is related to economic needs, to the spillover of their domestic competences into the international arena and in some cases to the need to manage ethnic or nationalist conflicts at their borders, with the security issues that these pose. However, this purely functional mode has to be divided into three spheres in order to comprehend its reach. The first sphere is related to economics and is arguably, seen from the central level side, positive and may potentially create investments and jobs. The second layer relates to cultural and ideational issues which may be much more conflictual and may lead to serious confrontation with the centre. The third layer is the geopolitical category which relates to the multiple scalar layers and actors involved in production of knowledge and geopolitical motives and objectives (Jackson 2018, 7).

The case of Gujarat is interesting since it is the third most internationalized in India after Maharashtra (which tops the list) and it has experienced high growth rates and cast itself under Modi as the Asian Lion. However, its growth miracle relying on neoliberal policies did not improve the living standards of the general population and according to critical voices it was 'growth without development' with no real progress in health and education indicators. The 'Make in India' project was an attempt to embrace foreign investors with what one observer (Ruparelia 2015) calls "minimum government, maximum governance". Its meaning and purpose as highlighted in the official website of the newly inducted prime minister stated that the government has no business to do business. Under the Modi government in Gujarat (2001–14), an effective judiciary, entrepreneur-friendly environment and less intrusive government had purportedly enabled the state to become "number one…in economic freedom in India" (Ruparelia 2015, 757).

When Chinese President Xi Jinping during his visit to India landed in Ahmedabad, Gujarat, PM Modi received him and narrated the importance of the Indian state and civilization in the Buddhist era. 'Buddha diplomacy' seems to have become a soft-power device of India's foreign policy and a way to forge links with countries in East and South Asia, not only to attract tourism but also to utilize Buddhism in foreign policy as a 'smart' device to create diplomatic leverage and interaction, especially with Japan and China. On one of his visits to China the chief minister of the state of Gujarat carried red business cards printed in Mandarin and declared that "China and its people have a special place in my heart" (The Economic Times 2011). Such enthusiasm has, however, died down during recent bilateral tensions over the border disputes between the two Asian countries, especially after the skirmishes between the armed forces in Ladakh.

The state used specific instruments in order to attract foreign direct investment and foreign tourists and promote the state in the domestic and international arena, and Modi himself became the symbol of the successful 'Gujarat model', which may have been one of the reasons enhancing his popularity to emerge at the national level and become the prime minister of India (Bywalec 2018). But, on the other hand, the experience from the 'Gujarat model' is also the tale of the present Modi government in power at the centre where policymaking has followed basic tenets of neoliberal ideas. As one analyst argues:

> Neo-liberal regimes frequently prioritize the civil liberties and political rights of individuals over collective socio-economic needs; deploy the rule of law and sanctity of the courts to protect private property; and privilege technocratic expertise over elected politicians to champion the liberalization, deregulation and privatization of markets at the expense of organized labour.
>
> (Ruparelia 2015, 775)

The secret behind Gujarat's relative success in forging external links and promoting the state in geoeconomic foreign policy terms was the close collaboration between the government and the corporate sector. Critics, however, have pointed out negative factors such as the low wages; the opportunities for investors to acquire land more quickly and at a better price and to obtain more tax breaks; the creation of export processing zones with no labour rights; and religious, caste and social polarization (Jaffrelot 2015).

One, however, has to keep in mind that this has been broadly the trend since India's economic reforms of 1991 and there are similar arrangements in Tamil Nadu and Maharashtra, with high expenditure on infrastructure and government corporate sector collusion and relatively high economic growth rates, but a far more inclusive social profile than the Gujarat example denotes. Prior to its fall in 2011, even the long-serving Left Front coalition government in West Bengal had initiated new policies in order to attract private and foreign investment, a policy which has been broadly continued by the present-serving Trinamool government. Competition between the states has become the order of the day, with aggressive and expensive campaigning through advertisements and frequently held investment summits.

The question is whether the federal element of foreign policymaking has been strengthened during the BJP government under Modi's jurisdiction or whether it has been weakened. The question is also whether there are examples of states pursuing geopolitical diplomacy which is contradicting the central government's foreign policy.

## Subnational foreign policy under the BJP government

It is interesting to note that, according to various opinion polls conducted by the media, the Modi government scores high in conducting foreign policy (Chaulia 2016, 2). Interestingly, many observers have compared Modi with Erdogan in Turkey and Putin in Russia as a staunch conservative, nationalist strongman. What, however, distinguishes Modi from these leaders is his clear vision of decentralizing parts of India's foreign policy by emphasizing cooperative federalism in foreign policymaking, at least in certain sectors. This was illuminated by the chief ministers of the states of Maharashtra and Gujarat who travelled to China, in April 2015, together with PM Modi. It is also interesting to note that, despite policy differences, the chief minister of the state of West Bengal joined Modi in Bangladesh in June 2015 where they signed the land boundary agreement between India and Bangladesh. In the beginning of the Modi government's term it was only BJP chief ministers who joined Modi on state visits abroad, but this pattern changed accordingly. Nor has this trend been initiated first by Modi. The former PM Manmohan Singh, for instance, had included four chief ministers from Northeastern states bordering Bangladesh during his trip to the country. According to some observers, Modi has used the 'cooperative federalism' and 'team India' cards to promote the centre's, i.e. BJP's, foreign policy agenda by including state chief ministers in crucial foreign affairs issues (Jain and Maini 2017, 296).

Such cooperation is, however, dependent upon personal relations and the level of internal political dynamics. In recent years, various policies undertaken by the government have largely alarmed the opposition, which has accused the central government of increasing its power at the expense of the federal structure. This has led to ruptures in cooperative policymaking.

## Concluding observations

Constituent units within a democratic federal structure can and do play a role in external relations. The development of subnational institutional arrangements to organize cultural, educational and commercial contacts make these governments a structural, integrative force in Marshall McLuhan's vision of the evolving 'global village' (Kelly 1996, vii). However, the idea of international relations being forged at the subnational level is not new as it goes back to the history of regional parties and local pressure groups and cabals having put pressure on the central decision-making process. Regional states as geographical spaces with land or sea borders interacted beyond the reach and capacity of the central political dispensations in the Indian subcontinent even during the pre-colonial and colonial periods. People-to-people contacts, itinerant trade and even cyclical labour and capital movement used to be the chief features of such contacts. Such contacts were by and large tolerated as long as they brought economic and commercial benefits to the central regimes and did not threaten its perceived sovereign status. Modern contacts, on behalf of the constituent state governments, also do not intrude with the sovereignty of the central federal government's prerogatives in terms of foreign policy decision-making. They cannot be seen as new modes of blurring the line or perforating the status quo of central government's autonomy and power in terms of core foreign policy decisions related to sovereignty and the fuzzy concept of national interest.

In the last three decades India's politics has been a period where deregulation, liberalization and the opening up of the Indian economy have created the conditions for the subnational entities to exercise specific foreign policy goals. Furthermore, the weakening of single-party dominance has created a fertile ground for the regional parties coming to the centre to form coalition governments. The states that share a border with a foreign nation have historical, cultural, linguistic, religious and ethnic links with the bordering nation that have made it imperative for their respective governments to indulge in some activities. These may have foreign policy characteristics, but it may be premature to call it an emerging trend of federalization of foreign policy. The most successful states have exercised some kind of economic foreign diplomacy while others have been involved in specific incidents where they have collided with shifting central government goals. However, these latter examples are few and scattered and it cannot be seen as a more general trend (Hazarika 2014).

A federal foreign policy may be divided into three categories. The first category is the border states which have historical connectivity across borders and pursue some degree of autonomy in terms of solving conflicts and pursuing harmony across borders in handling ethnic, religious, cultural and caste-related issues. Each state has their own history and political culture and in some cases also have economic reasons for employing aspects of subnational foreign policy and paradiplomatic manoeuvres in ways to accommodate complex relations with neighbouring states and entities (for details see Hausing 2014).

The second category is economic diplomacy pursued by the constituent states. Most Indian states have engaged in some form of economic diplomacy in one way or the other and that may be seen as a positive development by the central government as it acts as a catalyst for development itself and relieves the centre of some burden in terms of promoting India as a prime destination for foreign investment.

The third category is related to a slowly evolving process of decentralized foreign policymaking in India. This may be divided into two subcategories. The first is concerned with party politics and coalitions or regional political parties formed at the local level but with some impact on the formulation of national interest and sovereignty and thus foreign policy itself being pursued at the centre. The second category is also related to federalization of foreign policymaking, but in this case, there are significant examples of states pursuing their own foreign policy and in very rare cases even contradicting the official foreign policy at the central level.

This contribution also highlighted the BJP government's deliberate attempt to give more autonomy and power to the subnational level, but only in economic foreign policy, while the prerogatives of defence and security belong solely to the central government. In fact, under Modi's tenure there has been a tendency to restrict independent initiatives at ministerial level with key decision-making processes being initiated and monitored by the Prime Minister's Office, with the PM being assisted by key ministers and important advisors. Interestingly, some observers describe this trend as both 'competitive and cooperative federal foreign policy', meaning a more inclusive approach towards local governments in pursuing limited economic diplomacy and pro-investment policies but at the same time allowing competition between states in attracting foreign investment etc.

On the other hand, this explanation may be linked to the fact that India is considered more as a 'holding together' rather than a 'coming together' federation. This is reflected in its extreme diversity, its enormous variety in historical conjunctures such as the former 'princely states' striving for autonomy or even sovereignty, and the never-ending phase of dissolving and creating new state entities such as the recent new state Telangana which came into orbit in 2014. By and large, the evolving federalization of foreign policy is a key component of rapidly shifting political dynamics in India.

## References


Andersen, Walter K. 1983. The Domestic Roots of Indian Foreign Policy. *Asian Affairs* 10, no. 3 (Fall): 45–53

Appadorai, A. 1981. The Domestic roots of India's Foreign Policy, 1947–1972. Oxford: Oxford University Press

Asthana, Anamika and Jacob, Happymon. 2017. The Growing Power of States in India's Foreign Policy. *International Negotiation* 22, no. 2: 317–343

Bhattacharyya, Harihar. 2015. Indian Federalism and Democracy: The Growing Salience of Diversity-claims Over Equality-claims in Comparative and Indian Perspective. *Regional & Federal Studies* 25, no. 3: 211–227

Bhaumik, Subir. 2016. *The Agartala Doctrine: A Proactive Northeast in Indian Foreign Policy.* New Delhi: Oxford University Press

Bywalec, Grzegorz. 2018. Paradiplomacy in India As Exemplified by the State of Gujarat. In *Paradiplomacy in Asia: Case Studies of China, India and Russia*, eds Małgorzata Pietrasiak, Grzegorz Bywalec, Tomasz Kaminski, Dominik Mierzejewski, and Michał Słowikowski, 39–90, Lodz: Lodz University Press

Chari, P.R. 2014. India: Limits of Federalism. In *Federalism and Foreign Policy: Dynamics of Centre-State Dissensions in India*, *IFPS Special Focus*, ed. Ayesha Khanyari, 3–6, New Delhi: IFPS

Chaudhuri, Joyotpul. 1993. Federalism and the Siamese twins: Diversity and Entropy in India's Domestic and Foreign Policy. *International Journal* 48, no. 3: 448–469

Chaudhuri, Rudra. 2012. The Limits of Executive Power: Domestic Politics and Alliance Behavior in Nehru's India. *India Review* 11, no. 2: 95–115

Chaulia, Sreeram. 2016. *Modi Doctrine: The Foreign Policy of India's Prime Minister.* New Delhi: Bloomsbury

Haidar, Suhasini. 2014. MEA to oversee foreign investments in States. *The Hindu, New Delhi,* www.thehindu.com/news/national/mea-to-oversee-foreign-investments-in-states/article6530956.ece (accessed: December 16, 2019)

Hausing, Kham Khan Suan. 2014. Asymmetric Federalism and the Question about Democratic Justice in Northeast India. *India Review* 13, no. 2: 87–111

Hazarika, Obja Borah. 2014. Evolving Dynamics of Federalism and Foreign Policy Engagement of Indian States in External Affairs. *Indian Foreign Affairs Journal* 9, no. 1: 33–45

Jackson, Thomas. 2018. Paradiplomacy and Political Geography: The Geopolitics of Substate Regional Diplomacy. *Geography Compass* 12, no. 2: 1–11

Jacob, Happymon. 2016. Putting the Periphery at the Center: Indian States' Role in Foreign Policy. New Delhi: Carnegie India: 1–24 https://carnegieendowment.org/files/CP_282_Jacob_States_Roles_Final.pdf (accessed: January 29, 2019)

Jaffrelot, Christophe. 2015. What 'Gujarat Model'? – Growth without Development – and with Socio-Political Polarisation. *South Asia: Journal of South Asian Studies* 38, no. 4: 820–838

Jain, Purendra and Maini, Tridivesh Singh. 2017. India's Subnational Governments Foray into the International Arena. *Japanese Journal of Political Science* 18, no. 2: 286–312

Jenkins, Bob. 2003. India's States and the Masking of Foreign Economic Policy: The Limits of the Constituent Diplomacy Paradigm. *Publius: The Journal of Federalism* 33, no. 4 (Fall): 63–82

Kelly, John F. 1996. An International Foreign Policy Agenda for Subnational Government. Ph.D diss., MI: Wayne State University

Kincaid, John. 1990. Constituent Diplomacy in Federal Politics and the Nation-State: Conflict and Cooperation. In *Federalism and International Relations: The Role of Subnational Units*, eds Hans Michelmann and Panayotis Soldatos, 55–76, Oxford: Clarendon Press

Kincaid, John. 1991. Constituent Diplomacy: U.S. State Roles in Foreign Affairs. In *Constitutional Design and Power-Sharing in the Post-Modern Epoch*, ed. Daniel J. Elazar, 107–142, Lanham, MD: Jerusalem Center for Public Affairs and University Press of America

Kumar, Akhilesh. 2004. Federalism and Foreign Policy: The Indian Context. Ph.D diss., Pondicherry University

Lie, Peter Sean and Perwita, Anak Agung Banyu. 2019. The Modi Factor: The Role of Narendra Modi's Idiosyncratic Factors in India's Foreign Policy Responses Towards China Pakistan Economic Corridor. *Andalas Journal of International Studies* VIII, no. 2: 117–142

Mattoo, Amitabh and Jacob, Happymon. 2009. Republic of India. In *Foreign Relations in Federal Countries*, ed. Hans Michelmann, 169–187, Montreal and Kingston: McGill-Queen's University Press and Forum of Federations

Ministry of External Affairs (MEA). 2016, May 11. Gen. (DR) V.K. Singh (Retd)'s answer to the Lok Sabha Unstarred Question No.2970 to be answered on 11.05.2016, QUESTION NO.2970 NEW DIVISION FOR CENTRE-STATE

RELATIONS, Media Centre/Documents, www.mea.gov.in/lok-sabha.htm?dtl/26812/QUESTION_NO2970_NEW_DIVISION_FOR_CENTRESTATE_RELATIONS (accessed: November 12, 2019)

Mishra, Atul and Miklian, Jason. 2016, January. The evolving domestic drivers of Indian foreign policy. *Norwegian Peacebuilding Research Centre Report*: 1–9

Plagemann, Johannes and Destradi, Sandra. 2015. Soft Sovereignty, Rising Powers, and Subnational Foreign Policymaking: The Case of India. *Globalizations* 12, no. 5: 728–743

Roy, Srirupa. 2007. *Beyond Belief: India and the Politics of Postcolonial Nationalism*. Durham, NC: Duke University Press

Rudolph, Lloyd I. and Hoeber Rudolph, Susanne. 2010. Federalism as State Formation in India: A Theory of Shared and Negotiated Sovereignty. *International Political Science Review* 31, no. 5: 553–572

Ruparelia, Sanjay. 2015. Minimum Government, Maximum Governance: The Restructuring of Power in Modi's India. *South Asia: Journal of South Asian Studies* 38, no. 4: 755–775

Sen, Amartya. 2005. *The Argumentative Indian: Writings on Indian History, Culture and identity*. New York: Farrar, Straus and Giroux

Sharma, Chanchal Kumar and Swenden, Wilfried. 2018. Modi-fying Indian Federalism? Center–State Relations under Modi's Tenure as Prime Minister. *Indian Politics & Policy* 1, no. 1(Spring): 51–81

Stepan, Alfred Linz, Juan J. and Yadav, Yogendra. 2010. The Rise of 'State-Nations'. *Journal of Democracy* 21, no. 3(July): 50–68

Swenden, Wilfried. 2016. Centre-State Bargaining and Territorial Accommodation: Evidence from India. *Swiss Political Science Review* 22, no. 4: 491–515

The Economic Times. 2011, November 9. Narendra Modi seeks Chinese investments for Gujarat, https://economictimes.indiatimes.com/news/politics-and-nation/narendra-modi-seeks-chinese-investments-for-gujarat/articleshow/10667923.cms?from=mdr (accessed: June 28, 2020)

The Hindu Businessline. 2020, August 28. States up in arms over GST compensation, www.thehindubusinessline.com/news/national/states-up-in-arms-over-gst-compensation/article32468640.ece (accessed: September 2, 2020)

# Part IV

# Looking in – outside out: Northeast of India related to India's foreign policymaking

# 11 Manipur dynamics in India's Myanmar policy

## Politico-economic perspective

*Langpoklakpam Suraj Singh*[*]

## Introduction

Like any other outcome of globalisation, border states or regions today form a key aspect in any country's foreign policy. No longer are the regions considered a periphery or appendage of a country; rather they are complete entities with distinct identities of their own. And it is amid this newly emerging trend in the international order that India's Myanmar policy with Northeast India as the decisive factor came up within the broader perspective of its Act East policy (AEP). The recent developments in Myanmar, and India's renewed assertion for engagement with the country under Prime Minister Narendra Modi's second term in New Delhi, have brought to the fore the inseparable place of Manipur, a border state in Northeast India. Because of its geographical proximity, Northeast India and Manipur remain a top priority for the optimal success of India's new foreign policy of engaging overland with its immediate and distant Eastern neighbours. At this critical juncture, how Manipur will negotiate with these challenges and externalities pointing towards Myanmar within the broader framework of the AEP, in terms of its own shortcomings and overlapping ethno-national aspirations, is of immense importance. Besides, one can also see a clear interplay between domestic issues and external factors, which have serious ramifications for the country's foreign policy in this part of the country.

## Background

The geopolitical shifts in South and Southeast Asia and the increasing wave of globalisation after the Cold War brought about the need for a new orientation in India's foreign policy. This need for a more pragmatic and dynamic foreign policy culminated in India's 'Look East Policy' (LEP), the precursor of the present Act East policy, in the 1990s. The rapid multi-polarisation in the new sphere of geopolitics compelled the country to move nearer to the regional and sub-regional power centres in its distant and extended neighbourhood for security and economic interests. The policy resulted in growing cooperation in all fields ranging from comprehensive economic cooperation to combating terrorism and ensuring maritime security in the region. It was a key foreign policy doctrine which emphasises the significance of the countries to India's East, even including Australia, New Zealand and the South Pacific island states (Kaul 2010, 431).

It was the introduction of 'Structural Adjustment Programmes' in 1991 by Prime Minister Narasimha Rao's government for India's economic liberalisation that gave ground to formulate the LEP. The policy, thus, adopted both political and economic connotations of the larger policy framework associated with liberalisation, privatisation and globalisation (Sharma 2009, 201). The successful intensification of India–ASEAN cooperation paved the way for the second phase of the LEP from 2003 onwards. India became a summit-level partner of ASEAN in 2002 and a member of the East Asia Summit in December 2005. An extra dimension that emerges is the realisation of the increasing importance of Northeast India to Indian policymakers and diplomatic circles. Foreign policy analyst C. Raja Mohan aptly put it as: "India's search for a new economic relationship with South East Asia is no longer driven by considerations of globalisation, but by the domestic imperative of developing the Northeast by increasing its connectivity to the outside world" (Mohan 2002). In this phase, the essence of LEP goes beyond the economic imperatives and emphasises the eminence of connectivity and infrastructure facilities. The relevance of Northeast India has been enhanced as the workable overland gateway to Southeast Asia. Here, as developmental and infrastructural cooperation and projects could be sped up in the presence of proper land linkages, Manipur proves to be a viable option with Myanmar as the decisive variable across the border. The reciprocity inherent was made more apparent with the start of the formal border trade between the two countries in 1995 and the introduction of the cross-border *Free Movement Regime*. Centuries of racial and cultural affinity and politico-economic ties with the country has always linked Manipur to issues related to Myanmar.

All these factors have brought to the fore the increasing relevance of understanding the geopolitics of border territories as an indispensable part of a country's foreign policy. The same applies with Manipur as a part of the Northeast. But, interestingly, it reminds us of a reference to Northeast India in Professor James C. Scott's much talked-about region, the '*Zomia*' or the '*Southeast Asia Massif*', which is a complex and little-governed region inhabited by fugitives and runaway communities fleeing the subjugation of the state-building process (Scott 2009, ix).[1] Although that may not be the exact case with the region and the people today, yet a vestige of the past remains to some extent. Since the British administration put its imprint on the Northeast of India in 1826 (under the *Treaty of Yandabo*), till the present day, it is still a question in the mind of many in the state whether any policy of the Union government could forego the mindset of treating it as a frontier or boundary, though the new foreign policy strategy tries to show it otherwise. This is having a long-lasting consequence on any policy of the country towards the state, and its Myanmar policy is no exception.

How could one fit Manipur into the whole perception dynamics of the growing India–Myanmar equation? This question has become more relevant in its geopolitical bearing in the greater perspective of India's reoriented AEP and Modi's foreign policy doctrine of emphasising the '*Three Concentric Circles*' (Mohan 2006). Under the new initiative, the country started placing more emphasis on the security dimension and regional connectivity, besides the existing economic engagements. One could see India's intention of supporting an open and inclusive regional security architecture based on ASEAN centrality (Singh 2018). Conceptualisation of the implications associated with the question is not that easy. There is a need to dissect the related issues and thoroughly analyse the same.

## Manipur–Myanmar connection: the rationale

Manipur is situated between longitude 93.03° E to 94.78° E and latitude 23.80° N to 25.68° N, with an area of 22,327 sq. km. It touches Southeast Asia geographically on its 352 km boundary line with Myanmar. Beside the *Meiteis*, the majority community, it is occupied by many trans-border tribes, generalised into *Nagas*, *Kukis* and *Chins*, whose movements are not restricted by political boundary.[2] This state of Northeast India is, by location, in a very strategic point on the porous 1,643 km stretch of the international border shared between India and Myanmar. In fact, it remains comparatively the most viable land route for transit from India to Myanmar and the rest of Southeast Asia. The road NH 102 (earlier NH 39) of India reaches up to Moreh from where it continues on the Myanmar side and further to Thailand. Supplementing it is the age-old local belief of *Nongpok Thong Hangba*, or opening the 'Eastern Gate', as mentioned in the folklores and ancient texts of Manipur. For the people of this erstwhile princely state, the traditional belief is that its outlet to the world is through the 'Eastern Gate', i.e., through Myanmar and the rest of Southeast Asia. Because of the existing historical, topographical and strategic basis of the region, any issue concerning cross-border insurgency, narcotics, small arms proliferation, border trade, HIV/AIDS, animal-related diseases etc., which remain the main areas of concern in India's Myanmar policy, always reflect the long-term implications of the bilateral relations of Manipur and vice versa.

Manipur's relations with Myanmar date back in history. There was even a time when this native state was much closer to that country (then known only as *Awa* or *Ava* to the Manipuris) than to the rest of mainland India. There were instances of matrimonial relationships, coupled with politico-military competitions between the Manipuri rulers and the Myanmar kings. *Kabaw Valley* was one area for which there were hot contestations.[3] There were also trade relations. Not only was trade carried out between Manipur and Myanmar, but the former also acted as an important transit for trade between Myanmar and the rest of India, particularly the Bengali traders coming from Sylhet (now in Bangladesh). The state imported tea seeds, cattle and precious stones from Myanmar, and exported silk to the latter. This connection existed even during the British rule of Manipur. The state was a convenient land transit connecting British India and colonial Burma, with a motorable road built during the Second World War. But with the merger of the native state of Manipur with the Indian Union on 15 October 1949, and the subsequent limitation of the political boundary, the free flow was curtailed. In the later stages, the relationship was confined mostly to a limited informal border trade among the hill peoples and largely to illegal trade in contraband goods such as Chinese consumer items, narcotics, small arms and precious and semi-precious stones. The renewal of the border trade in 1995 allowed the two sides of the border to link formally, but the ongoing illegal activities persist.

However, any initiative taken up under the AEP with regard to Manipur will always have a direct or indirect inference for Myanmar and the reciprocity therein. Proper adjustment of Manipur to the measures of the AEP depends on how it tackles the many aspects related to Myanmar and also Southeast Asia's *Look West Policy*.

## India's Myanmar policy and Manipur perspective: common issues

At present, with lots of misgivings among the locals towards many of the national policies, Manipur has failed to make an effective contribution to India's Myanmar policy and vice versa. It remains a matter which needs serious rethinking by stakeholders. From the Manipur perspective, India's AEP is almost synonymous with that of its Myanmar policy. Many of the issues (both positive and negative) that come into the spotlight in Manipur's emerging relevance in the AEP point toward Myanmar, an aspect which can no longer be sidelined. Issues of both hues, negative and positive, form an unavoidable part of Manipur dynamics in India's growing Myanmar policy. Likewise, New Delhi's interest in the state is based on issues of immense national concern, extending beyond the national boundary. The same is likely also true for Myanmar. Another relevant aspect here is the impact of the state and its cross-currents on the overall foreign policy of India towards Myanmar. The natives still consider the policy an imposition for security and strategic reasons that has not taken the locals on board. Some issues need to be viewed closely before considering any of the likely implications of Manipur and its externalities on the foreign policy measures, and vice versa.

### *Cross-border trade: the maze*

The sudden closing down of the international transit gates along the Manipur–Myanmar border since 10 March 2020 because of the COVID-19 pandemic illustrates the simple fact of how fragile India's foreign policy is in this part of the country, as the cross-border trade and people's movement came to a complete standstill. At one time, the starting of the border trade at the Moreh-Tamu point was considered to be a significant event in India's Myanmar policy. The opening of this border trade in April 1995 brought Manipur directly within the purview of India–Myanmar relations, and beyond. In the immediate aftermath, Moreh started as the most important centre for border trade with the entire people of Manipur hoping for the ensuing economic prosperity. It changed from being a non-descript place to a well-known location in the entire Northeast of India. However, the volume of trade at the Moreh-Tamu border point, which gave a very positive picture in the initial years, gradually showed an overall declining trend although there have no longer been restrictions on tradable items since 1 December 2015.[4] The volume of trade, which was INR 623.6 million in 1997–98, dropped to INR 7.7 million in 2017–18, not in India's favour (Taneja et al. 2019; Khathing 2005, 51–57). What could be observed of the border trade is a zigzag, unbalanced and non-uniform pattern.

Besides, the Moreh-Tamu border trade has negative multiplier effects with far-reaching implications. Another side of the picture is that Moreh's official trade is only a fraction of its large and flourishing informal trade, with transactions in narcotics, small arms, precious stones, gold, electronic items and wildlife products with different origins. An estimate of the annual volume of unofficial trade comes to about INR 12 billion (Bose 2018). The primary reason for this large-scale illegal traffic is that Myanmar does not impose any rule of origin or other restrictions on third-country goods in transit (Verghese 2002, 189). Moreover, given the non-conducive situation in Moreh, business has gradually shifted to Tamu's Namphalong market. Adding to this is the excessive Chinese presence in the border trade. There is an onslaught of business groups, coming from as far as Yunnan. Products from the most sophisticated electronic goods to the simplest vegetables like garlic are brought to Manipur through the Moreh-Tamu transit from China.

Overall, the fact remains that, though barter trade has been abolished and border trade has shifted to normal trade, it has nevertheless failed to bring the minimum expected gain to the local people of the state. There is no coordination among the different Central authorities working in the state. The absence of a proper controlling authority with the right mechanisms for the control of whatever little benefit there is in terms of formal trade also adds to the problem. The stakeholders are at their wits' end with harassment and interference from the authorities themselves. Besides, with many blockades, strikes and open intra-factional and other conflicts, sometimes bordering on communal flare-up, a subdued but tense situation prevails in Moreh. And most of the projects touching this area are in disarray. The fact remains that the situation of the Indo Myanmar border trade could be a fulcrum for India, which could move either way, as a positive contribution or a declining negative trend.

### *Security issues on the border: insurgency, small arms proliferation and narco-trafficking*

Security issues form one of the focal points of India's Myanmar policy. Controlling insurgency through the destruction of safe havens across the border and controlling trafficking of small arms and light weapons as well as curbing the movement of drugs and human trafficking has always been on the agenda of India's increasing closeness to the country. Various security fallouts emanating from across the immediate border have a serious effect on governance and life in the region. One of the security dimensions of India's policy towards Myanmar is to overcome this problem by having a proper, developmental relationship and mutual understanding with the country.

Insurgency-related activities, inclusive of small arms proliferation, have become rampant, though some control has been seen very recently. Insurgency in Manipur is one of the longest-running movements in Asia. Besides, the state is also becoming home to the highest number of armed insurgent groups in the country. With an ethnic colour, insurgency in Manipur has gradually been institutionalised as an integral part of the socio-political system of the state, which makes the situation more complex. And adding to this problem is the Myanmar connection – availability of easy sanctuary and cheap arms. It is a well-established fact that most of the insurgent groups from the state have got their camps all along the India–Myanmar border, particularly across the border. Hope remains high in the corridors of power in New Delhi that, with power transferred to the Aung San Suu Kyi led National League for Democracy and an increasingly good rapport with Myanmar, army operations against the insurgents inside Myanmar territory will become more practicable. The Government of India is sending its National Security Adviser Ajit Doval time and again to pursue the expulsion of the insurgents from Myanmar soil. The recent handing over of 22 Northeast insurgents to the Indian authorities in May 2020 by Myanmar is taken as a positive outcome (*The Hindustan Times* 2020). Moreover, the fact that Manipur could not escape the characteristic of one of the most militarised regions in the world is very obvious. Without taking into account the large presence of Central security forces, the number of state security personnel alone came to 62,253 in 2019 (BPR&D 2019, 59). The state topped the security–civilian ratio chart of the country at 1:76, according to the latest government report available (BPR&D 2019, 23). In this situation, hoping for a vibrant foreign policy pushing towards cross-border cooperation and shared prosperity has become almost unfeasible, but at the same time remains unavoidable.

Aggravating this already complex situation of insurgency and consequent militarisation in the state is the influx of small and light weapons from Southeast and East Asia through Myanmar as part of large-scale arms trafficking in the region.[5] These weapons actually have their origin from two sources, one as remnants of the various civil wars in Southeast Asia and another as directly manufactured by Chinese companies, like NORINCO, along the Myanmar–China border. The critical aspect of the entire process is that those involved in arms smuggling have got their own established routes, which change from time to time and are hard to detect.

A sudden spurt of narco-trafficking in recent times is another negative dimension associated with security issues on the border. Though heroin and synthetic drugs are smuggled from the Myanmar side, a reverse trend can be seen in the form of raw material being supplied from the Indian side too. Many villages of Manipur along the border have adopted large-scale poppy plantations. It is estimated that the total poppy plantations in the remote hill areas of Manipur came to around 6,000 acres in 2017–18 (Kipgen 2019). Another modus operandi is the setting up of illegal drug manufacturing units, mainly in the border villages. The latest and the biggest haul was a capture of drugs (mainly WY or Yaba tablets) worth INR 4,000 million coming from across the Myanmar border on 24 August 2019 (*The Sangai Express* 2019).[6] Continuous effort on the part of the authorities to curb the same is to little or no avail, with no permanent solution in sight. Ultimately, drug and human trafficking along the border has resulted in collateral damage in the form of mass-scale drug addiction and AIDS/HIV, which has become common in Manipur.

### *Chinese threat perception*

Another serious concern for India's Myanmar policy is the China factor. At present, a disturbing trend is the gradual domination and occupying of the entire Moreh-Tamu border trade by Chinese goods, not to the penchant of New Delhi. But this is not surprising as China has been one of the major trade partners of Myanmar since the time it gained independence, and the first trade agreement between the two was signed in 1954. From then on there has been no looking back and for many years China has remained the biggest trade partner of Myanmar. In 2018, according to the World Bank, China's share of Myanmar's foreign trade was 32.17 per cent, while India's was a meagre 5.12 per cent (World Bank 2020). The same goes for the situation in Myanmar–China border trade. Consequently, China acts as a decisive factor in the overall India–Myanmar cross-border trade and has a direct or indirect impact on the socio-economic dimension of the Northeast region. So when the heavy influx of commodities from the Myanmar side became a phenomenon in the ongoing border trade in the Moreh-Tamu sector, the Chinese presence could no longer be underplayed. The gradual decline and disappearance of the Premnagar market (Moreh town) on the Indian side and shifting of the business to the Myanmar side in Namphalong market (Tamu town) has also to do with the involvement of Chinese capital and traders. Besides, every household in Manipur uses cheap manufactured goods manufactured in China in abundance because of their durability and price affordability as compared to Indian products.

Controlling the Chinese influence and continuous dumping of cheap consumer goods into the area is a serious issue that is hard to curb. The apprehension is that, as has happened in many of Myanmar's border areas and towns adjoining China, Manipur may gradually be transformed into a Chinese satellite region, particularly from the economic and cultural perspective. In addition, as already mentioned, its involvement in the fluid law and order situation of the state is also another established fact. In a disclosure by India's National Investigation Agency it has been proved that Chinese-made arms consignments are smuggled from the China border to South Myanmar by the Kachin rebels and handed over to the National Socialist Council of Nagaland (NSCN)-IM, who brought the same inside India, in Manipur (*The Sangai Express* 2015). Rajeev Bhattacharya, a veteran correspondent and long-time Myanmar watcher, also confirms the theory of Chinese involvement (Bhattacharya 2020). Better relations with Myanmar in order to challenge the increasing influence of China in the region is another aim of India's Myanmar policy.

### *In the midst of India–ASEAN connectivity agenda*

Infrastructure in the form of transport and communication connectivity makes up one of the priority sectors of India's Myanmar policy. Through Moreh, Manipur is soon expected to form a significant part of the *Trans Asian Highway* (TAH) and the *Trans Asian Railway* (TAR) under the ambitious *Trans Asian Movement*.[7] The inauguration of the 165-km-long Tamu–Kalemyo–Kalewa Road (named *Indo-Myanmar Friendship Road*) in February 2001 marked the first significant step. Another noteworthy move in this direction is the initiative for the earliest materialisation of the *India–Myanmar–Thailand Trilateral Highway* linking India's Moreh to Mae Sot of Northern Thailand through Bagan in Myanmar, and the TAR linking Jiribam in Southwest Manipur to Moreh then to Tamu.[8] With all these initiatives, an optical fibre telecommunication project, which will run along the Trilateral Highway, is coming up under the aegis of BIMSTEC (the Bay of Bengal Initiative for Multi-Sectoral Technical and Economic Cooperation). In the years to come the state could emerge as a significant regional hub of global trade and commerce linking South Asia with Southeast Asia and further to Southwest China, if all goes well. The basic goal is, in due course, to transform these connectivity corridors into important corridors of development and shared progress in India and Myanmar where the state could have a major chunk. Indeed, India is not only trying to improve its connectivity, but it is also undertaking various projects for development of connectivity in Myanmar. However, despite the initiatives, too much emphasis on the security dimension is hampering the speedy growth of linkages. The proposal for the Imphal–Mandalay bus service has been postponed time and again since 2012. On the other hand, in order to challenge the ever-proactive *One Belt One Road* or *Belt and Road Initiative* projects of China, the said Indian projects need to speed up within the broader perspective of the AEP, which again calls for giving utmost attention to the progress of these border areas.

### *Racial affinity*

Harnessing the existing racial and ethnic affinity along both sides of the border for more people-to-people contact and to promote other aspects of cooperation with Southeast Asia forms another important priority of India's foreign policy concerning Northeast India. Besides, the trans-border tribes of the region are not deterred by the man-made boundaries in maintaining relations with their groups.

The 16 km *free entry regime* for locals on both sides also gives freedom of movement to the different ethnic tribes living in the border areas of Manipur. This is because there are trans-border tribes like the *Kukis* and *Nagas*. Besides, many *Meiteis* (majority ethnic group of Manipur) have also been settled in many places of Myanmar since the 11th century (Bahadur 2018). Thus, the sense of ethnic affinity is further strengthened because of the presence of people belonging to the same ethnic groups on both sides of the border. In fact, the *Meiteis* went there as part of matrimonial alliances or as captives of wars. Myanmar called the Meitei people *Kathe*, which was derived from the Shan word 'Cassay' (Nwe Ni Hlaing 2015). Of the *Kathe*, who settled in Myanmar as non-war captives, *Kathe* Brahmans (*Ponnas*) were the most outstanding class and they served the king as the court astrologers, advisers and royal priests who arranged the royal coronations. Today, the *Meiteis* in Myanmar are included in the official list of 135 ethnic groups of the country under the name of *Meithei* or *Kathe* (Ananda Travel 2019). The Manipuris on the Indian side always hope to connect with their ethnic kith and kin in different parts of Myanmar. Besides, in many Manipuri villages along the isolated stretches of the border, the official rules and political boundaries have no meaning for the denizens.

## Foreign policy challenges: the missing links

The above issues, which point largely towards a cross-current of internal and external dynamics, negative as well as positive, illustrate the fact that India's foreign policy is likely to face serious challenges with Manipur and the Northeast. Further, the subject needs to be studied in the context of India's three well-established priorities in the region, as follows: (i) enhancing India's security advantage vis-à-vis the immediate neighbours across the border; (ii) harnessing the existing racial and ethnic affinity along both sides of the border for more people-to-people contact; and (iii) using cross-border trade to promote the above two priorities.

For the aforesaid priorities, understanding the same is necessary for synchronising the issues of the state with the policy measures – which is not happening. For instance, on prioritisation of security, the fact is that it is always on India's foreign policy agenda. In terms of changing the security and strategic scenario in and around the region, India aims to (i) establish friendly neighbours in Southeast Asia, and (ii) control negative externalities. However, the chances of external pointers disturbing the internal ground situation are very much there. In the quest for national interest there is an infringement of local interest leading to diametric contradictions: hurting ethnic sensitivities, heavy militarisation, sense of alienation, etc. As for the second aspect, as already discussed, harnessing racial affinity for connecting across the border is another priority area. This was very much the emphasis in one of the studies carried out by the Indian Institute of Foreign Trade way back in 1994–95. The study declared that the Northeast is Indian Mongoloid, but culturally part of Southeast Asia. The very essence of this measure is the cultural foundation of modern development. Besides the two priorities mentioned, developing border trade makes up another most significant priority for India in the region. It is one of the strategic initiatives of India's Myanmar policy and the most distinctive manifestation of Manipur in the policy measures. Starting up cross-border trade was prioritised to speed up the above two priorities, and the overall strengthening of its position vis-à-vis Myanmar's other neighbours, especially China. Understanding India's foreign policy measures towards the state and its present trend calls for an understanding of the dynamics of cross-border trade and of Moreh town itself.

Keeping these aspects in view, the gradually emerging reality now is the need to understand the pulse of the region to implement any national policy connected with Manipur. It calls for a serious and critical observation. So when measures concerning Myanmar are made in terms of the changing geopolitics and the recent developments in the country, this part of India, with its immediate proximity to Myanmar, needs to be taken with the utmost seriousness. The immediate concern is that the people framing foreign policy seem to lack the required depth of knowing the grassroots.

Manipur is a land of contested interests and complexities moving along ethnic, geographical and economic lines. The state and its surroundings, because of its deep-rooted ethno-culture, strong identity politics and different psychological plane, not to mention its geostrategic location, has a dimension and dynamics of its own that are very different from other parts of the country. The so-called impediments which are hampering the smooth process of the foreign policy through various diplomatic channels in this part are to a great extent the outcome of this disconnect. It has emerged as a vicious circle of sorts. The issue is not about a blame game or being anti-nationalist. The acute reality is the neglect of the region and its people and issues associated with it, which the national policies have failed to overcome. Except for investment or pumping in of central funds, no real effort or attention from a human angle to know the issues and understand the grassroots has been taken up. For many years the centre has always viewed the shortcomings of the states as a security issue and law and order puzzle.

Even the hype surrounding the cross-border trade in Manipur seems less to do with trade and commerce and more to do with security issues. The unfortunate part is that trade in its actual form is not at all operating in the state to its fullest. This is very clear from the fact that there are no proper orders or direction as to who actually should control the border trade and the affairs of the border. There has been a failure to understand under whose jurisdiction it lies. Though many central agencies have their stations open in the town for maintaining the border and border trade, they show very little interest towards the same. The foreign policy priority of border trade being used as a medium for achieving fruitful relations, both in terms of strategic considerations and people-to-people contact, between India and its neighbours through Manipur and the Northeast have not materialised.

When security is allowed to play an upper hand at international relations, as is the case in Manipur, thinking of improving a friendly and more people-to-people contact in the region is futile. The avenue for development remains low while an atmosphere of suspicion towards the people and place is the general psyche of the agencies. The room for a meaningful federal policy structure is absent, with no proper flow of communication between the grassroots and the policymakers at the regional and national administration.

## Understanding Moreh: going to the micro-level

Understanding Moreh, India's last frontier town at the Indo–Myanmar border, will be a contributory factor in presenting a clear vista to the principal theme of dealing with the interface of domestic and international issues in India's foreign policy. The characteristics of the town and the people itself speak a lot to what actually could be a scenario of border trade. The start of formal trade in this town was the first official manifestation of India's Myanmar policy. It is where the practical part of the AEP could be seen for many Indians. In other words, it acts as a practical window for the country's foreign policy towards Myanmar and beyond. What happens in and around Moreh town could act as real input into the subject matter of India's foreign policy in this part of the country. Recent happenings in and around Moreh, the politico-ethnic standoff among different communities, almost to the point of a communal flare-up but for the timely control, as well as the disconnect created by natural calamities, brought the smooth process of business in the border town to a standstill. Though normalcy has returned, the earlier vibrancy of trade is still missing. It also brought out the existing relationship between the border, trade, international relations, people's aspirations, and power contestations in the whole scenario.

The question is why Moreh. Here, any issue associated with India's Myanmar policy will be very unpragmatic without touching upon the dynamics of Moreh. What happens within the town or fallouts across the border could put the foreign policy in a whirlwind if related matters are not tackled. Moreh has a distinct facet of its own in the whole milieu of India's foreign policy initiatives. From socio-cultural and politico-economic angles Moreh has got a significance of its own. Besides being the strategic and commercial centre, the town is unique in the sense that it has a cosmopolitan character, with different communities settled there and engaged in the border trade. Apart from the different tribes like the Nagas, Kukis and the Meiteis, the place is also inhabited by the Tamils, Punjabis, Marwaris and other mainland Indians, making it appear a mini-India. The racial affinity among the majority tribes on both sides of the border also provides a conducive atmosphere for more people-to-people contact, thus suitable for Track-II diplomacy in India–Myanmar relations (Khundrakpam 2015).

At first glance, Moreh has a very surreal character, moving at its own slow pace. However, behind the facade of peace, one will not miss the strong undercurrents caused by opposing power centres if one looks a little carefully. The recent flare-up between organisations of two communities is an outcome of the long years of subdued and pent-up emotions consequent to neglect and an absence of effective policies and inclusive governance. When one compares it to the other town on the Myanmar side the growth differences in various aspects are starkly visible. It seems to be in a dilapidated condition. And the tragic part is, despite its multi-racial character, a sense of permanency by the locals is missing.[9] With time, Moreh has become a *hybrid of commercial rivalry and ethnic conflict*; a visible symptom of deep-seated socio-economic malady. Adding further to the uncertainty is that, regardless of the significance of the place in India's foreign policy, the requisite mechanisms commensurate to a border town of international repute are missing. The failed situation and the negative multiplier effects in and around Moreh town, added to the existing suspicion among the general masses of the state towards India's AEP, will prove detrimental for the same in the long run. And the problem will not wither away that easily.

## Repositioning Manipur: where does it stand?

The indispensability of Manipur has become more acute in India's foreign policy, largely following the initiation of the second phase of the Look East policy and the growing importance of Myanmar in the regional geopolitical context since the country's election in November 2010. Before that, the state was merely viewed from a security point despite the prevalence of border trade, which is also the major reason for the sense of alienation among many locals. The move has been further re-enforced with the introduction of *Northeast Vision 2020*. The concern is how to tap into distributive justice?

For India's measures towards Myanmar through Northeast India, Manipur has got its own competitive advantage. It is blessed with considerable opportunities and strength towards attracting foreign investment. The advantages are there in terms of ethnic affinity, geographical proximity, workable land connectivity to the neighbouring country, abundant untapped natural and human resources etc., which in themselves are added trade gains for the state. However, this can only be possible when the complicated social and political speed breakers are smoothed.

Professional skills based on the *Regional Specialisation Index* and the comparative advantages have to be rigorously developed to avoid social unrest. Otherwise, there is apprehension that trade dynamism may bypass Manipur. At most, it may be a 'transit corridor' or 'launching pad' (which may not be to the penchant of the country's foreign policymakers). The very internal commercial energy of the local economy may be threatened and exhausted. Its local people feel ignored and deprived. There is a strong need to increase capacity building of professionally organised trade groups to get them involved and engaged in the multi-dimensional trade services. What is needed is an 'inclusive trade model'. The liquidation of Prem Nagar Market at Moreh is a case in point. In fact, the onset of a liberalised economic engagement before the establishment of a sound foundation of the local economy amounts to open fight among 'business unequals', with a dismal future for the state in all aspects of trade and commerce.

At present one finds a running phenomenon characterised by (i) militant conservatism; (ii) extortion and improper payouts; and (iii) undue blockades by certain groups with the intention of establishing a new socio-economic platform for temporary gains at the cost of long-term prosperity. People in and around the border feel complacent with the bubbles of primitive transactions under traditional exchange. If Manipur is to be a meaningful stakeholder in India's Myanmar policy measures, then there needs to be proper enhancement of the socio-economic and political dynamics of the state.

Despite all the complexities associated with the border town of Moreh and the cross-border trade, re-whittling the same will be a positive starter, but this is not happening. Though it does not form a very large share of the total trade volume between India and Myanmar, yet it is considerably significant from the angle of India's AEP towards Northeast India. Though the Government of India and the Government of Myanmar have worked towards facilitating Letter of Credit (LOC) facilities at two banks, United Bank of India in Moreh and Myanmar Business Bank in Tamu, not much has been effective.[10] The Integrated Check Post in Moreh, built at an estimated cost of INR 1,360 million (Land Port Authority of India 2019), has started functioning, though it has failed to make a meaningful contribution to the policy measure. Besides, the two approved border *haats*[11] between Manipur and Sagaing Region at Behiang and New Somtal in Manipur have not materialised effectively.

In addition, the lack of regulation by Myanmar on transiting third-country goods, especially from China, and the threat of non-state actors hassling traders in strong turf wars have all left no incentive to develop commerce. As a result, trade has shifted to Tamu's Namphalong market in Myanmar, disappointing local entrepreneurs in Manipur. Besides, recent issues like illegal human trafficking, boundary fencing, border pillar controversies etc. have all presented challenges to India's Myanmar policy. Multi-dimensional problems with their negative multiplier effects prevent much positive development in this direction. Not only Moreh town, but the state itself lacks the basic requirements and the right mechanism for any cooperation across the border to surge forward. As for the border town, which is to be the torchbearer for India's foreign policy measures towards Myanmar and beyond, it is characterised by issues such as interrupted electricity supply, poor communication facilities, absence of a significant number of standard hotels and no sign of civic authorities, not to mention the prevailing poor law and order situation.

These are in the context of the present pattern of restrictive opening. The apprehension is about the condition of the state when the AEP becomes fully operational and Manipur is fully open for free movement from either side of the border. This is something that needs serious pondering. Various forms of insecurity from a global perspective can already be seen surging to Manipur from the Myanmar side.

## Assessment

Having discussed all the aspects, one can deduce that both India's Myanmar policy and the AEP can act as decisive mediums not only for establishing the country's link with the Southeast Asian countries or ASEAN as a group, but also for improving the economic and human security base of the region within its purview. Manipur finds itself in a very complex situation when one put its politico-economic dimension within the greater context of the AEP, of which Myanmar is also a significant determinant. At present, the most serious challenge for the state is the existing disconnect between India's foreign policy measures towards Myanmar and the ground realities of the area – the absence of proper synchronisation. Adding to this is the deficiency of security in the form of security of life, security of employment, security of production and security of income in the state, creating grave challenges to the foreign policy initiatives towards it. The problem does not stop at this point since the foreign policy cannot correct the shortcomings. A kind of vicious circle exists. Besides, once the state's Eastern gateways are opened, the region is likely to face economic challenges from two angles over and above the negativities: the ultra rich and powerful business groups from within the country, and the Chinese products (both legal and illegal) sent through Myanmar. The lack of a proper mechanism to deal with the changes may leave Manipur merely as a transit for goods going from mainland India to Southeast Asian countries and as a dumping area for Chinese-made cheap consumer goods. There are two lines of thinking in the state regarding its connection with Myanmar – one that believes that it will enhance prosperity, and another which believes the contrary. The dynamics of globalisation cannot be ignored whether one likes it or not. Changes associated with the policy measures have to be there. Locals need to be realistic and be ready for the change. For this what is required is that potentials need to be converted to actual development so that when the AEP is fully materialised in the region and Manipur opens up to Myanmar, the 'flyover' or 'corridorisation' symptom is avoided. The focused cross-border trade will fail to bring the right return without linking it to the productive base of the state's economy. Manipur cannot continue with its dependency syndrome towards the central government, and the latter could not think of initiating its policies without taking the people of the state into its confidence.

Structural transformation both in the political and economic set-up is a must. This could be supplemented more effectively, as suggested by Subir Bhaumik, by overcoming two lasting deficiencies of the region: *deficits of democracy and development* (Bhaumik 2009, 29). Prime Minister Modi talked about maximum empowerment and maximum technology penetration; however, it is yet to touch the state in earnest (PMINDIA 2015). To date Manipur has not benefitted in any significant way either from the AEP or from India's relations with Myanmar in particular. The interplay of domestic and external factors around the region influencing India's foreign policy do not at all allow Manipur and its people to benefit.

While moving forward with its broad AEP, the central government has failed to address the distinctive needs of the region and the state by dealing with human security rather than its current top-down approach, which seems to be the case prevalent in any policy implementation. Attempting to build an improved relationship with its neighbour and opening the border alone in the absence of proper policy implementation will neither solve the multi-faceted problems faced by New Delhi in Manipur nor bring socio-economic changes for the people. On the whole, apprehension is writ large on the part of the locals. Continuing with the colonial mindset of looking at the state as a frontier, using an army against its own people, and using the law and order situation as a valid pretext for the flawed development process with little concern for the participation and involvement of locals in governance will not help, nor promote, the foreign policy agenda. This is because, as Keping argues,

> governance can be distinguished from government in several ways. Government authority is unitary, while governance involves different levels and venues of authority. And although governance implies instrumentality toward given goals, it requires interaction with civil society and local populations for its effectiveness.
>
> (Keping 2015)

Combining political pragmatism with developmental realities in taking up any policy implementation and planning is what is expected of the foreign policy mandarins in South Block. Synchronisation of India's Myanmar policy in the interest of those who are directly linked with the issue is a must. Only then could the ongoing interface of domestic issues and international factors in India's foreign policy be overcome for the better in the region. A mechanism linking top-down and bottom-up initiatives is a must when it comes to foreign policy. Besides, efforts need to be made to create a congenial socio-political atmosphere where the general masses and the civil societies of the state become receptive to the developmental dynamics encompassing the region, with its ever-changing geopolitical realities. Strategic thinking and policy formulation requires farsightedness and overcoming the traditional notion of viewing every aspect purely from a security or business angle. Policies need to be more people-centric with provisions providing ample space for more people-to-people contact across the border. Only then will India–Southeast Asian cooperation become meaningful for Northeast India, and Manipur could make a positive contribution to India's Myanmar policy, both in terms of multilateral cooperation and economic connectivity, with the security issue being mutually settled.

## Notes

* The author would like to extend sincere gratitude to Dr Prasenjit Biswas for his insightful inputs in improving and enhancing the paper. Thanks also to Dr Iman Kalyan Lahiri for sharing his valuable viewpoints during the field interactions in the borderlands of Northeast India.

1 The term '*Zomia*' was originally coined by Professor Willem van Schendel of the Netherlands in 2002 (in an article published in the geography journal *Environment and Planning D: Society and Space*), and James C. Scott used it in his thesis. The word itself is an amalgamation of two terms '*Zo*' meaning remote or hill and '*Mi*' meaning people. Thus literally the term denotes a highland region, which is applicable to the Northeast of India. The concept of *Southeast Asian Massif* was introduced by the Canadian anthropologist Jean Michaud in 1997. The regions of *Zomia* and *Southeast Asian Massif* almost overlap with each other.

2 With the inclusion of six more tribes there are at present 39 Scheduled tribes (mostly Christians by religion) residing together in Manipur.

3 Kabaw Valley is an area of about 3,000 sq. miles covered with dense teak forest, located in the Upper Chindwin District in present Myanmar's Sagaing Division. It was a contested area which remained mostly under the Manipuri kingdom during the time of pre-colonial history. In the post-Independence period Prime Minister Nehru, under his foreign policy of having good relations with immediate neighbours, seceded the area to Myanmar on 30 March 1953, without taking into consideration the minds of the natives. This act has embittered the people of Manipur until the present day.

4 As per the Directorate General of Foreign Trade (Government of India) public notice no. 50 issued on 17 December 2015, it has been decided that the border trade at Moreh, Manipur would be upgraded to normal trade so as to promote bilateral trade between the two countries. This has indeed materialised.

5 Small arms and light weapons mainly enter Northeast India from Myanmar through Chandel, Ukhrul and Churachandpur districts of Manipur, though there are some instances where they come from the side of Mizoram state also.

6 WY stands for '*World Is Yours*', and is a psychotropic drug, mainly in tablet form.

7 Both the Trans Asian Railway (TAR) and Trans Asian Highway (TAH) are components of Asian Land Transport Infrastructure Development (ALTID). Most of the road network initiatives between the two countries will be along the alignment of TAH.

8 The Union Cabinet of India had already approved the signing and ratification of the inter-governmental agreement on the TAR on 8 March 2007. It signed the Agreement on 29 June at the UN Headquarters. India is to be linked with the TAH through its East–West Corridor Project under the National Highway Development Project.
9 As observed by the author during his frequent field trips in and around Moreh town since 2015.
10 Under the LOC the Indian Rupee and the Myanmar Kyat could be legally converted into dollars in the said banks.
11 A *haat* is a temporary open-air market held regularly on specific days. It serves as a trading venue for local people in remote villages or small towns in the border areas of India, Nepal and Bangladesh.

## References


Ananda Travel. 2019. *List of the 135 tribes and ethnic group in Myanmar*. www.ananda-travel.com/UK/myanmar_ethnic_group_uk.htm (accessed: 20 July 2020).

Bahadur, Mutua. 2018. *Manipuri diaspora in Myanmar: Past and present* – Part 1. www.e-pao.net/epSubPageExtractor.asp?src=manipur.Ethnic_Races_Manipur.Manipuri_Diaspora_in_Myanmar_Part_1_By_Mutua_Bahadur (accessed: 20 April 2020).

Bhattacharya, Rajeev. 2020. How China's 'aid' to rebel groups sustained Northeast insurgency. www.thequint.com/voices/opinion/northeast-india-sustained-insurgency-covert-chinese-support-weapons-supply (accessed: 14 August 2020).

Bhaumik, Subir. 2009. *Troubled Periphery: Crisis of India's Northeast*. New Delhi: Sage India.

Bose, Pratim Ranjan. 2018. At Moreh, trade with Myanmar borders on informal. *The Hindu Businessline*, 12 November. www.thehindubusinessline.com/news/at-moreh-trade-with-myanmar-borders-on-informal/article25478894.ece# (accessed: 13 August 2020).

BPR&D. 2019. *Data on police organisations (as on January 1, 2019)*. New Delhi: Ministry of Home Affairs, Government of India. https://bprd.nic.in/WriteReadData/userfiles/file/202001301028101694907BPRDData2019-19forweb-2.pdf (accessed: 16 August 2020).

Hindustan Times. 2020. 'HT Exclusive: Nudged by Ajit Doval, Myanmar army hands over 22 northeast insurgents'. *The Hindustan Times*, 16 May. https://bit.ly/3qLQdiJ (accessed: 12 August 2020).

Kaul, Man Mohini. 2010. India's Look East Policy. *World Focus* 31, no. 10: 431–436.

Keping, Yu. 2015. *Essays on the Modernization of State Governance*. Beijing: Social Science Academic Press.

Khathing, J.S.R. 2005. Indo-Myanmar Border Trade. In *Indo-Myanmar Border Trade, Status, Problems and Potentials*, eds., Gurudas Das, N. Bijoy Singh and C. Joshua Thomas, 51–57. New Delhi: Akansha Publishing House.

Khundrakpam, Padmabati. 2015. *Increasing Influx of Consumer Commodities from Myanmar's Side to Manipur and India's Look East Policy*. Unpublished UGC MRP Report.

Kipgen, Ngamjahao. 2019. Why are farmers in Manipur cultivating poppy? *Economic and Political Weekly* 54, no. 46. www.epw.in/engage/article/why-are-farmers-manipur-cultivating-poppy (accessed: 15 August 2020).

Land Port Authority of India. 2019. *Integrated Check Post Moreh*. www.lpai.gov.in/content/innerpage/icp-moreh.php (accessed: 5 June 2020).

Mohan, C. Raja. 2006. India and the balance of power. *Foreign Affairs* 85, no. 4: 17–32.

Mohan, C. Raja. 2002. 'Looking East: Phase Two'. *The Hindu*, 11 April. https://mea.gov.in/articles-in-indian-media.htm?dtl/15614/Looking+East+phase+two (accessed: 18 May 2020).

Nwe Ni Hlaing. 2015. The Meitei (Kathe) Crown Service groups in Myanmar from the earliest times to the end of Monarchical Rule. *Journal of the Myanmar Academy of Science and Arts* 13, No. 9: 65–86.

PMINDIA. 2015. Leveraging the Power of JAM: Jan Dhan, Aadhar and Mobile. Prime Minister's Office, Government of India. www.pmindia.gov.in/en/government_tr_rec/leveraging-the-power-of-jam-jan-dhan-aadhar-and-mobile/ (accessed: 20 January 2020).

Scott, James C. 2009. *The Art of Not Being Governed, An Anarchist History of Upland Southeast Asia*. New Haven: Yale University Press.

Sharma, Hanjabam Gyanendro. 2009. Look East policy: Its Gaze and Danger in the North East. In *Look East Policy and India's Northeast: Polemics and Perspectives*, ed., Thingnam Kishan, 200–209. New Delhi: Concept Publishing.

Singh, Udai Bhanu. 2018. Significance of India's Act East Policy and Engagement with ASEAN. *IDSA Backgrounder*, 4 December. https://idsa.in/backgrounder/significance-India-act-east-policy-and-engagement-with-asean-ubsingh_041218 (accessed: 3 April 2020).

Taneja, Nisha, Naing, Tin Htoo, Joshi, Sanjana, Singh, Thiyam Bharat, Bimal, Samridhi, Garg, Sakshi, Roy, Riya and Sharma, Manali. 2019. *India-Myanmar Border Trade*. Working Paper 378. New Delhi: ICRIER.

The Sangai Express. 2015. 'Chinese weapons being supplied to NE groups: NIA Arms smuggled via Manipur'. *The Sangai Express*, 2 April. http://e-pao.net/GP.asp?src=2..030415.apr15 (accessed: 10 June 2020).

The Sangai Express. 2019. 'Intl drug baron held; drugs worth Rs 400 Cr seized'. *The Sangai Express*, 26 August. https://bit.ly/33ZCbAo (accessed: 1 December 2020).

Verghese, B.G. 2002. *Reorienting India: The New Geo-Politics of Asia*. New Delhi: Konark Publishers.

World Bank. 2020. Myanmar Trade. https://wits.worldbank.org/CountryProfile/en/Country/MMR/Year/LTST/TradeFlow/Import/Partner/all/ (accessed: 14 August 2020).

# 12 Thinking, looking and acting

## Beyond East and Southeast to the 'other Asia'

*Sashinungla*

This chapter attempts to locate the critical role of the cultural dispersion of ethnic communities across transboundary South and Southeast Asia, who are substantive determinants of a variety of political and economic relations between nation-states in the said region. These ethnic groups remain substantive determinants in the form of giving rise to distinctive spatial imaginaries that negotiate resources and power relations across boundaries. India's Northeast, as another ethnically co-inhabited subregional fringe of the entire South and Southeast of Asia, combines cultural similarities as well as differences in terms of a continuous dualism between self and other, interior and exterior that potentially unsettles any mapping relation between communities, nation-states and boundaries in-between. Given this, the paper argues that India's Northeast constitutes a very special spatio-socio-politico context for critical geopolitics that goes far beyond enchanted policy paradigms and calls for a (re)understanding of the 'Other Asian' texture of a subregional formation that eludes mere looking and acting. In terms of India's foreign policy, India's relations with China and continental Southeast Asia as well as with Myanmar and Bangladesh are potentially affected by the political and cultural dynamics of India's Northeast, which largely presents a picture of alienation, distance and disconnect between mainstream India and its Northeastern periphery. The question is, can the 'Look/Act East' policy in some way establish a kind of 'reflective equilibrium' in terms of internal stability and good neighbourly relations?

Two distinct factors meet here: a critical geopolitical subregion (CGPSR) and its continual pressure on the limits of paradigmatic policy formulations. As far as the category 'Northeast India' is concerned, it has remained as a stranger, an Other being in the geopolitical subsumption of belonging to the South Asian and Southeast Asian political space. The category figured only as an ethnographic construct and not as a political economy space and far less as a foreign policy component. India's Look East Policy (LEP) turns the region into a mere corridor or a connective that joins South Asian territories with Southeast Asian territory. One would clearly note that in this concept of being, a 'corridor' launched from the heart of India's foreign policy establishment 'cannot allow itself to be appropriated' without being foreign to itself or to its self-image. That Northeast India is foreign to itself is amply demonstrated in its transborder flow of ideas, concepts, worldviews and identities that produce a picture of being-at-home and a certain sense of exteriority and therefore a deterritorialized entity. How the Indian state deals with such a space of multiple connections and meanings in a scheme of connecting itself both internally and externally with the neighbourhood remains a significant causal factor that never really attains the status of an ontological necessity. As a region of flow and flux, looked at from the Indian mainstream, and as a region of perpetual alteration in itself, looked at from its own location, India's Northeast assumes the place of a remainder that returns into some of the inter-state perturbances, which can never be exhausted within a policy frame. It enters an area of shadowy optical indeterminacy that falls in the domain of the incalculable. In terms of India's domestic policy, the incalculability is expressed in the form of 'carrot and stick' formulations that mark a document such as *ASEAN-India Vision 2020*,[1] or the place of Northeast India in the context of the ASEAN free trade agreement (FTA), which turn the space of the Northeast into a passive giver or a receiver of people, goods, ideas, capital and other such moving fragments.

As a calibrated response to long-standing ethnic insurgencies and political mobilizations against the experience of discrimination and neglect by the central government in India's Northeast, the Indian state assumes a realist-instrumentalist approach in terms of management of certain fixed objectives in India's Northeast. It is a 'view from nowhere' that assumes a third party position in its relation to people and statist politics of the region, while it attempts to control and dominate the region by playing the strategy of pump priming and claiming ownership over natural resources as part of 'national development'. The central government, after the deployment of elaborate security architecture in the Northeast region, leaves it to the mercy of internal dissensus as well as using the legitimate organs of legislative, judicial and executive powers to 'govern' it (Biswas and Suklabaidya, 2008: 36). The crux of organizing the region by acts of governmentality is to create a 'state of exception' as well as to appropriate it by using legal-juridical force of law. The foreign policy of the Indian state in relation to the neighbourhood of India's Northeast is bound by this fixed paradigm of governance that reduces the region to only a constituted element of the policy form without allowing an agency of constitution that potentially would have hinged itself upon the specific history, culture and economy of the region. One can characterize this policy slant as a deterritorializing subregionalism that has often found expressions in externalization of the region or in unwittingly taking hold of its politics and culture in a manner of guardianship by the Indian state. Needless to say, it subsumes the region under a bigger formation of the state that holds the centralizing power modelled after a Hobbesian Leviathan. The Leviathan is sustained by micro politics of a kind that subsumes the region in a state of just being a 'place' within the nation space, which takes the form of manoeuvring and manipulating the elite consciousness of ethnic masses by drawing sharp internal boundaries that are reinforced through legitimate and illegitimate forms of violence.

The voice and agency of its diverse people cancel each other out. Identities emerge in a space of contestation only to articulate a sense of negativity. The carrot part of the central government's policy indulges in a politics of accommodation and winning-over by using some of the collaborating threads within internecine fights between identities. As part of the state policy, the Indian state creates a collaborating class of actors from within ethnic identities and succeeds in raising them above marginalization that only perpetuates dominance within. Claims of belonging, nationhood and specificity are thus vulnerable to a state-sponsored politics of collaboration with the big brother.[2] As this politics of collaboration occupies the centre stage of Northeastern India's public political discourse, space for an alternative claims-making gets neutralized. The institutional management of political identities and their territorial claims of power by creating minority institutions[3] and by controlling them from above perpetuate a regimen of dependence that opens up the ethnic space to the logic of the state, market and capital.

## 'Thinking' India's Northeast and Look/Act East Policy

Recent historical development that throws up new opportunities and challenges is the growing realization that India must move closer to the countries to our east – closer economically, politically, emotionally and culturally. It will be justified to suggest that, without the active involvement of India's Northeast, it will be impossible to pursue these opportunities and address these challenges with any degree of wholesome national purpose. Anthropologist Peter Kunstadter described India's Northeast as a region where India "looks less and less India and more and more like the highlands of Southeast Asia" (Kunstadter, 1967). The ancestors of most of the ethnic groups that populate this 'remote' Indian region hail from Southeast Asia or Southwest China and are broadly of Mongoloid stock, which is why India's Northeast is seen as the country's 'Mongoloid fringe'.[4] The migration of ethnicities into what is India's Northeast today before the advent of the British was primarily east to west. The Ahoms who ruled Assam for several centuries, or most of the other ethnic groups who inhabit the various states of Northeast India, originally migrated from Southeast Asia or Southwest China into where they now live in India's Northeast (Bhaumik, 2009). Given the size and diversity of India and the historical and, in many cases, cultural distance of the region from the mainland, India's Northeast remains a widely misunderstood entity in the minds of most Indians. Post-independence, many issues relating to political and administrative arrangements, cultural, linguistic, ethnic identities and economic marginality came to the fore, often in violent forms, and occasionally even questioning the primacy of national identity. Many of these issues persist even today.

Most academic as well as policy discourse on India's Look East Policy (LEP) underlines both the 'centrality' of the Northeast and the urgency of an 'integrated' approach in its conceptualization. However, a slightly deeper analysis may hint at something very different. The nature of the conceptualization itself is problematic, when it sees India's Northeast as a 'land bridge' to connect the country's mainland with its Southeast Asian neighbours. Many analysts working closely on Northeastern tribal culture and politics, including social scientists and philosophers, have pointed out how such viewing of the Northeast as a 'land bridge' has also led to the fear among citizenry that development will pass through without doing much good to the region itself. Though views such as how India has been seeking to situate the country's 'troubled Northeast' at the heart of its LEP are well talked about and documented, it is not correct (both in theory and in practice) to argue that the LEP is 'centred' on the Northeast. The decision to reorient India's foreign policy towards its eastern borders came first, and the strategic location of the Northeast, useful for the implementation of this new ambition, came as a necessary corollary. The Northeast has historically been looked at as a means to an end, and herein lies the problem for any successful implementation of the LEP. Hence, "the many problems identified with the Northeast in the context of the LEP are symptomatic of the unequal focus on forward as well as backward integration and connectivity, which implies that internal developments must be concomitant to external developments" (Neog, 2014).

New Delhi may be driven to 'look East' as much by domestic as by foreign policy concerns, as many policy analysts would argue, but the question is – which and whose domestic concerns? This complexity is also evidenced by the Institute for Defence Studies and Analyses' (IDSA's) roundtable on the 'Northeast's Role in India's Look East Policy (LEP)', which stated,

> While rest of India has benefited from greater engagement with ASEAN under the LEP, the Northeast, which is the gateway to the Southeast Asian countries has been left behind…because of the week economic base and lack of proper infrastructure.
>
> (IDSA, 2013)

Very often, the notion of an 'integrated approach' is conflated with a mere politico-strategic and economic imperative, or often there are security concerns overriding the overall tone of the policy approach. Thus, it is important to be cautious of the claim that the LEP is 'multifaceted and multipronged' in its conceptualization and approach. There is a tendency to favour political statements over actual policy formulation. It should focus on initiatives that must be taken (both domestic and foreign) in order to seek an emotionally strong sense of belonging and togetherness in its engagement with the adventure of nation building, rather than merely trying to establish strategic links or extending its influence to fill the so-called power vacuum in Southeast Asia. Also, India's LEP needs to be viewed as a logical reawakening of India to the strategic reality in the post-Cold War era that India had 'Other Neighbours' too, besides South Asia. In most of the literature on the subject, concessions are made for a wide range of problems in seeking to situate the Northeast in the LEP; however, no concerted discussion has been made on why it remains India's 'troubled Northeast'. There is great impetus for taking India's Look East initiative forward. But it is also necessary to reexamine the paradigm in which the Look East thrust is conceived.

## Look(ed) at as an other

Both colonialist and Indian cultural nationalist discourses constituted the Northeast and the Northeastern subjects as the 'other'. The category 'Indian citizen' is a constitutive one with a normative ideal, and when the Northeastern tribes are compared to this normative ideal, they emerge as immigrants. For instance, Northeasterners were referred to as immigrants in the 2014 Bharatiya Janata Party (BJP) Election Vision Documents.[5] Colonial discourse represented India and the Northeast as binary opposites and the Northeastern tribes emerged as the 'Mongolian other' of Aryan India in this historiography (Kikon, 2009). India was represented through the categories of caste and religion; the Northeast was understood through the category of racialized 'Mongolian' tribes who migrated from China and Southeast Asia. Such anthropological analysis constituted the Northeastern tribes as different from the other tribes in the rest of the country, who emerged as *adivasis* or as indigenous to India. Thus, the nationalist historiography, by adopting the orientalist approach without dismantling the distinction between India and the Northeast, constituted the Northeastern tribes as belonging to another civilization, located in Southeast Asia, and different from the Indian or Indic civilization.[6] The Northeastern tribes were considered by the Indian cultural nationalist approach as too diverse and different, and unable to assimilate to the idea of the unity of India and therefore as still needing pedagogical training to be modern and national subjects. Thus, the Northeastern tribes emerge as immigrants who have to be 'accommodated' in the postcolonial nation-state. In post-independent India, this is articulated as the need to integrate the tribes into the national mainstream.

One could see here a kind of displacement and dislocation of Northeastern communities into a communicatively constructed and discursively negotiated space of politics that ironically brings out the possibility of a positive construction of being other to the statist nationalist policies, including both domestic and foreign policies. Although they are displaced into a differently constructed identity, which is deterritorialized in relation to mainstream India, yet they constitute a process of othering that is a transnational flow, operationally controlled by migrating non-state actors, who are to be recognized as part and parcel of being Indian. This difficulty of inclusion, as depicted in the recent film *Axone*[7] of the Northeastern subjects within the mainstream Indian cognitive frame of being Indian, comes as no surprise. In the film, actress Sayani Gupta, a Bengal woman appearing as a Nepali, does not relish fermented Axone, which is a misrepresentation, as Nepalis – a combination of various hill tribes and nontribal communities – do have an age-old fermentation practice in their own food culture. So a sense of difference through cultural difference over food within Northeasterners is portrayed, which gives a sense of internal difference among Northeasterners, while large number of communities sharing Akhuni, a Naga dish, creates a sense of shared culture and mutual respect for each other's cultural markers. Indeed, the film portrayed a shared cultural space of Northeasterners living in Delhi in their food habits and in other areas of life, where solidarity between groups and communities is the hallmark of this popular film. Theoretically this could be termed as a paradoxical reterritorialization that could only be legitimated by political, military and administrative control.

This mode of deterritorialization and enforced reterritorialization leads several armed-ethno sovereignty movements in the Northeast, such as the Naga sovereignty movement, to accept and respond to the Indian nationalist narrative of 'difference' by claiming a history distinct from India (Nuh, 2002). Consequently, building on the cultural nationalist narrative of Indian history, which did not include the Northeastern tribes within the category of 'Indian', constitutes the region as 'anti-state' or 'anti-national'. Put more allegorically, such ethnonational movements and their claims of sovereignty assume the form of claiming a status of 'nations-from-below' (Biswas, 2002: 140–162). The Indian state's military response to these 'nations-from-below' ethnic minorities' movements in the region needs to be seen as a hegemonic enterprise. Thus, the region emerged not only as the 'troubled Northeast' but also as a threat to India's internal and external security – a nefarious border region inhabited by anti-national elements whose loyalty to the Indian nation-state is suspect (Baruah, 2009; Bhaumik, 2009). This way of looking at the region as an other ironically acknowledges its right to be an other, while, at the same time, it denies it a place by looking and acting through it and above it. This creates a reign of impunity violating the personal and political freedoms of the members of Northeastern communities.[8]

This Indian cultural nationalist narrative of 'othering' the Northeast region and its subjects is also reflected in the nature of the conceptualization and approach the Indian state has towards the LEP or the 'LEP through Northeast'. It is obvious that the Northeast provides India with the *strategic, cultural and economic space* to the East. There is a genuine concern to engage and understand the region, but this distance is complicated further by India's LEP policy formulations couched in the colonialist and Indian cultural nationalist framework, both in its language and temperament, which is unable to imagine that the region's 'wholesome' participation is crucial. This problematic 'mainstream' India – Northeast relationship is clearly reflected in IDSA's view in the *ASEAN-India Vision Document 2020* and India's LEP – suggesting how people in the Northeast could be 'induced' to establish commercial linkages in Myanmar. It argues, "these will create economic interests for Myanmar in India and encourage it *to act against the Northeast insurgent groups* and keep the road networks secure" (IDSA, 2013, emphasis added). Such condescending and military approach of the Indian state and the policy analysts towards the region is commonplace. In India's LEP, the importance of security aspects is clearly discernible. Most vision documents and leading Indian policy analysts list the major lacunae in India's LEP through Northeast as: (i) absence of deep engagement with Myanmar, (ii) 'troubled Northeast', (iii) an unstable Bangladesh, (iv) porous borders, (v) ubiquitous corruption in the region, and so on (Bhaumik, 2014; Gupta, 2012). However, in the context of India's LEP and the Northeast, the paper argues that New Delhi's lack of effort or sincerity to overcome the democracy deficit in its engagement with its own 'Mongolian other', or the so-called 'troubled Northeast', is the major lacuna of India's LEP through Northeast.

For the country's 'troubled Northeast' to transform into the "gateways of opportunities of international trade and commerce" (Verghese, 2004), it will not be so wrong to suggest that a more understanding, purposefully open and entirely empathetic national involvement in the affairs of the Northeast would go a long way. Such an approach would facilitate a process of emotional alignment much more conducive to a firm and stable sense of common belonging, rendering the much required edge for India's Look East initiatives. A vibrant, self-confident, open and creative Northeast (both in terms of economy and culture) is vitally connected with the project of establishing mutually beneficial and multifaceted economic ties between India and our easterly neighbours. The Northeast cannot simply be a corridor for trade, commerce and other economic transactions and collaboration between India and our eastern neighbours. It must also be a substantial partner in these relations. Therefore, the policy formulation of India's LEP through Northeast must in a major way take into account policy initiatives to ensure the integrated economic development of the Northeast so that it is not just reduced to a peripheral role in the India–Southeast Asia economic partnership.

It is high time that Delhi overcomes its strange 'security mindset' in its approach to LEP through Northeast and paves the way for investment and development which has long been denied to the region and its inhabitants. As India tries to solidify its claims to success in institutionalizing pluralism and democracy and enhances its global positioning, it can no longer hide behind insurgency and security concerns and deny the people of Northeast even the basic infrastructure for a modern economy – rail, road and air links, water and power.[9] Delhi must stop portraying itself as 'an island of democracy in a sea of danger'.[10] In its approach to the 'troubled Northeast', India has always played this 'moral geography' (a term drawn from Michael Shapiro) – in which India views itself as a state of innocents subject to violent, unprovoked assault from insurgents. However, the locus of the armed ethno-sovereignty movements of the ethnic minorities in India's Northeast is the Indian cultural nationalist's 'othering' of its own 'Mongolian other'.

Even when India perceives and treats its own 'troubled Northeast' as a remote and dangerous frontier zone, how do we expect our neighbourly countries to make investment in it? Studies suggest that the ASEAN countries have shown tremendous interest in the Northeast. Even the Chinese made it clear on more than one occasion that their preferred investment destination in India is through the Northeast. The reasons are both economic and cultural, but they are deterred by the general perception of the security situation in the region. They also complain of lack of visibility or information about India's Northeast. It makes definite logistic and economic sense to Look East through Northeast. In a way, the success of India's LEP through Northeast would be dependent on the insurgency and conflict situation in the region. However, it is one thing to objectively and pragmatically outline the history of violent conflicts in the region and its immediate neighbourhood and try to find ways to resolve them, but it is another thing to cite 'strategic' reasons and deny the inhabitants of the Northeast their 'right to development' and their basic human rights. By proving its serious involvement towards the welfare of the region, Delhi can diffuse such doubts in the minds of prospective investors. It must move beyond the traditional muscular and security approach to the affairs of the Northeast. Commenting on the role of the Northeast in India's LEP, IDSA stated:

> Development of transportation and communication links in the Northeast should be considered as a *strategic issue* and accordingly greater resources should be allocated for such projects.
>
> (IDSA, 2013, emphasis added)

This is nothing surprising. Post-independence India has consistently 'dealt' with Northeast affairs from a strategic/security/military point of view, and never as a human issue – whether in regards to developmental projects or any administrative arrangements. The Indian state, according to the 'strategic' or 'security' demands or situations, actively 'encourages' or 'discourages' infrastructural and administrative arrangement in the region. For example, it opposed the opening of the Stilwell Route, citing that this could allow China great advantages in the event of a conventional war with India or that the road could be used by China to dump its goods through the Northeast. Therefore, Northeastern inhabitants' 'right to development' is 'hyphenated' with the ideology and policies of the state and changes according to the country's military or strategic situation.

Indeed, this is where the region is looked at as an other, an incalculable that can only be accommodated within a policy framework that 'deterritorializes' the region as an 'other' of India. This creates a relationship of othering:

> The politician arm-twisted every contractor for a cut and a deal for every contract work issued by his department and made money ... Meanwhile the number of poor people has increased because no opportunities were

> created for them. Governments only gave audience to mercenaries and collaborators in their wealth creation ventures.
>
> (Mukhim, 2015)

A stark otherness with a component of an internally alienating form of rent-seeking, wealth-mongering and neglect of the poor in the context of ethnic and tribal societies of the region assumes the form of crony capitalism that the Indian state patronizes. The right to development thus gets upturned by an inegalitarian exclusion of the larger majority of teeming subalterns within the frame of political economy that weakens the state structures in turn. The question is, can a weak local state collaborate with an influence-enhancing nation-state that aims to wield greater military, financial and political influence in the larger Southeast and South Asia?

Indian policymakers' approach to the LEP has been shaped by a culture that viewed geopolitics primarily in terms of agenda-setting 'Indian' spaces that are under threat from 'encroachments' from within and outside the border. This turns the internal state spaces within India's Northeast into a space of attrition against an imagined enemy who is breathing outside the borders. Herein, foreign policy and military strategy gets intertwined in organizing civic spaces into an imagined war zone by way of erecting checkpoints, booby traps and garrisons that co-exist with essential markers of place and identity. India's foreign policy sites assume a localized character of warfare against the supposed 'internal enemies' of ethnic insurgents, who act as the primary source of a 'bottom-up' policy of collaboration and contest with neighbours. Such localized low-intensity wars against internal enemies are treated by the Indian state as sites of a 'multiscalar' relational dynamic that tilts India's relation with its Asian neighbours.

Within this multiscalar bottom-up entrenchment with border sites, India's foreign policy assumes distinctive functional characteristics. On the one hand, India builds on a strategic multilateral cooperation with neighbouring nation-states such as Bhutan, Bangladesh or Sri Lanka on matters of tackling insurgency by ethnic groups. On the other, with states like Myanmar and China, a combined military-strategic relationship is continuously worked out in order to secure stability and peace rather than economic gains. This dual approach provides an interesting dimension to India's new found interest/focus in its 'troubled Northeast' that anchors directions of such a policy. The Look/Act East policy suggests both these directions of foreign policy with two different sets of neighbours. While looking East, India attempted to converge with China's Look West policy, while it does not converge with Myanmar's policy of military control on its Northern inhabitant ethnic groups. Seemingly India's inability to address the challenges posed by Northern Myanmar and the Myanmar–China entrenched relationship reduces India to a policy closure in and around Northeastern India.

The policy document of India's LEP reflects such a closure when it states, "the nature of political and intellectual discourse in the Northeast has to be changed from the anti-globalization and identity politics to one of economic growth and integration" (IDSA, 2013). Seemingly LEP makes hay out of a slogan like the idea of integrating Northeast India's economy with that of Southeast Asia. This suppresses the heterogeneity of Northeastern ethnic cultures and its historical and political complexity into a straitjacketed trade and commerce relationship that only becomes some kind of border trade.[11] The question is, can border trade ever assume the form of global multilateral trading, or it will only succeed as a people-to-people trade in the border region? Obviously current trading only shows the limited export potential of local goods that are reciprocally demanded by consumers (De, 2014). Such demand revolves around food and consumer items that are in short supply on the other side of the border and hence it does not really involve manufacturing and service sectors or any other form of comparative advantage.

Generalized statements about the affairs of the region not only ignore the complexities of the ethico-political history of the problem under discussion, but also overlook the fact that the socio-cultural structure and social arrangement of the Northeastern tribes are organically multicultural, fluid and open in orientation. They oppose oppressive hierarchies and cultural subordination. The discussion on India's LEP shows how 'mainland' India–Northeast dynamics involve complex interconnections between heterogeneous cultures. It also highlights how post-independence India struggled or continues to struggle to embrace its racial and cultural diversity within, underlining that the "unity in diversity" framework, within which the Indian nation is imagined, failed to accept Northeastern tribes as Indian in the political, racial, cultural and epistemic sense. The implication of this moral-cognitive failure of the Indian state manifests itself in pursuing a development agenda that turns the Northeast into a mere resource base. The Government of India's policy toward Northeastern India demonstrated this deficit of trust and lack of equal citizenship in its policy of dam-making in seismic zone IV on almost every river of the region. Such a paradigm of development only produces a sense of 'lack' that acts as a driving force behind formulations of domestic and foreign policy only to multiply the lack itself in many different ways. The most significant discourse about such a lack is the lack of the ethical in the constitution of the political in policy formulations of the Indian state.

Such 'lack' also produces 'imaginative geographies' which fold distance into difference and generate what Gregory calls "architectures of enmity" (Gregory, 2004). The interaction of the colonial racist narrative on the Northeastern tribes with the cultural nationalist narrative of 'Indian' history creates the 'space of exception' inhabited by those subject to the sovereign's power but excluded from equal protection, with incomplete rights and voice.[12] The 'troubled Northeast' cuts a Giorgio Agamben homo sacer figure,[13] and creates a space in what Gregory termed as the "colonial present" in which the mainstream cultures continue to privilege their own interests and mobility by denying the sovereignty of the uncivilized 'other'. Due to insurgents' responsibility for the attacks and separation or autonomy demands, the territory of the

Northeast could be viewed as a space outside civilization. Thus, the inhabitants of this space were reduced to targets on the Indian military/defence/security map – and subject to being monitored, controlled and secured by paramilitary troupes through watchtowers, checkpoints, roadblocks, separation walls and hilltop settlements. Northeastern society was viewed as located within uncivilized, barbarian space, allowing Northeastern civil infrastructure to be surveilled, targeted and destroyed through exceptional martial law such as AFSPA – where suspicion is enough for any armed forces personnel to shoot and kill citizens. What makes possible such draconian martial law within a democratic framework in the Northeast in the first place? It shows that citizenship is not merely a legal concept, but rather that there are critical political assumptions that underlie it. Within this context, the Northeastern tribes become 'hyphenate' in India's recent Look East politics and diplomacy. This history of inequality is intricately tied to the Indian state's approach (in both theory and practice) to its LEP through Northeast, and this is a major constraint (both internal and external) standing in the way of India's enthusiastic participation in and support of multilateralism in Asia-Pacific.

## Conceiving an 'other Asia'

The pigeonholed and limited perspective of the LEP symbolizes an impoverished constitutionalism that turns Northeast India's responsible dissent into an 'unrecognized ethnography' of everyday politics. One needs to understand how these limits are arrived at and further to what extent; these limits meet the geopolitically Asian reality. As has been stated, Northeastern spaces as a declared 'other' to the Indian mainstream generate an ontological insecurity for the Indian state. Such an ontological insecurity of the state at the institutional level creates 'cultural insecurity' in societies which are described as 'non-state spaces' (Scott, 2009) and successor societies, or agro-cultural complexes. As a region of multiple transnational flows, imageries such as riverine and hilly terrains across the Mekong delta to Chindwin and Irrawaddy to Tsiang, the Pang-Sau pass, Sela Pass and 'Lake of No Return' assume a distinctive (hydro)geopolitical space of signifiers, which the statist apparatuses of looking, thinking and acting cannot grapple with. Transborder, transethnic and transnational anaspora and diaspora of a large number of cultural, linguistic and religious communities complicate such a delimited vision such as LEP or Vision 2020. Further emphasis on cultural renewal of the interconnections between the people of the region and the mainstream may come as a happy consequence of building mutually respectful economic and human connections. Interestingly, the BJP's April 2015 Indian foreign policy resolution added "sanskriti evam sabhayata" (cultural and civilizational links) as one of the five cornerstones.[14] These pronouncements do not include cultural links between, say, the Buddhist Idu Mishmis and Tibet, nor do they talk about cultural linkages between Tangsa, Lisu and some other Arunachalee tribes and ethnic minorities in the Yunan province of China. The point is that cultural and civilizational links are selectively repressed from the same ontological-cum-cultural insecurity of the apparatus of looking, thinking and acting that the state has given rise to (Agamben, 2009: 14). The state does not return to an ontology of communities and cultures as it hastens to construct river dams and convert forests into roads and mines. Foreign policy grounds itself in this methodological alienationism that alienates the 'ontological sociality' of cultures and civilizations. Nevertheless, there is a beyond to this view with a delimited focus on an area that is deterritorializable.

This beyond needs to be conceptualized here. An opening towards an exilic regionalism would bring together the unrepresented and unspoken Asiatic connections that include India's Northeast as a conjunction between South Asia and Southeast Asia. The subregional contour of ASEAN, SAARC, IORARC, BIMSTEC, BRICS and many other such future bi- and multilateral formations needs to be explored through spaces and territories that are rarely paid any attention to. Following comparative methodologies of area studies and the transboundary character of subregional formations, it is possible to build an ontology of dynamics of flow and control in the region that Prasenjit Duara called "Asia Redux" (Duara, 2010a, 2010b). Duara argued for discovering points of encounter and mix that transcend the nation-states. In a slightly different vein, the Northeastern region could be conceived as a cusp region that criss-crosses South and Southeast Asia, making them both present and disperse into their territorial identities. This provides for the possibility of identifying a cusp region that loosely starts with Yunan and passes down the Mekong to reach Irrawady and rises up to the north of Tibet via the plains of Bangladesh to Pang-sau through an indeterminate and seismically volatile eastern fault, a land mass that establishes the missing links between the South and Southeast Asiatic state and social formations. From the foreign policy perspective, combination between cultural continuity and trans-Asiatic road, rail and energy linkages would make it an Asiatic resurgence. This would not only be a reenactment of the journey of Marco Polo and the present onset of an immaterial form of capital, but it would begin a process of conservation of natural and cultural resources by connecting Asiatic stakeholders in sharp contrast to a unilateral state-market nexus of extraction. To conceptualize such a possibility of a changed structure of inter-state relations through cultural and communicative relations, India's foreign policy needs to incorporate an element of federal subregionalism.

Such a federal subregionalism would transform existing rivalry structures and military competition into a bulwark of multi-state multi-partner sharing of resources and knowledges that would also avert the potential risk of appropriation and deprivation, an important element in warmongering in the Asiatic subregion. This would further a non-delineated and discreetly structured working with non-state ethnic and transethnic actors on the cusp that can take part in the interplay between cultural and civilizational factors. Indeed, critical geopolitical attitudes of nation-states can be reshaped in this humane way of looking at each other by weakening and lowering heights of regional jingoisms. Economically speaking, flows of remittances and flow of skill would interact with each other in this kind of subregionalistic sharing of the security, political and economic agenda. This would also ameliorate the present fear over appropriation of material resources such as rivers, mines and territories and would set up new infrastructures of mediation among disparate supply chains across borders. This would thwart any attempt to corner financial resources and social capital by more advanced countries by creating institutions of multilateral responsibility by way of an altruistic sharing of expertise that is gained abroad with local communities. The blueprint for action, therefore, would now include the right to sustainable development that the cusp cultural communities of the Northeastern region aim to host in their midst. Unusual circumstances of contesting demand pull and volatile military-political claims can be deterred by self-regulation through cultural and civilizational linkages that would exceed any attempt at building infrastructures of superpower control in South and Southeast Asia.

One would also mark out the dichotomy between India's agenda-setting policy formalism of security and development mix that gets subverted from within the corridors of power. Such formalism faces the daunting task of managing a porous border by turning it into a soft border, which the Asiatic subregional interconnections demand. India's vertical top-down multiscalar ontology local-subnational-national matrix of policy making and agenda setting is not only disabled to perform such a task in the cusp region of the Northeast, but it is yet to articulate a horizontal pathway of linking up factors and actors who are themselves arranged historically in a civilizational cusp in their linkages with South and Southeast Asia. Foucault's concept of apparatus applies in this case as India's foreign policy "ensemble consisting of discourses, institutions, architectural forms, regulatory decisions, and philosophical, moral and philanthropic propositions" (Foucault, 1980: 194) needs to take into account the spatial exterior of Northeastern India that it deterritorializes. The apparatus works from a certain rationale of thinking, looking and acting that can be sustained only by removing the obstructive hierarchies of power and control that create multiple oppositions. To remove this, the policy apparatus must have to yield places to responsible interlocutors such that the Northeastern enigma or 'protected ignorance' of the policy establishment can be illuminated by the idea of 'other Asia'. This 'other Asia' also could act as a category to remove the binary between non-state successor agro-cultural complexes versus settled societies in the South and Southeast Asia that would find its open field of possibilities in India's Northeast.

## Acknowledgements

Chapter 12 was originally written by Sashinungla and Prasenjit Biswas and presented at conferences in Copenhagen and Kolkata, 2015. I accept full responsibility for all revisions made. I can sincerely hope that they retain their original spirit and energy, which flowed from our collective effort.

## Notes

1 A document prepared as per the mandate of the Second ASEAN-India Summit held in Bali in October 2003, which called for the preparation of a long-term roadmap for the growing ASEAN-India partnership prepared by the think tanks of the region. See *ASEAN-India Vision 2020: Working Together for a Shared Prosperity*, RIS, New Delhi, 2004.

2 Olympic gold-medal-winning boxer Mary Kom's supposed confession in a TATA Salt advertisement that she had taken the 'salt' from India and so she cannot be 'nimak haram' (betrayer to the nation) becomes an interesting instance of compulsive collaboration with the larger nation-state and its abstract identity of the Indian people. The optics of the advertisement show how upcoming talent from the region will have to agree to the moral authority of the nation and, further, that they have no space to assume difference and separateness.

3 A large number of autonomous district councils controlled by tribes and ethnic groups all over Northeast India under various schedules and articles of Constitution create a sense of local autonomy, while these institutions and people belonging to them are subsumed within the larger framework of power of the Indian state.

4 Nandita Haksar, India's leading human rights lawyer known for her campaign against excesses by security forces in Northeast India, says "the northeast is very distinct from the rest of India essentially because of race". See Haksar (1996).

5 See 'BJP clarifies after vision document calls NE people "immigrants"', *Hindustan Times*, 4 February 2015. www.hindustantimes.com/india/bjp-clarifies-after-vision-document-calls-ne-people-immigrants/story-QB227t8fC5SDJnw2a28wLK.html (Accessed 12 June 2015).

6 A young lawyer from the state of Arunachal Pradesh was denied entry into the India Republic Day programme on 26 January 2015, where US President Barack Obama was a guest, by the Delhi police, who claimed she was not Indian. This is symptomatic of such constitution.

7 Nicholas Kharkongor's movie *Axone: A Recipe for Disaster*, is a stirring satire which revolves around a day's incident in the lives of a group of friends who are from the Northeast in a Delhi neighbourhood where racism is a regular experience. Food is the central motif and metaphor of the film, which explores migrants' lives. Various issues ranging from racial bias in subtle as well as threatening forms that the migrants have to encounter daily, intertwined with food, to the social aspirations of migrants, as well as the agency of the migrants to exercise their right, are raised through the movie.

8 The Report of the Manorama Death Enquiry Commission, set up by the Supreme Court of India, p.222. pt. no. 13, talks of the sense of impunity with which the security forces assume exercise of their power in the Northeastern region. The report was released in 2014 by the Supreme Court of India. Available at https://2019.hrln.org/wp-content/uploads/2018/07/report-of-commission-of-the-judicial-inquiry-manorama-death.pdf. Accessed 23 August 2020.

9 Anyone who has been to the region knows that the moment you enter India's 'troubled Northeast', your cell phone or your internet won't work or is barred, and if you tune in to your radio set, the Chinese and Rangoon's antenna signals automatically take over.

10 McAlister (2005) makes a similar argument in the context of US involvement in the Middle East.

11 Border trade points and sale of locally produced food and consumer items by local communities at Manipur's Moreh, Arunachal's Nampong in Changlang district, Mizoram's Sahia market etc. show brisk trading activity by the local community. Such markets are largely sellers' markets.

12 Besides extra-constitutional law like the Armed Forces Special Power Act (AFSPA), for over 50 years (till 2014), the governors of Nagaland had acted as 'super chief ministers' with extra-constitutional power by exercising sole executive control over the transfers and postings of bureaucrats. Also, Northeastern states have the strange situation of having retired Army generals and former directors of the intelligence agencies as governors.

13 The 'homo sacer' is a legal term referring to those viewed as outside the law. Appropriated from Giorgio Agamben's discussion of the figure of homo sacer in ancient Roman law, Derek Gregory uses this abstraction in his book *The Colonial Present: Afghanistan, Palestine, Iraq* as a means to depict the unrestrained actions of the US and Israel-led forces in Afghanistan, Palestine and Iraq.

14 See 'Panchsheel gives way to Panchamrit', *The Telegraph*, 4 April 2015.

## References


Agamben, Giorgio. 2009. *What Is an Apparatus? and Other Essays*. Trans. David Kishik and Stefan Pedatella. Stanford, CA: Stanford University Press.

Baruah, Sanjib (ed). 2009. *Beyond Counterinsurgency*. New Delhi: Oxford University Press.

Bhaumik, Subir. 2009. *The Troubled Periphery: Crisis of India's Northeast*. New Delhi: Sage.

Bhaumik, Subir. 2014. 'Look East through Northeast: Challenges and Prospects for India', *Observer Research Foundation's* Occasional Paper No. 51.

Biswas, Prasenjit. 2002. '"Nations from Below" and "Rebel Consciousness", The "New Subaltern" Emergence of North East India' in Ranju R. Dhamala and Sukalpa Bhattacharjee (eds.) *Human Rights and Insurgency: The North-East India*, New Delhi: Shipra Publications, pp.140–162.

Biswas, Prasenjit and Suklabaidya, Chandan. 2008. *Ethnic Life-worlds in North-East India: An Analysis*. New Delhi: Sage.

De, Sucheta. 2014. *Implications of government policies of industrialization and trade for the North-East: With special reference to India's look east policy*, Unpublished PhD thesis submitted to CSRD, JNU, New Delhi.

Duara, Prasenjit. 2010a. 'Asia Redux: Conceptualizing a Region for Our Times' in *Journal of Asian Studies*, 69, 4, 963–983.

Duara, Prasenjit. 2010b. 'Response to Comments on "Asia Redux"' in *Journal of Asian Studies*, 69, 4, 963–983 (pp. 1027–1029).

Foucault, M. 1980. *Power/Knowledge: Selected Interviews and Other Writings 1972–1977*. New York: Pantheon Books.

Gregory, Derek. 2004. *The Colonial Present: Afghanistan, Palestine, Iraq*. Oxford: Blackwell.

Gupta, Arvind. 2012. 'Myanmar's Critical Role in Bolstering India's Look East Policy'. Paper presented at International Conference on *Myanmar: Bringing South and Southeast Asia* held at Jamia Milia Islamia University, New Delhi – 30–31 January.

Haksar, Nandita and Navlakha, Gautam. 1996. 'Movement of Self Assertion in the Northeast' in Madhushree Dutta, Flavia Agnes and Neera Adarkar (eds.) *The Nation, the State and Indian Identity*, Kolkata: Samya, pp.127–173.

Institute for Defence Studies and Analyses (IDSA). 2013. 'Roundtable on Northeast's Role in India's Look East Policy'. Available at www.idsa.in/event/NortheastsRoleinIndiasLookEastPolicy (Accessed 3 April 2015).

Kikon, Dolly. 2009. 'From Loincloth, Suits, to Battle Greens: Politics of Clothing the "Naked" Nagas' in Sanjib Baruah (ed.) *Beyond Counterinsurgency*, New Delhi: Oxford University Press, pp.25–48.

Kunstadter, Peter. 1967. *Highland Societies of Southeast Asia*. New York: Alfred Knopf.

McAlister, Melani. 2005. *Epic Encounters: Culture, Media and US Interests in the Middle East since 1945*. Berkeley, CA: University of California Press.

Mukhim, Patricia. 2015. 'Old wounds reopened … Old hurts return to haunt', *The Shillong Times*, 13 March.

Neog, Ruhee. 2014. 'India's Northeast and the Look East Policy: Challenging Established Notions'. Available at www.ipcs.org/article/india/indias-northeast-and-the-look-east-policy-challenging-established-notions-4628.html (Accessed 3 April 2015).

Nuh. V. K. 2002. *The Naga Chronicle*. New Delhi: Regency Publications.

'Panchsheel gives way to Panchamrit'. 2015, 4 April. *The Telegraph*.

Scott, C. 2009. *The Art of Not Being Governed: An Anarchist History of Upland Southeast Asia*. New Haven: Yale University Press.

Verghese, B. G. 2004. 'Borders Matter more than Boundaries from the North East Looking out'. *Man and Society: Journal of North East Studies*, 1 (1, Spring).

# 13 Federalization of Indian foreign policy

## Recent trends

*Sreya Maitra and Shibashis Chatterjee*

### Introduction

For a considerable time, Indian foreign policy was remarkably bipartisan when it came to domestic differences. This is surprising given that India is a federal state betraying enormous diversities. Further, the state of India being born out of partition and vast population movements as a result of it, the linkages across the territorial borders of the new states, social and economic in particular, were clearly visible. Finally, state borders as artificial constructs were alien to the history of the sub-continent. Hence, the emergence of modern South Asian states through the complex processes of the colonial encounter created territorial (political) and anthropological (social) mismatches that must have posed difficulties for social communication and created challenges for India's foreign policy in the immediate neighbourhood. However, the painful birth through vivisection and bloodshed, coupled with the prospect of internal fragmentation and implosion, led to the crafting of a federal polity with a clear unitary bias. Hence, the arguments born out of variety and fluidity were trumped by those of consolidation and unity. Foreign policy became the template where the nation can speak as one, despite bordering states having their own experiences in dealing with neighbours. The political dominance of the Congress party reinforced the constitutional framework of unitary federalism. However, this unitary character of the federal order was also decidedly accommodative in its social and political commitments. It sought to create an inclusive polity where minorities and underrepresented groups acquired a legitimate political voice. Hence, India's foreign policy was also sensitive to deviations from accommodative and inclusive practices in its neighbourhood (Sridharan, 2016: 70).[1] In another critical probe, Madhan Mohan Jaganathan (2019) has shown how the state transformation process, in conjugation with the specificity of the issue and the dynamics of coalition politics, has increased the salience of some states in the making of India's neighbourhood policy. In a counter-intuitive argument, he finds that the growing importance of the provinces makes the Centre nervous since it lacks the capacity to discipline and bring in line the states that have become very proactive in foreign policy. In a nutshell, while their presence has become more visible and they have become more vocal on the need to be consulted in foreign policy decisions that directly impact on them, the states show a variable degree of autonomy vis-à-vis the Centre when it comes to having an effective role in shaping India's neighbourhood policy (see Jaganathan, 2019).

With the gradual unravelling of the Congress system and regional political parties coming into prominence, the political dynamic underlying the Centre-heavy federal architecture suffered a major setback. Three changes coincided over a period of time. First, the regions came of age and became politically vocal; second, the one-party dominant system gave away to a multi-party system of coalition politics; and third, a new politics of globalization emerged that began to leverage provinces and regions as never before. A change in the federal character was, therefore, underway. While this had major domestic repercussions, the foreign policy consequences were also far from being trivial in nature.

Indian federalism finds itself at a crossroad in the current political scenario. Theoretically, it assumes the same contours that had been rendered by the makers of the Constituent Assembly. But in practice, it is caught between the dialectical pulls of increasing centralization and state assertions for greater participation. Scholars cannot help but critically interrogate these trends and pressures, contributing to the debate on the merits of each side (the Centre and the states), and speculating on future trends. The present paper offers an overview of the Indian federal experiment as it is poised at present. In two sections, it straddles the historical-constitutional evolution of federalism in India and its implications, and the current challenges in which the federal provisions are mired. The paper ends with a summary of the arguments while conceding that any definitive conclusion of the theme under study might be premature in academia.

## The changing contours of Indian federalism

Indian federalism has undergone many changes in the last three decades, not all of which are relevant to foreign policy (see Sharma and Swenden, 2017). Of these, three changes demand some investigation. We shall discuss these three features and trace their foreign policy implications. First, federalism was meant to accommodate India's manifold diversities such as language and ethnicity (Bhambhri, 1993). The linguistic reorganization of the Indian provinces was the first major political move to realign the federal structure in the line of linguistic sentiments (Lacina, 2014; Majeed, 2003). Over the years, the state realized that, while this formula worked successfully in many provinces, tensions prevailed in a few others due to different factors, mostly related to identity questions. In states like Assam, autonomous councils were created to resolve autonomy and secessionist demands by ethnic communities whose political demands could not be met within the standard federal structure. A few large provinces like Uttar Pradesh, Madhya Pradesh and Bihar were split into a number of new provinces on the pretext of better governance and social justice. While these proved to be relatively peaceful and less controversial exercises, similar attempts in Andhra Pradesh and West Bengal met with stiff resistance. Though Telengana was curved out of Andhra Pradesh after protracted political and legal-constitutional battles, the West Bengal government resisted the Gorkhaland movement despite the Centre's fleeting sympathy with the cause.

Two consequences can be derived here. First, the political experiments in the interest of accommodation of groups and various collective identities have considerably changed the federal structure. The local has gained more political salience though commensurate financial autonomy has not devolved to them. This has hastened political mobility and encouraged relatively smaller identities to cohere and articulate their political grievances more effectively. The democratic space within the federal structure has widened. Second, this has emboldened provinces to bargain harder with the Centre on all issues, be it political, economic, or identity ones having economic and political ramifications. Bordering states have thus become vocal on a whole range of issues, including foreign policy, since these apparently have consequences for the governance of the province. The strategically located states have demanded a right to voice if not a veto on all policies, domestic or external, that affect their resources and overall governance capacity to deliver. As the Centre requires more cooperation from the recalcitrant provinces that fear increasing interference and possible structural changes in their boundaries, it must placate states lest things go out of bounds in quick time (Ruparelia, 2015).

The second change relevant to federalism and foreign policy is that globalization and liberal reforms have altered the federal dynamics significantly (see Sharma and Swenden, 2017: 5–10). As the states are directly related to global capital flows and investments, the equation of power between the Centre and the provinces has been considerably realigned. But there is no uniform trend in this complex transformation. Financially powerful states have benefited from the economic reforms and made good headway in regional economic developments. In contrast, the poor states have suffered due both to stringent demands imposed by the institutions and agencies of global capital and to decreasing federal support from the Centre. States that have gained in the process have become politically more assertive and exercised influence on many foreign economic policy decisions undertaken by the Indian state. In contrast, economically disadvantaged states have created more noise on foreign policy matters that directly affect them. The Indian state's inability to subsidize the weaker provinces has actually weakened its bargaining capacity vis-à-vis the noisy provinces since it cannot either buy off dissent or compensate the latter in some other beneficial way. Financial weakness does not *ipso facto* translate into political frailty. In quite the reverse, economically underperforming states may become non cooperating and obstinate, prioritizing their immediate and local interests above the national ones (ibid: 5–7).

The third change is that Indian federalism functions on a much re-worked political landscape. Four trends are visible. First, the decline of the Congress has been a gradual process and the space vacated by the Congress has been usurped by many new political forces, led by the regional parties and the Hindu right-wing outfits (see Seshia, 1998; Datta, 1999; Chhibber, 1997). The regional parties have highlighted provincial issues and mostly offered diverse narratives of representation. The decline of the Congress has also resulted in the weakening or questioning of the fundamental pillars of the Indian state, particularly the commitments to secularism, state planning and a non-aligned foreign policy. Regional states have not necessarily challenged these core values but have sought to appropriate and regionalize them. Second, the Hindu right has steadily grown in Indian politics and the Bharatiya Janata Party (BJP), heir to the erstwhile Jan Sangh, had steadfastly espoused an alternative narrative based on the Hindutva philosophy that emphasizes a unitary and ethnic nationalism and a muscular statism based on the notions of cultural vitality, virility and purity and fullness (Hansen, 1999). It had fashioned a coalition called the National Democratic Alliance (NDA) that brought together both right-wing regional parties and anti-Congress formations across the country. The coming into power of the Narendra Modi-led BJP majority government in 2014 has created a new political environment that has had major consequences for the states (see Thachil, 2014; Jaffrelot, 2013). The regime brought back a solid majoritarian government after 1989 and initiated a number of controversial policies in keeping with its political leanings and core commitments. However, this has not fundamentally altered the federalizing trends in Indian foreign policy and the governments of West Bengal, Tamil Nadu and Punjab have retained their visibility in Indian foreign policy narratives vis-à-vis the neighbouring states. In fact, in the cases of Assam and Tripura, the BJP has apparently dilated the salience of the regional response to Bangladesh by securitizing the migration discourses (see Baruah, 2003; Tillin, 2007).

The third trend resulting from the re-worked political landscape is that the politics of recognition and redistribution in India, despite its myriad limitations and shortcomings, has mobilized new social forces, given them a voice to articulate their case, and made some difference to their lives that society refused to give them for centuries (Ruparelia, 2008). The empowerment of the under-classes and Dalits in India has proceeded qua an outright political process that has looked up to the state rather than civil society as a locale of both demands and protests. While the rise of the Hindutva forces has caused setbacks to the politics of the Dalit assertion, the state-led redistributive policies have significantly increased the political mobilization of the lower strata of society and the locus of agitational politics has increasingly riveted to the state. While this trend has no direct foreign policy derivative, it has increased the need for accommodative politics and given more space to regional politicians to bargain harder against the Centre. Finally, the periphery of Indian politics has oscillated between periods of intermittent peace and large-scale violence[2] (see Madhavan, 2012: 203–220; Behera, 2000; Ganguly 1996; Widmalm, 2014; Kolas, 2017: 22–37; Baruah, 2009).

This violence is manifest in the defiance of the red corridor in the face of state operations against the militant cadres. It has also engulfed the Kashmir valley where the Indian state's legitimacy remains dubious and contested and where a state of emergency has become the norm. The ebb and flow of insurgencies in some of the troubled states of India's northeast is also indicative of the apparent failure of the federal democracy to satisfactorily answer the grievance of the alienated surplus, those who cannot be folded into the logic of the mainstream Indian nationalism through the available resources of the state. This has resulted in increasing intermeshing of the domestic and the international despite the wholehearted efforts by the state to insulate the outside influences from fomenting trouble in the zone of sovereignty.

## Current episode in Indian federal experiences

Having outlined the incorporation and changing mosaic of the principle of Indian federalism, the stage is now set for undertaking an analysis of the challenges which are confronting it today. It must be mentioned at the outset that the Constitution ordains the specific jurisdictions and areas of functioning for the Centre and the states in distinct constitutional Articles. However, in real terms, the actual federal functioning meets with recurrent test cases that would challenge any water-tight compartmentalization. Political developments crop up which involve stakes at the national and regional levels (one or more states). In this light, the key element of federal functioning becomes a strong need for coordination between the Centre and the states. 'Coordination' itself is a term with positive connotations; it is goal-oriented albeit context-driven. Two forces may coordinate for a relatively negative objective leading to disastrous consequences. But coordination between two units for a positive goal can catapult growth. In either case, the merit of 'coordination' itself holds.

Ideally, coordination should not only be administrative and institutional, but also personalistic; that is, the willingness of the two or more sets of political authorities [at the Centre and the state(s)] to mutually consult, conduct dialogues, cooperate and compromise for greater benefits. Needless to say, this is acutely complex and influenced by a combination of politico-socio-economic factors. And it is here in the very scope of the requirements of coordination that its limitations can also be discerned. Thus, to begin with, in the current political scenario, the problems in the functioning of Indian federalism may be generalized as problems of coordination; its absence or its abeyance in the form of a deadlock. Broadly, two categories of decisions fall victim to this. First are moves that the Centre initiates, which require the cooperation of the state(s). The second category includes those decisions that require the participation of both the Centre and the state(s) as stakeholders. In either case, certain factors can impair smooth federal functioning by influencing the scope of coordination. The first would be a game of one-upmanship. The Centre could take a unilateral policy, justifying it in the interest of the nation, with perceptible bulldozing tactics. In this case, the states might not cooperate at the ground level (even though constitutionally they may be obliged to) due to political differences. However, smaller states may be forced to give in to the Centre's tactics, fearing financial repercussions.[3] Similarly, a regional party may try to arm-twist the Centre through agitations to effect a change, catering to vested interests like gaining electoral popularity or public sympathy. Second, there may be practical considerations that problematize the implementation of the policy undertaken by the Centre at the regional level. The outcome, very simply, is the lack of coordination between the Centre and the state(s) and unresolved crises spanning various spheres of policy making. Indian federalism has witnessed all of the above-mentioned cases, especially since the era of coalition politics. Federalism in economic issues and fiscal federal structure are cases in point.

There is sufficient literature on Indian federalism that recognizes that the 'unitary bias' in the constitutional provisions has translated into conscious centralization (see Chatterjee, 2014; Singh and Verney, 2003). Singh and Verney observe that centralization meant that the Government of India directed the economy. It exercised this function through a Finance Commission that was set up every five years to produce a formula for the distribution of revenues to the states, and by a Planning Commission that implemented five-year plans of economic development. The states were therefore heavily dependent on Delhi. Centralized management accompanied this economic direction. Members of the Indian Administrative Service were in charge of much of the public sector (Singh and Verney, 2003: 2).

A major issue of concern for many Indian constituent states was the signing of the World Trade Organization (WTO) agreement by the Government of India in 1995. Many states claimed that by signing the WTO agreements on 'Agriculture', the Union government has encroached state's power on agriculture policy. Some states even took the Government of India to court demanding a reinstatement of the constitutionally mandated division of powers in which agriculture is categorized as a state subject (Jenkin, 2003: 607; Jain, 2009). In another instance, the state government of Chhattisgarh opposed the Union government plans to disinvest the public sector BALCO (2009). The state government took the matter to the Supreme Court, though it lost there. But such actions by the state government forced the then Prime Minister Atal Behari Vajpayee to hold a meeting of state chief ministers to discuss with them their concerns regarding WTO and its impact on agriculture (Vasudeva, 2001 cited in Jain, 2009).These certainly serve as examples of collaboration and consultation between Union government and states on matters of economic diplomacy. Sridharan observes that, between 1989 and 2014, the Indian National Congress and the BJP had to build large executive and/or legislative coalitions which included many smaller parties. Executive coalition is limited to the parties directly allied and present in government while a legislative coalition is a broader alliance with external supporters that have committed to a pre-electoral power-sharing arrangement but have decided to opt out of government participation. This legislative coalition is also further cemented if the party at the Centre has established electoral alliances at the state level with regional/local parties. In effect, this creates 'mutual electoral interdependencies' between the nation-wide party and smaller parties, making it difficult for either of them to withdraw, without running the risk of losing their electoral support in national or regional elections. This creates 'locked-in alliances' and to some extent has an impact on policy output (Sridharan, 2014; Blarel, 2019).

Regarding foreign direct investment (FDI), states are primarily and legitimately interested in ensuring that their foreign economic engagements are unencumbered by the central government. Dating back to the onset of liberalization, a number of Indian states have actively pursued FDI from abroad and other foreign economic opportunities. Gujarat, Madhya Pradesh, Tamil Nadu, West Bengal and other states have regularly organized investor summits in order to gain foreign investment. Andhra Pradesh Chief Minister Chandrababu Naidu has been a key player in this regard. In April 2015, the Union government asked him to lead a high-level Indian delegation to China on its behalf. However, certain instances in recent times have exposed the pulls and pressures underlining federalism in India. The state of Odisha signed a Memorandum of Understanding (MoU) with POSCO (a Korean company) in 2005 to construct an integrated plant to manufacture steel, mine iron ore and build the necessary infrastructure for constructing a port in Odisha. The total worth of the project was $12.6 billion, and it was the biggest FDI deal in India till then. With the Congress-led United Progressive Alliance (UPA) government at the Centre, the project ran into trouble with the Environment Ministry for violating forest laws and causing displacement of the tribal population. The project finally saw the light of the day in 2014, when the central government intervened after South Korean President Geun-Hye visited New Delhi (Basu, 2016). The coinciding of this development with the change in government at the Centre in 2014, and the close relations between Odisha's Chief Minister Navin Pattnaik and the BJP fanned a critique on the role of the Centre in Indian federalism.

In another instance, the UPA-II government in 2012 decided to allow 51 percent FDI in multi-brand retail. This encountered strong opposition from the Trinamool Congress in West Bengal (even though it was a UPA ally) and several state governments. The Department of Industrial Policy and Promotion wrote to governments of all states and Union territories in June 2012 to invite their views. West Bengal Chief Minister Mamata Banerjee asserted that reforms need not amount to 'selling out everything'. On the contrary, Omar Abdullah, who ran the Jammu and Kashmir government in alliance with Congress, congratulated the Centre for leaving the final say with the states because 'Why should Mamata [Banerjee] or [Uttar Pradesh Chief Minister)] Akhilesh Yadav decide what is bad or good for J&K?' In sum, the UPA-ruled states hailed it as a 'bold initiative'. Lalu Prasad Yadav argued that it would let the farmers get a fair price for their produce. But the states with non-Congress governments assailed the measures as 'anti-people' as it threatened massive job losses. Interestingly, Shiromani Akali Dal which governed Punjab with BJP as a junior partner initially welcomed the move but later threw in its lot with the BJP-ruled states opposing it (Basu, 2016: 225). Finally, after a prolonged stand-off, the issue had to be put to vote in the Lok Sabha on the BJP's initiative. The UPA government convincingly won as the Samajwadi Party and the Bahujan Samaj Party (BSP) walked out, alleging that the motion ignored the interests of the farmers and small retailers (ibid). The significance of party alliances and overlapping political agenda between the Centre and the states in Indian federalism was unequivocally asserted. In yet another recent instance of this trend, West Bengal has opposed the new policy announced by the Centre on allowing 100 percent FDI in coal mining, processing and sale. Chief Minister Mamata Banerjee resisted the ancillary move of the government to shift the desk offices of four of the subsidiary companies of Coal India from Kolkata to their headquarters in other regions. She also stated that it contradicts the spirit of self-reliance or 'Atmanirbhar Bharat', which the Modi government has helmed in recent times. However, BJP national secretary Rahul Sinha defended the move by asserting that the FDI in the coal sector will benefit West Bengal and the state government the most. He also insinuated that the lack of work culture in the state was the underlying cause for the decision to shift offices away (Hindustan Times, 26 June 2020). The constant, virulent sparring between the state and the Centre has continued since the former launched massive protests against the Citizenship Amendment Act (CAA) initiated by the BJP government in 2019. This shall be discussed in the following sections. Another non-BJP-ruled state, Chhattisgarh, has also opposed Modi's auction of five coal blocks, saying this move will hit their Lemru elephant reserve plan in the ecologically sensitive Hasdeo Arand and the catchment area of Mand river. The Congress government at the state further alleged that the Central Ministry had remained unresponsive to several pleas (Hindustan Times, 9 July 2020).

The predisposition towards centralization in financial matters witnessed a reversal through the recommendations of the 14th Finance Commission (2013), which ushered in a new era of fiscal federalism in India. Devolution to the states significantly went up from 32 percent to 42 percent. The government followed it up with the constitution of the National Institution for Transforming India (NITI Aayog, 2015; replacing the Planning Commission) to promote 'cooperative federalism'[4] and enacted a constitutional amendment to establish the Goods and Services Tax Council (2017). The allocation ratio of Centrally Sponsored Schemes was restructured from 75:25 to 50:50 to provide greater flexibility and ownership to the states. In turn, the states were mandated to pursue zero revenue deficit, fiscal deficit not exceeding three percent of Gross State Domestic Product (GSDP), interest payments-to-revenue receipt ratio not exceeding 10 percent and debt-to-GSDP ratio not exceeding 25 percent. But as of 2018, most states have witnessed an upward trend in fiscal deficits. The NITI Aayog has pointed out that despite an increase in total central transfers to the states (21.9 percent), social sector expenditure has increased only marginally. The autonomy of the states in spending and borrowing has combined to obstruct consolidation of public finances. There is little incentive for states to improve revenue performances. The states are predisposed to indulge in unproductive expenditure for political gimmick, ideological symbolism or other vested interests. The tax buoyancies have been affected by the transition to Goods and Services Tax (GST). GST compensation to states will continue till 2022. The 15th Finance Commission (27 November, 2017) has the responsibility of equalizing the widening gap between richer states and the low-income states. A large part of this drive has to be through grants-in-aid rather than devolution (Firstpost, 14 January 2018). This further complicates the federal equations and strengthens the practical power inequalities between the Centre and the states.

Commenting on the loopholes in the present fiscal federal structure, West Bengal Finance Minister Amit Mitra stated in a recent interview that the Union budget cut off (funds for) 58 projects (fully sponsored by the Centre), which includes police training and the Integrated Child Development Services. There is another category of projects where states have to pay a proportion; in twenty-eight such projects, the proportion has been increased.

Mitra complained that while the Centre 'give 10% more in devolution [as per the 14th Finance Commission], on the other, you take away ... We found out that they [the Centre] have introduced a new process in which 50% of the weightage was on surveys done among businesses in the state ... We were not consulted' (Financial Express, 14 January 2018).

Amidst the massive economic losses and pressures on health infrastructure suffered by the states due to the COVID-19 pandemic in early 2020, the West Bengal government has pointed to the lack of cooperation from the Centre to financially assist the affected state at dual levels. On the one hand, it had refused to clear earlier dues which amounted to Rs11,000 crore under the devolution of central taxes; and Rs 36,000 under various pending schemes. Also, it had not released any funds to the state to assist the state in dealing with the pandemic. Mamata Banerjee urged for a grant of at least Rs 25,000 crore from the Centre to Bengal without any delay as the state was in 'dire situation with practically no revenue flows after the closure of almost all business' (The Telegraph, 10 July 2020). Other virus-ravaged states like Punjab and Tamil Nadu, ruled by opposition parties, have criticized the Centre for sanctioning amounts that were 'chicken feed' compared to the magnitude of the states' needs. The animosity towards the Centre is heightened by the fact that the country's sudden lockdown in March 2020 was imposed without consulting with the state governments (The Economic Times, 9 July 2020).

The rather surprising launching of demonetization by the Modi-led NDA government in November 2017 garnered the stiff opposition of the states. However, the reactions were soon hijacked and tailored along party lines, allowing little scope for much academic analysis or reflections on federalism as such. Three years on, Prime Minister Modi himself defended the move in an interview, stating that demonetization was not done for elections, but the opponents of BJP in Uttar Pradesh who cried foul only because they 'lost a lot in the note ban'. He further asserted that the move had brought down inflation in the entire country and 'changed the mindset of the people about black money, convincing them to opt for honesty' (Business Today, 26 April 2019).

In yet another notable centralizing move by Modi, non-BJP-ruled states expressed anxiety that the 'Swachchata app' launched in 2019 was stealthily making the local municipal corporation officials accountable to the Union Ministry of Housing and Urban Affairs for addressing sanitation issues. As per the Constitution of India, sanitation has remained the domain of the states and any Central intervention without legislation alters the basic federal balance (New Indian Express, 13 May 2019). Also, in 2016 Arunachal Pradesh was put under the president's rule, after rebel Congress legislators sided with the BJP. Subsequently, the People's Party of Arunachal Pradesh formed a government, which is an ally of the BJP. The sudden constitutional amendment to declare Jammu, Kashmir and Ladakh as Union territories after a prolonged period of governor's rule since June 2018 drew critical attention. This brings us to a discussion of three separate, albeit interconnected, political decisions imposed by the Centre in the last year, with far-reaching implications for India's federal balance as well as federalization of foreign policy. The fallout is still unravelling.

The first has been the decision of the BJP-led Centre to repeal Article 370 of the Indian Constitution, which grants special status to the state of Jammu and Kashmir. It was declared that the state would be bifurcated into two Union territories – Jammu and Kashmir, which will have a legislature, and Ladakh, which will be without a legislature. Additionally, Article 35A (which gives special rights and privileges to the citizens of the state, and the discretionary power to the legislature to decide who are the permanent citizens of the state) was annulled as a 'discriminatory provision against non-permanent residents and women of Jammu and Kashmir' (The Economic Times, 5 August 2019). Prior to the implementation of the move, the Centre deployed additional paramilitary troops and also put various political leaders including former Chief Ministers Farooq Abdullah, Omar Abdullah and Mehbooba Mufti under house arrest. Mobile internet services were barred (Business Standard, 26 November 2019). While these piecemeal moves were defended on grounds of security, in hindsight they seemed a crucial step to manage the widespread shock and turmoil because of the declaration of the abrogation. Significantly, while the people in Jammu were supportive of the scrapping, all Kashmir-based parties remain opposed to it. BJP's Defence Minister Rajnath Singh defended the move as a fulfilment of its decade-old promise and its commitment to the development and growth of Jammu and Kashmir; oppressed people like refugees from Pakistan-occupied Kashmir and west Pakistan and the Valmiki community would get equal rights after more than 70 years of independence (Hindustan Times, 14 June 2020). What has remained problematic and controversial is the process of executing this move;

the recommendations of the constituent assembly of Jammu and Kashmir were not sought, neither was political support solicited from local leaders, civil society or other stakeholders. For a state within India which enjoyed asymmetrical federal arrangements under 'special status' in the Constitution since independence, the entire bulldozing of the process seemed, *prima facie*, unconstitutional. Though numerous petitions were filed and heard, including a bench of the Supreme Court, the BJP remained steadfast in its stance that the abrogation has become a *fait accompli.* BJP General Secretary Ram Madhav recently asserted that a legislative assembly for the Union Territory of Jammu and Kashmir would be formed 'very soon', dispelling any notions of a possible rollback of the decision (The Economic Times, 13 July 2020).

Not only did the move flout the federal balance within India, it has had severe implications for neighbouring countries, including Pakistan-occupied Kashmir. There was much apprehension in the international media about India's ability to 'take back' Pakistan-occupied Kashmir by military means, if necessary. There was worldwide criticism of the treatment of citizens in Jammu and Kashmir, the prolonged detention of mainstream Kashmiri leaders, the communications shutdown and the lack of access to independent observers. Though the Indian government tackled the 'internationalization' of the Kashmir issue through high-powered diplomacy, including visits by External Affairs Minister S. Jaishankar to China, Europe and the United States, the issue was repeatedly raised and contested in the UN Security Council (on China's insistence), the European Parliament and the UN Human Rights Council (Haidar in The Hindu, 2 November 2019). The cudgel persisted on India's relations with Pakistan as insecurity and terrorism continued to reign in Jammu and Kashmir; it faced one of the worst terror attacks in February 2020 when a Central Reserve Police Force bus was blown up by Pakistan-based terror group Jaish-e-Mohammad, killing 40 *jawans* (soldiers). India retaliated with bombing of terror camps in Balakot in the same month (The Economic Times, 27 December 2019).

Maintaining chronological order as well as consistency of commitment to their election manifesto, the BJP next launched the Citizenship Amendment Act (CAA) in the winter session of Parliament 2019. The bill piloted by the Ministry of Home Affairs under Amit Shah was ultimately approved by the Parliament amidst nation-wide protests and criticisms. The transition from the Citizenship Amendment Bill (CAB) to CAA continued to grab bitter attention by the suddenly 'excluded' communities. Shah explained the core of the bill in the Lok Sabha – that it sought to give Indian nationality to non-Muslim refugees from Pakistan, Bangladesh and Afghanistan, who were facing religious persecution there. According to the amended citizenship law, members of Hindu, Sikh, Buddhist, Jain, Parsi and Christian communities who came from Pakistan, Bangladesh and Afghanistan till 31 December 2019 and were facing religious persecution there would be eligible for Indian citizenship (Business Today, 30 May 2020). What is of particular significance is that the CAA alters the bargaining positions of the Muslims, one of the largest minority communities in the country as well as in South Asia. Additionally, the legislation turns a blind eye to refugee communities in India seeking justice and repatriation, such as the Tamils and Rohingyas. This has had severe repercussions for the Centre's equations with the non-BJP-led states with high density of Islamic people (transient or enjoying domicile) like West Bengal, Tamil Nadu and Punjab. Terming the CAA as violative of the basic character of the Constitution of India, five states have passed a resolution till May 2020 in their respective Cabinets against the legislation – West Bengal, Kerala, Punjab, Rajasthan and Madhya Pradesh – and urged the Union government to revoke it (India Today, 5 February 2020). At the same time, the special status of the Muslims in Kashmir already being altered by the constitutional amendment of the largest Muslim 'state' in the country, and its vindication as 'an internal matter', a strong message has been sent to the neighbouring Islamic states, its purported implications ranging from consciously changing demographics (and an altered projection of secularism of the nation) to an emboldened stance against illegal migration by Muslims into border regions.

The Chinese Army's 'intrusion' in the Galwan Valley in Ladakh in June 2020 and India's strong retaliation, both militarily and diplomatically, are based on the claim that the embankment on the Galwan river-bend is in Indian territory, where the Indian army has patrolled for decades. Subsequent to this high-pitched man-to-man combat, Sino–Indian relations have plummeted, attracting critical international attention and speculations about changing power dynamics within Asia. Of relevance to the premise of the present chapter is the assumption that the audacious move by the Chinese can be directly linked to the abrogation of Article 370; the Chinese saw Indian action in Kashmir as affecting its position in Ladakh, AksaiChin, and a unilateral assault on the uneasy status quo with Pakistan (see Sinha, 2019; Grossman, 2020). Having leveraged control over the Doklam plateau in 2017 through military fortifications and facilities, experts observe that Galwan is another target in its series of 'salami-slicing' (Chellany, 2020; Tellis, 2020; Nautiyal, 2020). Coinciding with the COVID-19 pandemic, the military stand-off has elongated the already hyphenated relationship between the two countries, stalling efforts at trade and cooperation. It is interesting to note that New Delhi's recent infrastructure enhancement along the Line of Actual Control may have sparked off insecurities on the Chinese side, implying a reiteration of 'cartographic assertions' by the Indian government in the area. The 'posterchild' of such developments is the completion of the strategic road known as Darbuk-Daulat-Beg-Oldie which improves travel between Leh and Daulat-Beg-Oldie located in the Karakoram pass, a potential back-door entry into Aksai Chin (Grossman, 2020: 4–5). The border areas continue to remain vulnerable to the threat of escalation of tensions. The accusations by Kashmiri local leader Mehbooba Mufti, that the BJP had 'unconstitutionally' abrogated Article 370, so that it could 'gift the territory to China' and disempower locals, heightens the sense of vulnerability of the people. But Ram

Madhav's clarification about legislatures being formed in the newly formed Union territories has put an end to any possibility of the Centre acknowledging the salience of the interconnected issues.

Having explored the possibilities of coordination through cooperation, and the challenges of coordination through one-upmanship as manifested in economic policies, we may now turn to the second factor impairing coordination: that is, genuine differences in chosen approaches of the Centre and the state(s), which cannot be mitigated. This has been evidenced in the realm of foreign policy, particularly involving resource sharing or management. The dynamics of this could be easily borrowed from the analysis of federal play-offs in the economic sphere; central bulldozing, states' non-cooperation and the issue remaining in abeyance; or political party alliances and electoral understandings to save the deal. Certain examples may be discussed in this vein. But prior to that, a note on the nature and provisions for the participation of states in foreign policy may be articulated.

The Indian parliament has exclusive powers to legislate on foreign affairs and security and all matters concerning the Indian Union's foreign relations: diplomatic, consular and trade representation; the Union participation in international conference, war and peace; citizenship, foreign loans and trade and commerce with foreign countries and so on. There are three more provisions which give the federal government full power with respect to foreign affairs. First, the Indian parliament has power to make any law for the whole or any part of the territory of India for implementing any treaty, agreement or convention with any country (Art 253). Second, the Union has full executive powers for the implementation of its laws, treaties and agreements (Art 73). Third, to prevent the states from obstructing the administration of laws by the Union, the executive powers of the states are to be so exercised as not to impede or prejudice the exercise of the executive power of the union (Art 257). Thus, in practice the central government has exercised control over India's external relations since the constitution came into force in 1950. Indian states historically have not been closely involved in the country's foreign policy.

Verney and Frankel asserted in 1986 that Delhi cannot allow trans-border regional negotiations for a number of reasons. India's neighbours are not federal states; there are unresolved controversies between the new states of South Asia, and especially between India and Pakistan; there is a border dispute with China which, like the tensions with Pakistan, involves the power equation in Asia; and there are many border regions which are porous, being the location of tribal skirmishes, guerrilla warfare and the infiltration of immigrants. Finally, India is a country of diverse ethnic, linguistic and religious groups, many of which have ties that cross frontiers (Verney and Frankel, 1986).

However, recent trends indicate that this may be changing at least partially. In October 2014, the Indian government announced the creation of a new States Division within the Ministry of External Affairs (MEA), to be headed by a senior officer with the rank of joint secretary. Designed 'to coordinate facilitation of efforts ... between ... Mission/Post(s) and State/Union Territories' Governments as well as foreign diplomatic and trade missions in India', this new division was unprecedented and indicative of the newfound recognition in New Delhi of the significant role that states have come to play in the country's foreign policy engagements. Moreover, since October 2013, in what was viewed as his first major speech on foreign policy, the then Prime Ministerial candidate Narendra Modi criticized the incumbent Congress Party's approach as Delhi-centric. He reminded the audience that 'India is not just Delhi. The foreign policy should be decided by the people and not by some politicians sitting in Delhi'. He emphasized the importance of creating a new spirit of cooperation and collaboration between New Delhi and the states, arguing: 'Team India shall not be limited to the Prime Minister led team sitting in Delhi, but will also include Chief Ministers and other functionaries as equal partners'. As the prime minister of the country, Modi has invoked the importance of instilling a spirit of 'cooperative federalism' in the relationship between the central government and various state governments. In November 2015, Modi stated: 'In a break with over sixty-five years of tradition we have involved states even in foreign policy. The Ministry of External Affairs has been asked to work with the States' (Jacob, 2016: 3).

Further, in coping with the ongoing pandemic, Prime Minister Narendra Modi reiterated to chief ministers and lieutenant governors of 21 states and Union territories that the fight against coronavirus is a 'fine example of cooperative federalism' (India News, 16 June 2020). But contrary perspectives have emerged; M. Govind Rao, economist and adviser to two Indian state governments, has pointed out that instead of coming out with a COVID-19 grant to help states tide over the financial crunch, the Centre has only allowed states to borrow more, conditional to the incorporation of economic reforms outlined by them. 'That's not cooperative federalism' (The Economic Times, 9 July 2020). Moreover, Modi's 'Neighbourhood First' policy, which stressed connectivity and infrastructure development (see Xavier, 2020) and was largely successfully in the first term, seems to be attracting censure owing to the exclusion of the affected states, increasing border skirmishes and controversies as witnessed in recent times. This may also be attributed to a neglect of smaller neighbours in the second term of Modi's rule (Business Standard, 10 July 2020). What remains of significance is that both regional equations and foreign policy seem to be bearing the brunt of the wave of deliberate lack of federalization and jingoistic assertions.

We may now turn to critically analyse the cases which illustrate the dynamics of coordination between the Centre and the states.

The UPA government signed a Land Boundary protocol with Bangladesh in 2011 to introduce the 119th Constitution Amendment Bill in the Lok Sabha. But an attempt to implement this in 2013 witnessed stiff opposition from the West Bengal Government and the North East MPs Forum. Chief Minister Ms. Mamata Banerjee asserted that the transfer of nearly 17,000 acres of land from West Bengal in return for approximately 7,000 acres from Bangladesh was not acceptable without formal consultation with the affected people. She made it clear that while having friendly ties with Bangladesh was important, it should not come at the cost of the interests of the people of West Bengal. Similar sentiments were voiced by Asom Gana Parishad in Assam, Khasi Students' Union in Meghalaya and several other political outfits from Tripura and Mizoram. The BJP too, under pressure from its Assam unit, sought to prevent the bill being tabled and its spokesperson Arun Jaitley went to the extent of invoking the Keshavanada Bharati judgment (1973) in which the Supreme Court precluded the parliament from amending the basic structure of the Constitution and argued that the territory of India was a part of the Constitution which could not be reduced or altered by a constitutional amendment (see Jacob, 2016; Basu, 2016).

After the NDA government assumed power in 2014, Prime Minister Modi made 'Neighbourhood First' a major plank of his foreign policy. Nurturing better relations with India's neighbourhood in South Asia was accorded top priority. Ms. Mamata Banerjee finally agreed to support the agreement on the condition that the Centre would grant a substantial financial package for rehabilitation and resettlement of the people once the process of exchange of enclaves was completed. The shift in her stance was also influenced by the multi-crore Saradha chit fund scam which compromised the credibility of the Trinamool Congress, the rise of the BJP in West Bengal politics, and unearthing of a terror plot in the state reportedly targeting the Sheikh Hasina regime in Bangladesh in October 2014, causing diplomatic embarrassment (see Basu, 2016: 224).

Although the Asom Gana Parishad (BJP ally) remained recalcitrant for a while on the question of land alienation, the matter was finally resolved in June 2015 during Modi's visit to Dhaka. The 1974 India–Bangladesh Land Boundary Agreement was finally operationalized including the exchange of enclaves and 'adverse possessions' from the Indian states of Assam, Meghalaya, Tripura and West Bengal. The state governments thus played a key role in brokering a win–win situation at the political level.

However, electoral calculations and differences in party alliances continue to highlight the problems of federal coordination. Recently, while tabling a Bill in the State Assembly (19 November 2018) to grant land rights to the residents of fifty-one enclaves of Chitmahal, Chief Minister Ms. Banerjee took the opportunity to point out the Centre's apathy towards monetary support for the development of the new Indian citizens. "The Land Boundary agreement is an international treaty between two countries and MEA has a role to play. When the 51 enclaves in Cooch Behar were included, the MEA promised that they will provide funds of around Rs.1,002 crore". She complained that West Bengal received only Rs 426 crore though the outstanding claim amounts to 576 crores. She further pointed out that the government has already spent Rs101 crore on constructing houses for these people (Millennium Post, 19 November 2018).

Another example involving the Centre's impaired coordination with the West Bengal government, influencing diplomatic relations with Bangladesh, is on the issue of Teesta water sharing. The Teesta River, which originates in the Indian state of Sikkim, flows to Bangladesh via West Bengal. In 2011, under the UPA government, the two countries nearly agreed on a 50–50 water-sharing arrangement. But the accord could not be signed due to stern opposition from Ms. Mamata Banerjee, who dropped out of the prime minister's official delegation to Bangladesh at the eleventh hour. The West Bengal Irrigation Minister Rajib Banerjee said in 2014:

> Not enough water is flowing into the Teesta to meet our irrigation needs. We have to increase the area under irrigation in North Bengal to boost agricultural production. We will achieve our target of bringing 1.5 lakh acres of farmland.
>
> (The Times of India, 9 April 2017)

In 2017, Banerjee stated,

> If we share Teesta water, the people of Siliguri, Jalpaiguri will not get water and the farmers will not be able to carry out agricultural activities … But we cannot share it from a source which does not have water. I have already put forward an alternative proposal in this regard.
>
> (Daily Star, 30 June 2018)

Ms. Banerjee proposed sharing the waters of other rivers, like the Torsa River. As North Bengal is completely dependent on the Teesta, she said, rivers like the Torsa, which are closer to the border of India and Bangladesh, are good options. The Torsa, in fact, has connectivity with Bangladesh's Padma River. She proposed that the two countries set up a commission to ascertain the level of water flowing through the Torsa and the quantum of water that can be shared (The Times of India, 9 April 2017).

The matter remains unresolved. However, throwing light on the rising significance of state consent in Indian federalism, the former Indian External Affairs Minister Sushma Swaraj had said that the signing of an agreement on sharing Teesta water would not be possible without taking West Bengal on board. The solution cannot be achieved merely by two central governments. The West Bengal government is a key stakeholder and they were trying to engage with West Bengal Chief Minister Mamata Banerjee on the matter[5] (see Daily Star, 30 June 2018; NDTV, 7 June 2015; Chatterjee in Ganguly, 2016: 76–104). However, during her visit to India in October 2019, Prime Minister Sheikh Hasina reiterated that the people of Bangladesh are awaiting early signing and implementation of the Framework of Interim Agreement for sharing of the Teesta waters, as agreed upon by both governments (at the Centre) in 2011. In response, Prime Minister Modi informed her that his government is working with 'all stakeholders in India for the conclusion of the

Agreement soonest possible' (NDTV, 6 October 2019). Any deal remained unforthcoming till the end of Hasina's visit, as Mamata Banerjee remained uncooperative, more so in the renewed climate of agitations with the BJP over the implementation of the National Register for Citizens in the state.

A fresh ground for differences has opened up between Ms. Banerjee and the Centre since 2017 over the migration of *Rohingyas* from Myanmar. The NDA government has been weary of the crossing over of the ethnic community and has sought their deportation. In 2017, there were murmurs of the Rohingyas being termed a 'security threat' by the Union home minister, linking them to terror organizations like ISIS and Lashkar-e-Taiba. In the wake of these developments, Ms. Banerjee supported the UN call to the international community to help the Rohingyas, and opposed the approach of the Centre. She stated that,

> It is not the right decision by the Central Government to deport them [Rohingya Muslims], as not everyone is a terrorist ... There is a difference between commoners and terrorists, and that terrorists should be firmly dealt with but commoners should not suffer.
>
> (News18, 18 September 2017)

The West Bengal government is clearly against the idea of 'pushing back' the Rohingyas trying to cross the border and insists that they should be arrested instead. However, matters reached a sensitive turn earlier this year when central agencies wrote to the Union Home Ministry alleging that the Trinamool Congress has flouted federal policies not only by facilitating the entry of Rohingyas from Myanmar into the state but also by sheltering them. These agencies claimed that a few Muslim groups backed by the ruling party have set up camps to shelter Rohingyas in South 24 Parganas district. At Baruipur area in South 24 Parganas, a local NGO has provided makeshift shelter to at least twenty-five Rohingyas. But official news reports stated that the Border Security Force (BSF) has foiled attempts by at least three teams of ten to twelve Rohingyas to enter the country illegally from Bangladesh at border points like Swarupnagar and Bongaon in North 24 Parganas districts (The Economic Times, 16 January 2018). The matter remains unresolved, as the state government has not altered its official stance. Meanwhile the Union Home Ministry has sent an advisory to state governments to enumerate, observe and collect biometric data of Rohingya migrants living in India, and told the Lok Sabha that the government had received reports of their involvement in illegal activities. The government also made it clear that Rohingyas were 'illegal migrants' and not 'refugees'. The BSF and Assam Rifles have also been sensitized over not allowing in more illegal immigrants (The Hindu, 1 August 2018). In December 2019, the South Bengal Frontier of the BSF revealed that seventy-two Rohingyas were apprehended along the Indo-Bangladesh border between December 2018 and November 2019. It was also reported that the shelters and camps for Rohingyas in West Bengal had been 'shutting down' in West Bengal, and the Rohingyas 'simply disappeared' (The Times of India, 3 December 2019). The Ministry of Home Affairs ordered mandatory health screening of all those who attended the Tablighi Jamaat congregation in Delhi at the beginning of March 2020, though none of the Rohingyas who attended the convention tested positive (Athray, 7 July 2020). The Centre continues to remain firm in its decision to deport the community from India. They have not been included in the list of six (religious) minorities who shall be granted citizenship in India, under the CAA. They also do not belong to any of the three neighbouring countries – Pakistan, Bangladesh and Afghanistan. Union Minister Jitendra Singh asserted that they must go back to Myanmar, where they came from (The Wire, 4 January 2020). Bangladesh has found an ally in India in this regard, as the latter has expressed support on its repatriation stance on the forcibly displaced Rohingyas and supported the need for a 'sustainable and lasting solution to the crisis' (Outlook, 11 July 2020). It may be surmised that the bludgeoning CAA has stifled the scope of the affected states to opt for an oppositional stance on the matter.

Yet another state that has significantly dented the Centre's unilateral decision-making in foreign policy is Tamil Nadu. On the one hand, the central government has been pressurized by the parties in this region to moderate its diplomatic moves with Sri Lanka. In the 1990s, when the civil war in Sri Lanka was witnessing a thaw, the DMK tried to convince the Centre to mediate in Sri Lanka and broker a permanent ceasefire between the government and the LTTE (Liberation Tigers of Tamil Eelam) rebels. India was also unable to pursue a specific foreign policy of neutrality towards post-war Sri Lanka between 2012 and 2013, fearing ethnic repercussions in Tamil Nadu.[6] India was compelled to support the United States-sponsored UNHRC resolution in Geneva seeking accountability for the deplorable excesses the Sri Lankan security forces perpetrated against the minority Tamil population. Again, in November 2013, Prime Minister Dr. Manmohan Singh decided not to attend the Commonwealth Heads of Government Meeting as both the ruling All India Anna Dravida Munnetra Kazhagam (AIADMK) party and the opposition Dravida Munnetra Kazhagam party (DMK) demanded that India boycott the meeting. However, things took a turn in 2013 when Washington brought a stronger resolution in the international forum. This time DMK demanded that New Delhi should not only support the resolution but actually amend it, accusing Colombo of genocide and war crime. DMK's shrill pitch was not only meant to upstage the ruling AIADMK but also respond to the regional emotional uproar against film footage depicting the killing of the LTTE supremo's minor son, presumably by Sri Lankan soldiers. However, no consensus was reached in the parliament regarding the appropriate response on the part of the Government of India, although a series of statements denouncing the Sri Lankan government's atrocities against the Tamils came from a host of ministers as well as from the UPA chairperson Sonia Gandhi. The DMK was openly displeased and chose to pull out of the government in March 2013 (without, however, destabilizing the central government). Interestingly, following the walkout by the DMK, the UPA-II was no longer compelled to vote in the UNHRC in 2014. India once again reverted to its age-old policy of abstaining from voting (see Jacob, 2016; Basu 2016). Given India's own experiences with the UNHRC processes on the Kashmir issue in 2019 (even before the abrogation of Articles 370 and 35-A), experts comment that New Delhi may now be more circumspect in the continued internationalization of Sri Lanka's ethnic issue, otherwise an 'internal affair'. Moreover, the ruling AIADMK and opposition DMK in Tamil Nadu have maintained a stoic silence on the regime change in the Sri Lanka election (of Gotabaya Rajapakse as the President and Mahinda Rajapakse as the Prime Minister between 2018 and 2019), as well as on the prospects of the Tamil National Alliance in Sri Lanka allying with the Centre for buttressing a political solution for the Tamils (Moorthy, 26 November 2019). While the two national governments deepen their exchanges through high-level political visits and trade, the role of the state-level parties seems to have been relegated off-centre for the time being.

However, the case of Sri Lanka continues to raise diverse issues straddling domestic and foreign policy concerns. For one, the popular narrative of India's dilly- dallying on Sri Lanka is that Tamil regional political parties have sensitivity on how Tamils are treated in Sri Lanka that puts constraints upon India's leverage vis-à-vis the island nation. In a way, this fits into India's accommodative federal model; any deviation from inclusiveness is unacceptable to the state. Hence, even if Colombo moves closer to Beijing, or warms up to the United States, as it has tried in the past, India's critical stance towards Sri Lanka's exclusionary political practices would be a natural corollary to its own normative commitments. Sridharan argues that India's equivocations on Sri Lanka are not only the result of the Union government's efforts to placate Tamil regional parties. They can be traced rather to India's fears of secessionism and attendant national security concerns that bedevil the foreign policy thinking of a democratic post-colonial state (see Sridharan, 2016: 70–71).[7]

Federalization of foreign policy involves not only regional parties and India's immediate neighbourhood but also parties that are ideologically distinct as part of a rumbustious national coalition on matters of global partnerships. The near collapse of the Congress-led UPA-1 government over the Indo–US civilian nuclear deal is a case in point. The nitty-gritty of the deal and the ensuing political drama did not detain us here see Ghosh, 2007; Cherian, 2007; Tripathi, 2007). The debate centred on the idea of an autonomous foreign policy in the post Cold War era. The mainstream perspective on Indian foreign policy as articulated by the Congress leadership was based on a unipolar reading of the international system, one that visualized India as a major global power and a fledgling regional hegemon, following naturally from India's military power, democratic credentials, sustained economic performance and geopolitical significance. The mainstream vision was concerned with the gradual transcendence of the constraints facing India's foreign policy and thought close ties with the United States to be the guarantee to remove some of these bottlenecks, particularly those related to the projection of India's power within the Asian theatre. The mainstream considered China to be the most crucial, long-term threat to India's power and prosperity. It imagined a new strategic partnership of democratic states as a deterrent to the rise of the People's Republic of China. The enormous expansion and maturity of the Indian diaspora in the US was also a critical driver of this policy. Like all major immigrant communities in the US, they wished to pursue a proactive partnership between their home country and the US, based on shared economic, commercial and professional interests. The mainstream also believed that a policy deemed to be good in the national interest of a state was by natural extension beneficial to the interests of the people residing within. The underlying argument was simple: the greater the economic linkages between India and the US, the more pervasive the benefits that would accrue to the Indian people at large.

Against this mainstream narrative, the left was wedded to the idea of a multipolar world, where the principal threat consists of the hegemonic proclivities of the United States. In a parliamentary democracy with little mass support, the left had difficulties synchronizing global class issues in line with national interest. Therefore, the left ceased to engage with the possibility of India's rise in association with the United States in any sustained manner. The underlying leftist thesis was that the US never had an intrinsic policy towards India. India was always factored in as part of US global strategic interests, and that exercise remains constant. The left refused to see any concrete benefit following from a closed relation with the United States for the Indian people at large. The left considered the US as an imperial outfit and believes that bandwagoning with Washington would drag India into a series of misadventures which would seriously undermine India's foreign policy autonomy. At present, the current government is facing opposition from certain states in its energy and security policies with other countries. For example, the BJP's coalition partner in the state of Maharashtra, the Shiv Sena, has opposed the Modi government's decision to fast track the revival of the Jaitapur nuclear power project since 2015.Its persistent opposition to the project could create problems for Modi's ambitious nuclear energy plans (The Economic Times, 12 January 2015). Similarly, the government of Tamil Nadu, led by Chief Minister Jayalalithaa Jayaram, also consistently opposed the Kudankulam nuclear power project in the state until 2012 (The Economic Times, 19 October 2011). Thereafter it executed a sharp U-turn on the matter. At the time, then Prime Minister Manmohan Singh had to personally ask Jayalalithaa to allow the project to go forward (Jacob, 2016: 10).

The role of the border states deserves special mention in political bargaining with the Centre and overall foreign policy. On the one hand, many traditional trade routes and modes of economic exchange involving border states have been disrupted due to the partition of the subcontinent in 1947. But they continue to enjoy ethnic, familial and economic affinities with neighbouring territories. On the other hand, they face problems of illegal migration and cross-border terrorism. Thus, to maximize the opportunities and minimize the challenges, the border states negotiate special treatment in the federal structure. Illegal migration from Nepal and Bangladesh evokes strong emotions in the northeastern states, with economic and security implications. In this context, the case of the Madhesis in the Terai plains which border India has been controversial, especially since the demands for constitutional amendment by the Madhesis in 2015. But there is no major difference between the approaches of the Centre and the state on the matter. Both maintain that it is the 'internal matter of Nepal' though the government must include all stakeholders in the political process (The Hindustan Times, 16 May 2017). The recent attempts by Nepal to redraw its map to include the contested areas of Lipulekh Pass, Kalapani and Limpiyadhura (western Nepal) have also been met with strong opposition by India's MEA. Triggered by the inauguration of the 80 km upgraded road on the Lipulekh Pass connecting it with Dharchula in Uttarakhand in May 2020, China has become a party to the conflict as the pass connects to the Tibet region also. While there are some allegations that the claims made by Nepal are boosted by China's prospective economic support, India remains steadfast in its claims on the region since the Lipulekh Pass has tremendous security implications in its borders with China (BBC, 10 June 2020). Needless to say, the rift between Nepal and India played a key role in Chinese forays in the Galway Valley. As Nimmi Kurian points out, despite its enthusiastic rhetoric about featuring border states as bridges with its neighbours, the curious paradox remains that, in actual practice, India's neighbourhood policy remains unambiguously top-down and continues to be firmly led and steered by New Delhi, excluding the proximate border regions from being sites of cooperation (Kurian, 2019: 122)

## Conclusion

The argument advanced in this paper, inspired primarily by Eswaran Sridharan's study, is that internally India's tight federal model has tried to be accommodative and inclusionary and the turn towards coalition politics has only strengthened this trend. It has remained sensitive to its neighbourhood and got involved when groups have been excluded in the political process in states like Sri Lanka, Bangladesh and Nepal. This is not necessarily because there is a strong commitment to liberal multiculturalism in India's democracy. Federalism was necessary to accommodate the country's many diversities so that people enjoyed constitutional guarantees and might claim a share in the operating dynamics of the state. Hence, India's sensitivity to exclusionary policies and practices in its neighbourhood stems from its possible long-term consequences within the body politic of the Indian state rather than altruistic considerations of political rights and legitimacy in its neighbourhood.

However, the so-called seamless national interest parleyed by the Indian state has often been strongly critiqued if not resisted by the bordering provinces, which are sensitive on resource sharing and economic forces across territorial lines. Federal calculations have, therefore, often been at variance with those of the provinces on the border. Immediate consequences and short time horizons have motivated the political decisions of such states far more than the abstract and sanitized approach of the Centre. This has exposed the implications of the operational dynamics of federalism, rendering clear that it is not just the constitutional division of powers as etched in black and white. It involves the actual dynamics of coordination between the two levels of authorities and its illustrations in everyday politics. The maturing of Indian democracy over more than six decades and the era of coalition politics and liberalization since the 1990s have set a certain trend in motion, whereby the nascent states of 1947, which required the support of a strong Centre, have been transformed into fully developed, assertive constituent units of the nation with distinct political and sociological compositions and ethnic configurations. They are strongly represented by experienced political leadership, well-trained in the languages of political bargaining and adept at claiming stakes in national politics through negotiations, agitations and, if required, manipulation. Further, globalization and economic liberalization have strengthened some states against the Centre while making others vulnerable to a wide array of forces. The decrease in central assistance automatically has complicated Centre–state relations. The impact of this on foreign policy has, interestingly, varied. Financially weak states were often more vocal than the stronger ones in criticizing national foreign policy, fearing further burdens, both economic and political. Finally, the foreign policy of the BJP-led NDA government since 2014 has complicated citizenship issues domestically and, despite commanding a clear majority, encouraged states like Assam to harden their stance on cross-border migration and demographics. This selective encouragement to join with the Centre has dilated the federalization of foreign policy in India and divided the political responses of provinces to bilateral concerns like the Rohingya issue. In brief, this study describes the evolution of India's federalism and traces how this process has impacted on a range of foreign policy issues both in South Asia and beyond.

## Notes

1 In the words of Eswaran Sridharan,

> It adopted a secular, federal, multi-lingual constitutional dispensation with explicit minority rights and protection against caste discrimination, in addition to equal rights and non-discrimination in general. Political practice has flowed from this constitutional dispensation and from the inclusive, umbrella character of the Congress Party that ruled India for over four decades since independence, in that the unity of the nation and the inculcation of a sense of identification with the nation and the state have been based on policies of accommodation and inclusion … The foreign policy counterpart of such a national integration strategy (and national unity is the foundation of internal security and hence national security) would inevitably be a policy of sensitivity

> to the feelings of any section of the people of India, if agitated or mobilized, as far as discrimination or maltreatment of ethnic kinfolk is concerned.
>
> (Sridharan 2016: 70)

2 On the Maoist challenge, see Mahadevan (2012: 203–220). On Kashmir, see Navnita Behera (2000); and Ganguly (1996: 76–107). A recent addition to the vast literature is Widmalm (2014). On the northeast, see Kolås (2017: 22–37). On Assam, see Baruah (2009: 951–974).
3 States like Arunachal Pradesh and Nagaland before their political configurations got aligned with the ruling party at the Centre are cases in point.
4 The detailed theoretical literature on cooperative federalism is beyond the scope of this article.
5 For details, see Daily Star (2018). The 2015 state visit by Indian Prime Minister Narendra Modi, accompanied by West Bengal's Chief Minister Mamata Banerjee, although it failed to change the fundamental dynamics of Indo–Bangladesh ties, yet successfully addressed two major concerns: Bangladesh's craving for equal and dignified treatment and assurance from India of serious commitment to invest in the Teesta Agreement. As a major boost to connectivity, both countries agreed to allow Indian cargo vessels to ferry goods through Chittagong port, bypassing Singapore in the process. The Kolkata–Dhaka–Agartala and Dhaka–Shillong–Guwahati bus services inaugurated by Prime Ministers Modi and Hasina, in company with Mamata Banerjee, underlined India's commitment to further connectivity (NDTV, 2015). Another crucial outcome of the visit was the exchange of Instruments of Ratification of the 1974 Land Boundary Agreement. While implementation of the agreement has remained widely undefined, the fact that India could cede 10,000 acres of land to Bangladesh despite strong protests from state BJP in Assam is a major achievement. Mamata Banerjee's support for the deal, announced during her visit to Bangladesh in February 2015, greatly facilitated the ratification process on India's side. Thus, the positive vibes exchanged between the two countries indicate that while the priorities of geopolitics will remain, commerce and connectivity have seriously started to rival the recursive dynamics of power. Federalizing foreign policy has helped create the political capital necessary for sustaining the relationship despite much bitterness and resentments on both sides. On issues like water and demographic profile, it is impossible to placate local fears by invoking the seamless idiom of national interest. A foreign policy that is out of sync with ground realities cannot deliver the goods. Hence, contrary to the popular view, the active involvement of the politicians of West Bengal and other neighbouring states in India's dealings with Bangladesh is not necessarily a reprehensible constraint. Rather, it is in conformity with the logic of accommodation and inclusive federalism that characterizes Indian federalism. For details, see Chatterjee (2016: 76–104).
6 The UPA government was found to vote in favour of this resolution, in a departure from India's longstanding practice of not voting for country-specific motions, apparently to placate the DMK, still its coalition partner.
7 In the words of Sridharan,

> I would argue … the centre's own sensitivity to the perceived requirements of national unity as the foundation of national security, and not only pressure from Tamil Nadu parties – that explains the broadly Tamil-sympathetic policy stance of India's Sri Lanka policy since the July 1983 riots.
>
> (Sridharan, 2016: 70–71)

## References

Athray, Dharika. (2020). 'The plight of refugees in India during COVID 19', Observer Research Foundation, 7 July [online]. Available at www.orfonline.org/expert-speak/the-plight-of-refugees-in-india-during-covid19-69287/ (Accessed: 11 July 2020)

Baruah, Sanjib. (2003). 'Protective Discrimination and Crisis of Citizenship in North-East India', Economic and Political Weekly, 38(17), p. 1624–1626.

Baruah, Sanjib. (2009). 'Separatist Militants and Contentious Politics in Assam, India: The Limits of Counterinsurgency', Asian Survey, 49(6), p. 951–974.

Basu, Partha Pratim. (2016). 'Federalism and Foreign Policy in India: Experiences of UPA and NDA-II Regimes', India Quarterly, 72(3), p. 216–234.

BBC. 2020. 'India and China: How Nepal's new map is stirring old rivalries', 10 June [online]. Available at www.bbc.com/news/world-asia-52967452 (Accessed: 11 July 2020)

Behera, Navnita. (2000). State, Identity & Violence: Jammu, Kashmir, and Ladakh. New Delhi: Manohar Publishers.

Bhambhri, C.P. (1993). 'Cohesion, Conflicts and Contradictions within the Indian State', Social Scientist, 21(5/6), p. 25–35.

Blarel, Nicolas. (2019). 'Coalition Politics and the Making of Indian Foreign Policy: A New Research Program', India Review, 18(5), p. 582–595, 27 January [online]. Available at https://doi.org/10.1080/14736489.2019.1703367 (Accessed: 11 July 2020)

Business Standard. (2019). 'Explained: What are Articles 370 and 35A? Why they are important for J&K', 26 November [online]. Available at https://bit.ly/33ZZtWw (Accessed: 13 July 2020)

Business Standard. (2020). 'India is paying the price for neglecting its neighbours', 10 July.

Business Today. (2019). 'PM Modi exclusive interview: Demonetisation changed people's mindset on black money', 26 April [online]. Available at www.businesstoday.in/current/economy-politics/prime-minister-narendra-modi-exclusive-interview-demonetisation-changed-people-mindset-on-black-money/story/340919.html (Accessed: 11 July 2020)

Business Today. (2020). 'One year of Modi govt 2.0: CAA< abrogation of Article 370, other key decisions taken by BJP govt', 30 May [online]. Available at www.businesstoday.in/current/economy-politics/one-year-of-modi-govt-20-caa-abrogation-of-article-370-other-key-decisions-taken-by-bjp-govt/story/405398.html (Accessed: 13 July 2020)

Chatterjee, Rakhahari. 2014. 'Foreign policy and federalism', Observer Research Foundation, 23 January [online].Available at www.orfonline.org/research/foreign-policy-federalism/ (Accessed: 11 July 2020)

Chatterjee, Shibashis. (2016). 'India–Bangladesh Relations' in Ganguly, Sumit (ed.) Engaging the World: Indian Foreign Policy since 1947. New Delhi: Oxford University Press, p. 76–104.

Chellany, Brahma. (2020). 'As in 1962, 1965 and 1999, China's latest encroachments in Ladakh have taken India by surprise at "the strategic and tactical levels"' @Chellany, Twitter India, 28 May.

Cherian, John. (2007). 'The deal should not be seen in isolation', Interview with CPI(M) general secretary Prakash Karat, Frontline, Chennai, 24(17) [online]. Available at https://frontline.thehindu.com/cover-story/article30192649.ece (Accessed: 30 November 2020)

Chhibber, Pradeep. (1997). 'Who Voted for the Bharatiya Janata Party?' British Journal of Political Science, 27(4), p. 631–639.

Daily Star. (2018) 'Likelihood of Teesta watersharing', 30 June [online]. Available at www.thedailystar.net/opinion/likelihood-agreement-teesta-water-sharing-1597378 (Accessed: 25 November 2018)

Datta, Rekha. (1999). 'Hindu Nationalism or Pragmatic Party Politics? A Study of India's Hindu Party', International Journal of Politics, Culture, and Society, 12(4), p. 573–588.

Financial Express. (2018) 'Amit Mitra interview: More important than who aligns with whom is why do so. Mamata Banerjee has a major role', 25 November [online]. Available at www.financialexpress.com/india-news/amit-mitra-interview-more-important-than-who-aligns-with-whom-is-why-do-so-mamata-banerjee-has-a-major-role/1392815/ (Accessed: 25 November 2018)

Firstpost. (2018). 15th Finance Commission: A Challenge and an Opportunity', 14 January [online]. Available at www.firstpost.com/business/from-fiscal-deficits-to-slow-down-in-economy-15th-finance-commission-stares-at-many-challenges-4287397.html (Accessed: 24 November 2018)

Ganguly, Sumit. (1996). 'Explaining the Kashmir Insurgency: Political Mobilization and Institutional Decay', International Security, 21(2), p. 76–107.

Ganguly, Sumit (ed.). (2016). Engaging the World: Indian Foreign Policy since 1947. New Delhi: Oxford University Press.

Ghosh, D.N. (2007). 'Nuclear Debate, National Interest and Political Drama', Economic and Political Weekly, 42(38), p. 3823–3825.

Grossman, Derek. (2020). 'Chinese Border Aggression Against India Likely Unrelated to Pandemic: The Chinese Approach to India Represents Continuity in Behavior,' The Diplomat, 5 July, p.1–7.

Haidar, Suhasini. (2019). 'The perils of post-370 diplomacy', The Hindu, 2 November [online]. Available at www.thehindu.com/opinion/lead/the-perils-of-post-370-diplomacy/article29857257.ece (Accessed: 13 July 2020)

Hansen, Thomas Blom. (1999). Democracy and Hindu Nationalism in Modern India. Princeton, NJ: Princeton University Press.

Hindustan Times. (2017). 'India "shifts" stance, asks Madhesis to drop demand for changes in constitution', 16 May [online]. Available at www.hindustantimes.com/india-news/india-shifts-stance-asks-madhesis-to-drop-demand-for-changes-in-constitution/story-29xYUN0YoCCnRFTSiyOWOP.html (Accessed: 15 December 2018)

Hindustan Times. (2020). 'Mamata writes to PM Modi, says 100% FDI in coal sector contradicts spirit of self-reliance', 26 June [online]. Available at www.hindustantimes.com/india-news/mamata-writes-to-pm-modi-says-100-fdi-in-coal-sector-contradicts-spirit-of-self-reliance/story-WGlPRak1JeDUGaKB2AZKLM.html (Accessed: 9 July 2020)

Hindustan Times. (2020). 'Centre writes to Chhattisgarh govt over coal blocks in Hasdeo Arand', 9 July [online]. Available at www.hindustantimes.com/india-news/auctioning-of-coal-blocks-near-hasdeo-arand-halted/story-Yp1I1FQZPygRlVsu3H8RqI.html (Accessed: 10 July 2020)

Hindustan Times. (2020). 'Article 370 an old stain, done away in a blink of an eye: Rajnath Singh', 14 June [online]. Available at www.hindustantimes.com/india-news/article-370-an-old-stain-done-away-in-a-blink-of-an-eye-rajnath-singh/story-TjgXZE9BMlxurQrVVQccRO.html (Accessed: 13 July 2020)

India News. (2020). 'Fight against Coronavirus fine example of cooperative federalism: PM Modi tells Chief Ministers', 16 June [online]. Available at www.india.com/news/india/fight-against-coronavirus-fine-example-of-cooperative-federalism-pm-modi-tells-chief-ministers-4059773/ (Accessed: 10 July 2020)

India Today. (2020). 'Madhya Pradesh becomes 5th state to pass resolution against CAA', 5 February [online]. Available at www.indiatoday.in/india/story/madhya-pradesh-anti-caa-resolution-1643512-2020-02-05 (Accessed: 13 July 2020)

Jacob, Happymon. (2016). 'Putting the Periphery at the Center: Indian States' Role in Foreign Policy', Carnegie India.

Jaffrelot, C. (2013). 'Gujarat Elections: The Sub-Text of Modi's 'Hattrick' – High Tech Populism and the 'Neo-middle Class', Studies in Indian Politics, 1(1), p. 79–95.

Jaganathan, Madhan Mohan. (2019). 'Can Constituent States Influence Foreign and Security Policy? Coalitional Dynamics in India', Third World Quarterly, 40(8), p. 1516–1534.

Jain, S.K. (2009). 'Federalization of Indian Foreign Policy', Paper presented at IPSA, World Congress, 12–16 July.

Jenkin, Rob. (2003). 'How Federalism Influences India's Domestic Politics of WTO Engagement', Asian Survey, 43(4), p. 598–621.

Kolås, Åshild. (2017). 'Framing the Tribal: Ethnic Violence in Northeast India', Asian Ethnicity, 18(1), p. 22–37.

Kurian, Nimmi. (2019). 'The Future is Federal: Why Indian Foreign Policy Needs to Leverage Its Border States', in Centre for Policy Research (ed.) Policy Challenges 2019–2024: Chartering New Course for India and Navigating Policy Challenges in the 21st Century, p. 122–123.

Lacina, Bethany. (2014). 'How Governments Shape the Risk of Civil Violence: India's Federal Reorganization, 1950–56', American Journal of Political Science, 58(3), p. 720–738.

Mahadevan, Prem. (2012). 'The Maoist Insurgency in India: Between Crime and Revolution', Small Wars & Insurgencies, 23(2), p. 203–220.

Majeed, Akhtar. (2003).'The Changing Politics of States' Reorganization', Publius, 33(4), p. 83–98.

Millennium Post. (2018). 'Bill tabled to grant land rights to Chitmahal Enclave residents', 19 November [online]. Available at www.millenniumpost.in/kolkata/bill-tabled-to-grant-land-rights-to-chitmahal-enclave-residents-328089 (Accessed: 13 July 2020)

Moorthy, Sathiya N. (2019). 'Sri Lanka: Rajapaksas' return and 'Tamil Nadu factor' in India relations', 26 November, South Asia Weekly Report, XII(47) [online]. Available at www.orfonline.org/research/south-asia-weekly-report-58116/ (Accessed: 12 July 2020)

Nautiyal, Annapurna. (2020). 'India's Foreign Policy in the Backdrop of Covid-19 Pandemic: Challenges and Opportunities', Online Special Lecture, 16 June 2020 (Google Meet), Bengal Institute of Political Studies, Kolkata.

New Indian Express. (2019). 'PM Modi takes centralisation of powers to new heights', 13 May [online]. Available at www.newindianexpress.com/states/tamil-nadu/2019/mar/13/pm-modi-takes-centralisation-of-powers-to-new-heights-1950437.html (Accessed: 10 July 2020)

News18. (2017). 'Centre should not deport Rohingya refugees, says Mamata Banerjee', 18 September [online]. Available at www.news18.com/news/politics/centre-should-not-deport-rohingya-refugees-says-mamata-banerjee-1521619.html (Accessed: 15 December 2018)

NDTV. (2015). 'PM Narendra Modi Returns Home after Two-Day Bangladesh Visit', Press Trust of India. June 7 [online]. Available at www.ndtv.com/india-news/pm-modi-returns-home-after-two-day-bangladesh-visit-769582 (Accessed: 15 June 2015)

NDTV. (2019). 'Early signing of interim agreement on Teesta River awaited: Sheikh Hasina', 6 October [online]. Available at www.ndtv.com/india-news/bangladesh-prime-minister-sheikh-hasina-early-signing-of-interim-agreement-on-teesta-river-awaited-2112513 (Accessed: 11 July 2020)

Outlook. (2020). 'India assures support for Rohingyas "repatriation": B'desh', 11 July [online]. Available at www.outlookindia.com/newsscroll/india-assures-support-for-rohingyas-repatriation-bdesh/1892692 (Accessed: 12 July 2020)

Ruparelia, Sanjay. (2008). 'How the Politics of Recognition Enabled India's Democratic Exceptionalism', International Journal of Politics, Culture and Society (Special Issue on the Work of Charles Taylor), 21 December (1–4), p. 39–56.

Ruparelia, Sanjay. (2015). Divided We Govern: Coalition Politics in Modern India. New York and New Delhi: Oxford University Press.

Seshia, Shaila. (1998). 'Divide and Rule in Indian Party Politics: The Rise of the Bharatiya Janata Party'. Asian Survey, 38(11), p. 1036–1050.

Sharma, Chanchal Kumar and Swenden, Wilfried. (2017). 'Continuity and Change in Contemporary Indian Federalism', India Review, 16(1), p. 1–13.

Singh, Mahendra P. and Verney, Douglas V. (2003). 'Challenges in India's Centralized Parliamentary Federalism', Publius, 33(4), p.1–120.

Sinha, Rajesh Kumar. (2019). 'The abrogation of Article 370 and its Implications', Foreign Policy News, 20 August, p.1–9.

Sridharan, E. (ed.). (2014). Coalition Politics in India: Selected Issues at the Centre and the States. New Delhi: Academic Foundation.

Sridharan, Eswaran. (2016). 'Indo-Sri Lanka Relations: Geopolitics, Domestic Politics, or Something More Complex?' in Ganguly, Sumit (ed.) Engaging the World: Indian Foreign Policy since 1947. New Delhi: Oxford University Press, p. 49–75.

Tellis, Ashley. (2020). 'The Sino-Indian Border: Escalation &Disengagement', Zoom Webinar with Ashley J. Tellis and Gautam Bambawale, moderated by Rudra Chaudhuri on 24 June, Carnegie, India.

Thachil, Tariq. (2014). 'Elite Parties and Poor Voters: Theory and Evidence from India', The American Political Science Review, 108(2), p. 454–477.

The Economic Times. (2011). 'Jayalalitha blames Centre for Kudankulam nuclear plant impasse', 19 October [online]. Available at https://economictimes.indiatimes.com/news/politics-and-nation/jayalalitha-blames-centre-for-kudankulam-nuclear-plant-impasse/articleshow/10408345.cms (Accessed: 25 November 2018)

The Economic Times. (2015). 'Shiv Sena continues to oppose 9,900 MW Jaitapur nuclear project', 12 January [online].Available at https://economictimes.indiatimes.com/news/politics-and-nation/shiv-sena-continues-to-oppose-9900-mw-jaitapur-nuclear-project/articleshow/45854026.cms (Accessed: 1 December 2018)

The Economic Times. (2018). 'Central agencies accuse Bengal of rule breach in Rohingya shelter', 16 January [online]. Available at https://economictimes.indiatimes.com/news/politics-and-nation/central-agencies-accuse-bengal-of-rule-breach-in-rohingya-shelter/articleshow/62520123.cms (Accessed: 15 December 2018)

The Economic Times. (2019). 'Article 370 no more: BJP on way to fulfill its long-standing promise', 5 August [online]. Available at https://economictimes.indiatimes.com/news/politics-and-nation/article-370-no-more-bjp-on-the-way-to-fulfill-its-long-standing-promise/articleshow/70531929.cms?from=mdr (Accessed: 11 July 2020)

The Economic Times. (2019). 'Year-end review: Pulwama, Article 370, CAA kept MHA busy', 27 December [online]. Available at https://economictimes.indiatimes.com/news/politics-and-nation/year-end-review-pulwama-article-370-caa-kept-mha-busy/articleshow/72988009.cms?from=mdr (Accessed: 13 July 2020)

The Economic Times. (2020). 'Virus-ravaged states clamor for more funds from Modi', 9 July [online]. Available at https://economictimes.indiatimes.com/news/economy/finance/virus-ravaged-states-clamor-for-more-funds-from-modi/articleshow/76869192.cms (Accessed: 11 July 2020)

The Economic Times. (2020). 'No rollback on Article 370 abrogation, legislative assembly for J&K will be formed "very soon": Ram Madhav', 13 July [online]. Available at https://economictimes.indiatimes.com/news/politics-and-nation/no-rollback-of-article-370-abrogation-legislative-assembly-for-jk-will-be-formed-very-soon-ram-madhav/videoshow/76932351.cms (Accessed: 13 July 2020)

The Hindu. (2018). 'Centre tells States to count Rohingya migrants', 1 August [online]. Available at www.thehindu.com/news/national/centre-tells-states-to-count-rohingya-migrants/article24566817.ece (Accessed: 15 December 2018)

The Telegraph. (2020). 'Didi writes to PM for 25,000 cr.', 10 July [online]. Available at www.telegraphindia.com/west-bengal/mamata-writes-to-modi-for-rs-25-000cr/cid/1761240 (Accessed: 11 July 2020)

The Times of India. (2017). 'Teesta river dispute explained in 10 points', 9 April [online]. Available at https://timesofindia.indiatimes.com/india/the-teesta-river-dispute-explained-in-10-points/articleshow/58091320.cms (Accessed: 25 November 2018)

The Times of India. (2019). 'West Bengal: BSF flags Rohingya infiltration worry, 72 nabbed in 12 months', 3 December [online]. Available at https://timesofindia.indiatimes.com/city/kolkata/bsf-flags-rohingya-infiltration-worry-72-nabbed-in-12-months/articleshow/72340252.cms (Accessed: 11 July 2020)

The Wire. (2020). 'After passing CAA, Centre to focus on deporting Rohingya refugees: Union minister', 4 January [online]. Available at https://thewire.in/rights/jitendra-singh-rohingya-refugees-jammu-caa (Accessed: 11 July 2020)

Tillin, Louise. (2007). 'United in Diversity? Asymmetry in Indian Federalism', Publius, 37(1), p. 45–67.

Tripathi, Purnima. (2007). 'Their opposition is ridiculous', Interview with Kapil Sibal, Union Minister, Frontline, Chennai, 24(17). Available at https://frontline.thehindu.com/cover-story/article30192652.ece (Accessed: 30 November 2020)

Vasudeva, P.K. (2009). 'Chief ministers conference on WTO mixed results', 2 July 2001; cited in Jain, S.K. 'Federalization of Indian Foreign Policy', Paper presented at IPSA, World Congress, 12–16 July 2009, p.8–9.

Verney, Douglas V. and Frankel, Francine R. (1986). 'India: Has the Trend Towards Federalism Implications for the Management of Foreign Policy? A Comparative Perspective', International Journal, 41(3), Foreign Policy in Federal States (Summer), p. 572–599.

Widmalm, Sten. (2014). Kashmir in Comparative Perspective: Democracy and Violent Separatism in India. London: Routledge.

Xavier, Constantino. (2020). 'Modi's Neighbourhood First push is being pulled down by decades of stagnation', 15 February [online]. Available at https://theprint.in/opinion/modis-neighbourhood-first-push-is-being-pulled-down-by-decades-of-policy-stagnation/365895/ (Accessed: 13 July 2020)

# Index

*Note*: Page numbers in *italics* indicate figures, **bold** numbers indicate tables, on the corresponding pages.

For Product Safety Concerns and Information please contact our EU representative GPSR@taylorandfrancis.com
Taylor & Francis Verlag GmbH, Kaufingerstraße 24, 80331 München, Germany

www.ingramcontent.com/pod-product-compliance
Lightning Source LLC
LaVergne TN
LVHW021120300926
849160LV00010B/791

*9780367641351*